THE
DUCATI
STORY

THE DUCATI STORY

FOURTH EDITION

RACING AND PRODUCTION MODELS FROM 1945 TO THE PRESENT DAY

IAN FALLOON

FOREWORD BY ING. FABIO TAGLIONI

First published by Patrick Stephens Limited in 1996
Reprinted in February 1997
Reprinted in July 1997
Second edition published by Haynes Publishing
   in August 1998
Third edition published in February 2000
Reprinted in April 2003
This reformatted fourth edition published in July 2006

A catalogue record for this book is
available from the British Library

ISBN 1 84425 322 8

Library of Congress catalog card no. 2005935271

Published by Haynes Publishing, Sparkford, Yeovil,
Somerset, BA22 7JJ, UK

Tel: 01963 442030 Fax: 01963 440001
Int. tel: +44 1963 442030 Int. fax: +44 1963 440001
E-mail: sales@haynes.co.uk
Website: www.haynes.co.uk

Haynes North America, Inc.,
861 Lawrence Drive, Newbury Park,
California 91320, USA

*All photographs are from the author's collection
except where credited separately.*

Page build by G&M Designs Limited,
Raunds, Northamptonshire
Printed and bound in England by
J. H. Haynes & Co. Ltd, Sparkford

CONTENTS

FOREWORD

by Ing. Fabio Taglioni

When Ian Falloon asked me to write the introduction to his new book on the history of Ducati motorcycles, I was delighted to oblige. He and his wife visited me at my home in Bologna where we discussed many details about the history of the company and my designs.

When I started at Ducati in 1952 the only development work that was being done was on the Cucciolo, but as I began my collaboration with the company and started on my first projects, the work on the Cucciolo was suspended. The first Ducati motorcycle design of mine to be built was the 100 cc Marianna, then the 125, 175, 250 and 350, all with a single overhead camshaft. My final designs were the Pantah series 500, 600, 750, 850, 900, until the 955, all unequalled and memorable because they have been the only engines to use the indestructible desmodromic valve system.

My best motor, and the best looking motorcycle, was the 750 twin, made world famous by many Italian riders such as Bruno Spaggiari, and foreigners Paul Smart and Mike Hailwood. Nearly all the riders of the racing Ducatis were excellent, and enthusiastic, because these motorcycles fulfilled their ambitions. They gave everything, and I tried to contribute by giving them the best equipment possible.

I have designed many motorcycles over my 40-year period at Ducati, and all have gone into production except the 1,000 cc V Four, which was considered too expensive.

I hope Sig. Falloon has a lot of success with this book.

Ing. Fabio Taglioni
Bologna
October 1995

INTRODUCTION AND ACKNOWLEDGEMENTS

For the best part of my adult life I have had an association with Ducati motorcycles bordering on the obsessional. There is no rational explanation for it, and I have been badly hurt crashing them, but the seduction of their superb engineering and their excellence as motorcycles persists. However, not all Ducatis are great motorcycles, and in this story, while endeavouring to document most models, I have also made judgements regarding their relative excellence or historical importance. More than most manufacturers, Ducati has had peaks and troughs, and this is largely part of their appeal. The Japanese or Germans rarely build a bad motorcycle, but then their products seldom achieve the level of inspiration that is found in the best Ducatis. The peaks are undoubtedly associated with racing success, either directly with the actual bikes themselves, or the spin-off with street versions of race replicas. The troughs occurred when the bureaucrats, rather than the engineers, decided what the public wanted. This happened more than once, but throughout the history of Ducati it was the conviction and brilliance of Fabio Taglioni that kept the company on the right track. It is no coincidence that Taglioni has been associated with all the peaks, including the most recent successes.

The constraints of this book have been such that inevitably there will be exclusions. There are just too many individual models to detail individually, and I have concentrated on the more recent history because the earlier period has been comprehensively covered by other commentators. Only the motorcycles from Bologna get mentioned, and the racing bikes are either the factory bikes or particularly significant privateer machines. The plethora of Ducati singles, both four and two-stroke, overhead valve and overhead camshaft, have by necessity been covered only briefly, and not exhaustively. They have an importance historically, but to most enthusiasts they are not as relevant as the later twins, and I have concentrated on those particular models that I feel are of more historical interest. I apologise to any singles fanatics who feel that

their bikes are hard done by. While I have endeavoured to be as accurate as possible, often factory power and weight figures are conflicting, a scenario that has existed from the first Ducati motorcycles and continues today. Therefore I have aimed for consistency in quoting figures, generally using workshop manual data in preference to that from brochures.

This book would not have been possible without the help of many Ducati enthusiasts around the world, and I would like to thank everyone who has supported this project. From Italy, my good friend Maurizio Bavaresco, of the Bikers' Restaurant at Valle San Liberale; Ing. Fabio Taglioni, and his wife of more than 50 years Narina, who entertained us so lavishly at their home in Bologna; Nadia Pavignani of Ducati's Public Relations Department; Virginio Ferrari, who gave me valuable time during a World Superbike race meeting, and another enthusiastic friend, Gerolamo Bettoni. In Germany, Rolf im Brahm, was happy to let me use his magnificent range of photographs from ten years of Ducati calendars; Hartmut Snoek for his help and encouragement, and Thorsten Schulze. Phil Schilling in the USA has been most enthusiastic and the editor of *Two Wheels,* Jeremy Bowdler allowed access to photographic archives.

For this fourth edition, many more have assisted. At Ducati and Ducati Corse, Federico Minoli, Pierre Terblanche, Paolo Ciabatti, Livio Lodi, Julian Thomas, Ludovica Benedetti, Claudio Domenicali, Sonia Braggio, Livio Suppo, Corrado Cecchinelli, and Francesco Rapisarda. Alan Cathcart, Nico Georgeoglou, Roy Kidney, Mick Woollett, and Phil Aynsley all contributed new photographic material for this updated edition. Finally, I must thank my wife Miriam, and sons Ben and Tim, who have put up with the many hours of work, and constant Ducati conversation over the ten years between the first and fourth editions of this book.

Ian Falloon
Spring 2006

Taglioni's first masterpiece: the
98 cc Gran Sport of 1955. *Phil
Aynsley*

1 ORIGINS

Back in 1922, when 19-year-old physics student Adriano Cavalieri Ducati was conducting his first experiments with radio, the production of motorcycles could not have been further from his mind. By 1924, from his house in Bologna, he had established radio contact with the United States, a considerable feat at the time, and on 4 July 1926, with his two brothers Bruno and Marcello, he set up a company called the Società Scientifica Radio Brevetti Ducati, building condensers and other radio-graphic components. While Adriano was a brilliant technician, Bruno assumed the role of manager and administrator, and Marcello that of designer. At this time Bologna was a centre of radio development, with Guglielmo Marconi, the inventor of the radio, being one of Bologna's most famous sons. Under the fascist dictator Mussolini's policy of modernization, the Ducati brothers' business expanded considerably, and by 1935 they had acquired a new site at Borgo Panigale, an industrial district on the outskirts of Bologna.

On this site they built a huge modern factory to manufacture radios and electronic components, and the prosperity of the company was undoubtedly aided by Mussolini's interest in the widespread availability of radios to further his propaganda. By 1940 Ducati also had a large research department and had diversified to include optical and mechanical divisions alongside the electronic, starting to produce cameras and lenses as well as cash registers and electric razors. Because Italy was largely untouched by the early years of the Second World War the company continued to grow, until the Italian government sought an Armistice with the Allies on 8 September 1943.

That was when things started to go wrong for the Ducati brothers. On the day after the Armistice, German soldiers commandeered the factory at Borgo Panigale, eventually transferring much of the plant and machinery to Germany. There was a further disaster on 12 October 1944, when Allied bombing almost destroyed the factory completely. After the war the Ducati brothers were briefly involved with Allied Naval Intelligence, but attempts to rebuild the company were stricken with financial problems caused by the expense of reconstruction and the general difficulties of the immediate post-war period. On 1 December 1947 the Società Scientifica Radio

The three Ducati brothers during the 1980s: Marcello, Adriano and Bruno.

Below left: A Ducati 18 x 24 mm 'Sogno' camera. These came with Vitor interchangeable lenses and are now collectors' items.

Below right: This radio is one of many post-war electrical products produced by Ducati.

Brevetti Ducati went bankrupt. However, it was considered too important by the IRI (Istituto di Ricostruzione Industriale) to be allowed to collapse completely, and a joint Government and Vatican financial consortium came to its rescue in 1948, when control of Ducati passed from the brothers to that of the FIM (Fondo Industrie Meccaniche) and IMI (L'Istituto Mobiliare Italiano). Now under government control, the history of Ducati would be affected by a mixture of good and bad political decisions for the next 40 years. In the meantime the Bologna plant had been rebuilt and started producing 'Cucciolo' motors, condensers, cameras, and cinema projectors, while Milan became the centre for Ducati radios and electronics. The 18 x 24 mm format rangefinder camera, with its assortment of screw-mount lenses, was of particularly high quality, being hailed as a miniature Leica.

Below: The 48 cc Cucciolo T1 was the first motorcycle engine produced by Ducati. This is an early example (No. 14502), but is not one of the first as the cylinder fins are horizontal rather than diagonal. *Phil Aynsley*

THE CUCCIOLO

The 'Cucciolo' (or puppy) was an engine designed for Siata of Turin during the Second World War by a lawyer called Aldo Farinelli. 1945 was a very opportune time to produce such a motor: it was easily installed in a bicycle frame, thus providing cheap and economical transportation. Somehow, amidst the chaos of post-war Italy, the Borgo Panigale plant came to produce these engines, presenting their first example, the T1, at the Milan Show in September 1946. Using the FIAT foundry at Cameri near Milan, the Cucciolo was so successful that it became the cornerstone of the Ducati company's revival.

The 48 cc four-stroke Cucciolo engine was intended as a cheap, reliable, and economical unit. With only a 6.5:1 compression ratio, the 39 x 40 mm engine, with its 9 mm Weber carburettor, could run easily on the post-war low octane fuel and provide exceptional fuel economy. Perhaps the most interesting feature of the engine was that the 12 mm valves were operated by pullrods rather than pushrods. Starting was by the usual moped method of pedalling while the engine was in gear, and there were two speeds, selected by the pedals via a handlebar mounted clutch lever.

By 1948, with the injection of capital from the new controllers, the Borgo Panigale plant had been rebuilt and was operating at increased capacity. Demand for the Cucciolo was so strong that a T2 was offered in two versions, Turismo and Sport. With capacity still at 48 cc, the Turismo was detuned slightly with a 5.5:1 compression ratio to produce a mere 0.8 bhp. The Sport retained the 6.5:1 compression of the T1, and power was up to 1.2 bhp at 4,250 rpm. The valve timing was very moderate, and not particularly accurate, with the inlet opening 5°–15° before top dead centre, closing 25°–30° after bottom dead centre, and the exhaust opening 45°–35° before bottom dead centre, and closing 0°–20° after top dead centre.

The T3, which appeared at the Milan Show of 1948, was almost identical to the T2 but with fully enclosed valve gear and a slight bore increase to 43.8 mm, to yield 60 cc. More importantly, this engine was displayed in an entirely new vehicle called the Girino, an unsuccessful three-wheeled device that gave Ducati the impetus to construct their own complete motorcycle. So, with no experience in motorcycle design and construction, they went into a partnership with Aero Caproni, a company that had built aircraft before and during the war but was looking to diversify. This appeared a strange choice, because Caproni were also totally inexperienced in the field of motorcycle design and only one 60 cc motorcycle arose from this alliance. By May 1950 Caproni decided to market their own machines in an expanding, but increasingly competitive market.

In order to maintain sales of the Cucciolo, Ducati supported an attempt on some 50 cc speed records at Monza in March 1951. Ugo Tamarozzi set 12 new 50 cc world records, returning two months later with

By 1950, Ducati was producing complete motorcycles of which one of the earliest was the 60TL. This example has a Caproni-style frame. *Phil Aynsley*

co-rider Glauco Zitelli to achieve 20 more, notably the 12-Hours' at 67.156 km/h (41.73 mph). Not content with these, a team of five riders took another 27 records in November, with Tamarozzi collecting the final two in January 1952. These 50 cc world records were to last five years, demonstrating to the public the durability and reliability of the Cucciolo.

They also had the desired effect of keeping the Cucciolo in production for several more years, with small modifications. The final versions, the 55/r and 55/e, were marketed from 1954 as true mopeds, with leading-link forks and swinging-arm rear suspension. The power was now up to 1.35 bhp, but, with its popularity waning, the little Cucciolo was discontinued during 1956. Many thousands had been built over a

ten-year period, and while not being of a particularly sporting orientation, they did much to establish the name of Ducati as a motorcycle manufacturer.

THE FIRST SINGLES

Even before the brief relationship with Caproni had soured, Giovanni Fiorio had designed another engine, a 65 cc four-stroke with pushrod-operated valves. Introduced in March 1950 and called the 60 Sport, it was the first real Ducati motorcycle. This engine would form the basis of a complete range of pushrod singles lasting through until the 125 Cadet of 1967.
The 44 x 43 mm three-speed engine produced 2.5 bhp at 5,500 rpm, and soon became the 65TS. 1951 was a

With its 17-inch wheels the 1952
65TL looked like a *real*
motorcycle. *Phil Aynsley*

significant year for Ducati, with all production now concentrated at Borgo Panigale and the company headquarters moving from Largo Augusto 7, Milan. In addition, in October that year Dottore Giuseppe Montano was made director. Montano, while a government appointment, was a motorcycle enthusiast and a racing supporter, and he could see the promotional benefits of a successful racing programme.

The 65 soon grew to 98 cc and was displayed at the Milan Show in January 1952 in two forms, the 98N and 98T (with twin seat). With a power output of 5.8 bhp at 7,500 rpm, this 48 x 52 mm engine with its 8:1 compression ratio was the most sporting Ducati yet. The 98s had a pressed-steel spine type of frame, telescopic forks, and swinging-arm rear suspension.

With 17-inch wheels, their weight was 89 kg (196 lb) and they were good for 87 km/h (54 mph).

The other model displayed at the Milan Show was the complete antithesis, and ultimately a failure. Attempting to compete directly with Vespa and Lambretta scooters, the Cruiser, as it was known, was the world's first four-stroke scooter, with a 7.5 bhp 175 cc ohv engine designed by Fioro. Among the features of the Cruiser were an electric starter and an automatic gearbox, both contributing to its excessive weight and complexity. Within two years the Cruiser was dead, the first of several poor marketing decisions by Ducati, and one they would amazingly repeat in the next decade.

Both the 65 and 98 continued to be produced during 1953 and 1954, and the first more sporting

Although advanced for its day, one of Ducati's first serious mistakes was this ambitious Cruiser of 1953.

model, the 98S or Sport, appeared at the Milan Show of 1953. This had a finned oil-cooler attached to the front of the sump and produced 6.8 bhp for a top speed of 90 km/h (56 mph). By this time Ducati Meccanica had been created as a separate organization alongside Ducati Elettrotecnica. They both still operated in Borgo Panigale, but in adjoining factories on a street renamed Via Antonio Cavalieri Ducati. (Antonio was the father of the three Ducati brothers and had been an eminent engineer and designer of water systems.) Ducati Meccanica gave Montano the opportunity to hire a new designer to spearhead a racing programme. He could see that the potential of the ohv 98 was limited as a competition design, so he looked at some of the other successful motorcycle manufacturers in Bologna and found, at nearby Mondial, a 32-year-old engineer by the name of Fabio Taglioni. It turned out to be an inspired choice. Taglioni was a brilliant designer, and Montano gave him the freedom to develop his own ideas. It was also a bonus for Ducati. They would now achieve results totally out of proportion to their size and influence, and eventually become the premier Italian motorcycle

manufacturer. None of this would have been possible without Fabio Taglioni.

FABIO TAGLIONI AND THE GRAN SPORT

Born on 10 September 1920 and a graduate of Bologna University, Taglioni had been involved with the FB Mondial racing team. With designs by Alfonso Drusiani, Mondial had just won three successive 125 cc road-racing World Championships, and Taglioni came to Ducati with impressive credentials. Montano decided that they needed a motorcycle capable of success in the important Milano–Taranto and Giro d'Italia races, so Taglioni set about designing a completely new, bevel-gear driven, overhead camshaft engine that would not only be a successful racing engine, but would also provide a basis for future development. The 100 cc Gran Sport, nicknamed the Marianna, was an instant success and would be the foundation for a line of classic singles lasting two decades.

Fabio Taglioni with Battilani, Vighi, Villa and Lelli at the release of the Gran Sport at Imola, prior to the 1955 Giro d'Italia. *Walter Breveglieri*

By February 1955 the prototype Gran Sport was being tested at Modena. One month later it was officially released, and a team was entered in the Giro d'Italia only a few weeks later. Gianni Degli Antoni easily won the 100 cc class for the nine-day event at an average speed of 98.90 km/h (61.5 mph). In its debut, the Gran Sport had performed beyond even Taglioni's expectations.

The reasons were not that difficult to see. From the outset the Gran Sport had been designed as a racing engine of the highest quality and was of considerably more advanced specification than the Ducati ohv 98, or the Laverda pushrod ohv singles that had beaten them so convincingly in 1954. This approach would also serve Ducati well 30 years later, when they designed the eight-valve twin also as an uncompromised racing design that could be adapted for street use. By using bevel-gears to drive the overhead camshaft, Taglioni chose the best engineering solution, but it was an expensive one. Bevel-gears required careful manufacture and assembly, so the first Gran Sports were high-priced, limited-production racing bikes, albeit with a horn and headlight to comply with Italian FMI regulations.

Displacing 99.66 cc, the 49.4 x 52 mm Gran Sport, with its 8.5:1 compression ratio and 20 mm Dell'Orto carburettor, produced 9 bhp at 9,000 rpm. It featured many design specifications that would not only carry through to the production overhead camshaft singles, but also the later V-twins. Some, like the vertically split crankcases with unit gearbox and finned sump, along with the predominance of ball and roller bearings, are even present today in the Pantah and current eight-valve engines. The cylinder head had the same 80° included valve angle that would last until the Mille V-twin of 1985, as would the camshaft drive by a vertical shaft and bevel-gears from the right side of the pressed up three-piece crankshaft. Like all the ohc singles, the finned alloy cylinder was inclined forward 10°, but the Gran Sport had exposed hairpin valve springs with the cam box cast separately from the cylinder head. The bevel and primary gears were straight cut and the Gran Sport had a four-speed gearbox.

The frame was also a prototype for the range of Ducati singles that was to follow, in that it was a single down-tube open cradle type using the engine as a stressed member. With 17-inch wheels and weighing a

Below: The 98 cc Gran Sport soon became a 125, and was just as successful in the Giro d'Italia. This is Nello Mandini in the 1957 event, one of many riders of these catalogued racers. *Walter Breveglieri*

mere 80 kg (176 lb), the 100 Gran Sport had a top speed of 130 km/h (81 mph). Success continued for the Marianna in the Milano–Taranto road race of 1955, with Degli Antoni winning the 100 cc class of the 1,400 km event at 103.172 km/h (64.1 mph). This continued until 1958, when, because the Gran Sport had been so successful, the 100 cc class was scrapped altogether. Fortunately, Taglioni always envisaged a larger engine for his masterpiece, and even for the 1955 Milano–Taranto event had produced a prototype 125 Gran Sport.

The 125 was simply achieved by boring the 100 unit to 55.3 mm, and with a 22 mm carburettor 12 bhp was produced at 9,800 rpm. Apart from the use of 18-inch wheels and larger brakes, the 125 was very similar to the 100, and both continued into 1956 with moderate power increases (12 bhp for the 100 and 14 bhp for the 125). There was success again in the Giro d'Italia, with Giuliano Maoggi winning the event

outright in 1956 on a 125. In the final Milano–Taranto race, once again both the 100 and 125 Gran Sports were dominant, Alberto Gandossi winning the 100 cc class at 99.744 km/h (62 mph), and Degli Antoni the 125 class at 103.176 km/h (64 mph). As expected, the Gran Sport engine grew again during 1956 to 175 cc. By both boring and stroking the 100 to 62 x 57.8 mm, the 175 produced 16 bhp at 9,000 rpm, and was the prototype for the 1957 175 cc road bikes, 175 Bialbero, and the later Formula 3 bikes. Taglioni's influence was also becoming evident in the range of pushrod ohv bikes, most notably with the first sporting Ducati, the 98S of 1953. By 1956 this had a small fairing, and was joined by the 125TV with a full cradle frame. The 1956 98S in particular was a very purposeful-looking sporting motorcycle and headed the year's line-up of three 65 cc bikes (65T, TL, and TS) and four 98s (98N, T, TL, and S) alongside the 125TV.

The dominance of the 100 Gran Sport in its class was emphasized in November 1956, when the streamlined private machine of Mario Carini and Sandro Ciceri took 44 world records at Monza. Apart from a 25 mm Dell'Orto carburettor, the engine was standard and the bike was timed at an amazing 171.910 km/h (106.8 mph). The Marianna's reliability was displayed over the 1,000 km at an average speed of 154.556 km/h (96 mph).

The first production overhead camshaft road bikes appeared in 1957 (covered in a later chapter), and not only the end of the 100 cc class, but also the final Giro d'Italia following the tragedy in the Mille Miglia car race only a week later when De Portago's Ferrari 315 ran off the road into the crowd after a tyre burst, killing nine spectators. In this last Giro d'Italia, Graziano won the event outright, with Mariannas filling the first 12 places. While the single overhead camshaft racers were now superseded by the double overhead versions, there was still one important success

left for the 125 Gran Sport, a clean sweep in the 1957 Barcelona 24-Hour endurance race. Here Bruno Spaggiari and Alberto Gandossi completed 586 laps at an average speed of 57.66 mph (92.8 km/h) on a bike intended for the cancelled Milano–Taranto race, with Gran Sports also filling second and third places. The following year Mandolini and Maranghi led home another Gran Sport dominated field: while the number of laps completed was identical, 125 cc Gran Sports this time took the first five places. The stage was set for Ducati's years of dominance in this esteemed event.

However, during 1955 Ducati had decided to contest the 125 cc Grand Prix class, and while the Marianna was ideal for street races and for establishing Ducati's reputation, a more sophisticated engine would be needed. Taglioni would also be given the opportunity to put into practice his idea for desmodromically-actuated valve operation, an idea that he had been working on since 1948.

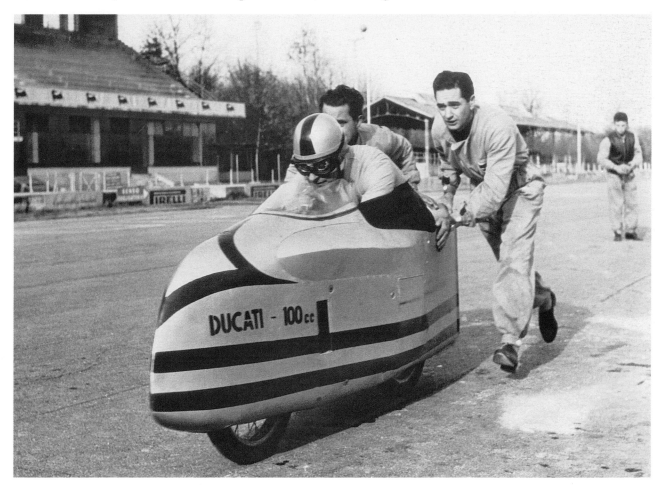

The double overhead camshaft
125 cc Grand Prix Bialbero.
Rolf im Brahm

2 DESMODROMICS

On 25 February 1956, barely one year after the debut of the Gran Sport, a double overhead camshaft version, the Bialbero, was unveiled. It was now Ducati's intention to enter not only the Italian modified sports class with this new racer, but also the World Championship 125cc Grand Prix. This was a massive step for a small company with little racing experience. The mid-1950s was a golden age for Grands Prix in all classes, and competition between MV and Mondial in the 125 class was fierce, with DKW, Montesa, and Gilera also vying for the victor's laurels. Essentially a Gran Sport apart from the cylinder head, the Bialbero was raced in the early Grands Prix of 1956, but with little success.

While the Bialbero was significantly more powerful than the Gran Sport, initially producing 15.5 bhp at 10,500 rpm and soon increased to 16 bhp at 11,500 rpm, it was still no match for the MVs, let alone the Mondials and Gileras, and with sustained high revs its reliability suffered. The problems of valve float and the minimal valve-to-piston clearance meant there was no room for error if a rider missed a gear, so Fabio Taglioni sought to eliminate valve-springs entirely by a method of positive valve control – desmodromic valve gear. Mercedes-Benz had successfully used desmodromic valve gear on their W196 Grand Prix and 300 SLR Sports racing cars in 1954 and 1955, but apart from Mercedes only Taglioni has managed to make desmodromics work reliably and successfully.

Using the Bialbero engine from the cylinder head downward, Taglioni was able to create his 125 desmodromic racer in an astonishingly short time. Its debut at the non-championship Swedish Grand Prix at Hedemora on 15 July 1956 was one of Ducati's greatest race triumphs. Gianni Degli Antoni, on the fully-faired little desmo, easily won the 125 race, lapping the entire field. This was no hollow victory either, because the competition included a number of privately entered MVs and Mondials. While this first desmo wasn't significantly more powerful than the Bialbero, with 17 bhp at 12,500 rpm, it was the increase to over 14,000 rpm that the desmodromic system safely provided that had made the difference. A shortened big-end life was the only price paid for exploiting this capability. Taglioni's desmodromic system differed from others in that it used three camshafts mounted in a magnificent one-piece cambox

7.5 mm), and 7.4 mm for the exhaust (compared with
7.0 mm). Carburation was either a 27 mm Dell'Orto
like the Bialbero, a 29 mm unit for faster circuits, or as
small as 22 to 23 mm for the Italian street circuits.

Setting a precedent that would become a feature of
all factory racing singles (and the later Imola twins),
twin plug ignition was used. The usual 14 mm spark
plug was supplemented by a 10 mm plug mounted near
the bevel-gear tube, allowing the ignition advance to be
reduced from 42 to 36°. Ignition was by a total loss
6 volt battery and twin 3 volt coils. The compression
ratio was 10:1, and much of the lower part of the engine
was shared with the Gran Sport. A five- or sometimes
six-speed gearbox was fitted, but because there was no
room inside the Gran Sport engine-cases for more than
four, the fifth or sixth gears were mounted inboard of
the clutch in the primary drive compartment. The street
origins were also displayed by a blanked-off kickstart
and an empty space on the left side of the crankshaft
where the Gran Sport carried a generator.

Ducati hoped to create a big impression at the
Italian Grand Prix at Monza in September 1956, but
tragedy struck when their star rider, 26-year-old Gianni

and cylinder head casting. As with the Bialbero, the
opening camshafts were carried on the outer shafts, but
the desmo's closing cams were mounted on the single
central camshaft, operating the valves by forked
rockers. The closing camshaft was driven by a vertical
shaft and bevel-gear, this being geared directly to the
two opening camshafts. The 31 mm and 27 mm valves
were the same size as the Bialbero, but desmodromics
allowed more lift, 8.1 mm for the inlet (up from

Right: When raced during 1956
the desmo 125s were fully
streamlined; Degli Antoni raced
with a matching helmet. *Ducati
Motor*

Below: Dave Chadwick on the
start line for the 1958 Isle of Man
125 TT. *Mick Woollett*

Degli Antoni, was killed while testing at Monza in
August. In the race itself none of the Ducatis performed
particularly spectacularly, ending the year on a
disappointing note after their magnificent display in
Sweden. For 1957 it was decided to spend a year
developing the desmo for an all-out assault on the
Grands Prix in 1958. This also gave Taglioni time to
concentrate on the production of the new overhead-
camshaft road bikes. Meanwhile, a limited number of
double overhead-camshaft 125s, called the 125 Grand
Prix, were made available to privateers, and these
featured a number of changes from the previous year,
most noticeably in the frame, which now had an
additional twin-loop subframe under the engine. The
engine also received new crankcases. About 50 of these
125 Grand Prix racers were made between 1957 and
1959, and they were the most competitive 125 racer a
privateer could buy at the time. A double overhead-
camshaft Bialbero 175 cc version was also available.

While the only 1957 World Championship event
that the desmos raced in was the Italian Grand Prix at
Monza, this, like the previous year, was a disaster.
Alberto Gandossi fell while in the lead on the first lap,
bringing down most of the field. Non-desmo Ducatis
were also entered for the non-championship Swedish
Grand Prix (where this time they took the first five
places), but in the Italian Formula 2 and 3 classes
Franco Farnè and Bruno Spaggiari were virtually
unbeatable. The 125 desmo now produced 18 bhp at
12,500 rpm, and, with a new double-cradle frame, was
ready to take on the might of the other Italian factories.

However, before the start of the 1958 season Moto
Guzzi, Gilera, and Mondial announced their retirement
from Grand Prix competition. This would leave MV
Agusta as Ducati's principal opposition, but with Carlo
Ubbiali being joined by reigning World Champion
Tarquino Provini they would be a formidable team.
Ducati's own team was headed by Luigi Taveri, and
consisted of Alberto Gandossi, Bruno Spaggiari,
sometimes Romolo Ferri and Franco Villa, Dave
Chadwick for the opening Grand Prix at the Isle of
Man, and, later, trials ace Sammy Miller. The fully-
streamlined 'dustbin' fairings of the previous two years
were now banned, and in several pre-season events the
desmos performed impressively. Ducati went to the Isle
of Man with an air of confidence, and a speed
advantage over the MVs.

Ubbiali on the MV won at the shorter Clypse Isle of
Man circuit after Taveri retired, but Gandossi retaliated

with a win at Spa in Belgium. After the Isle of Man
new, higher-lift camshafts had given the desmo single
an increase to 19 bhp, and throughout the season the
motorcycle was continually developed. No two were
identical, with not only different petrol tanks and seats,
but also crankcase castings and frames. Further Ducati
victories came in Sweden and at Monza, where
Spaggiari led a top-five clean sweep. His winning speed
was 155.827 km/h (96.8 mph), and this was one of

Left: Australian Ken Kavanagh
rode this 220 cc Bialbero to
considerable success in 1960 in
Australia. *Ducati Motor*

English newcomer, Mike Hailwood.

After the success of 1958, everyone expected 1959 to be a repeat performance, but, unfortunately for Ducati, this didn't materialise. Hailwood's success in 1958 on a dohc Grand Prix, along with his father Stan Hailwood's setting up of Ducati Concessionaires in Manchester as distributors, prompted the factory to loan Hailwood a 125 cc desmo single for the season. It was only Hailwood's exploits that brought any real results, and he won his first ever Grand Prix victory at Ulster in August, eventually ending up third in the 125 cc World Championship. At the end of the 1959 season Ducati retired from racing, selling off the works desmos but substituting the desmodromic heads for the dohc valve-spring type. These continued to be successfully raced for many years, often with the single down-tube Gran Sport type frame of 1956 and 1957 rather than the later full-cradle double down-tube.

There was one more interesting development to the 125 Grand Prix that needs to be documented, and this occurred at the end of the 1959 season. Australian Ken Kavanagh had successfully raced a 125 Grand Prix

Ducati's greatest triumphs. Unfortunately, while humiliating MV in front of their home crowd, Gandossi still just failed to beat Ubbiali for the 125 cc title. However, on the domestic front Ducati won all the 125 cc championships in 1958. Having proved that desmodromics worked, the factory decided to contest the 1959 series of Grand Prix and Italian Championship races on a reduced scale with both the single cylinder desmo, and the new twin. Joining Gandossi and Spaggiari were Taveri and a promising

Below left: At the 1958 Isle of Man TT Romolo Ferri (6) and Dave Chadwick (26) finished second and third in the 125cc GP. It was won by Ubbiali (20) on the MV Augusta. *Mick Woollett*

Below: Complex and heavy, the 125 desmodromic twin was not as successful as the Desmo single. *Alan Cathcart Archive*

during 1959 and persuaded the factory to supply him with a 220 – built out of a 69 mm bored 175 dohc Bialbero – to use to help promote Ducati in Australia in a series of races held during the antipodean summer season. Displacing 216.13 cc, and with a 9:1 compression ratio, the 220 produced 28 bhp at 9,600 rpm. Carburation was by a 29 mm Dell'Orto, and because of its success several similar 220 cc machines were later built.

RACING TWINS AND FOURS

The first indication that Ducati were interested in building larger, multi-cylindered motorcycles came at the Milan Show in December 1956, with the unveiling of a 175 cc double overhead camshaft parallel twin with exposed valve springs. This was raced by Leopoldo Tartarini in the final, 1957, Giro d'Italia, but it retired in the third stage. Originating from drawings first sketched by Taglioni in 1950, it was an interesting, if complicated design, with the pressed up crankshaft consisting of two flywheel assemblies clamped by Hirth

(radially serrated) couplings. A jackshaft was driven off the middle of the crankshaft, and this drove the twin overhead camshafts by a train of spur gears. While the 49 x 46.6 mm 175 produced considerably more power than the 175 cc single cylinder Gran Sport – 22 bhp at 11,000 rpm – the narrower power band and increase in weight to 112 kg (247 lb) largely negated this benefit. The 175 became the basis for a 125 cc Grand Prix machine first raced by Franco Villa at the Italian Grand Prix at Monza in 1958, where it finished third in that remarkable Ducati first-five clean sweep.

This 125 was intended to replace the single by producing more horsepower through increased revs, and the 42.5 x 45 mm engine produced 22.5 bhp at 13,800 rpm. A similar three-camshaft desmodromic valve system to the single allowed the engine to rev to an amazing (for the time) 17,000 rpm, but the power band was extremely narrow and the bike difficult to ride despite having a six-speed gearbox. As with the 175 twin, the 125 was also too heavy at a claimed 92 kg (203 lb), and the handling was less than satisfactory. Compared with the single, the twin (of which only

Below: One of the two desmodromic 350 cc racing twins built in 1960. Later, they were sold to John Surtees who commissioned this Reynolds frame with leading-link forks. *Rolf im Brahm*

three were built) didn't achieve much success. Breakages in the camshaft drive gear-train often occurred, with disastrous results, and the bikes were sold at the end of the 1959 season, two of them ending up being raced by Mike Hailwood.

It was during 1959 that Stan Hailwood commissioned a 250 cc version for Mike to race in 1960. Revealed to the press in February 1960, the 250 shared the same 55.25 x 52 mm dimensions with the 125 cc single, but in other respects was a scaled-up 125 twin. The power was 43 bhp at 11,600 rpm, and it was a very fast motorcycle with a top speed in the region of 218 km/h (135 mph), but it handled poorly and was considerably overweight. At about the same time, Ken Kavanagh, about to undertake his successful series in Australia, persuaded the factory to build a 350 cc desmo twin for the 1960 season. This appeared in time for Kavanagh to race at Imola in April but an accident

prevented him from riding it until the Isle of Man, by which time Hailwood also had a similar machine. With a bore and stroke of 64 x 54 mm, the 350 produced 48 bhp, but the engines vibrated badly and the bikes needed a lot of development to be competitive. At the end of the season John Surtees bought both Hailwood's 250 and 350, followed a few months later by Kavanagh's. They received new frames and leading-link forks by Ken Sprayson, and Phil Read rode a 350 at the Isle of Man in 1962 where it blew up in practice. They were raced unsuccessfully for a couple more domestic British seasons.

There was, however, to be one more multi-cylindered disaster. Seeing the limitations of a single, or even twin, at Grand Prix level, Taglioni designed a 125 cc in-line four-cylinder engine in 1958. This idea was advanced for the time, but with Ducati's withdrawal from competition at the end of 1959 the design languished until the Spanish Mototrans concern persuaded Ducati to produce it five years later, in 1964, by which time it was obsolete in a few design areas. There were four non-desmo valves per cylinder and a very wide 90° included valve angle. The double overhead camshaft 125 used a train of gears on the left side of the engine to drive the camshafts. With a compression ratio of 12:1 and four 12 mm Dell'Orto carburettors, the 34.5 x 34 mm engine produced 23 bhp at 14,000 rpm, hardly outstanding considering that the 125 cc twin had produced 22.5 bhp in 1958. Even with 12 months of development the power was only increased to 24 bhp at 16,000 rpm, and Ducati realized that it would never be competitive at Grand Prix level. Only two bikes were built, and during 1966 the 125 four quietly disappeared.

The entire parallel twin and four cylinder episode was interesting in that they were the first Ducatis designed exclusively for racing bearing no relationship to any road bikes. Because they were so unsuccessful compared to the Gran Sport derivatives none of their features ended up on the production line, but they certainly had the effect of creating a Taglioni philosophy that would prevail in the future: that of producing a motorcycle with a balance of power and weight. There was no point in an unnecessarily complex and heavy motorcycle if this did not translate into improved lap times. Also, what good was a powerful motorcycle if it did not handle well or the powerband was so narrow that it was unridable? Not only was it significant that the desmodromic Grand Prix racer was closely derived from a road bike (albeit a catalogued racer with lights), but all future Ducati success would emphasize a broad range, rather than outright power, and a balance between power and weight.

The 175 Sport of 1957 was the
first production overhead
camshaft bevel-gear Ducati.

3 PRODUCTION OVERHEAD

CAMSHAFT SINGLES (NARROW-CASE)

Following the success of the Gran Sport in the 1955 and 1956 Giro d'Italia and Milano–Taranto races, it was inevitable that the Gran Sport engine would be used as a basis for a range of production motorcycles. Given Taglioni's ability to generate designs amazingly quickly, it wasn't surprising that Ducati's first production bevel-gear motorcycle, the 175 Sport, was on display at the Milan Show in December 1956. This was followed shortly afterwards by a slightly detuned version, the 175T.

100/125/175/200

The 175 engine was to form the basis of the entire range of production singles (and also the subsequent Spanish Mototrans versions) until their demise in 1974. It differed from the Gran Sport in a number of design details, most notably in the use of enclosed, rather than exposed, hairpin valve springs. With a bore and stroke of 62 x 57.8 mm, and a compression ratio of 8:1, the 175 Sport produced 14 bhp at 8,000 rpm. The weight was 104 kg (229 lb), and though only a four-speed gearbox was used, performance was lively with a claimed top speed of 130 km/h (81 mph). The 175T had a 7:1 compression ratio and produced 12 bhp at 6,000 rpm. Top speed was 109 km/h (68 mph). The Sport featured the distinctive scalloped petrol tank that would last through to the 200 Elite.

In September 1957, 100 and 125 cc Touring and Sport versions of the overhead camshaft single were displayed, to go into production during 1958. The 125 Sport, sharing its 55.25 mm bore and 52 mm stroke with the Grand Prix, produced 10 bhp at 8,500 rpm with a compression ratio of 8:1. The 100, with the same 49.4 x 52 mm bore dimensions as the first Marianna, produced 8 bhp at 8,700 rpm. Both these Sports were styled after the F3 and weighed 100.5 kg (221.5 lb), with the 125 having a surprising maximum speed of 112 km/h (69 mph). The 175S of 1958 continued with the scalloped petrol tank, and was the first to feature the strange dual muffler that would also categorize the later 200 Elite. After about a year of

The 1957 175T was similar to the Sport, but slightly detuned.
Phil Aynsley

Below left: The 125 Sport was styled along the lines of the racing F3. *Roy Kidney*

Below right: For 1959 the 175 cc engine grew to 200 cc, and powered the sporting 200 Elite.

One of the more unusual models
of this period was the 200
Motocross, only a few of this
1960 model being produced.
Phil Aynsley

production the 100 was discontinued, but the model range actually expanded during this period as the 125TS and 175TS were added, and the 175 grew to 200 cc. The 125 Sport remained a popular model, particularly in Italy, until 1965.

By simply boring the 175 by an additional 5 mm, to 67 mm, the 200 Elite was created for the 1959 season. With 18 bhp at 7,500 rpm, the 111 kg (245 lb) Elite had a claimed top speed of 135 km/h (84 mph). The styling followed that of the 175 Sport, but for 1959 both models received 18-inch wheels. The Elite soon gained a reputation as a first rate sporting motor-cycle and did much to establish the Ducati name in export markets. There were other 175 and 200 models for 1959, notably the Americano sharing the dual muffler

and valanced mudguards. The 175 Americano was an extraordinary motorcycle with its twin air horns, high 'cowboy' style handlebars, and chrome-studded seat. It was difficult to imagine that beneath that exterior lurked much the same engine and running gear as the 200 Elite. Another significant, if not totally successful, model was the 175 and 200 Motocross. Though this lasted only through to 1961, it was a prelude to a much more successful range, the Scrambler or SCR, later to become the backbone of the overhead camshaft line-up.

During this period a wide variety of specifications was offered with the range of 175s and 200s, much depending on the requirements of importers in specific countries. In the UK they even had different names,

Below: The 175 F3 was a catalogued racer sharing little with the production models. The front brake was a magnesium Amadoro. *Phil Aynsley*

Right: The first production overhead camshaft 250 was the four-speed Diana of 1962. *Roy Kidney*

with the 125 Monza and Monza Super, 175 Silverstone and Silverstone Super, and 200 Super Sports and Elite being listed in 1960. For the domestic Italian market there was also the touring 175TS and 175 'Due' Selle with an 11 bhp engine.

As the engine grew to 250 cc, the 175s and 200s were phased out. The 125 engine eventually became a 160, and by 1962 the 175 was discontinued. The 200 Elite soldiered on for a few more years, still being offered until 1965, while in 1962 the 200GT was created out of the new 250 Diana. Perceived as an underpowered 250, this was a sales disaster, and was dropped after only a year. The writing was on the wall for the smaller-engined Ducatis, and the success of the new 250 only reinforced this. The public then, as now, wanted larger engines, with more performance.

125/175/250 FORMULA 3

In 1958 the Formula 3 became Ducati's production racer, superseding the Gran Sport that had been available since 1955. If one were to make an analogy with modern Ducatis, the Supermono would be the closest equivalent to both the Gran Sport and the F3. They were intended for the non-Grand Prix privateers and were made in very limited numbers, being assembled by racing mechanics. Also they were extremely expensive and used unique components. 175 F3 owner Phil Schilling estimates that less than 100 of all types (125/175/250) were built over a five-year period, perhaps some 50 of them being 175s.

Looking like racing versions of the 100 and 125 Sport, the F3 actually owed more to the Gran Sport than the production bikes. Unlike the street bike, the engine-cases were sand-cast rather than die-cast, and internally the engine was completely different. From the Gran Sport came the straight-cut primary and bevel-gears, along with special camshaft, rockers, con-rod, piston, clutch, and gearbox. Virtually nothing was interchangeable with the street 125/175 Sport. The frame was lighter, lower, and longer than the standard model, and used different forks and shock absorbers. The dimensions were such that neither the petrol tank nor seat were interchangeable between the two. However, by far the most startling differences on the 175 and 250 were the brakes. They had the same double-sided Amadoro front, and vented rear, brakes that were used on the Bialbero and factory racers. These were so unusual that Phil Schilling always referred to his 175 F3 as the Ducati 'with the funny front brake'.

Interestingly, all the F3s came with complete street equipment that included a headlight, muffler, tail light, and number-plate holder, but the intention for the bike was clear. It was meant for the track. The 125 F3 featured the same engine specifications as the 125 Gran Sport (but with enclosed valve gear), and the 175 shared its 62 x 57.8 mm engine dimensions with the 175 Bialbero and 175 road bikes. The 175 F3 produced 16 bhp at 9,000 rpm, with a maximum of 9,800 rpm, and was able to achieve 100 mph (161 kph).

Given the specifications, one could assume that the 175 F3 had a spectacular racing career, but generally only factory-prepared bikes were successful. Franco Villa won the supporting Formula 3 race at the 1958 Italian GP (where Ducati had filled the first five places in the 125 Grand Prix), and Franco Farnè the Class 4 Lightweight race at Daytona in 1959. At the Barcelona 24-Hour race of 1960 eight 175s were entered, with victory going to Franco Villa and Amedco Balboni at an average speed of 59.25 mph (95.35 km/h). Most F3s were raced by privateers, but they were too expensive for many. The lightweight class eventually grew to 250, so the 175 became obsolete, and a limited number of 250 F3s were made during 1961. Pressure from

Ducati's export markets, particularly Berliner in the US, had led Taglioni to develop a 250 cc version of the 175 F3 in 1960. With a special 74 mm cast iron liner, the 250 F3 produced 32 bhp at 9,000 rpm, and Franco Villa was sent to contest a series of road races in the US. So successful was this racing effort that it established Ducati in the US as a manufacturer of reliable and competitive racing machines, and also paved the way for the release of a production 250.

By 1962, production of these beautiful and purposeful racing motorcycles was finished, but they remain as some of the best examples of Ducati's commitment to fine engineering and exquisite construction. There would be no more catalogued production racers, apart from a small number of 250 and 350 SCs Mach 1/Ss and the SCD in 1965, 1966 and 1967, until the 600TT2 of 1982.

250 MONZA, DIANA, AND SCR

Following on from the success of the prototype racing 250 F3, a 250 street bike was displayed in April 1961. This new motorcycle would form the basis of the overhead camshaft production range until the wide-case single of 1968, and was available in two versions, the touring Monza and more sporting Diana. The first Monza had high handlebars and the new engine shared

The British version of the 250
Diana was called the Daytona,
but was otherwise similar.

the same bore and stroke (74 x 57.8 mm) as the 250
F3. With a Dell'Orto UBF 24BS carburettor, and an 8:1
compression ratio, the claimed power was a pretty un-
realistic 22 bhp at 7,200 rpm. Weight was only 125 kg
(276 lb), so the performance was more than respectable
for its day, and top speed was claimed to be 80 mph
(129 km/h). The Diana (Daytona for the UK), with
clip-on handlebars, had a claimed power output of
24 bhp. Its weight, at 120 kg (265 lb), was slightly less
than the Monza, and top speed was in the region of
85 mph (137 km/h). There was also the option of a
larger, SS1 27A remote float-bowl carburettor for the
Diana. The styling for the 250 was completely new,
with a different petrol tank, seat, and side panels from
the 175s and 200s. The third 250 cc model to emerge
during 1962 was the 30 bhp 250 Motocross, the 250
SCR. Primarily intended for the US market, this was
based very closely on the earlier 200 Motocross.

With Ducati dubiously preoccupied throughout
1962 and 1963 with the new range of two-strokes, the
only new ohc model was the 250 Mark 3 Super Sport
for the US in mid-1963. This modified Diana was a

true production racer and offered the 30 bhp, 10:1
compression ratio engine, with the SS1 27A carburettor
and 40 watt flywheel magneto ignition, of the 250
SCR. Full racing equipment, including clip-ons, racing
guards and tyres, and a competition plate, were also
included. In April 1964 the Mark 3, Monza and
Motocross received a five-speed gearbox along with the
250GT (essentially a Diana with a Monza engine). A
few months later one of Ducati's all-time classics, the
250 Mach 1, was released.

250 MACH 1

There have been several occasions throughout Ducati's
history when one particular production model has
stood out like a beacon from the rest of the range, and
the Mach 1, first displayed in September 1964, was
undoubtedly one of these. Purely from a performance
point of view the Mach 1, based on the US 250 Mark 3
Super Sport, was outstanding, with its claim of a top
speed of 106 mph (170.6 km/h). In 1964 this placed
the Mach 1 firmly at the top of the 250 cc class, but it

wasn't a claim that was always substantiated. In February 1965, for instance, *Motor Cycling* could only manage a best of 83 mph (134 km/h), because the bike was too overgeared.

Of all the production street narrow-case singles, the Mach 1 was the most outstanding. It was the first top-of-the-line limited production street Ducati developed from a successful racer and offered the highest standard of performance for its day. Because of its significance, the Mach 1 justifies more detailed examination.

While Ducati had officially withdrawn from Grand Prix racing at the end of 1959, the factory continued to support various racing events that would help develop the road bike range. The most notable venue was that of Montjuich Park in Barcelona for the annual 24-Hour endurance race, and it has always been one of Ducati's

Below: One of the all-time classic Ducatis: the Mach 1.

happiest hunting grounds. The first 250 had been entered in 1962, when Ricardo Fargas and Enzo Rippa took a prototype Mototrans 250 to victory, but a more significant win was in 1964 when Spaggiari and Mandolini rode a 284 cc factory prototype. With a bore of 79 mm, this was the first Ducati displacing more than 250 cc, and its success prompted the factory to release a limited number of SC (Sport Corsa) production racers. Like the F3, these had straight-cut primary and bevel gears, and special sand-cast crankcases. Those of the SC were stronger than earlier designs, and a forerunner of the subsequent wide crankcase of 1968. A 250 and 350 SC was offered in January 1965, and they had a twin spark-plug cylinder head producing 34 bhp at 8,500 rpm for the 250, and 39.5 bhp at 8,000 rpm for the 350. Because they had been designed to be strong and reliable in endurance events, they weren't a particularly light or compact bike at 280 lb (127 kg) on a 56-inch (1,422 mm) wheelbase. The most notable feature of the SC was its double down-tube full-cradle frame and much wider engine mounts, both front and rear. The 1965 version used a Mach 1 style petrol tank, but was not particularly successful. The SC was also offered in 1966, when it had an Oldani front brake and a special fibre-glass racing petrol tank. It may not have been the ideal racer for the privateer, but its street derivative, the Mach 1, was definitely the bike that Ducati enthusiasts had been waiting for.

The Mach 1 engine had a higher compression piston, giving a 10:1 compression ratio, and had larger (40 and 36 mm) valves along with a grey coded camshaft. As with all the overhead camshaft singles, the valve springs were the hairpin type, and the valve timing figures were inlet opening 62° before top dead centre and closing 76° after bottom dead centre, and exhaust opening 70° before bottom dead centre and closing 48° after top dead centre. With an unfiltered Dell'Orto SS1 29D carburettor, the claimed power was 27.6 bhp at 8,500 rpm. The five-speed gearbox was operated by a rear-set rocking gearchange pedal, and while clip-on handlebars were specified, there was also the bizarre option of a Mach 1 with rear-set foot controls and high, touring-style handlebars.

Despite the output of the alternator being increased to 60 watts (from 40) for the five-speed 250s, the electrics remained a cause for concern, with the six-volt 25W headlight particularly poor. But Marzocchi suspension front and rear, a light weight of 116 kg (256 lb), and a short wheelbase of 1,350 mm (53.15 inches), ensured that the Mach 1 had the right ingredients for a top 250 cc sporting streetbike in the style of the 500 cc BSA DBD34 Clubmans Gold Star and Velocette Thruxton. Brakes were the 180 x 35 mm front and 160 x 30 mm rear drums fitted to the rest of the range, as were the 18-inch wheels with steel rims, but the red and silver Mach 1 was the only one with a red frame. It was also noted for a wildly optimistic 150 mph (241 km/h) Veglia speedometer.

For the US market the 250 Mark 3 continued to be the top performance model as it had been during 1963 and 1964, but for 1965 it was very much a renamed Mach 1 (with magneto ignition). The factory even claimed a higher top speed of 177 km/h (110 mph) for the Mark 3, which also came equipped with a

supplementary 100 mm white-faced Veglia tachometer and a racing plate over the headlight. The weight for the Mark 3 of 1965 was slightly less than the Mach 1 too, at 112 kg (247 lb). *Cycle World*, testing a Mark 3 in August 1965, achieved a top speed of 97 mph (156 km/h).

The Mach 1 continued in production until 1966, as did the Mark 3, now with normal foot-rests rather than rear-sets. The Mach 1 was discontinued in 1967, leaving only the Mark 3, but with battery and coil ignition rather than the flywheel magneto. However, even with the new wide-case replacement imminent, the Mach 1 (and narrow-case Mark 3) continued to be the favoured choice amongst privateer racers because they were so much lighter, and the problems of a fragile kickstart mechanism less significant. In 1969, Alistair Rogers on a Mach 1 racer gave Ducati its first TT victory – the 250 at the Isle of Man – at an average speed of 83.79 mph (134.84 km/h).

160/250 MONZA, 250GT, 250 SCR, 350 SEBRING

The importance of the US market for Ducati really became evident from 1964 with the release of a number of basically non-sporting models. The 160 Monza Junior was created out of the earlier 125 by increasing the bore to 61 mm, while retaining the 52 mm stroke, to achieve 156 cc. With an 8.2:1 compression ratio and a Dell'Orto UB 22BS carburettor, this engine was placed in the same frame as the 250 Monza, where it looked too small and out of place. The 160 also received 16-inch wheels front and rear, and there was still only a four-speed gearbox. The 106 kg (234 lb) machine was only able to reach a top speed of 102 km/h (63 mph). Most commentators couldn't understand the logic of putting a smaller engine in a 250, but Ducati kept making the 160 Monza Junior until 1966; then, in 1967, with US demand at an end, 1,800 were dumped on the UK market as part of a consignment of 3,400 motorcycles purchased by Scottish entrepreneur Bill Hannah. They were still being sold at a discount price in 1972.

The styling was altered for 1965 with a new square petrol tank, side covers and seat, and there was a similar third, and final, edition in 1966, now with a square headlight surround. Otherwise the 160

The 250 Motocross was produced primarily for the US market. *Roy Kidney*

remained unchanged throughout its production and was definitely not one of Ducati's triumphs.

The 250 Monza mirrored the 160, but for some reason the squarish styling changes happened a year later. So the five-speed 250 Monza appeared in 1964 looking identical to the earlier four-speed model, and continued unchanged through 1965. Engine specifications were the same as the first version, and for 1966 the 250 Monza shared its styling with the 160 Monza Junior.

Fitting in between the Monza and Mark 3, the 250GT was essentially a Mark 3 with the detuned Monza engine (along with battery and coil ignition), and was only available for 1964 and 1965. The final model in this range of rather mundane touring singles was the 350 Sebring. Like so many Ducati engines, the largest narrow-case single, the 350, had its origins on the race track. Franco Farnè had taken a 350 Mach 1/S racer to victory in the 350 class (and tenth overall) at an international race run in conjunction with the Sebring 12-Hour car race, in central Florida, in April 1965. Hardly a high profile event, it was, however, considered sufficiently prestigious to name the new 350 the Sebring.

Unfortunately, the production version shared little with the racer, and was in reality a Monza with a larger engine. By boring and stroking the 250 to the almost square dimensions of 76 x 75 mm, 340.327 cc was obtained. With an 8.5:1 compression ratio, and the Dell'Orto UBF 24BS carburettor of the 250 Monza, the 123 kg (271 lb) Sebring was a particularly sluggish performer with a top speed of only 125 km/h (78 mph). There were two versions for 1965, the US model almost identical to the 250 Monza, and the European model mirroring the 250GT. For 1966 the Sebring had the square styling of the 160 and 250 Monzas of that year, and, with no change in engine specification, the claimed top speed had amazingly risen to 142 km/h (88 mph).

Throughout the continuing changes to the range over this period, the 250 Motocross (SCR) remained in production, largely in the same form as it had appeared in 1962 but now with the five-speed gearbox. With a more highly tuned engine than the Monza, the Motocross had a 9.2:1 compression ratio, a Dell'Orto SS1 27A carburettor with air cleaner, and a totally open exhaust system. For 1965 there were 19-inch wheels front and rear, and the weight was 109 kg (240 lb). The 1966 version had a different headlight,

an 18-inch rear wheel, a battery to power the lights, and the weight was up to 120 kg (264.5 lb).

By 1968 the entire range of narrow-crankcase models had been superseded by the new wide-crankcase type, even though unsold stocks continued to be available long after production had finished. There had been too much emphasis placed on the mundane touring models, and problems with reliability and finish did little to endear these to the motorcycle-buying public. The only lines to continue as a wide-case were to be the 250 Monza, the Mark 3, and the Scrambler.

Throughout the 1950s and into the 1960s, pushrod singles like the 1958 98TS were offered alongside the overhead camshaft models.

4 ODDBALLS

While today the name of Ducati motorcycles is associated with the production of some of the best-ever sporting and racing motorcycles, throughout its history the company has produced a surprising variety of unmemorable products. Most of these lesser models were produced during the 1960s, being the more mundane overhead camshaft bevel-gear singles outlined in the previous chapter, and an even less noteworthy range of entry level motorcycles. These outnumbered the entire line up of ohc bikes, both in production and model range. Some had two-stroke engines, while others had four-stroke engines with pushrod-operated valves. The two-strokes were born in 1958, finally dying in 1977 with the 125 Six Days, while the pushrod singles finished in 1968. As part of a period of diversification of Ducati products that included outboard motors, lawn-mowers, and even the distribution of British Triumph cars, they were the result of poor management decisions. As would happen in the future, Taglioni refused to be involved with most of these projects, and he was ultimately proved right.

PUSHROD SINGLES

Until the advent of the Gran Sport in 1955, Ducati's road motorcycles were built around a range of pushrod overhead valve singles, which formed the basis of production until 1957, when the first overhead camshaft street bikes were released. Even after this, the overhead valve models continued to be sold in a range of capacities, and in 1957 the 85 Turismo and 85 Sport joined the 65, 98, and several 125s. At the request of Berliner in the US, the 98 cc Bronco appeared in 1959, and by 1960 the ohv model range was the 85T and S, 98 Bronco, Cavallino and TS, and 125 Aurea. The Aurea was an unusual model in that it used the twin cradle frame of the 1956 125TV, with the more sporting headlight and petrol tank of the 125 cc overhead camshaft bikes. The overhead valve motorcycles were definitely budget Ducatis, as the 125 Aurea, despite looking like a 125 Sport, only developed 6.5 bhp at 6,500 rpm from its 55.2 x 52 mm engine. The compression ratio was 6.8:1, and an 18 mm Dell'Orto carburettor was used. Performance didn't match that of the contemporary overhead camshaft 125TS with its 10 bhp.

The final pushrod single was the
125 Cadet/4 of 1967.
Phil Aynsley

The 98 Bronco and 98TS used the 48 x 52 mm 98 cc engine that had first appeared in 1952. With a compression ratio of 7:1, they made 6 bhp at 6,800 rpm. Both these, and the 125 Aurea, had a four-speed gearbox, and the TS boasted a more sporting riding position. The 98s weighed 87 kg (192 lb) and the top speed for the TS was about 53 mph (85 km/h).

The Bronco continued to be produced in 125 cc form and during 1964 it received a slightly restyled 125 cc engine, with square finning, but still with the engine specifications of the 125 Aurea. Then in 1966 a new 125 cc overhead valve engine was designed, with dimensions of 53 x 55 mm. This 121.3 cc engine was installed in a model known as the 125 Cadet/4 Lusso (the 4 denoted four speeds, while lusso means 'luxury'). There was a more powerful engine (with 8.4:1 compression), able to propel the 72 kg (159 lb) Cadet to a top speed of 95 km/h (59 mph). By 1967 the Cadet/4 was joined by the Cadet/4 Scrambler, with a high-rise exhaust system and a 16-inch rear wheel. Very few were made, and production didn't continue beyond 1968.

So ended the pushrod single that had started out 15 years earlier and had been entirely eclipsed by Taglioni's Gran Sport and its successors. As with the complete range of two-strokes, these final pushrod 125s weren't missed. They have become categorized with other failures, the later parallel twins, the Giugiaro 860, and the Weber carburetted Pantahs.

TWO-STROKES

In an endeavour to expand their customer base for motorcycles, Ducati decided in 1961 to market a range of moped and lightweight two-stroke motorcycles, initially in 50 cc but later joined by an 80 cc sports model. There had been a two-stroke 48 Sport offered briefly during 1958, and the new engine was based on this design. The 50 cc range of five models started with the single speed 48 cc Brisk, and culminated in the three speed 48 cc Sport. The Brisk/1 (single speed) certainly didn't live up to its name, and was a moped of very modest specification and performance. The single cylinder 38 x 42 mm two-stroke displaced 47.633 cc, and with a 7:1 compression ratio produced 1.34 bhp at 4,200 rpm. Weighing only 45 kg (99 lb), the top speed was a mere 40 km/h (25 mph). Subsequent versions had slightly more power (1.5 bhp) and went a claimed 50 km/h (31 mph). The frame was of pressed steel, but, unusually for a moped, the Brisk had telescopic forks and a swing-arm with dual shock absorbers.

Using the same 1.5 bhp engine, but with a three-speed gearbox and dual seat, was the Piuma 48 Export. For the British market the Piuma was called the Puma, and released in 1962 with a single seat. The 48 cc Sport models were also based around the same power unit, but with a 9.5:1 compression ratio, and a larger Dell'Orto UA15S carburettor without an air filter, power was increased to 4.2 bhp at 8,600 rpm. Using a double cradle tubular-steel frame, the Sport also looked like a smaller version of the then current 125/175/200 overhead camshaft model, right down to the shape of the petrol tank and the red and gold paintwork. The basic Italian market Sport 48 was styled as the 125 Sport, with clip-on handlebars, a dual seat, and the speedometer in the front headlight. It was a real motorcycle in miniature, but some had pedals, rather than a kickstart, for starting, which looked out of place. The performance of this 54 kg (119 lb) machine was up considerably on the regular Brisk or Piuma, with the top speed a claimed 80 kph (50 mph).

Other markets received slightly different versions. There was the Sport 48 Export, identical but for a fuel tank styled along the lines of the 200 Elite, and the Sport 48 USA (called the Falcon 50) that had the Italian market version's petrol tank, but higher handlebars and a single seat. According to the factory brochures, all models had a 'voluminous toolbox'.

Below: Although powered by an
unremarkable 50 cc two-stroke,
the 1967 50 SL/1 was styled like
a racer and included twin fuel
filler caps.

The Setter 80 (Super Falcon 80 in the US) appeared at the same time as the 48 and used a similar two-stroke engine displacing 79.807 cc. The bore and stroke were 47 x 46 mm, and with a 7.1:1 compression ratio power was 4.25 bhp at 7,200 rpm. The weight was 62 kg (137 lb), and the top speed 75 km/h (47 mph), even less than that of the 48 Sport. Needless to say, the Setter 80 wasn't a spectacular success and was discontinued during 1964. In its place was a new range built around a 94 cc engine.

Several new models joined the Brisk 48/1, Piuma 48 (three-speed), and 48 Sport (now with a fan-cooled engine). Because of Italian laws prohibiting 50 cc motorcycles to exceed 1.5 bhp and 40 km/h (25 mph), the 48SL was created using a fan-cooled version of the Brisk engine (with only 1.3 bhp at 4,300 rpm), mounted in the full cradle frame of the 48 Sport. The same motorcycle, with the new 94 cc engine in place of the 48 cc unit, became the 100 Cadet and would last, with minor changes, until 1968. The fan-cooled 94 cc engine had a bore and stroke of 51 x 46 mm, and produced 6 bhp at 7,000 rpm.

In addition to the Cadet there was also the 100 Mountaineer and two scooters, the 48 and 100 Brio.

The 100 Mountaineer was similar to the Cadet, but for a high-level exhaust, rear rack, and 16-inch wheels, while the Brio was a genuine scooter in the Vespa and Lambretta mould. Harking back to the disaster of the Cruiser, the equally uninspired Brio used the three-speed engine of the Piuma and Cadet.

Small changes occurred for the 1966 season, most noticeably with the creation of the Piuma Sport 50, which had a pressed-steel frame and used the three-speed 4.2 bhp engine of the 48 Sport. The styling was similar to that of the larger sporting Ducatis, but without the performance to match. The 49 kg (108 lb) machine had a top speed of 80 kph (50 mph). The 48SL was uprated to the 50SL. No longer with fan-cooling, and with a larger 38.8 mm bore, capacity was now 49.66 cc, and it had a four-speed gearbox. The compression ratio was 9.5:1, and the styling was similar except for the exhaust now being on the right side. Both the 100 Cadet and Mountaineer retained the fan-cooled engine, but with a foot-operated four-speed gearbox rather than the previous hand change.

While the 94 cc Brio continued into 1967 largely unaltered except for a name-change to 100/25, it still had the fan-cooled engine. The rest of the range came

The 1968 100 Mountaineer used an air-cooled cylinder head. *Phil Aynsley*

Below: The 100 Cadet, also of 1968, was similar to the Mountaineer. *Phil Aynsley*

Right: One of the last Ducati two-strokes: the 125 Regolarità. *Phil Aynsley*

in for some revision. The 50SL/1 received a higher compression ratio of 11:1, lost its air filter, and gained a new style of petrol tank with twin filler caps, a styling feature that would be used on the first Mark 3 Desmo singles a year later. The 100 Cadet and Mountaineer were no longer fan-cooled, and received a new air-cooled cylinder head with a chrome bore. The capacity was increased to 98 cc with a 1 mm bore increase.

The Brio continued through to 1968, when it was joined by the 50 cc Rolly moped, and some new 50 cc sporting bikes. Following on from the 50SL/1 came the 50SL/1A, identical but for a different petrol tank, and the 50SL/2 and 50SL/2A. These were styled more like the Cadet, with a square type of headlight, the 2A getting higher handlebars. The 100 Cadet and Mountaineer were available into 1969, and the last versions, 50 and 100 cc Scramblers, finished production in 1970. While there had been significant numbers of these two-stroke machines made, most weren't exported, and they have done little to enhance the reputation of Ducati as a premier motorcycle manufacturer. It must be borne in mind, though, that a good proportion of Ducati motorcycle production through the 1960s was that of two-strokes, but if the management hadn't finally listened to Taglioni and re-

entered the world of competition in 1970 with new designs the company might have faded from the scene altogether.

Amazingly, considering its lack of success, the two-stroke was resurrected in 1975. As in the 1960s, some poor managerial decisions were made at this time. Not only was production of the 750 and 250/350/450 singles being ended, but their replacement by the Giugiaro-styled 860 and the parallel twins was a dubious move. Two 125 cc two-strokes were proposed, the 125 Sperimentale street bike and the 125 Regolarità. Only the Regolarità Six Days made it into production, but because it wasn't a real enduro bike, it didn't sell well. This wasn't really surprising considering Ducati had no real experience in off-road competition. It had a completely new 54 x 54 mm, 123.7 cc engine with a 10.5:1 compression ratio, a Dell'Orto PHB 30 carburettor, and a six-speed gearbox. The weight was 108 kg (238 lb). In 1977 an improved 125 Six Days was offered, with a larger 32 mm Bing carburettor and a 14.5:1 compression ratio. The revised 125 Six Days had a new petrol tank, and laid-forward twin Marzocchi shock absorbers. The weight was much less than the Regolarità, at 97 kg (214 lb), but this also wasn't a success. Both Six Days

Below: Ambitious but advanced,
the Apollo, of which only one
complete example has survived.

had obsolete suspension, and were unremarkable bikes competing against some highly specialized off-road motorcycles. They were definitely not among Ducati's more memorable models, and served only to prove that the company should concentrate on what it had always done as well as, if not better, than other manufacturers.

THE APOLLO

During the 1960s the US market became increasingly important to Ducati, which had appointed Berliner as its US distributor in 1957. Berliner's aggressive approach gave them considerable influence with the Ducati management. One of the results of this influence was the Apollo, and even though it was a joint project, ultimately it created more financial problems for the company.

At the instigation of Joe Berliner, Ducati was commissioned to build a police bike that could compete with Harley-Davidson. This was no problem for Fabio Taglioni, who had always been a very prolific designer, and a 1,260 cc V-4 five-speed engine was soon on the drawing board. By the end of 1963 a motorcycle had been constructed, and from a firm that was known primarily for single cylinder motorcycles of up to 250 cc, this was a dramatic departure. It was also the largest capacity motorcycle to emanate from a European manufacturer since the Second World War.

In retrospect the Apollo was many years in advance of its time. Even if it had been built ten years later it may have been more successful, but it was far too heavy and powerful for the available tyres of 1964. Typically of Taglioni, it was a brilliant concept. Two siamesed 90° V twins created a 1,257 cc V-4. To keep the engine as compact as possible, the stroke was very short, and with cylinder dimensions of 84.5 x 56 mm it was also extremely oversquare for the day. The bore/stroke ratio of 1.5:1 was greater than that of any other Ducati before or since, except for the racing 926 of 1993. The Apollo also featured the different cylinder finning on the front and rear cylinders that would later appear on the 750 twin and Pantah. Every advantage was taken of the benefits of the V-4 layout, and the crankcases were only 19 inches (483 mm) wide. The valve gear was not driven by bevel-gears and an overhead camshaft, but followed the practice of the contemporary range of utilitarian singles by using the simpler pushrods and rockers. The specifications of the Apollo were such that it was a very advanced motorcycle. It had a five-speed gearbox, a Marelli electric starter, duplex chain final drive, and Ceriani suspension, front and rear. With a modest 1,537 mm (60.5-inch) wheelbase, the dry weight was 270 kg (595 lb).

There were to be two versions of the Apollo, one with twin Dell'Orto carburettors and an 8:1 compression ratio producing 80 bhp at 6,000 rpm, and the other, a sports version, with four Dell'Orto carburettors, producing 100 bhp at 7,000 rpm. Unfortunately the Apollo made too much power for the 5.00 x 16 Pirelli white-wall tyres, so it had to be reduced to 65 bhp. Because it was still a heavy bike, reducing the power affected its performance in comparison to the Harley-Davidsons and BMWs that were its competition as a police bike, and Berliner had a lot of difficulty in selling the concept. Only one

This 500 cc parallel twin
prototype was produced in 1967
for the Italian police but it never
went into production.
Ducati Motor

example, and another engine, survived, the bike staying
with Berliner at their New Jersey headquarters. Later
it was sold to Domiracer in the US, and it is now
in Japan.

500 PARALLEL TWIN

The influence that Berliner wielded over Ducati was
such that they were responsible not only for the Apollo,
but also for a 500 cc twin. Intended for the US market,
and displayed at the Daytona Show immediately after
the US Grand Prix in March 1965, the latter was
poorly received. Overweight at 190 kg (419 lb), its
performance was sluggish. The 497 cc 360° twin had
pushrod overhead valves and dimensions of 74 x 57.8
mm. These were very oversquare for the day and very
similar to the 500 Pantah of 15 years later. In other
respects too, it was very advanced, having an electric
starter and five-speed gearbox. With two 27 mm
Dell'Orto SS1 carburettors, claimed maximum power
was 40 bhp at 6,000 rpm. There was a large twin

leading shoe front brake, along with 19-inch wheels,
but it wasn't a project that Taglioni was too interested
in so it didn't get into production. Another version
appeared three years later, in 1968. A lighter bike at
177 kg (390 lb), it was an improvement over the earlier
model, but there wasn't enough dealer interest to justify
putting this into production either. Amazingly, the
500 cc parallel twin was resurrected seven years later,
and was again a disaster.

Taglioni did design a more interesting parallel twin,
and a prototype was constructed in 1967. In two
capacities, 500 and 700 cc, this bike was intended for
the Italian Carabinieri, as a replacement for their Moto
Guzzi Falcone singles. The 700 was built in two
versions. One, a sports version with chain-driven
double overhead camshafts, was claimed to produce
80 bhp at 7,500 rpm, while the pushrod police version
produced 70 bhp at 6,500 rpm. Still, the question of
vibration wasn't addressed, and it came at a time when
the overhead camshaft singles were being updated, so
the resources weren't there for it to go into production.

The wide-case singles grew out
of the limited-production
desmodromic SCD of 1967.
Phil Aynsley

5 DESMODROMICS REBORN

AND THE WIDE-CASE SINGLES

The prototype wide-case Ducati single was displayed at the Cologne Show in September 1967. This revised engine would not only improve on some of the weaknesses of the earlier design, but also allow Ing. Fabio Taglioni to make his dream a reality: the first production engine with desmodromic valve gear. Additionally, the new engine allowed for the capacity to be eventually increased beyond that of the 350 cc of the previous narrow-case, to 436 cc.

While Franco Farnè had debuted a desmodromic 250 at the Italian season opener at Modena on 20 March 1966, this bike was based on the 250 SC. It had used crankcases of a new design, with wider front and rear frame mounts, and would form the basis for future designs. There was then a full year of development, during which time Cere and Giovanardi won the 250 cc class at the FIM *Coupe d'Endurance* Imola 6-Hour race on a factory bike, but it wasn't until 1967 that the desmo single was raced again, now with an even stronger, wide-crankcase engine. Initially 350 cc, the new desmo was raced by Gilberto Parlotti and Roberto Gallina at Modena in March 1967. Soon a 250 version joined the 350, and Farnè took it to Daytona to ride in the Expert Lightweight event, but was not allowed to start as the desmodromic single was deemed to be not derived from a road-going model. These 250 and 350 desmodromic bikes were raced in several Italian early season events on street circuits with a reasonable amount of success. The 74 x 57.8 mm 250, with its 36 mm Dell'Orto carburettor, produced 35 bhp at 11,500 rpm, and the 76 x 75 mm 350, with a 40 mm Dell'Orto carburettor, 45 bhp at 10,500 rpm. In 1968, now with Bruno Spaggiari riding, the 250 and 350 desmos achieved more encouraging results, notably fifth in the Italian 350 Grand Prix, but still no outright victories. Making its debut at Rimini in March 1968 was the first 450, actually 436 cc, sharing the dry clutch, twin-plug ignition and straight cut primary and bevel gears with the smaller versions. With a 42 mm Dell'Orto carburettor, power was up to 50 bhp at 9,000 rpm.

In 1969 Gallina, Parlotti, and Spaggiari again rode the 250 and 350, with the best results being Spaggiari's two second-place finishes behind Pasolini's Benelli four at Modena and Cesenatico. While the racing results

Right: The famous glass-sided
Ducati transporter with a
selection of scramblers and
outboard motors, 1971.
Ducati Motor

Below: The 450 Scrambler
appeared in 1969, and was
extremely popular.

may not have been spectacular, they were a very useful proving ground for developing the range of street desmos. A similar scenario existed through 1970, but instead of being special factory-prepared engines, Spaggiari's 450 and Parlotti's 250 and 350 derived from the new range of road machines, and had the regular wet-clutch of these bikes. The 450 still featured twin-plug ignition, larger valves, 42 mm Dell'Orto carburettor, and a 10:1 compression ratio, but used die-cast rather than sand-cast engine-cases. It also had a reinforced swing-arm and a 210 mm Fontana front brake and weighed 264 lb (120 kg). They were entered under Franco Farnè's semi-official team quaintly called Scuderia Speedy Gonzales. Once again, while results were encouraging, particularly at Rimini, Modena, and Riccione, the new singles were no match for the multi-cylindered MVs, Benellis, Lintos, and Patons. For this reason the factory stopped development of the desmo single to concentrate on the 500 V-twin. Ironically, it was the privateers who benefited from all the factory development on the desmo racer, and Ducati singles were, and still continue to be, highly successful in the

various classes for which they are eligible. The culmination of this was Charles Mortimer's win in the 1970 250 Production TT at the Isle of Man aboard the Vic Camp Mark 3 Desmo. Here he won at an average speed of 84.87 mph (136.6 km/h).

By 1968, production of the new series of singles was underway. The wide crankcase increased the capacity of the sump to 2.5 litres (0.55 imperial gallons), and there were improved kickstart gears, a problem with five-speed narrow-case engines. There was also a larger crankpin, at 27 mm, and the drive-side main bearing enlarged to 30 x 72 x 19 mm. Because of the wider rear engine mounts and a twin down-tube rear frame section, the frame was stronger at the rear, but this was at the cost of an increase in weight.

125/250/350/450 SCRAMBLER

The first production versions of the wide-case engine appeared in early 1968 as the 350 cc Scrambler, and in

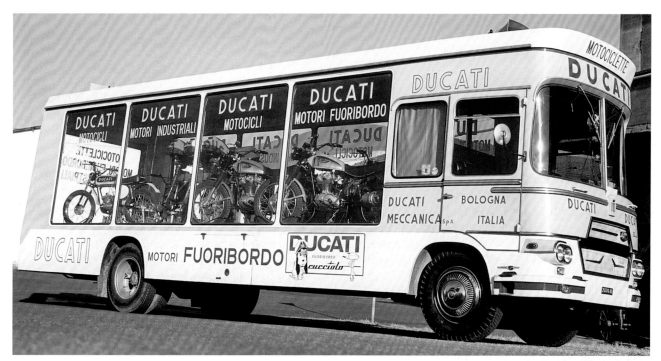

the US as the 350 Sport Scrambler. This was followed shortly afterwards by the 250 Scrambler. The Scrambler was to become the most popular of all the wide-case singles, particularly in Italy. It offered full street equipment, with no pretensions for off-road competition as had been evident in the prototype 350 Scrambler of 1967, and the 250, 350, and even the later 450 versions, were essentially similar.

This 350 cc wide-case engine shared the same dimensions of 76 x 75 mm with the 350 Sebring and 350 SC racer, and had a 10:1 compression ratio and a high performance camshaft (coded white/green). This had valve timing figures of inlet opening 70° before top dead centre and closing 84° after bottom dead centre, and the exhaust valve opening 80° before bottom dead centre and closing 64° after top dead centre. They certainly required the decompression lever operated from the left handlebar. The 250 had a 9.2:1 compression ratio and no compression release. Using 35 mm Marzocchi forks, the 1968 versions of the 250 and 350SCR had their Veglia speedometer mounted in the Aprilia headlight. They came with 315 mm Marzocchi shock absorbers, later replaced by 310 mm items, with the option of stiffer suspension available. Very soon after they were released they were restyled, with a new petrol tank and seat design that would carry through until 1974. The 350 then became the 350SSS (or Street Scrambler Sport) for the US market.

In 1969 the 450 (actually 435.7 cc) became available, and featured a new crankcase, cylinder, and cylinder head castings to accommodate the 86 x 75 mm dimensions. The reason why a full 500 wasn't created was that the 75 mm stroke was the largest that could

be used for the throw of the crankshaft to miss the gearbox pinions. To make the engine larger would have required a redesign and retool. Interestingly enough, even though the 450 shared the 75 mm stroke with the 350, the 450 used a con-rod with an eye-to-eye length of 140 mm, rather than the 136 mm con-rod that was used by both the 250 and 350. Certainly with a rod length to stroke ratio of 1.81:1, the shorter rod was not ideal for the longer stroke 350, accentuating piston acceleration.

For the 450 there was also extra gusseting along the top frame tube, exactly like Spaggiari's 1968 450 racer, and a wider chain and sprockets, allowing the use of a 5/16 x 3/8 inch final drive chain. With a 9.3:1 compression ratio, and white coded camshafts of the 250SCR, the 450SCR (and identical Mark 3) produced a moderate 27 bhp at 6,500 rpm. The valve timing was inlet opening 27° before top dead centre, closing 75° after bottom dead centre, and exhaust opening 60° before bottom dead centre, and closing 32° after top dead centre. In 1969 the US model of the 450 Scrambler was marketed by Berliner as the Jupiter. With the 450 came slightly longer (515 mm) Marzocchi forks, and these were also fitted to subsequent 250 and 350SCRs.

All the carburettors were changed during 1969, with the Dell'Orto SS1 29D being replaced by a new square-slide VHB. The 250 received a smaller VHB 26AD (from 27 mm), and the 350 and 450, a VHB 29AD. This required a new air filter and the traditional rounded muffler became the cut-off Silentium type, either long or short. At the start of 1970 the crankpin diameter was increased to 30 mm, and the Scramblers then remained unchanged until 1973, when they became very similar to the range of Mark 3 roadsters. They now had Borrani 19-inch and 18-inch alloy wheel-rims, and the 350 and 450SCR the same double-sided front brake, headlight, and instruments as the Mark 3. They also featured Marzocchi forks with exposed staunchions and new side-covers. The 250 still had the single brake and fork gaiters (though US versions differed), and all now went back to using the older rounded muffler. In 1973 they received the Ducati Elettrotecnica electronic ignition, and finally a larger, 32 mm diameter crankpin in 1974.

For a short while during 1971 a 125SCR was actually built in Bologna with a narrow-case Spanish Mototrans five-speed engine, complete with Spanish Amal carburettor. This wasn't a success and was soon discontinued, but the final 250 Scramblers of 1974 also used Spanish-built engines.

250/350/450 MARK 3 AND MARK 3 DESMO

Soon after the 350 and 250 Scramblers appeared with the new wide-crankcase engine in 1968, so did the Mark 3 and 250 Monza. The Monza was of similar specification and styling to the unremarkable narrow-case version, but the Mark 3 was now quite distinctively styled with a twin filler petrol tank (like the two-stroke 50 SL/1). The 250 engine remained in the same state of tune as it had in the Mach 1, with the same grey-coded camshaft, 10:1 compression ratio, and Dell'Orto SS1 29D carburettor, while the 350 Mark 3 had the even more highly tuned (white/green camshaft) 350 engine from the 350SCR.

For the wide-case Mark 3s the weight was up from the earlier models, at 128 kg (282 lb), so the 250 didn't perform as strongly. Only 143 km/h (89 mph) was claimed for the 250, a far cry from the Mach 1 and Mark 3 of 1965–67. While the 350 Mark 3 was considered the performance model with its top speed of 170 km/h (106 mph), waiting in the wings to enhance Ducati's reputation was Taglioni's engineering *tour de force*, desmodromic valve gear.

During 1968, Fabio Taglioni's dream was fulfilled: Ducati produced the first production motorcycle engine with desmodromically-operated valve gear. Unlike the 125 Grand Prix desmos with their three camshafts, only one was used, incorporating both opening and closing lobes, and hairpin valve springs were retained to assist in starting. These were from the 160 Monza Junior, and lighter than standard, but were still considerably stronger than the small closing springs fitted to the later desmo twins. Apart from the cylinder head the engines were identical, and there really wasn't much of a performance differential between the two models in standard trim. The desmo engine was fitted to the 250 and 350 Mark 3, creating two new models, the 250 Mark 3 Desmo, and the 350 Mark 3 Desmo. These were virtually indistinguishable from the regular Mark 3 apart from a 'D' on the side-panels and different colours.

All the Desmos used the same white and blue coded camshaft with the inlet valve opening 70° before top dead centre, closing 82° after bottom dead centre, and the exhaust valve opening 80° before bottom dead centre and closing 65° after top dead centre. The performance was up on the Mark 3, with 150 km/h (93 mph) claimed for the 250D, or 160 km/h (99 mph) with megaphone exhaust. The 350D became the fastest production Ducati single offered with its top speed of 180 km/h (112 mph) with megaphone exhaust, but with the standard silencer the maximum speed was 165 km/h (103 mph). Several options were available for the Desmo, these being a high, touring-style handlebar, or a racing uprating kit containing a racing camshaft, a range of main jets, a megaphone, and a full racing fairing. The 1968 models, with their twin filler petrol tanks, Dell'Orto SS1 carburettors, and auxiliary white-faced Veglia tachometer, were amongst the finest Ducati singles, and each bike was provided with a test certificate. All they needed were rear-set footpegs to go with the clip-on handlebars.

With the release of the new 450 engine in the Scrambler in 1969, it wasn't long before there was also a 450 Mark 3 and 450 Mark 3 Desmo. The 450 Desmo used the same camshaft as the other Desmos, and the lower, 9.3:1 compression ratio of the 450 SCR. All the 450s had the new type of Dell'Orto VHB 29 square-slide carburettor, a single filler petrol tank, and the cut-off Silentium muffler, and soon these were shared with the 250 and 350 Mark 3 Desmo. The 450 also had an individual speedometer and tachometer, rather than the headlight-mounted speedo and white-faced Veglia, and these too would become standardized throughout the range of Mark 3s and SCRs during 1970. For the US, Mark 3s and Desmos were fitted with a Scrambler petrol tank and the higher

The 350 desmo of 1986 had twin filler caps and a Dell'Orto SS carburettor.

handlebars. *Cycle* tested all three Desmos in February 1970, and found the power characteristics distinctly different, with the 250 and 450 having wide powerbands, and the 350 tuned as 'a street dragster' with power coming in at 6,500 rpm. As they all used the same camshaft and carburettor, this was probably a function of the short con-rod. The 450 was the strongest performer, with a standing quarter-mile time of 16.60 seconds, followed by the 350 at 17.63 seconds, and the 250 at 18.94 seconds. Because they shared cycle parts, the kerb weight ranged from 299 lb (136 kg) for the 450, to 292 lb (132 kg) for the 250, with the 350 in between at 292 lb (132 kg). They found all bikes overgeared, and strangled by the Silentium exhaust system, and with a megaphone the 350 went through the quarter mile in 15.15 seconds.

Also during 1970, a street replica of Spaggiari's racing desmo was offered but unfortunately not put into production. Called the 450 Desmo Superbike, it was to have been available on special order only. While based on a production 450 Desmo, this magnificent machine had genuine rear-set controls and Ceriani racing forks with twin hydraulically-operated Campagnolo disc brakes, surely a first for a street bike. The engine was virtually identical to Spaggiari's, but for a slightly smaller 40 mm remote float bowl Dell'Orto carburettor (which necessitated a cut-out in the petrol tank). It had larger valves, stronger crankshaft and bearings, 10:1 compression, and the option of twin ignition. With a short Silentium exhaust, power was claimed to be 40 bhp at 9,000 rpm. Its 18-inch Borrani alloy rims were fitted with Dunlop KR83 racing tyres, and the claimed weight was only 297 lb (135 kg), with a top speed of 120 mph (193 km/h).

450 R/T

Certainly one of the more interesting bikes emanating from Bologna during this period was the 450 R/T. While using a production 450 Desmo engine, it had a

The other version had lights, instruments, and the normal Scrambler exhaust system. With its 21-inch front and 18-inch wheels mounted with Pirelli Cross tyres, the R/T was aimed more at the off-road market than the street, and the specification of a sump guard, chain guide, and chain oiler confirmed this, as did the tiny 160 mm front brake from the 160 Monza Junior.

When it came down to it, at 128 kg (282 lb) the R/T was still too heavy to be considered a serious dirt bike, and it didn't remain in production as long as the non-desmo Scrambler. Production had ended by 1973.

239/250/350/450 MARK 3 1971–74

Whereas the Mark 3 and Mark 3 Desmo were virtually indistinguishable from 1968 until 1970, they both came in for a significant redesign in 1971, and in the process two distinct models were created. But for a new petrol tank the Mark 3s of 1971 were still quite similar to those of 1970, and these continued through 1972. For 1973 they were restyled with a new seat, side-covers, instruments, and headlight. More importantly they now received the 35 mm Marzocchi forks of the Desmos along with the Grimeca double-sided front brake and Borrani alloy wheel-rims. The final Mark 3s of 1974 had tank badges rather than decals, along with steel wheel-rims, just like the 750GTs of the same era.

The US market singles of 1973 differed to those elsewhere, with two models complementing the 450 R/T. After a year in which no street singles had been imported, in October 1972 Berliner advertised the new 250 Road, with the exclamation, 'It's back!' The 250 and 350 Roads used a combination of parts from the Scrambler, Mark 3, and R/T. Styled very much like a Scrambler, they had a dual seat like a Mark 3, Mark 3 instruments and headlight (with chrome wire 750GT headlight holder), and 18-inch Borrani alloy wheels with a single leading shoe front brake. While the frame was that of the Scrambler, the swing-arm incorporated the snail cam chain adjusters of the 450 R/T. Engine-wise, these US models were similar to their European counterparts, using electronic ignition, but an Amal 30 mm carburettor and a new silencer. Like the R/T they also had a steel sump guard, but they weren't a success and ceased to be available for 1974.

There were also two touring models in 1971 and 1972, based on the Mark 3 and designed primarily for

frame and cycle parts totally unlike any other Ducati. The frame owed more to the 750GT, and was almost half that of the larger bike, also using tapered roller steering-head bearings in place of the ball-bearings of all the other singles. First displayed at the 1970 Bologna Show, the R/T was, like so many Ducatis, created primarily for the US market.

R/T was meant to stand for 'Road and Track', but as *Two Wheels* magazine stated in January 1972, it could also have been interpreted as 'Race and Trail', 'Rorty Thumper', or even 'Revenge on Two-strokes'. The R/T was a much more serious dirt bike than the Scrambler, and this was demonstrated in August 1971 when, with Morini unable to prepare a team of bikes for the International Six Day Trial, Ducati provided a complete line-up of seven 250, 350, and 450 R/Ts for the Italian Trophy team. Looking very much like standard 450 R/Ts, these factory bikes had an unusual twin muffler reminiscent of that of the 200 Elite, but were no match for the CZ and Jawa two-strokes.

The engine of the R/T was identical to that of the 450 Desmo previously described, except for a compression release valve fitted behind the bevel-gear tube. It was available in two versions, the first being without lights and having an open high-level exhaust.

police forces. The T and TS (differentiated only by their camshaft) had a shorter and rounder petrol tank, valanced mudguard, and panniers. Rather heavy at 160 kg (353 lb), the performance wasn't too exciting either, with 140 km/h (87 mph) claimed for the TS and only 128 km/h (80 mph) for the T. The only redeeming feature of the T and TS was in the use of a 12-volt electrical system, and they were discontinued during 1973.

One rather unusual model of 1974 was a 239 cc Mark 3 built specifically for the French market to circumvent taxes on motorcycles over 240 cc. With a 72.5 mm piston, these 239s also used a Dell'Orto PHF 30 mm carburettor, and had regular coil valve springs replacing the hairpin type, along with 12-volt electrics. The 239 also received the reinforced 450 frame, and in many ways was the most developed of the overhead camshaft singles.

250/350/450 DESMO 1971–74

The Mark 3 Desmo became an even more sporting motorcycle with the creation of a new Desmo single for 1971 and 1972. This was the model nicknamed 'The

Silver Shotgun' by the Australian magazine *Two Wheels* in their long-term test of a 450 in January 1974. While the 250, 350, and 450 cc desmodromic engines were unchanged (apart from larger timing side main bearings), the rest of the motorcycle was considerably updated. Most obvious was the metalflake silver paint scheme for the fibreglass petrol tank, side covers and solo seat, but the Desmo was now a genuine cafe racer with rear-set footpegs to complement the clip-on handlebars.

Most of the improvements came with the running gear. Borrani 18-inch alloy wheel-rims replaced the previous steel type, and the front brake became a Grimeca double-sided single leading shoe instead of the rather weak single leading shoe that had been fitted from 1957. The forks were considerably uprated from the previous spindly 31.5 mm units, with a new type of 35 mm Marzocchi fork with exposed staunchions. As expected, the performance was similar to that of the earlier Mark 3 Desmos. *Motociclismo* managed a maximum speed of 158.632 km/h (98.57 mph) from their totally standard 450 Desmo test bike in 1972.

For some reason the silver Desmos have become an endangered species and not too many are to be seen

Another classic: the 450 desmo of 1971, known as the 'Silver Shotgun'.

Below: For 1973, the desmo single was restyled along the lines of the 750 Sport.

these days. This is probably because they were mainly sold on the local market, and is a pity because I prefer these to the later yellow type. They had a more pleasing Aprilia headlight (with the speedometer mounted in the shell), the white-faced racing Veglia tachometer on its individual bracket, and more attractive levers and controls. They still used contact breaker and coil

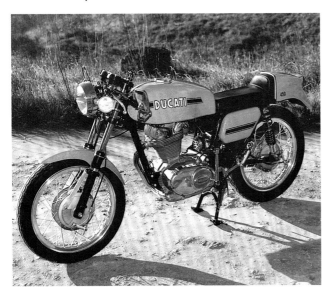

ignition, the smaller tail-light of the 750GT and 750 Sport, and I find the styling of the seat more in keeping with the overall design.

The Desmo single was given to ex-racer Leopoldo Tartarini (of Italjet) for a slight restyle for 1973. Thus appeared the distinctive yellow colour scheme, to match the 750 Sport, along with a new seat incorporating the tail-light. This final version featured electronic ignition, by either Ducati Elettrotecnica or Spanish Motoplat, and the larger 32 mm crankpin. They also received a revised instrument panel with Smiths instruments, and a new style of CEV headlight. With the new colour scheme came replacement of the fibreglass petrol tank by one in steel.

In all other respects the specification was identical to that of 1971–72, but in 1974 Ceriani 35 mm forks, with a 280 mm Brembo disc and 08 caliper, replaced the Marzocchis and their Grimeca double-sided single leading shoe drum brake. These forks were not fitted to any other models in the Ducati range and were unique to the Desmo single. Because of the use of the front disc brake and 750 style hub, the 18-inch WM2 Borrani had 40 spokes rather than the 36 of the drum-braked versions, and the fibreglass front mudguard was bolted, rather than clamped, to the fork legs. New con-rods

The 1973 350 desmo. For 1974 it
was similar but for a Ceriani front
fork and disk front brake.
Rolf im Brahm

and pistons were also used in some of the final 450s when the 86 mm piston of the 860GT, with its 20 rather than 22 mm gudgeon pin, was fitted.

These very last Desmo singles were an intriguing contradiction between ancient and modern. With a race-bred chassis, lightweight Borrani alloy rims and a disc brake, along with a hand-built engine featuring items like polished rockers, it still had 6-volt electrics and an 80 watt alternator. In 1974 there weren't many bikes available with a modern electronic ignition and a 1950s lighting system. The basic design was beginning to show its age and even the fuel crisis of 1974 couldn't save the exceedingly fuel-efficient single without a major redesign. It was unfortunate that Ducati decided to replace these singles with the unremarkable parallel twin, because the changes made to the French market 239 showed that there was development life left in the design.

The yellow Desmos were more widely exported than the silver versions, and tested by several magazines. *Bike* tested a 350 Desmo with a non-standard exhaust and achieved a top speed of 98.47 mph (158.5 km/h) in August 1974, and in April 1975, they managed 99.97 mph (160.9 km/h) out of a 450 Desmo, again with a non-standard exhaust. These were still light

bikes, with all Desmos weighing a claimed 127 kg (280 lb) dry. *Bike* weighed their 350 test bike at 294 lb (133 kg) with a gallon of fuel, and their 450 at 308 lb (140 kg) with a full fuel tank.

In standard trim none of the singles, not even the Desmo versions, were particularly fast motorcycles. A lot of earnest modification was required to obtain serious performance from a Ducati single and at higher speeds they were a decidedly lively device due to the light weight, short wheelbase, stiff suspension, and quick steering – quite unlike the later larger twins renowned for their slow steering and more stable handling. Having owned one of the last 450 Desmos myself, I am not overly enthusiastic about such spirited motorcycles on the road, preferring the stability of the larger Ducatis. The intoxication of a Ducati single is on tighter roads (preferably smooth) where the directness of the steering combines with the torquey engine and excellent handling. There was something inherently correct about the balance of these motorcycles, which have achieved cult status in consequence of many commentators waxing lyrical about them. Unfortunately, while the final Desmos were beautifully crafted they were, by 1974, obsolete, and no longer a serious commercial proposition.

The first production 750GT of
1971 with metalflake paintwork.

6 THE BIRTH OF THE V-TWIN

THE 750 ROUND CASE

On 20 March 1970, Ing. Fabio Taglioni made his initial sketches of an idea for a V-twin. This would be the classic round-case 750 engine and was, in his view, his best design. The basis of the 750 was essentially that of taking two singles and placing them on a common crankcase with the cylinders 90° apart. For Ducati to create a larger capacity twin the easiest and cheapest way was to utilize technology from the current range of singles, and, as always, Fabio Taglioni sought an uncompromised and unique engineering solution.

Taglioni could well remember the racing success, not only of the singles and fours from Moto Guzzi, Gilera, and MV, but also the 120° 500 cc Moto Guzzi twin. This bike retained the horizontal front cylinder of a single to maintain a lower centre of gravity with the rear cylinder facing slightly rearward. There were other advantages too, not the least of these being a good flow of air to cool the rear cylinder. When Ducati decided it was time to move into the large capacity market, as Moto Guzzi, Honda, and all the British manufacturers were doing, these ideas influenced him.

Taglioni only had limited resources at his disposal, and there was a certain marketing risk involved in developing and trying to sell a larger capacity bike when the company was known only for smaller singles. There was also the stigma of the failure of the 1,260 cc V-four Apollo, a concept that in retrospect had been 25 years ahead of its time. Because of this failure Taglioni first developed his 'L' twin not only as a street bike but as a racer, both for 500 cc World Championship events and 750 cc events. He was always a true believer in the premise that 'racing improves the breed'.

Being an engineering purist, Taglioni chose the 90° layout for several reasons. He liked the wide cylinder angle for the same reasons that Moto Guzzi had used it in their racers, but preferred 90° because it offered perfect primary engine balance. With this layout the engine could be very smooth, with only some high frequency secondary imbalance, and with a narrow crankshaft there was virtually no rocking couple. In addition, theoretically the twin could be no wider than a single so the engine could be kept low in the frame while maintaining good ground clearance. Cooling to the rear cylinder was less of a problem, and the main

Below: Fabio Taglioni displays an
early-production 750GT to
Ducati's directors in July 1971.
Ducati Motor

Right: Ermanno Giuliano on the
Seeley-framed 500 GP racer at
Ospedaletti, at the end of 1971.
Ducati Motor

concerns were carburation and keeping the inlet tracks
of equal length with a good shape.

Taglioni's second drawing was completed exactly
one month later, on 20 April 1970, and here he
indicated a projected power output of 80 bhp (SAE) at
9,200 rpm from 750 cc. The inclination of the cylinders
was to be 15° from the horizontal, exactly as the
Apollo. Development of a prototype took place almost
immediately. The engine was running within two
months and a complete bike was on the road by
August. This had a 250 mm double-sided twin leading
shoe Fontana front brake, and an unusual forward,
rather than rear-set, footpeg arrangement. On a later
version the front brake was from a Scrambler, while
another had double front discs with the calipers cast
into the fork legs, similar to that of the Dunstall
Nortons of the time. This bike was displayed at the
Olympia Show in London in January 1971. The first
version featured remote float bowl Dell'Orto 29 mm
SS1 carburettors, but these became 30 mm Amal 930
concentrics on subsequent models. Many of the
ancillary components, such as the Silentium silencers,
were sourced from the contemporary range of singles.

THE 500 GP BIKES

At a Ducati board meeting in October 1970, the
decision was made to re-enter the world of motorcycle

competition. The management at this time – director
Arnaldo Milvio and general manager Fredmano
Spairani – were particularly enthusiastic about racing,
and they had been instrumental in encouraging Taglioni
to develop the 750 twin. The plan was to initially build
ten 500 cc V-twin bikes, and race in Italian
Championship events and some of the 1971 Grands
Prix, but only five bikes actually ended up being made.
The intention was not so much to win races as to prove
that the V-twin idea was sound, and to promote sales
of the 750. Spairani wanted a frame developed by
Colin Seeley in England, and a set of 500 cc prototype
engine-cases was despatched to him, his brief being to
develop a racing frame along the lines of his successful
G50 Matchless version. The frame he developed was
displayed in February 1971, then raced with limited
success as a 500 Grand Prix bike by Bruno Spaggiari,
Ermanno Giuliano, and Phil Read during the 1971 and
1972 seasons. In the meantime Fabio Taglioni and his
team managed to design and build a complete racing
bike, from scratch to race debut, in under six months.

While many of the technical specifications of the 500
were identical to the 750, it had a much shorter stroke,
at 58 mm. With 74 mm pistons and 10.5:1
compression, it initially produced 61.2 bhp at 11,000
rpm. All the 500 GP bikes built used two-valve engines
with desmodromic valve gear and an 80° included
valve angle. Carburation was by remote float bowl
Dell'Orto 40 mm SS carburettors, and they used a six-
speed gearbox with a dry multi-plate clutch.

Ignition was electronic, provided by nearby Ducati
Elettrotecnica, but this was generally unreliable in early
races. When first raced, they used a Ducati-designed
chassis with a single Lockheed disc brake on the front
and a twin leading shoe Fontana at the rear. Dry weight
was 297 lb (135 kg) and 18-inch wheels were fitted
front and rear with 3.00 and 3.25 tyre sizes. Wheelbase
was a moderate 56.3 inches (1,430 mm). In June 1971,
Phil Read tested the bike with the better-handling
Seeley frame, and this was then adopted on
Spaggiari's bike.

Besides the two-valve head, Taglioni also produced a
four-valve version, still with the single overhead
camshaft driven by vertical shaft and bevel-gears. These
heads were taller and had twin splayed exhaust ports,
but ultimately they didn't produce as much power as
the two-valve versions. Thus they contributed to
Taglioni's suspicion of four-valve cylinder heads, even
though he persevered with their development through

to 1973. Initial power from the four-valve heads gave 65 bhp at 12,000 rpm, but by the end of 1972 this had only risen to 69 bhp at 12,500 rpm. Over the same period the power from the two-valve engine increased to 71 bhp, so the four-valve version was never raced.

Race results during 1971 were disappointing due to a spate of gearbox and ignition problems. The best results had been Phil Read's second to Agostini in the San Remo Grand Prix, and a fourth, also by Read, at Monza in the Grand Prix delle Nazione, where Spaggiari had looked like taking second before breaking a valve. In May 1972, Bruno Spaggiari finished third at Imola, this time beating Paul Smart into fourth. They had finished the other way round one month earlier in the Formula 750 race (see Chapter 7). Unfortunately, no matter how tractable and light it was, nor how well it handled, a twin was never going to match Agostini on the MV triple. Ducati realized this and already had plans to produce a water-cooled 350 triple, and 500 four.

Taglioni had always been a fan of fuel injection, and direct injection was tried on the 500 Grand Prix bike in March 1972. It was then outlawed by the FIM, which ruled it was a form of supercharging. Twin discs now graced the front end. The final 500 appeared in 1973, with belt-driven double overhead desmodromic camshafts, but it was still no MV-beater. This bike is described in Chapter 10.

The MV-beater proposed by Spairani was the previously-mentioned 350 triple, and 500 four. The government controllers of Ducati wouldn't sanction the 500, but a water-cooled 350 cc double overhead camshaft, 12-valve three-cylinder engine, with a seven-speed gearbox, was built and developed throughout 1972. It ran to 16,000 rpm in bench tests, but barely achieved 50 bhp at 14,500 rpm. Already obsolete, and brought in from the British Ricardo company, Taglioni wasn't too keen on the project. By now Spairani was no longer in control, and all racing projects (500 four and 350 triple), along with the 500 GP, were scrapped early in 1973.

A 750 cc version of the 500 with the Seeley frame was tested by Mike Hailwood at Silverstone in August 1971, but Hailwood elected not to ride the bike

Below: Mike Hailwood in
discussion with Franco Farnè
prior to testing the 750.
Mick Woollett

Below: The first 750 cc racer was
built out of the 500GP bike and
appeared at Silverstone in 1971.
Mick Woollett

because the handling needed more development. Taglioni had already developed another frame, based on the Seeley, that found its way to the production 750GT, and evolved into the largely unchanged 750 Sport, 750SS, and lasted through to the final 900SS and Mike Hailwood Replicas of 1982. It formed the basis of the 1972 Imola race-winning 750s and the 1978 Mike Hailwood Isle of Man F1 bike. All these frames have typical Seeley features such as the solidly-mounted chain adjusters.

750 GT

When the production prototype 750 appeared, it had a single Lockheed disc with the distinctive polished aluminium leading axle Marzocchi forks with 'Ducati' cast into the sliders. The first production models appeared in June 1971 and were the epitome of 1970s styling, with silver-painted frames and garish metalflake paintwork in either orange, green, or blue on the fibreglass tank and side-covers. The instrument layout was more like a dashboard, the Smiths instruments being surrounded by plastic and warning lights. What was undeniable now, though, was the way

the designers had managed to tidy up the styling of the engine-cases, with beautiful castings for the side-covers and ignition housing. It was obvious that the aesthetics of the engine were as important as the look of ancillary components. In this respect the 750 twin carried on the tradition of Italian engines of the past, that even if the internals were rather ordinary (as they were on many popular small Italian motorcycles) the motors still looked purposeful and functional. In the case of the 750, however, there was nothing mundane about the internals and, with the MV Agusta 750, it was the most exotic engine in production at that time.

Although obviously utilizing much from the contemporary line of wide-case singles, the 750 'L' twin, as it was called, was considerably uprated. The hairpin valve springs were replaced by single coil springs, to keep the rocker box narrow and allow sufficient air-flow over the individually-cast cylinder heads. The finning on the horizontal head was longitudinal, while on the rear cylinder it was radial. The two 80 mm pistons moved through a 74.4 mm stroke via one-piece connecting rods, not unlike the singles. Compression ratio was a very mild 8.5:1, the pistons being quite heavy full skirt designs with three rings, one of which was a slotted oil scraper. The small end bronze bush size was 22 mm, and eye-to-eye length on the con-rod 150 mm, giving a theoretically perfect stroke:rod ratio of 2:1. The crankshaft itself was a three-piece pressed-up item with the two connecting rods on one 36 mm pin, rotating on two rows of 18 caged 5 mm rollers. Thus the two cylinders were slightly staggered, the rear to the right and the front to the left, to allow a slimmer overall width and bring the exhaust pipes closer in for better ground clearance. The main bearings were considerably uprated from the 250/350/450 single, being an expensive fibre-caged axial thrust type, 80 x 35 x 21 mm. The crankshaft was additionally supported by two smaller outrigger ball-bearings in the alloy outer cases. Drive to the gearbox was by helical primary gears, the first series having 29 teeth on the crankshaft driving a 71-tooth clutch basket. Unfortunately, Ducati got it wrong with this ratio of 2.448:1, and early engines were prone to clutch slip. From 1974 all round-case engines had the revised primary drive ratio of the 750 Super Sport. Inside the primary drive gear a large, 5 lb flywheel resided, filling up the space between the gear and the main bearing. Removing this seemed to have no detrimental effect to performance, or idling, and was generally the first modification any prospective racer made. The gearbox and all bearings were stronger. In order to keep the engine as short as possible, Taglioni had chosen to use a direct type gearbox with the layshaft above the mainshaft necessitating that the engine rotated in a reverse direction. The gear selector mechanism on the right side of the engine was identical to that of the singles, fine while new but rather prone to wear, especially if the bike had been ridden in the rain for long periods. Water would then enter the selector box, washing out the grease.

The cylinder-head design owed more to the singles than any other aspect of the engine, and was arguably obsolete before it was even put into production, the wide included angle of 80° having been inherited from the 1955 Gran Sport. Thus while valve sizes were a reasonable 40 mm for the inlet and 36 mm for the exhaust, there would be problems getting sufficiently high compression from racing engines using these heads in the future. Valve adjustment was by replaceable shims on top of the valve stem. Large squish bands were provided, and the offset of the ports (15° inlet and 30° exhaust) contributed to excellent swirl characteristics. Due to the space limitations imposed by the frame the swirl in the front cylinder was clockwise, as the ports were offset to the right, while in the rear it was anti-clockwise with left offset ports. This swirl contributed to excellent cylinder filling and allowed the use of a moderate 38° of ignition advance, even though ultimate horsepower was limited by the cylinder head design.

Surprisingly, the camshafts were particularly racing orientated for such a low compression touring engine. Timing figures were inlet opening 65° before top dead centre and closing 84° after bottom dead centre, and exhaust opening 74° before bottom dead centre and closing 58° after top dead centre. This gave an inlet valve duration of 329°, exhaust valve duration of 312°, and valve overlap of 123° – figures more appropriate for a high performance engine. It was a tribute to the design characteristics that the engine was still eminently tractable with excellent mid-range torque, despite these camshafts.

The camshafts were supported by three identical ball-bearings, and the larger, 17 mm bevel-gear shafts by a double row, self-aligning ball-bearing at the top and two ball-bearings and sleeve at the bottom. The distributor shaft was placed in between the two camshaft drives, driving an ignition cam inside an exquisitely cast and machined housing. The points may have been difficult to set up because they were both mounted on one backing plate and access was difficult, but the casting was undeniably artistic. The condensers too were located in this housing, not the most practical place if one was trying to ensure that they didn't get too hot. However, the use of points was obviously considered a temporary measure, because the cases were drilled and tapped for electronic ignition installation beside the drive side main bearing, and the 35 mm outlet hole for the wires plugged up. Electrical power was provided by a marginal 150 watt alternator mounted on the right side of the crankshaft. 150 watts was obviously its peak output because those who rode around at night using low revs would be plagued by a flat battery the next day.

The bevel-gear layout on these first V-twins was magnificent, but time-consuming to assemble correctly. A set of nine helical toothed bevels was used for both camshaft and distributor drive, with the hunting-tooth principle used to distribute the shock load of valve opening over several teeth. The difficulty in assembly occurred because all the lower bevel-gears were dependent on one another for correct meshing. If too

Below: By 1972 the 750GT was adapted for the US market, and received new colours.

tight, the gears whined excessively, overloading the bearings. If they were set up too loosely, they rattled and affected the valve timing, causing power loss. In addition, the heat expansion of the alloy engine-cases needed to be factored in. The lower bevels came as a matched set, with dots machined to assist correct valve timing during assembly. The earliest bevel sets were also heavily dished underneath, and the very first sets came without timing marks.

The oil filtration and lubrication system was carried over from the singles. The only provision for filtration was a gauze filter in the sump, and the centrifugal sludge traps in the webs of the crankshaft. The transmission too was lubricated by engine oil flung off

the big-ends. The oil pump was driven off the crankshaft on the right-hand side and was, in deference to the widespread use of ball and roller bearings, a low pressure device. It has to be said that here was an area in which the design was not thoroughly up to date. An owner needed to be scrupulous with the maintenance schedule and heavyweight oil was specified because of the churning by the bevel-gears. Leaving oil in longer than 1,000 miles (1,600 km) risked problems with the big-end bearings due to loss of viscosity and contamination.

The wet clutch comprised 16 plates, and was a slight problem. The clutches on the early bikes in particular, with the lower primary drive ratio, were prone to slipping. It wasn't long before the factory racing bikes were using a dry multi-plate clutch, but it would be over ten years before these made it to the production line.

With two tower shafts of bevel gears driving the single overhead camshaft in each cylinder head from a set of bevel-gears originating at the crankshaft, and primary drive by helical gear, there wasn't a chain in the engine (at least until the advent of an electric start version first displayed early in 1972). All bearings were ball or roller and every shaft, be it crank, gearbox or bevel, was shimmed individually for the correct end float or backlash. This was truly an engine from a different era, designed without any concession to

production economics. It was so labour-intensive to assemble (particularly the bevel-gears, which had to be set up individually from the crankshaft) that it took up to eight hours to assemble one engine at the factory and two days for a racing one. Consequently it wasn't possible to produce many, and over the four-year production period (1971–74) only 6,159 were made, around 1,500 a year including 750 Sports and 750SSs. Even contemporary Italian manufacturers were moving towards less expensive engines in the early 1970s. Moto Guzzi was building a pushrod twin and the Laverdas had chain primary drives and cam chains like British bikes and Hondas. The Ducati singles and twins, and the MV fours, were really the only bikes left with their roots in the great racing designs of the 1950s. However, a beautiful engine is worthless if placed in a mediocre chassis, and this is where Ducati came up trumps. The Seeley-inspired frame using the solid sand-cast engine as a stressed member, though not light, was strong, and utilized mainly straight tubes. Steering was slow due to the 29° fork rake and the 60.2-inch (1,530 mm) wheelbase, but stability was unquestioned. The wheelbase length, which resulted from the long engine, was considerably greater than that of the contemporary 500GP Twin racer. In a time when most large bikes used forks with tiny diameter staunchions and small diameter plastic swing-arm bushes, the 750GT was very advanced with its 38 mm staunchions and large bronze bushes. Not only that, but Taglioni had designed the bike with his typical commitment to balance and symmetry. The crankshaft was placed exactly mid-way between the axles and on the same line, and high quality components such as Borrani alloy rims were fitted to reduce unsprung weight.

All these factors contributed to many commentators at the time claiming that no bike in the world handled better than the 750GT. The testers at *Cycle* magazine in the USA were particularly enthusiastic about the Ducati 750. To quote from their road test in October 1972: 'When the right-side peg nicks down in an 80 mph sweeper and the bike never bobbles … you know that a motorcyclist designed this machine, and he got it right'. Admittedly, the quality of certain components, such as the Aprilia switchgear and the general standard of chroming, was questionable. However, features like the straight pull spokes laced to strong cast hubs, Tommaselli throttle, and stainless steel guards, showed that Ducati had different priorities when it came to building bikes.

It may have handled better than any other bike, but to those brought up on British motorcycles it looked long and weird. By the standards of the day the single opposed piston Lockheed front brake was excellent (most calipers at that time were floating piston types), but even though weight was moderate at 185 kg (408 lb), it was down on power compared to a Norton Commando or Triumph Trident. With heavy 8.5:1 pistons, and tiny 30 mm Amal carburettors (made in Spain) with extremely restrictive air cleaners, the bike was slow. A rider was hard-pressed to coax more than 180 km/h (112 mph) out of it, even though the factory claimed 200 km/h (124 mph). Maximum power was quoted as 55 bhp, and maximum revs as 7,800 rpm.

With a dealer network that was very poor outside Italy, the bike proved a slow seller until its victory at Imola in April 1972. As Ing. Fabio Taglioni observed in 1974: 'When we won at Imola we won the market too'.

The GT, rather than the singles, became the mainstay of the production line-up, but it underwent numerous changes during its manufacture. The very first few examples built in 1971 featured a twin leading shoe rear brake. Those up to engine number 404 had engine-cases with a bolt through the sump (this was also to mount the forward-set foot-rests of the first prototype). The very earliest bikes also had a clutch cover without an inspection plate, and the engine-cases were sand-cast. The first 500 bikes were considered pre-production. In 1972, new paint schemes appeared, the silver frame and metalflake paint giving way to a black frame and red or black fibreglass petrol tanks. Veglia instruments replaced the Smiths. There were new seats, and the rear tail-light from the singles.

Problems with the kickstart lever cracking the engine cover led to the installation of a longer kickstart shaft, and new lever after engine number 1500. By now, with Berliner serious about distributing the bikes, US versions had appeared, slightly different to their European cousins. Larger tail-lights and higher, wider handlebars were the most notable alterations.

Some commentators have made the observation that the 750GT appeared with a random selection of equipment from 1974, but this is incorrect. All bikes can be dated from the range of brakes or suspension fitted, bearing in mind that at Ducati batches of engines are always made separately to the bikes, and engine and frame numbers do not coincide. There was nothing random about the way the bikes were assembled, though the shipment of bikes from Italy may have been less methodical. By mid-1973 the glass-fibre fuel tank had been replaced by a steel one, with a new colour scheme, and the Lockheed front disc and master cylinder had given way to an Italian Scarab that was essentially a Lockheed copy.

Earlier, the Smiths instruments had been replaced by Veglia, the tachometer in particular becoming a rather unreliable electronic type. I can remember that the 750GT I bought in 1973 had three of these replaced under warranty. The tacho drive on the first series had been similar to the singles, with a floating drive mounted on the front camshaft end cover, and was rather prone to leaking oil. In addition new camshafts were fitted at this time, with the same opening and closing specifications but a new profile, and the new type of Dell'Orto PHF 30 AD and AS carburettor of the type fitted to the 750 Sport. Though these didn't help the bike develop any more horsepower, they certainly aided starting, and they didn't leak fuel as much as the Amals. The stainless guards now made way for a painted steel variety.

At this point – late 1973 – about 2,500 bikes had been built (GTs and Sports), and they all featured the leading axle Marzocchis, which were painted black for the European market but rendered as polished alloy for the USA. Some of these had an electric start mounted over the clutch cover, but they were unusual and it is rare to see one today. The next stage in production demonstrated the greatest variety, which was caused by variability in supply from Ducati's sources of proprietary components.

In the search for a shorter wheelbase, the racing bikes had moved away from the leading axle forks during 1973, and this filtered through to the production line. By early 1974 some GTs appeared with 38 mm centre-axle Cerianis and a single Brembo 280 mm cast iron front disc and forward-mounted 08 caliper. They still had the Borrani wheel-rims, and had

reverted to a cable-driven Veglia tachometer with the drive housed in a one-piece cover from the front camshaft. As supply from Ceriani became difficult, Marzocchi also produced a centre-axle fork, but with a Scarab brake caliper mounting for the 278 mm iron disc. These Marzocchis had modified top triple clamps to provide the same trail as the centre-axle models, and steel rims rather than the Borranis. Marzocchi also produced a centre-axle fork with a forward-mounted Brembo 08 caliper, but fewer GTs had this arrangement.

By now not only had the Borrani rims disappeared, but quieter Lafranconi mufflers had replaced the loud, but lovely, Contis. The valve adjustment followed the practice established by 860 of being by screw and locknut, rather than shim. All engines from mid-1974 had the higher crowned rocker covers, whether they were GT, Sport, or SS, irrespective of their method of valve adjustment. Also, the revised primary ratio of the 1974 750 Super Sport was standardized throughout the range. With 32 teeth on the crankshaft and 70 on the clutch drum, the ratio was now 2.187:1, and helped alleviate problems of clutch slip. This ratio was retained until the advent of the Mille in 1985.

The final examples shared much in the way of ancillary components with the 860 that was in production simultaneously. They had the revised CEV switch-gear and throttle, with the ignition switch now placed under the tank, not between the tank and seat. They also shared the 860 wiring loom and 860 instrument panel with the intriguing 'city/country' horn button switch. The last models had lost a lot of the individual features of the original and it set a precedent that Ducati was to follow in the future. Often it is the earliest examples of particular models that are the most appealing. Throughout the subsequent history of the marque this has happened time and again.

By late 1974, US legislation was making left-side gear shifts mandatory, so the round-case engine was phased out to make way for the square-case 860 that had a left-side gearshift by a crossover shaft behind the engine. The round-case was also too expensive and time-consuming to manufacture, and by 1975 its production had ended, though, like the last singles, it continued to be sold until stocks had run out. Interestingly, demand occurred again three years later, in 1978, when the Australian importers, Frasers in Sydney, requested a batch of both 750GTs and Sports. The factory responded by building 40 GTs and 23 Sports out of spare parts. These, along with some police bikes, were the last of the round-case models.

For some reason the GT has become one of the forgotten members of the Ducati family. Considering the exotic nature of the engine, and its beautiful castings, it is surprising how little status it has in the Ducati classic hierarchy. Once again it comes down to the sporting heritage. Ducatis are perceived as sporting motorcycles, not touring bikes. However, it is

The first production 750 Sport
used a 750GT frame, and only a
few were manufactured.
Thorsten Schulze

had been displayed, largely based on the GT but with clip-on handlebars and rear-set footpegs, and a more highly-tuned engine. The first prototype was shown to Italian concessionaires in 1971 by the then Ducati directors, Arnaldo Milvio and Fredmano Spairani. It was little more than a sporty GT with a deeply-scalloped tank, and a second prototype appeared in early 1972. This was black with a white frame, had Nippon Denso instruments as on the Honda 750, 32 mm Amal carburettors with no air cleaners, and unique curved Conti mufflers. Braking was by a single Lockheed disc up front, and a single Lockheed rear disc. Alternative versions were also shown, some with a half-fairing, twin Lockheed front discs, and Veglia instruments. The colour scheme was the one eventually chosen for the production bikes, yellow with black frame and 'Z' stripes. By the end of 1972 the 750 Sport was in production, and today it is one of the most sought-after of the older Ducatis. There is no denying that Ducati got it right with the Sport.

The first production Sports used 750GT frames with the wide rear sub-frame, Veglia instruments, single Lockheed 278 mm iron disc, and the single rear drum brake as on the GT. The strange curved Contis never made it to production, and by 1973 the frame was replaced by a neater-looking one with a narrower rear sub-frame. All 750 Ducatis at this time came with leading axle Marzocchi forks, but there were a number of details that differentiated the Sport from the GT. It must also be remembered that the 750 Super Sport had not yet appeared, and the 750 Sport was the company's top-performance, and top-of-the-line, model.

The appearance of the Sport created quite a stir in the motorcycle press. Everyone was still amazed by the MV-beating performance of the 750 Desmos at Imola, so naturally the bike was expected to perform considerably better than the GT, and they were not disappointed. With only minimal changes to the engine the 750 Sport now vied for the title of the best-performing 750 on the market. Not only was this a respectably fast bike for its day but it probably handled best too.

The 1973 version looked stunning with its yellow fibreglass tank, seat, and matching guards contrasting with the black-painted engine side-covers. I can clearly remember seeing one in 1973 and thinking how narrow the bike was compared to Honda 750 fours and Kawasaki triples. As a factory option a small half-fairing was available, but as this was only frame, and

important to remember that even the most revered sporting Ducatis had more humble origins. Historically the 750GT is perhaps one of the most important Ducatis ever, the first of the long line of highly successful 90° V-twins. They were also powered by an engine rated by Taglioni as his best design.

DUCATI 750 SPORT

When Ing. Fabio Taglioni conceived the 750 Ducati in 1970, he always had it in his mind to develop this design as a sporting motorcycle. An early prototype 750 cc engine carried 35 mm carburettors and spun to 9,500 rpm, far removed from the eventual 750GT, and indicating that sometime in the future a higher performance version would appear. Even before the historic Imola victory in 1972, prototype 750 Sports

One of the classic sporting
Ducatis, the 1973 750 Sport,
with black engine cases and a
leading axle fork.

Right: By 1974, the 750 Sport
had a centre-axle fork and
polished engine cases.

not steering head, mounted, its effectiveness looked
better than it was. At high speed it moved around
unnervingly, and with all the instruments and the
headlight still mounted on the fork legs and triple
clamp, no advantage could be made of any reduced
steering inertia. Another problem was caused by the
clip-on handlebars being splayed out at an
uncomfortable angle because the petrol tank lacked
sufficient clearance on full lock. Starting was by
kickstart only, using a revised, swinging out lever, and
fold-up foot-rest. This was a far more satisfactory
arrangement than the kickstart on the GT, which more
often than not resulted in bruised shins.

However, it was in the engine department that the
Sport really showed most improvement over the GT.
While engine changes consisted purely of lighter (by
around 70 gm) slipper, pistons matched to a
correspondingly lighter crankshaft, and larger
carburettors without air cleaners, the change was
dramatic. The very earliest models also had milled and
polished con-rods, but without the dual strengthening
rib around the big-end that characterized the later 750
Super Sport rods. The increase of compression to 9.3:1
was much better suited to the quite radical camshaft
profiles of the GT, and the use of the new type of
Dell'Orto PHF 32 mm carburettor with unfiltered
velocity stacks allowed the engine to breathe more

freely. While power was only up to a claimed 60 bhp,
the difference in performance between a GT and Sport
was considerable. In all other respects the Sport engine
was identical to the GT, despite various claims of hotter
camshafts and larger valves.

The cycle parts were identical to the GT, except that
the rear 305 mm long Marzocchi shocks were without
the top spring covers. All the guards were fibreglass,
like the seat and petrol tank, and were of dubious
quality. In the search for lightness even the rear
number-plate holder was made of plastic. Wheels with
19-inch Borrani WM2 front and 18-inch WM3 alloy
rims were the same as for the GT, as were the single
278 mm iron disc and single drum rear brake. With
these early Sports no provision was made for any
pillion passenger, and like the GT, Scarab brake
components appeared during 1973, as did the
electronic tachometer. They were still an
uncompromised sporting motorcycle, with no provision
for turn indicators.

By 1974 the 750 Super Sport had entered
production, and the Sport was no longer the range
leader. Changes in specification began to mirror those
of the GT. First there were Ceriani centre-axle forks
with a single Brembo front disc. Then, in deference to
the UK market, where fibreglass petrol tanks were
illegal, came a steel tank in the same shape. Some of

these had appeared in 1973 on US market Sports. During 1974 the black-painted cases were replaced by polished cases like the GT and SS. Also like the GT, Marzocchi centre-axle forks with a Scarab front disc were fitted throughout 1974, still with the flat triple clamps, but unlike the GT Brembo-equipped centre-axle Marzocchis were not specified. While engine specifications remained unchanged except for a longer-stemmed inlet valve and the use of the revised primary drive, the very last 750 Sports featured a range of differences. To pull the widely splayed clip-on handlebars back to a better angle, they became offset forward of the forks. This was a considerable improvement over the strange riding position of the earlier models, and made the bike more similar in feel to the 750 Super Sport. The switch-gear and wiring mirrored the final 750GTs and first 860s, with the boxy CEV items and two-into-one throttle. The last item was definitely a retrograde step as throttle action was poorer and the cables were under more stress. The last Sports also featured a dual seat as an option. US models now had indicators and large tail-lights, but fortunately the Borrani alloy rims stayed. The earlier Sports, while essentially the same, were a purer display of the sporting concept.

As a sporting motorcycle, the 750 Sport was superb. Lighter than the GT, at 182 kg (401 lb) due to the widespread use of fibreglass, and with more power, it was a stronger performer. Handling was the same, but the riding position lent itself to more spirited riding. To quote *Cycle* magazine in its June 1974 issue: 'The 750 Sport has a great engine packaged with a brilliant chassis'. *Cycle* went on to say: 'The Ducati 750, in any of its three incarnations, is still the best handling street machine available.' Elsewhere, too, praise was heaped on this motorcycle. The Australian magazine *Two Wheels* stated in October 1974: 'The Ducati 750 Sport is not just a good bike – it is a truly exceptional motorcycle'. In England, *Motorcyclist Illustrated* said, in July 1974: 'The Ducati Sport stands level with the very best that history can offer to match it, and as a sporting machine probably better than almost any other big roadster in production'.

Fifteen years later Ducati acknowledged the importance of the Sport when they released the Nuovo 750 Sport, a bike that was unfortunately only a shadow of the original. The round-case 750 Sport epitomizes the very best of Ducati, uncompromised engine and chassis performance, equal to the best in its day. If it hadn't been for the 750 Super Sport, or if it had possessed desmodromic rather than valve spring heads, the 750 Sport would have a higher status among *Ducatisti*. As it is, not many Sports were made and they are amongst the most desirable street Ducatis.

The 1973 Imola 750 racer was considerably more compact than that of the previous year's, here ridden by Bruno Kneubühler who crashed out after setting the fastest lap. *Mick Woollett*

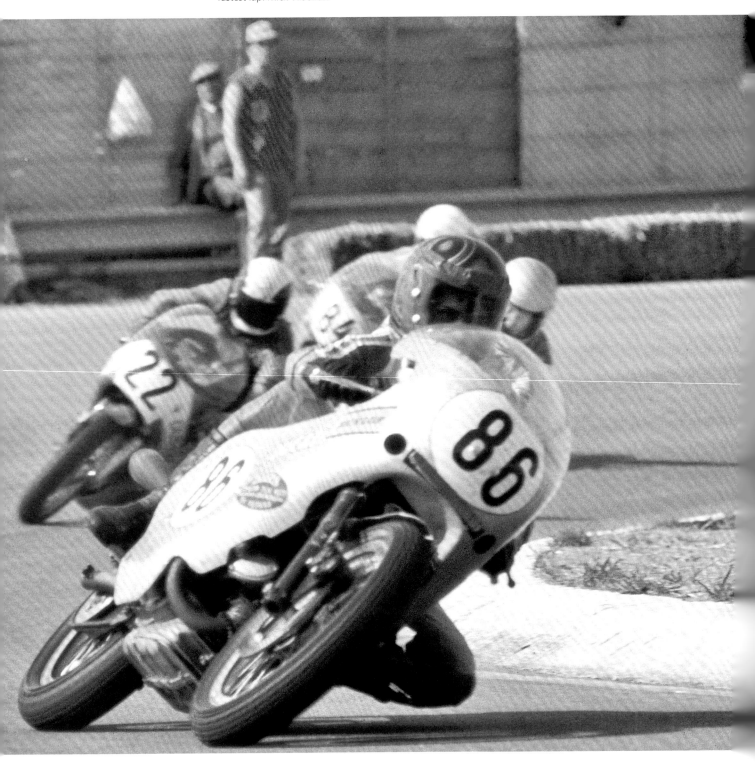

7 IMOLA AND THE DESMODROMIC 750

April 23, 1972 was the day when a brace of specially-prepared desmodromic 750 racers took on the best the world's manufacturers had to offer, and trounced them convincingly. It was the inaugural Imola 200, the 'Daytona of Europe', for Formula 750 machines, racing 750 cc machines with production-based motors. The win at Imola marked the transition for Ducati, from a relatively small and unknown Italian manufacturer, primarily of small-capacity single-cylinder bikes, to that of a marque equal to any other. Within Italy, and to certain *cognoscenti* in other countries, Taglioni and Ducati were respected for technical excellence and innovation. Yet, in production terms, Ducati was a minor manufacturer of motorcycles. Imola changed that.

The impetus for developing a racing 750 had occurred back in July 1971. In a one-off ride, Mike Hailwood was to race a prototype Formula 750 machine at Silverstone in August 1971. However, although Hailwood tested the bike, and recorded a sixth-fastest practice lap for the F750 race, he elected not to race it in the event, telling *Motor Cycle* that 'it did not handle well enough. This isn't surprising because it is only three weeks old and has never been raced before; it just needs a bit of sorting out. It should be good then'.

This 750 was more closely related to the 500 racer than the 750 street bike that had only just gone into limited production. The sand-cast crankcase was identical to that of the 500 Grand Prix bike, but it had the bore and stroke, 80 x 74.4 mm, of the production bike. It also had the dry clutch and six-speed gearbox of the 500, and a single overhead camshaft driven by bevel-gears. This was also the first 750 twin with desmodromic valve gear, and it reputedly allowed 75 bhp to be developed, with the engine revving to 11,500 rpm, using 40 mm SS Dell'Orto carburettors. The frame, likewise, was from the 500, being one of the batch made by Colin Seeley earlier that year. Up front, only a single Lockheed disc graced the Marzocchi leading axle front end, and this was insufficient for the more powerful 360 lb (163 kg) machine. The handling problems mentioned by Mike Hailwood were obviously the result of slotting a 750 engine into a 500. The bike would need to be redesigned for the inaugural Imola 200 the following year.

Below: Paul Smart's 1972 750
Imola racer was built out of a
750GT. *Ducati Motor*

With the support of Fredmano Spairani, Fabio Taglioni was given the brief to make an all out assault on this important race. It was being heavily promoted, and nine different factories had entered works-supported teams. In order to assess the level of competition, Taglioni made the trip to Daytona in March 1972, and came away impressed by the well developed Japanese racers. He realized that he couldn't tackle them head-on, he didn't have the resources. Utilizing proven technology from the 350 Desmo and 500 racers, he aimed to build a balanced machine, with handling and braking matched to usable horsepower.

Upon his return from Daytona, serious work began on developing the Imola bikes. Surprisingly, Taglioni started with standard 750GT street bikes. They had 750 engine numbers, indicating that bikes were just taken off the production line and into the racing department. The frames still had centre-stand mounts. They also had machined production leading axle Marzocchi forks, but there was more to these bikes than met the eye. The engines, while using standard 40 mm inlet and 36 mm exhaust valves, used

desmodromic valve control enabling the engine to run to 9,200 rpm. These were the first bikes to use the 'Imola' desmodromic camshafts with figures of inlet opening 65° before top dead centre and closing 95° after bottom dead centre, and exhaust opening 95° before bottom dead centre and closing 60° after top dead centre. Inlet valve lift was 12 mm. Power of 84 bhp at 8,800 rpm was claimed at the rear wheel, but more importantly it was the spread of power that was so advantageous. At 7,000 rpm the engine was said to make 70 bhp. Compression was up to 10:1 and these engines still used the wide, 80° included valve angle. They also used the first versions of the new 40 mm Dell'Orto PHF concentric carburettor.

In order to keep combustion temperatures down, an oil-cooling system was fitted that cooled the oil to the cylinder heads, and dual plug ignition installed with an additional 10 mm Lodge spark-plug. This enabled ignition advance to be cut back to 34° before top dead centre. With the alternator removed from the right side of the crankshaft, total loss battery and coil ignition, still by dual points, was employed. Since his experience with electronic ignition on the 500, Fabio Taglioni was wary of employing it on the 750 for Imola, and was also worried about heat build-up inside the fairing over such a long race. Thus the condensers were mounted on the front frame down-tubes, away from the heat of the engine.

Apart from the stronger connecting rods machined out of solid billet, 50 gm lighter than standard, the lower end of the engine was early 750GT. There were straight cut primary drive and clutch gears (with a drilled clutch basket to save weight), but it had the same gearbox. There was no six-speed gearbox, or dry clutch, as on the 500 racers. The primary drive ratio differed from the GT and the later SS, being 31/75, or 2.419:1. Further weight was saved by completely removing the kickstart mechanism, which also served to increase ground clearance on the right side. Braking was uprated to two Lockheed front discs, and a rear 230 mm disc replacing the road bike's drum. With only left-side calipers in stock from the street bikes, these were used all round, the right-side front having an unusually long brake hose. A high-rise exhaust pipe was on the left, but not on the right. Imola had predominantly left-hand corners, but ground clearance was still a problem because racing tyres required an 18-inch front wheel instead of a 19-inch. Total dry weight of these racers was 392 lb (178 kg), and they were reputed to pull the tallest available gearing, giving 169 mph (272 km/h).

Seven bikes were built. To ride one of them, Ducati had approached firstly Jarno Saarinen, Renzo Pasolini, and then, in February, Barry Sheene. All had declined, not feeling that the Ducati would be competitive. Ducati already had the evergreen 39-year-old Bruno Spaggiari, who had raced every factory bike since the 1950s, and knew the Imola circuit intimately. To partner Spaggiari would be the younger Ermanno Giuliano, who had raced the 500 Ducati throughout 1971. English rider Alan Dunscombe, who had already been racing a modified 750GT for English importer Vic Camp, filled the third berth. Spairani now only required a top-line F750 racer to ride the last bike, and, through Vic Camp, managed to secure Paul Smart at the last minute. Originally planning to ride a Triumph Triple, the deal fell through, and reluctantly Smart flew to Italy. While a 750 Desmo with Sport bodywork had been tested at Modena in March, with further tests by Spaggiari with revised bodywork on 6 April, it wasn't until 19 April that the Imola racers were started up for

the first time at Modena, too late to correct any defects. However, Taglioni was quietly confident. Smart had equalled Agostini's lap record, set on a 500 cc MV Agusta Grand Prix bike. In their specially-constructed glass-sided transporter, all seven Ducatis – two each for Smart and Spaggiari, one each for Dunscombe and

Giuliano, and one spare – were transported the 40 km (25 miles) to Imola.

On race day, 70,000 spectators crammed into Autodromo Dino Ferrari at Imola. With works machines in abundance from MV Agusta, Honda, Norton, Moto Guzzi, Triumph, and BSA, alongside works-supported Kawasaki, Laverda, Suzuki, and BMW, they had hopefully come to see the Italian factories beat the Japanese teams that had dominated Daytona. The best riders in the world were there too: Giacomo Agostini, Phil Read, Roberto Gallina, Walter Villa, Ray Pickrell, Tony Jeffries, John Cooper, Percy Tait, Ron Grant, and Daytona winner Don Emde. In practice, Spaggiari, followed by Smart, had set the fastest time. With its fast sweeping curves – some smooth, others bumpy – and its up-and-down topography, Imola seemed to suit the Ducatis. Unlike Daytona this was no mere horsepower circuit. This was Imola before the advent of chicanes, a fast European circuit in the traditional style.

Agostini, on a specially-prepared 750 MV, led at the start. This MV, while still with the shaft-drive of the road bikes, had a Grand Prix style frame with 500GP

forks and brakes. At the end of the fourth lap Smart overtook Agostini, followed a lap later by Spaggiari. From then on the two Ducatis were untroubled out in front, and in the final five laps they were both racing for the lead. Spaggiari nipped in front, but on the final lap his bike started to misfire as he was low on fuel. He ran wide on a sweeper, allowing Smart to take a comfortable victory. It had been a great day for Ducati. It wasn't so bad for Paul Smart either, as he took home 7,080,000 Lire in prize money. Spairani was so excited that he donated the winning bike to Smart. Spaggiari's bike ended up being sold to Ron Angel, Ducati distributor in Victoria, Australia, where it was campaigned by Kenny Blake during 1973. The race speed over 200 miles had been an astonishing 97.76 mph (157.35 km/h), with the fastest lap of 100.1 mph (161.11 km/h) being shared equally by Smart, Spaggiari, and Agostini.

After the race, Ducati promised 'Imola' replicas, but these were slow to appear. In the meantime the 750 racers were displayed at selected events around the world as part of a promotional exercise for the 750 road bikes. In June, three bikes were entered at

Below: Spaggiari at Imola in
1974, now with a full face
helmet. His best result this year
was an eighth in the first leg.
Mick Woollett

Daytona, followed in July by the Canadian GP at
Mosport, where they were raced unsuccessfully by
Bruno Spaggiari and Percy Tait. Then in October,
Smart won the Greek GP on the island of Corfu.
Meanwhile, Smart had raced his own bike at various
races in England throughout 1972, with moderate
success. One was also taken to South Africa to race
over the northern winter, where local rider Errol
Cowan had some reasonable results in highly
competitive fields that included Giacomo Agostini.

For 1973, despite the replacement of Arnaldo Milvio
as general manager by Ing. de Eccher, Taglioni was
given the authorization to build brand new racers,
considerably removed from the street bikes. He knew
that the 1972 bikes were too close to the road bikes to
be competitive against the new wave of two-stroke
Yamahas and Suzukis, so a completely new bike was
designed, this time a real racer. As Formula 750
regulations only stipulated that the crankcases of the
production bike must be retained, he designed a
shorter, lighter frame, and a more powerful and
compact engine. The frame featured eccentrics in the
swing-arm bosses for chain adjustment, along with

positions in the swing-arm to select one of three
different wheelbases. The chain adjustment system
ultimately found its way through to the next generation
of road frames, the 860GT, yet the wheelbase selection
remained peculiar to this 1973 racer. Also, to shorten
the wheelbase even further, the distinctive Marzocchi
leading axle forks were replaced with those of a centre-
axle type after Spaggiari complained of front end
instability at the first test session at Modena. Thus,
without the time to experiment further, the centre-axle
Marzocchis were installed along with the flat triple
clamps of the leading type. Though it meant an
enormous trail increase (to nearly 6 inches), and despite
reservations, it cured the wobble, and the bike
subsequently handled well. Taglioni was so impressed
with this suspension set-up that when the production
750SS appeared the following year it had this front end
on the standard frame. Indeed, this front end geometry
was fitted to the entire range of 750/900 Super Sports
throughout their nine-year model life.

As he was still committed to the 90° twin, Taglioni
needed more horsepower as well as a lighter, shorter
bike. Here, by taking the 86 mm pistons of the 450 racer

Spaggiari's 750 in the pits at
Imola in 1974. Although
outclassed, this was a
magnificent machine.

of 1970 that were readily available, he was able to shorten the stroke to 64.5 mm. This enabled revs to increase by 1,000 rpm, from the 9,200/9,500 rpm of the 1972 bike to 10,200/10,500 rpm. To take advantage of this more oversquare bore/stroke ratio, a new head was designed with a 60° included valve angle, rather than the 80° that had been a feature of all previous Ducatis. Preparation was left to the last minute, this time due to the endless strikes that occur in Italy from time to time. Because of delays in signing the 1972 metal-workers' contract, it wasn't until March 1973 that the strikes ended and work could begin on the new engine, barely a month before the Imola 200. The cylinder heads, new camshafts (now giving 14 mm of intake valve lift), connecting rods, and rockers were all specially machined out of solid billets or castings, and a new vented dry clutch took the place of the previous oil-bath type. Carburettors remained the same 40 mm Dell'Ortos of the previous year, but instead of the unusual one-up, one-down exhaust system, both exhausts were now the high-rise type. Weight was down significantly, to 325 lb (147 kg). Front brakes were now forward-mounted Italian Scarab, a Lockheed pattern that would also eventually be seen on the 750 Super Sport.

On the dyno, the engine power dropped off at 9,500 rpm, yet in testing Spaggiari reported it happy to rev beyond 10,400 rpm. These problems with the Ducati dyno room meant that no one knew exactly how much power this new engine actually made, but claims in the region of 93 bhp were made. While testing at Modena, Spaggiari set an absolute record, beating Agostini's previous best on the MV 500 by 0.3 seconds, and demolishing the 750 record, set by Smart in 1972, by two seconds. With only three days to go before the race, the last engine was finished. It had to be run-in during qualifying and ended up in Spaggiari's bike.

Race day was 15 April 1973, and even without the presence of Giacomo Agostini and his MV, 100,000 people streamed in to see the second Daytona of Europe. The Ducati team consisted of three riders, Bruno Spaggiari, Bruno Kneubühler, and Mick Grant. There was also another Ducati, entered under the NCR banner for the first time, but it wasn't a short-stroke racer, and was a prototype for the production 750 Super Sport to be released later in the year. Ridden by Claudio Loigo, it finished 15th. Even without Agostini, the competition was much stronger, particularly with Jarno Saarinen on a Yamaha 351 two-stroke, and the

Franco Uncini rode a short-stroke
750 for Bruno Spaggiari during
1975. *Ducati Motor*

decision to run the race in two 100-mile stages also helped the two-strokes. Still, in the first leg Kneubühler set the fastest lap at 1:49.1, almost three seconds faster than the Ducatis in 1972, and an average speed of over 103 mph (166 km/h). In the second race he crashed while catching Saarinen. Mick Grant burnt his clutch at the start of the first race, but Bruno Spaggiari again finished second overall, with a second place in the first leg, followed by a third in the second. It was a magnificent result considering the level of competition, but was to be the final race for the silver 750s as official factory bikes.

At the Imola race of 1974, Spaggiari rode one of the same bikes as in the previous year, but they were entered under his own team. With no more development they were totally outclassed and the best he could manage was an eighth in the first leg, retiring in the second. They were raced again in 1975, Spaggiari this time electing to manage the team rather than ride. With 1972 winner Paul Smart and future 500 cc World Champion Franco Uncini riding them, the best result was Uncini's 21st overall. Smart crashed out, breaking his leg and prompting his retirement. Uncini went on to compete in the Junior Italian

Championship on the Team Spaggiari 750SS, winning 15 out of 21 races. It was a pity that these bikes bowed out with such a whimper, because if they had been developed further they could have been possibly the most successful bevel-gear two-cylinder racers, and many of the engine design features may have found their way onto the production bikes. Even without that development, the short-stroke 750 racers were amongst the finest Ducatis ever built. If only they had made a short-stroke street 750 Super Sport with the 60° valve angle in 1975.

DUCATI 750 SUPER SPORT 1974

Even more than the MV Agusta, the 1974 Ducati 750 Super Sport epitomizes the Italian sporting motorcycle of the 1970s. Whereas the production MV four-cylinder bike was intentionally designed to be as far removed from the genuine Grand Prix racers as possible (to avoid customers converting them into competition for the factory bikes), the Ducati was as close a replica to the Imola 200 winning racer of 1972 that could be built and still be street legal. Immediately after the 1972 Imola race, Spairani promised 'Imola' replicas, but in typical Ducati fashion these were slow to materialize.

A prototype emerged in late 1972 that was very much a modified GT, just like the first racer. It had the leading axle forks, wide rear sub-frame, and the distinctive fibreglass petrol tank with the instant fuel gauge clear strip. Braking was by triple Scarab discs and the engine was a detuned version of the Imola racer. Because an 18-inch front wheel was fitted to the Marzocchi forks designed for a 19-inch, the fibreglass front guard was clamped to the fork legs. The engine itself was a work of art, still with the 40 mm Dell'Ortos, desmodromic camshafts (with 11 mm of intake valve lift), and the race connecting rods milled, machined, and polished from solid chrome-molybdenum steel billet. The desmodromic system was

different to that of the singles. Instead of hairpin valve springs, to provide the light pressure to seat the valves to assist starting, springs that curled around the lower rocker were fitted. The early ones tended to break, and adjustment of the closing valve clearance was now by a one-piece shim. Along with the Laverda SFC750, the 750SS pioneered the standard fitting of fairings to a production streetbike. The racing style half-fairing also had the instruments (including ammeter) and headlight mounted in it, and was supported by the steering headstem to reduce steering inertia. This prototype had the black engine-covers of the 750 Sport. The silver bodywork was matched to a green/blue frame, quite unlike any Ducati before or since. As such, these models have earned the nickname the 'Green Frame'.

When 1973 came everyone waited expectantly for the production bike. At the Milan Show at the end of the year another 750 Super Sport was displayed, now

Below: The 1974 750 Super
Sport – the definitive factory cafe
racer and now considered one of
the finest production Ducatis.
Roy Kidney

with polished engine-cases and the centre-axle Marzocchis. Earlier, a few bikes had been built and three were airfreighted to the USA in late-1973. Phil Schilling and Cook Neilson of *Cycle* magazine got one of them, Neilson eventually modifying his into the 'California Hot Rod' and racing it to victory in the Daytona Superbike race of 1977 (see Chapter 9). These bikes also had the black engine-cases, but with the centre-axle forks, and were basically modified 750 Sports, using Veglia instruments (now without the ammeter). They had rear-mounted Scarab front calipers and an underslung Lockheed rear caliper.

It wasn't until early-1974 that the one and only batch of round-case 750 Super Sports was produced. They were built as homologation specials for the FIM, regulations requiring 200 to be manufactured. Although engine numbers go up to 411, recently found production records indicate 401 were manufactured. A

significant proportion (88) went to the US. Other countries were less fortunate, with the UK getting 24 and Australia 33. Germany only received 12. There were only the barest concessions made for street legality. Silencing was minimal from the Conti silencers, and the 40 mm Dell'Ortos lacked any form of air filtration. There was no provision for turn signals, let alone an electric start. Whereas the quality of the fibreglass and some of the ancillary components was dubious, the engine was a masterpiece. A special machine was installed at the factory to machine from billet each individual con-rod, just as with the Imola racers, and all the rockers were highly polished. No other contemporary machine offered comparable performance, for while the power output of 72 bhp (at the rear wheel) was modest, the light weight – barely 397 lb (180 kg) – in combination with an extremely narrow frontal area ensured a top speed of around

130–35 mph (210–17 km/h). *Motorrad* in Germany was one of the few magazines to comprehensively test one and they achieved a top speed of 216.7 km/h (135 mph), while *Motociclismo* in Italy achieved a standing 400 metre time of 12.215 seconds at 176.47 km/h (109.7 mph).

All these 1974 bikes were identical, and they were quite different to the GTs and Sports. The engine-cases were generally drilled for an oil-cooler and had extra internal webbing, as did the side-covers. The frame dimensions too were different, as the optional high-rise exhaust system bolts on perfectly to the SS but doesn't fit a Sport. They had the higher-domed rocker covers of the 860 and later 750s, higher primary drive ratio and the same 9.5:1 Mondial pistons as the 750 Sport, even though compression was listed on some brochures at 10:1. Valve sizes were standard 750, at 40 mm and 36 mm, but the desmodromic camshafts featured higher lift (11 mm) and different timing, with inlet opening 63° before top dead centre and closing 83° after bottom dead centre, and exhaust opening 80° before bottom dead centre and closing 58° after top dead centre. Despite being desmodromic these camshafts were actually slightly milder than the 750GT, with inlet duration of 326°, and valve overlap of 121°. There were lots of individually fabricated parts, like the welded steel inlet manifolds – hardly weight-saving, but indicative of a limited edition machine. These bikes had the same Marzocchi front forks and forward-mounted Scarab calipers that had been used on the 1973 Imola racers, and an overslung rear Lockheed brake caliper. The front Scarab master cylinder wasn't the best quality, and invariably leaked brake fluid over the tank. Instruments were English Smiths, and tyres were the only V-rated ones available at the time, Metzeler C7 Racing, in identical sizes of 3.50V18 front and rear. It must be said that these tyres were not really suited to the bike, making the steering ponderously heavy, as well as being quite slippery. They were mounted on identical Borrani WM3 18-inch rims front and rear.

For those who bought a 750 Super Sport, there was also the factory option of a racing uprating kit. This highly comprehensive kit contained a full fairing and brackets (patterned after the 1973 racer, not the boxier 1972 version), high-rise open megaphones, oil-cooler, 12 mm 'Imola' desmodromic camshafts, a selection of eight rear sprockets from 34 to 42 teeth and a range of main jets from 150 to 152. There was even a set of racing Lodge spark-plugs and a Renold racing chain. For engines fitted with the 'Imola' camshafts but still with Conti silencers, the maximum revs increased from 8,800 rpm to 9,000 rpm. With the megaphones, revs increased to 9,200 rpm.

However, even as the 750SS was being produced the round-case engine series was being phased out in favour of the Giugiaro-inspired square-case 860. Economics, and forthcoming legislation regarding noise and left-side gearshifting, would leave the 750SS of 1974 as the only desmodromic version of the round-case engine and the rarest and most special of all production street Ducatis. It also represented the end of an era for production engines, the era where cost and government legislation had minimal influence on the design or execution. Where the 750 Super Sport also scored was that it was, in effect, a racing bike with lights and a horn, so it had all the hallmarks of a racing machine in handling and braking, as well as the looks of a racer. This machine is the perfect example of form following function, and successful aesthetics being not the result of stylists, but of subconscious evolution. To many it still remains the best-looking Ducati ever produced.

DUCATI 860 SUPER SPORT

After Imola in 1973, the future looked quite bleak for four-strokes in Formula 750, especially with the prospect of the Yamaha TZ700 for 1974. Endurance racing was really the only avenue left for Ducati, and as this didn't have any capacity restriction, Taglioni reasoned that he would need a larger engine to combat the Hondas and Kawasakis. So by the simple expedient of using the 86 mm 450 racing pistons in a 74.4 mm stroke 750 Desmo, an 864 cc twin was created and first raced in the Barcelona 24-Hour race of 1973. Held at the twisting 2.25 mile (3.62 km) street circuit of Montjuich Park in July, this bike was essentially an overbored 750SS road bike. Ridden by Salvador Canellas and Benjamin Grau it won in record time, completing 720 laps at 71 mph (114.3 km/h). So dominant were they that they beat the second place Bultaco by 16 laps. Like the Imola racers of 1972, the bike used early 750 crankcases, but had the dry clutch and centre-axle Marzocchis with Scarab brakes of the 1973 Imola bikes. Claimed power was 86 bhp at 8,200 rpm. After such success it was inevitable that a road version of the 860 prototype would appear.

The road version that was shown at the Milan Show in November 1973, however, was not the 860 Super Sport, but the 860GT (covered in Chapter 8). While the 750 Super Sport went into production, another 860 endurance bike raced at the 1974 Montjuich 24-Hour race, again ridden by Grau and Canellas and now producing around 90 bhp. Unfortunately, after 16 hours they retired with a failed gearbox while leading. In 1975, now with an 88 mm 905 cc engine with heavily-machined crankcases to allow the use of low exhausts, Canellas and Grau won yet again, at an average speed of 71.74 mph (115.45 km/h), beating their previous record by another 11 laps. By now Ducati were competing in the entire World Endurance Championship, and this is covered in Chapter 9.

In the meantime, a round-case 860 Super Sport ridden by Kenny Blake had won the 1975 Easter Bathurst Production Race in Australia. According to Ron Angel, the importer and entrant, the one-off 860SS was actually built for the Castrol Six-Hour production race of October 1974, but it was declared ineligible (as was the 750 Super Sport, the organizers thinking that such a limited production race replica was outside the spirit of the event). So, rather than airfreight the bike

The Kenny Blake 860SS was
visually similar to the 750SS but
with 860 camshaft bearing
supports.

out, they sent it by sea, in time for the 1975 round of
Australian production races. As raced by Kenny Blake
it was visually identical to a stock 750SS, the only
differences being square '860' camshaft bearing mounts
on the cylinder heads and the words '860 Super Sport'
on the side-covers. Carrying 750SS frame and engine
numbers, this 860SS had a close-ratio gearbox and
other special racing parts. To most other competitors it
must have appeared as a 750SS fitted with the 86 mm
pistons and barrels from a 450 single, and it was hardly
a production model because it was the only one in
existence. In the 20-lap race Blake completely
demolished the opposition of Kawasaki 900s, and was
immediately disqualified by the organizers pending
confirmation from the Ducati factory that the 860SS
was indeed a production bike. This duly arrived and
Blake's victory reinstated. However, when the 860SS
did appear as a production model, the 900SS, it was
based on the square-case 860 engine, not the round-
case 750.

DUCATI 900 SUPER SPORT

By taking the square-case 860 engine and placing it in
the 750SS running gear the 1975 900SS was created.
The 750SS continued, but was now merely a sleeved-
down 860. Whereas the 860GT had been designed with
US noise and left-side gearshift regulations in mind, the
1975 750/900SS continued where the 1974 bike had
left off. With the right-side gearshift, small CEV tail-
light, glass-fibre tank (without the clear strip), open
bellmouths, Conti silencers, and no provision for turn
indicators, these bikes were still very much a limited
edition factory production racer. They even had the
Aprilia switch-gear and the ignition switch between the
tank and seat, like the earlier 750s. Because they used
the square-case engine, they had the 5 mm shorter
connecting rods, with a 20 mm gudgeon pin rather
than the 22 mm gudgeon of the round-case. Thus the
milled connecting rods made way for regular forged
items, still with a dual strengthening rib around the

Below: The production 900SS of
1975 had a square-case engine
but was still a hand-assembled
race replica.

big-end eye, and apart from the desmodromic heads of
the 1974 750SS, with polished rockers, the engine was
as the 860GT, covered in the next chapter.

Unfortunately this series of Super Sports inherited
some of the ignition problems and poor build-quality
of the 860. Also, while the shorter con-rods of the
square-case engine helped boost mid-range torque, the
increased rod angularity put more strain on the big-
end. Coupled with the abrupt ignition advance of the
first series of Ducati Elettrotecnica electronic ignition,
and the additional reciprocating weight of bigger
pistons, the model had a reputation for poor reliability,
and was prone to premature big-end failure.

All these 1975 bikes used 750SS frames and frame
numbers, though they differed in detail from the earlier
bike. Brakes were now Brembo 08s with larger 280 mm
drilled front discs. The rear drilled disc was slightly
smaller at 229 mm. The centre-axle Marzocchis with
the flat triple clamps remained, as did the rear
Marzocchi shock absorbers, though to help improve
ground clearance they were now 5 mm longer, at

310 mm. The tyres specified were still the Metzeler C7
Racing, and wheels were the same 40-spoke Borrani
WM3 x 18. These bikes had silver frames, and silver
and blue paintwork, the 750 with a silver fairing and
blue stripes, and the 900 with a blue fairing and
silver stripes.

Because they couldn't be sold in many countries,
only 246 750SSs and 249 900SSs were made in 1975.
With 198 going to Australia, it was obvious that they
were made with Australian production racing in mind.
The Castrol Six-Hour race had become the premier
motorcycle event in Australia but success had eluded
Ducati. Its limited edition 750SS hadn't been eligible in
1974, and it had been disqualified in previous years, so
a purpose-built production racer seemed the ideal
solution. This was to be the last truly raw sporting
motorcycle you could buy completely uncompromised
by legislation.

However, the 900SS never did manage to win the
Castrol Six-Hour. John Warrian's best effort in four
years was a second place (shared with Terry Kelly) in

Left: The 1976/77 900SS had a
steel petrol tank and a left-side
gear shift, but the soul was
unchanged.

Below: While the 750SS
continued for 1975 it too now
had a square-case motor.

1978, still on the 1975 model bike. He had almost won
in 1975 until big-end failure robbed him of victory in
the final hour. While not actually winning this
prestigious race, the 900SS had nevertheless established
its credentials as one of the strongest-performing bikes
on the market. It could certainly meet the Kawasaki
Z900 and later the Z1000 head-on and not be
disgraced, and combining this performance with the
renowned brakes and handling of the 750SS, Ducati
had created undoubtedly the best all round sports bike
of its day. Unfortunately, the Six-Hour race had also
showed up the bike's prime weakness, reliability. Yet it
would be three more years before the big-end and
ignition problems were addressed.

For 1976 it was decided to put the 900 Super Sport,
and its sleeved-down sister the 750, into regular
production. Thus the bike needed to be modified to be
acceptable for sale throughout the world. It was the
next step in altering the bike and diminishing its appeal
to the purist, a compromise seen at Ducati so often

before and since. Now the fibreglass 'Imola'-shaped tank was replaced by a 750 Sport style steel one, and the Conti silencers by the Lafranconis of the 860. Indicators on stalks appeared from the fairing along with new Aprilia switch-gear and an ignition switch mounted on the dashboard. 32 mm Dell'Orto carburettors and air-cleaners were fitted onto the now cast aluminium inlet manifolds, and Veglia instruments replaced the Smiths. No longer did the engine breathe directly into the atmosphere, but into a catch-tank moulded into the fibreglass seat. The gearshift was also moved to the left via the sloppy crossover shaft arrangement of the 860, the gear-selecting mechanism still residing in the right outer cover like the 750 (and the singles). The rear brake lever was thus moved to the right. It wasn't a very tidy conversion and the rubber foot-rests and levers were clumsy. While a display bike that appeared in early 1976 had a blue frame, colours for the production models were the same as for 1975, but with different graphics on the tank.

To fit a Super Sport with quiet mufflers and small carburettors really destroyed the character of the bike, but fortunately many came with the 40 mm Dell'Ortos and Contis packed in the crate. This restored the power to that of the 1975 bike, as the engine specifications were still the same. The 900SS was a strong-performing motorcycle, even if weight was up from the 750 to 414 lb (188 kg). *Cycle* magazine, testing a 1977 (the same as 1976) bike in July 1978, achieved a standing quarter mile time of 12.91 seconds at 104.16 mph (167.6 km/h) with Lafranconis and 32 mm carburettors. The kitted bike ran 12.4 seconds at 109 mph (175 km/h). *Cycle* 'marvelled at its almost hydraulic power.' *Revs* in Australia tested both the standard and kitted versions in 1977, coming away with the conclusion that, with the 40 mm Dell'Ortos and Contis, Ducati had created an engine that was 'truly brilliant – a real credit to the Italian motorcycle industry'. They achieved a 17% overall power increase over the detuned version, with even greater gains in the mid-range. The engine was

For 1979 the 900 Super Sport gained an attractive black and gold colour scheme while the wire-spoked wheels made way for a cast-alloy type. *Nico Georgeoglou*

obviously designed to run in this trim. Even today, the 900SS is a brilliantly-performing motorcycle and it is no wonder that it is considered an all-time classic.

A lot of the details of the 1976–77 bikes were tidied up in 1978. The SD900 Darmah had just gone into production with a revised left-side gearshift and Bosch ignition. It also had a new big-end with a larger, 38 mm crankpin and correspondingly smaller rollers in an effort to improve reliability. These changes were now incorporated in the Super Sport, which still retained its kickstart and alloy Borrani rims. By now, with full production underway, the polished rockers disappeared, but the 1978 bikes were better than in 1976–77. The gearshift was improved, as the crossover linkages tended to develop a lot of slop with wear, and the footrests and levers were neater. The engine was also smoother, with the Bosch ignition and its revised ignition advance. Unfortunately it now needed a fully-charged battery. The earlier system was notable in that it was self-generating, and if required the bike could be

run without a battery at all. A dual seat was also listed as an option at this time.

In parallel with the 900SS, production of the 750SS continued, although on a much smaller scale. The 1975–77 bikes were identical to the respective 900, save for the silver fairing, smaller pistons and 750 bearing-covers on the cylinder heads. The last 750SSs appeared in 1979, with the Bosch ignition and Goldline Brembo 08 calipers. They were the last Ducatis with Borrani rims, as by now the 900SS was fitted with alloy Speedlines. Very few were made, and total production for the 750SS was only about 1,000 over five years.

During 1978 the 900SS appeared with a black and gold paint scheme along with the alloy wheels of the Darmah. This mirrored the striping of the previous year, but with gold stripes over a black petrol tank. The engine remained as before, with the option of 40 mm Dell'Ortos and Conti mufflers. The Speedline wheels were prone to cracking and soon replaced with alloy

The final 900SS of 1981/82 with
Silentium mufflers, FPS wheels
and a restyled seat.

FPS ones. By now some Super Sports had the 40 mm carburettors they deserved, and the use of alloy wheels meant a 280 mm disc was now fitted at the rear. The small CEV tail-lights made way for the larger US-style ones.

The final 900SS was shown at the 1980 Bologna Show and released during 1981, now with a dual seat only, a black frame with silver bodywork, and new decals. There were lots of detail changes, but unfortunately quality control could have been better at this time. Bikes appeared with incorrect speedo drives and 'A' pistons in 'B' barrels. Some had a handle on the frame to help in putting the bike on the centre-stand, and others had early petrol tanks and front guards. Its Silentium silencers were better-looking than the Lafranconis, but still not a Conti replacement. Yet the engine and running gear remained the same, so the basic ingredients were still there. Unfortunately, the constant modernization of the Super Sport had also diminished its original appeal as a race replica. While

the last bikes had better paint and fibreglass, much better electrics, cable-mounted chokes, even locking petrol caps, they lacked the raw appeal of the original, and lost a lot of the character. They also became hard to sell and in 1982 were dumped at bargain prices in markets like Australia.

So, ten years after Imola the same basic bike remained in production, but time had caught up with it. Buyers now wanted electric start and an easier bike to live with. The Super Sport had already evolved into the Mike Hailwood Replica and they both merged to become the S2. But now we are a long way from Imola. The early 750 and 900 Super Sports reflected the very best of the Italian concept of a sporting motorcycle, genuine unadulterated race replicas built irrespective of regulation and, to some extent, cost. However, the later bikes were inevitably compromised by increasing legislation, fashion, and economics, and they were no longer race replicas. The next generation of race replica Ducatis lay in another bloodline, the Pantah.

A restyled seat appeared on the
Darmah for 1979, and it lost the
kickstart.

8 PRODUCTION MAINSTAYS

With the success of the 860 cc version of the 750 Super Sport at Barcelona in July 1973, it was obvious that the 864 cc engine would eventually make it into production. Here was an opportunity to meet increasing noise legislation and still maintain the performance levels of the 750. However, the shape of the prototype took everyone by surprise when it was displayed at the Milan Show in November 1973. Instead of entrusting the styling to Leopoldo Tartarini, who had done the rear-seat design of the last desmodromic singles, they gave it to the car stylist Giorgetto Giugiaro, of Studio Italdesign. In the 1960s, Giugiaro had worked for Bertone and designed the beautiful 105 Series Alfa Romeo coupés, but his designs of the 1970s were less flowing, and more angular. These ideas were transported through to the 860, even to the design of the engine-cases and Lafranconi mufflers. While journalists raved about the 860 at the time (they generally assume that anything new is better than the old), the 860 hasn't aged well, and today is considered an inferior model to the 750.

The Milan Show bike differed slightly to the eventual production models, in that it had a small bikini fairing, right-side gear-change, and Borrani 18-inch alloy rims. The frame was standard 750 Sport (with the narrower rear sub-frame). It also featured an electric start, with the starter motor between the cylinders, as it had been on the few 750GTs so fitted. When the 860 went into production it had a new frame, with bowed front down-tubes, and the eccentric adjustment at the swing-arm pivot for chain adjustment, just like the 1973 Imola racers. Steel rims and a single Brembo 11-inch disc with Ceriani forks also appeared on the production models. The style of the bike was different to the 750GT, with much higher, wider handlebars, and less of a sporting riding position. Colours were typical mid-1970s – orange, green, or blue.

It was in the engine department that most of the changes took place. Apart from the obvious external appearance, the bevel-gear camshaft drive layout was completely revised. Instead of the expensive and difficult-to-assemble train of bevel-gears of the 750, there was now a straight cut gear keyed to the crankshaft, driving two more straight cut gears mounted in ball-bearings on an alloy outrigger plate.

A prototype 860, with small fairing and electric start.
Ducati Motor

These two gears keyed directly with a set of helical bevels matching the towershafts. The ignition contact breaker of the 750 was eliminated, so there was no longer the need for a central bevel-gear between the two vertical shafts. While the new bevels were better-supported than in the 750, they also added considerable width to the engine. The primary advantages came through the much greater ease of assembly, because each bevel shaft could now be shimmed independently. Another advantage came with the use of a straight cut gear from the crankshaft. If, through wear, crankshaft endplay developed, this no longer affected valve timing – not a problem with constantly rebuilt racing engines, but possibly one with higher mileage street bikes. Camshafts were new, and more touring orientated than the 750, with figures of inlet opening 37° before top dead centre, and closing 74° after bottom dead centre, and exhaust opening 75° before bottom dead centre and closing 38° after top dead centre. Thus valve duration (for the same size valves) was 291° for the inlet and 293° exhaust, with valve overlap at only 75°. These milder camshafts enabled peak power to be developed at a lower, 6,900 rpm.

With the loss of the contact breaker, there was now a space for an oil filter, still not a full flow type as it only filtered oil to the rear cylinder head, but better than no filtration at all. Although the stroke, at 74.4 mm, remained the same, the connecting rods were 5 mm shorter, giving an eye-to-eye length of 145 mm, reducing the rod/stroke ratio to 1.95:1. The cylinder barrels too were correspondingly shorter. The diameter

of the small end eye was reduced to 20 mm to compensate for the increase in reciprocating weight due to the larger 86 mm pistons. These pistons were the slipper type as fitted to the 750 Sport, not the full skirt 750GT design. Compression ratio was 9.3:1. The same 36 mm crankpin and big-end bearings from the 750 were also used, as was the 750's 150 watt alternator for the first 1,683 engines, after which a 200 watt type was fitted. Ignition was now by the Ducati Elettrotecnica that had been tried on the 500 racers, with the stator being bolted onto the crankcases as had been intended on the 750. The magnetic rotor was incorporated in the flywheel on the primary drive side. Primary drive ratio was also the revised 32/70 of the 750SS. There were several revisions to the primary drive and clutch during the production of the first 860s, mainly in the type of bearings in the clutch housing. The revisions occurred at engine number 1194, with new bearings, then at number 2179, when even larger bearings were fitted into the clutch drum. There were also alterations to the clutch plates and fifth gear (after number 1194).

The valve adjustment mechanism was changed to incorporate a screw and locknut, just as with the last series of 750GTs. This aggravated the problem with the cylinder head design that only allowed for short, not particularly well-supported valve guides, and they were prone to premature wear. The cylinder head design was really designed for desmodromic valve actuation and there also wasn't much room for valve springs of a decent length. Not a problem with street bikes, but certainly one for racing.

In the electrical department the 860 was completely revamped from the 750, and not entirely successfully. New CEV switch-gear was the same as fitted to the last 750GTs and Sports. There were regulator problems, and melting switch-gear and fuse boxes, particularly on the electric start 860GTE. The instrument panel with the city/country two-level horn switch was also shared with the last 750s. To meet US Federal legislation the gearshift lever was moved to the left side via a crossover linkage behind the engine. It was a rather crude conversion and the precision of the right-side shifting bikes was lost in the process. The crossover system for the rear brake was even worse, the cross-tube being simply welded to the engine plates. The result of this was that the rear lever was set so low that the clamp severely affected ground clearance.

Despite the extra capacity, higher compression, and the use of the 750 Sports 32 mm Dell'Orto PHF32

Below: The production 860GT of
1974 which was a departure, but
not an improvement over the
750GT. *Ducati Motor*

carburettors (still with restrictive air-cleaners), the 860 didn't perform any better than the old 750GT. The weight increase to 454 lb (206 kg), or 478lb (217 kg) with electric start, more than offset any gains in maximum power. The harsh Ceriani forks and steel rimmed 18-inch wheels front and rear also didn't improve the handling over the 750, and the seat height, at 31.5 inches (800 mm), was very high. *Cycle World*, in July 1975, achieved a top speed of only 109 mph (175 km/h). The 860 didn't meet with universal approval, and there were criticisms of the riding position and the styling. Many of these were answered with the 860GTS later in 1975.

860/900 GTS

The GTS was a successful attempt to make the 860 more appealing to European markets. It was still basically an 860GT but now had a new petrol tank

design with knee indentations and a lower, wider seat. The colour was a more classical dark blue with silver stripes, and low handlebars along with a twin Brembo braking set-up at the front contributed to its more sporting emphasis. Several features from the 750s were reintroduced, notably an instrument panel modelled on the 750 Sport, with the Smiths instruments held in separate clamps on a bracket attached to the top triple clamp. The ignition key was placed on this panel along with a set of warning lights and the city/country horn switch. The headlight was mounted on the same chrome wire brackets as the earlier 750GTs, giving a lighter, more airy look, and the indicators too were the round type from the earlier bike. The electric starter was now fitted as standard, and a chrome rail was provided to aid putting the bike on the centre-stand.

New to the GTS was the choke mechanism, with a plastic lever pulling out at right angles, mounted to the left of the headlight, rather than the handlebar-mounted

The 860GTS was produced in response to the poor reception to the angular 860GT.

type of the 860GT that had been carried through from the singles. In other respects the GTS was as the 860GT – Ceriani 38 mm forks, Marzocchi 320 mm shocks, same engine and frame (except for the rear section), wheels, side-covers, and painted steel mudguards. Transfers appeared on the tank in place of badges. Initially it was sold alongside the 860GT and GTE, but by the end of 1976 both these models had gone, leaving the 860GTS as the sole V-twin besides the 750/900SS.

For 1977 the bike was essentially unchanged. From number 3670, Marzocchi forks with more offset triple clamps replaced the Cerianis, and stainless steel mudguards replaced the painted steel ones. Tank badges came back again along with new switch-gear, as fitted to the Super Sports of the same period. There was also a slightly revised instrument panel, no longer with the two-volume horn switch. Reprofiled camshafts and double valve springs were fitted after engine number 3788. The new valve timing figures, giving more duration and 97° of overlap, were inlet opening 51° before top dead centre, closing 75° after bottom dead centre, and the exhaust opening 74° before bottom dead centre, closing 46° after top dead centre. Later in

the same year the 860GTS became the 900GTS with new colours, red and silver, or black and silver. The definitive 900GTS appeared in 1978 when it received the engine of the Darmah, but still had the valve spring heads. Along with this engine came an improved electric start mechanism, Bosch ignition, and a proper left-side gearshift. These improvements are detailed in the next section. The 900GTS, which was to be the last bevel-gear valve spring twin, was sold until 1979, by which time it had developed a reputation as one of the most reliable of all Ducatis. Unfortunately, it was a bit too late to save the GTS, as the problems with the very first GTs had hurt their reputation badly. The success of the desmodromic racers, along with the larger numbers of desmo engines being built, also meant that the public now associated Ducati with desmodromics, and it was time for the Darmah.

DARMAH 900 SPORT DESMO

While most attention has been placed by enthusiasts on the various Super Sport models, it could be argued that the Darmah was more significant. The Darmah,

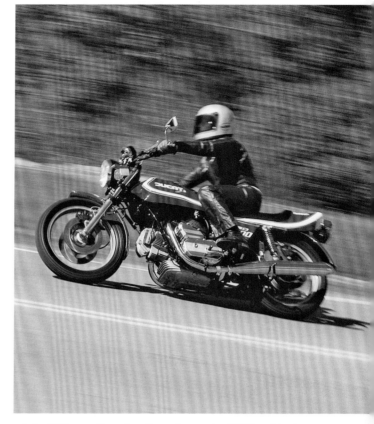

Many engine improvements were introduced with the 900SD Darmah in 1977, making it an excellent street motorcycle.

because it was sold in such large numbers (by Ducati standards), and at a price competitive with equivalent Japanese bikes, introduced desmodromics and the charisma of Ducati to a wider range of riders, not just the serious sporting fraternity. For the five-year period between 1977 and 1982, the Darmah formed the mainstay of Ducati production, and with its release a real attempt was made to combine traditional features with civility and reliability.

Ducati had often sent designs outside for styling and, apart from the 860GT of Giugiaro, these usually went to Leopoldo Tartarini of Italjet. Tartarini had not only restyled the last desmo singles, but also the 500 Sport Desmo in 1975. In 1976 he was also given the brief for the SD 900, or Sport Desmo 900, and he styled it along similar lines to the 500 (covered in the next section). It was to be a sport touring version of the 900SS, using an electric start 900 engine along with desmodromic heads, but with smaller, 32 mm Dell'Orto carburettors. The bike came out looking significantly different to previous touring Ducatis, in red and white with a ducktail seat and – what was a first for Ducati – cast alloy wheels. When first displayed, at the Bologna Show in 1976, it had FPS wheels, similar to the Moto Guzzi Le Mans, and a Plexiglass screen. By the time the first production bikes appeared in August 1977 it wasn't just the styling that set the Darmah apart. There were many other changes, particularly in ignition and ancillaries. It was called the Darmah after the name of a tiger in an Italian children's story.

While the basic Darmah was really an 860GTS with desmo heads, it represented a big step forward with its electrical system. In an attempt to compete with the Japanese there were now warning lights for the side-stand and neutral, as well as indicators, generator and head and tail-lights. Additionally, the electronic ignition was provided by Bosch, with transducers and coils and all associated wiring tightly squeezed under the front of the fuel tank. While the warning lights often failed, the ignition was a definite improvement over the Ducati Elettrotecnica fitted to the first square-case bikes.

The first model of 1977 came with very light five-spoke Campagnolo magnesium wheels, changing to Speedline in 1979. Both types were the cause of a serious safety scare in Australia in 1981, when various wheels started disintegrating. This initiated a nation-wide recall, and free replacement with aluminium FPS six-spoke wheels. The earliest versions also had Ceriani forks that became Marzocchis in 1978, and all had

triple 280 mm Brembo discs. Later, in 1978, a black and gold version appeared with the tiger insignia on the side-panels.

The introduction of the Darmah also brought the first upgrade of the square-case engine. Not only did the ignition change to the Bosch system but the gearshift selector mechanism was moved to the left side behind the clutch housing, eliminating the need for the sloppy crossover shafts. The electric start mechanism was properly integrated into the primary drive system, greatly improving the effectiveness and reliability. Initially all Darmahs came with a kickstart as well but by 1980 this had disappeared. To endeavour to overcome the problem of big-end failure on the 900 series the crankpin was enlarged to 38 mm along with a reduction in roller diameter. This was the remedy long tried by Ducati with its singles, and in the case of the Darmah it was successful. These engines didn't suffer the premature crankshaft failure that had been a problem with the early 860s and Super Sports, but some of the increased longevity would have been due to the more gentle advance curve of the Bosch ignition. The Darmah didn't get the dual rib strengthened con-

Below: The 900 Super Sport
Darmah combined the user-
friendly features of the Darmah,
with a Super Sport-style fairing
and riding position. *Rolf im Brahm*

rods of the Super Sport. With the better gearshift selection and the more progressive ignition curve, coupled with instant starting and easy idle, the Darmah indeed seemed far more refined than previous Ducatis.

As longer forks and Marzocchi shocks (300 mm to bike number 989, 315 mm from bike 990) were fitted, the Darmah was quite a lot taller than a Super Sport, but did offer better ground clearance. However, it still handled in the best Ducati tradition with rather slow steering (31° of rake and 4.3 inches of trail). A Paioli hydraulic steering damper was fitted on the right-hand side, more for cosmetic reasons than practical usefulness, as it was leaky and ineffective. This was a replacement for the equally ineffective friction damper fitted to Super Sports, which could no longer be fitted because of the new instrument console with Nippon Denso instruments. All the switch-gear was Japanese too, but the headlight was an excellent Bosch halogen. In many respects the Darmah represented a departure from traditional Ducati practice. The factory had relied

almost totally on Italian suppliers in the past, but there was now evidence of increased use of Japanese and German components. This would continue right through to the present day.

The Darmah created a big impression when it first appeared in 1977. Here was an electric start Super Sport, but performance was never in the same league as an SS. Despite the same desmodromic cylinder heads and 9.3:1 pistons as the 900SS, but with smaller inlet throats, even with Conti mufflers they only offered a marginal performance increase over a 750 or 860GT. 32 mm carburettors, huge air filters (with solid plastic intakes rather than the previous pleated type) and double-walled smaller diameter exhausts didn't help either. In 1979 (from number 3026) the cylinder heads became 900SS ones, with the larger inlet ports which enabled 40 mm carburettors to bolt on easily. This allowed the engine to produce 900SS horsepower, but the size and weight (216 kg, or 475 lb, dry) of the motorcycle blunted the performance. However, the

At the end of 1981 the Darmah was displayed with a fairing and panniers, but these were never made available. *Ducati Motor*

appeal of the Darmah was not as an all out sportster, more as a sport touring bike capable of covering long distances or short ones – the Italian answer to the Universal Japanese Motorcycle. The emphasis was definitely on shorter trips though, the 15-litre tank generally running onto reserve at about 180 km (112 miles), and the seat had marginal padding. They were all supplied with very low gearing (15/38 teeth sprockets for the final drive) that limited top speed. The English *Motorcycling Monthly* only achieved 112.2 mph (180.6 km/h) from their early model in July 1978, even less than a valve-spring 860GTS. *Cycle* magazine, in April 1980 – known for their editorial sympathy towards Ducatis, and 750 Super Sports in particular – liked the Darmah, but had to admit that to 'purists and owners of 750s, it wasn't a true Ducati, merely a facsimile'. Standing start quarter-mile times were close to that of a 750GT at 13.13 seconds, with a terminal speed of 101.35 mph (163.1 km/h).

In 1979 practicality took over from styling considerations, and the pretty ducktail seat was altered for more comfort. Silentium silencers replaced the ugly Lafranconis and the kickstart disappeared. Colours were still red and white, or black and gold, with most in the latter. The rear shock absorbers were now (from number 2960) the Marzocchi 315 mm oleo-pneumatic type.

At the same time the Darmah SS appeared, essentially an identical bike but with a Super Sport style half-fairing, offset clip-ons, and rear-set foot-rests. Other changes included three 280 mm drilled Brembo discs with six bolt mounts. This model was painted in an attractive two-tone blue, but not that many were made. It was a bike that lacked identity, not being a proper Super Sport or a sports tourer. Introduced at the Bologna Show at the end of 1978, it kept the same ducktail seat throughout its model life. Due to the improved aerodynamics, *Motor Cycle News* attained a top speed of 117.18 mph (188.6 km/h) in March 1979, still some way off the speed of a 900SS. Not particularly popular, the 900SS Darmah only lasted until 1980.

This was now a time of diminishing motorcycle sales worldwide, and as Ducati was concentrating its efforts on developing the Pantah series, it was clear that the days of the bevel-gear engines were limited. After a peak in 1980 sales declined significantly, and to many the Darmah was still the bike it had been in 1978. By now all the bevel-gear models had been largely unchanged for several years apart from colour schemes.

However, at the Bologna Show of November 1981, in an effort to broaden the appeal, Darmahs were displayed with optional fairing and panniers. It was obvious that the Darmah was near the end of its production life because the frame now appeared with an SS style swing-arm with the Seeley-type chain adjusters, as well as the eccentric adjustment at the swing-arm pivot. Along with the last 900 Super Sports, these final Darmahs were sold off at heavily discounted prices in some markets right through until 1983. Some of the last ones were parts-bin specials, with at least one example fitted with a 900 dry clutch Mike Hailwood Replica engine.

It's important to place the Darmah in its historical perspective. Ducati had gone through some lean years previously, with some very poor managerial decisions between 1975 and 1977. The singles and round-case bikes were stopped in favour of parallel twins and the square-case 860, and only the 750 and 900SS continued to uphold their sporting tradition. Neither the 860 nor the parallel twins sold particularly well and Ducati desperately needed a mainstream bike to take over from where the 750GT had left off. With the Darmah they succeeded, but this model is generally underrated when compared to the more glamorous Super Sport models.

350/500 PARALLEL TWINS

The history of the parallel twin Ducati went back to the 175 cc racing twin of 1957, followed by the racing 250 and 350, and finally the 500 and 700 cc prototypes of the 1960s. All of these had been completely overshadowed, both on the road and track, by the overhead camshaft singles, so Fabio Taglioni wasn't too interested when it was suggested in 1972 that the wonderful singles be replaced by a new parallel twin. He wanted nothing to do with the design – he already had designs for his Pantah with belt-driven overhead camshafts. In retrospect, the termination of the singles was a little premature when the oil crisis hit in 1974, creating an emphasis on fuel economy, but by this stage all the decisions had been made.

As with the 860 taking over from the 750, a decrease in production costs was largely the impetus behind the parallel twin. The problem was, they fitted awkwardly into the Ducati range of singles and V-twins, and as such were never a success. Because Ing. Taglioni would have nothing to do with their initial design, the work was entrusted to Ing. Tumidei, who took the basic 1965 500 engine design and updated it. The 360° crankshaft was replaced by a 180° one, and a single overhead camshaft, driven by a chain rather than push-rods and rockers. Engine dimensions were even more oversquare than the first 500, at 78 x 52 mm. The similar 350 was 71.8 x 43.2 mm. This was the first production Ducati engine to use a forged crankshaft with plain big-end bearings (45 x 22 mm) but only two plain main bearings were used, there being no centre bearing between the cylinders. These too were large at 50 x 25 mm. Because of all these plain bearings, a real departure for Ducati, the oil pump was uprated, and two oil filters supplied. The new twin also had the revised cylinder head layout, with (for the 500) two 37 mm and 33 mm valves set at the shallower included angle of 60°, as used on the 1973 Imola racing bikes. The 350 had smaller 35 mm and 31 mm valves. Valve adjustment was by screw and locknut, and primary drive still by helical gear. To keep engine width down, the camshaft drive sprocket was not from the crankshaft, but from a countershaft sprocket behind the cylinders, with the chain running up a narrow sleeve between the two barrels. The camshaft itself was in two pieces, coupled to the central sprocket, with valve timing, for the 500, of inlet opening 32° before top dead centre, and closing 70° after bottom dead centre, and the exhaust valve opening 68° before bottom dead centre, and closing 39° after top dead centre. The 350 had less conservative valve timing (44/85/70/27). The claimed compression ratio was 9.6:1, and the die-cast engine crankcases vertically split, with a small electric starter motor fitted in front of the engine. Carburation was by Dell'Orto as usual, PHF30 on the 500 and the older style VHB26 for the 350. Surprisingly, given the use of electronic ignition on the 860s, ignition was by battery, coil and contact breakers.

It was quite a tidy design, but when the first 350/500GTL examples were displayed during 1975 they incorporated many of the Giugiaro styling characteristics of the 860GT. In some respects the GTL sported the best quality equipment – Borrani alloy rims, 35 mm Marzocchi forks with twin Brembo 05 calipers (single on the 350) and 260 mm front discs. Yet they were not a replacement for the singles, even if they did work well as motorcycles. The single down-tube frame still used the engine as a stressed member, and the bikes were a reasonable weight at 170 kg (375 lb). Instruments and switch-gear were similar to the 860GTS, and colours were similar to the 860GT – blue, green and, later, red.

The performance of the 500 wasn't startling, and the 350 even less so. *Cycle World* only managed a standing quarter-mile of 14.92 seconds at 85.87 mph (138.2 km/h) in their test of November 1977. They found handling to be its best feature. Somehow the GTL seemed to be aimed at a different market to that of previous Ducatis, and this was its problem. In endeavouring to widen the bike's appeal, Ducati's traditional customer-base had been neglected: they didn't want a nondescript Ducati. Fortunately, some of their misgivings were overcome with the 500 Sport.

With the adoption of desmodromic heads and a new frame with twin down-tubes, the 350/500 was sent off to Leopoldo Tartarini of Italjet for styling. His prototype featured a theme of matt black with white exhaust pipes and FPS alloy wheels (similar to the Moto Guzzi Le Mans), and was displayed at the Milan Show in November 1975. Fortunately, by the time the bike made it into production it was more tastefully styled, and altogether more satisfactory than the GTL. While the actual weight increased to 185 kg (408 lb) the desmo engine was more powerful. The desmodromic camshafts had different timing specifications, with the inlet valve opening 32° before top dead centre, and closing 75° after bottom dead centre, and the exhaust opening 60° before bottom dead centre, and closing 45° after top dead centre. *Motorrad* had only managed a top speed of 162.2 km/h (100.8 mph) from their 500GTL in August 1976, yet their 500 Sport Desmo the following year went 180 km/h (112 mph).

The Sport Desmo was fitted with Paioli 35 mm forks with 330 mm long Marzocchi rear shocks, and FPS wheels with a rear disc brake. Certainly the engine vibrated, as you would expect of a 180° parallel twin without balance shafts, but it possessed excellent brakes and handling. Finish on the matt black-painted Lafranconi mufflers could have been better, but for a design that was intended to be economic to build, ultimately its price killed it. In England the red/white or blue/white 500 Sport Desmo was sold at the same price as the valve-spring 860GTS. The yellow/black or blue/black 350 was aimed at the Italian market.

A racing version of the Desmo Sport was also produced in 1977, called the 500 Super Sport. The electric starter was removed, and an oil-cooler fitted in the front of a half-fairing. With 40 mm Dell'Orto carburettors and larger valves (39 mm inlet, 35 mm exhaust), along with racing camshafts, power was up to 61 bhp at 10,500 rpm, and the weight down to 160 kg (353 lb). Claimed maximum speed was 220 km/h (137 mph).

In an effort to broaden the appeal of the parallel twin, Ducati replaced the GTL with a valve-spring version of the Sport Desmo in 1978. Called the GTV, this also came in 350 and 500 cc engine capacities and was essentially a Sport Desmo with a GTL engine. While they were sound in concept, there were too many mechanical problems with the parallel twin. Crankshaft failure and short-lived valve gear were among the problems that afflicted them all.

The GTL soldiered on until 1978, and the Sport until 1980, with only minor changes to instruments and switch-gear as with the 860/900GTS. Surprisingly, after an absence of three years, 67 500 Desmo Sports were built for the Australian market in late-1983. They had later instruments and switch-gear, along with 600 Pantah Oscam wheels and Marzocchi forks, and were sold at a bargain price. However, they were still no match for a Pantah. By 1984 the Pantah was already a success on and off the track, and had completely eclipsed the parallel twins. While not necessarily bad motorcycles, to most Ducati enthusiasts the latter were never really the genuine article.

900/MILLE S2

The early 1980s were not the best time for Ducati under the VM group. VM specialized in diesels, and much of the Ducati manufacturing plant at Borgo Panigale was taken up with diesel engine production at

An unsuccessful example of style
over function: the 900S2.

this time. In the lead up to 1982 there had been two failures within the motorcycle division, and two significant success stories. The successes were the Super Sport and Mike Hailwood Replica line, along with the Pantah. The parallel twins and 860s had been failures, not because they were bad designs, but because there had been reliability problems and their styling had not proved popular. The Darmah, while a better motorcycle, had been in production for five years by now, and was being discontinued. To rationalize production, a hybrid model was created to run alongside the Super Sport line. Called the S2, it was basically a Darmah SS frame and running gear, with a restyled seat, and the fairing from the 600SL Pantah. Eventually the S2 would replace the Super Sport and became the basis of the revised Mike Hailwood Replica in 1983. The last S2s and Mike Hailwood Replicas were essentially the same, and they became the last bevel-gear twins.

The first 900S2s of 1982 had the option of either a kickstarter, as with the 900SS, or an electric start. During 1983 new alternators and regulators appeared on both versions, while earlier the shifting drum had

also been modified. Either Dell'Orto PHM 40BD and BS carburettors, or Dell'Orto PHF 32AD and AS were fitted, but most S2s had the electric start and the 40 mm carburettors. The main problem with the S2 was that, while it was a motorcycle in the mould of the 900SS, it *wasn't* a 900SS, and didn't perform or handle as well. It was taller and heavier, at 419 lb (190 kg) dry. Also, the frame wasn't as rigid, as the rear down-tubes were bowed and recessed to allow the use of the larger battery (even on the kickstart version). This meant that if you removed your hands from the handlebars at a modest 50 mph (80 kph), the bars would start oscillating disconcertingly. The same problem afflicted all the last Mike Hailwood Replicas with electric start, and was a sufficient problem for the German TüV authorities to consider a ban on these models in 1985. While not quite a 900SS, *Motor Cycle Weekly*, in 1983, achieved a best one-way speed of 123.94 mph (199.5 km/h) from a 900S2 with 40 mm carburettors and Silentiums.

The 1982 S2 was painted bronze, with yellow, orange, and red stripes, and for 1983 there was a black or red option. Oleo-pneumatic Marzocchi shock

The Mille S2 looked similar to the
900, but featured a new engine.

absorbers also appeared this year, along with a red frame. The last 900 version of 1984 was largely unchanged, in red with the red frame, and tank badges rather than transfers. They all featured a new fuel cap that was particularly prone to allowing water to enter and most 900S2s have suffered rusted petrol tanks. While it was still fitted with the regular Giugiaro-inspired square-case engine, these final models had the spin-on oil filter of the last 900MHR, along with an oil-level sight glass in place of the dip-stick. The most peculiar addition to these last 900S2s was a belly pan bolted underneath the engine, and if there was ever a case of style before function, this was it. By now all bikes were electric start. Running gear for 1984 was as the MHR, with the new type 18-inch Oscam wheels that allowed the fitting of tubeless tyres.

In 1984 the 860 engine received one last overhaul by Ing. Taglioni and his new assistant, Ing. Massimo Bordi. These changes are covered in detail in Chapter 9 with the Mike Hailwood Replicas, and this new engine was shared in 1985 by both the Mille Mike Hailwood Replica and the Mille S2. It has to be said that while the engine was updated for the 1980s, the

rest of the bike was obsolete. It was even heavier than before (at 198 kg, 436 lb, dry), and didn't steer or handle as well as the old Super Sports. This was brought home to me when I had an opportunity to ride the first 750SS of 1974 back to back with the last Mille S2 when they first came out. While the torque from the Mille engine was magnificent, carburation and smoothness were inferior. The older bike was so much more responsive, and handled better, and it was obvious that the future of the big-twin was limited in that form, and without a more modern chassis, the Mille wouldn't last. However, no-one expected the bevel-gear twins to disappear so quickly, and within one year the Mille was finished.

These last S2s were all black with the same red, orange, and yellow stripes, and still featured the belly pan. Engine, frame, suspension and wheels were the same as the Mille MHR detailed in the next chapter. They were not as popular as the MHR and not as many were built, and when looked at now, more than ten years later, the S2s share, with the Darmah SS, the problem of a lack of identity. They were neither Darmahs, nor real Super Sports.

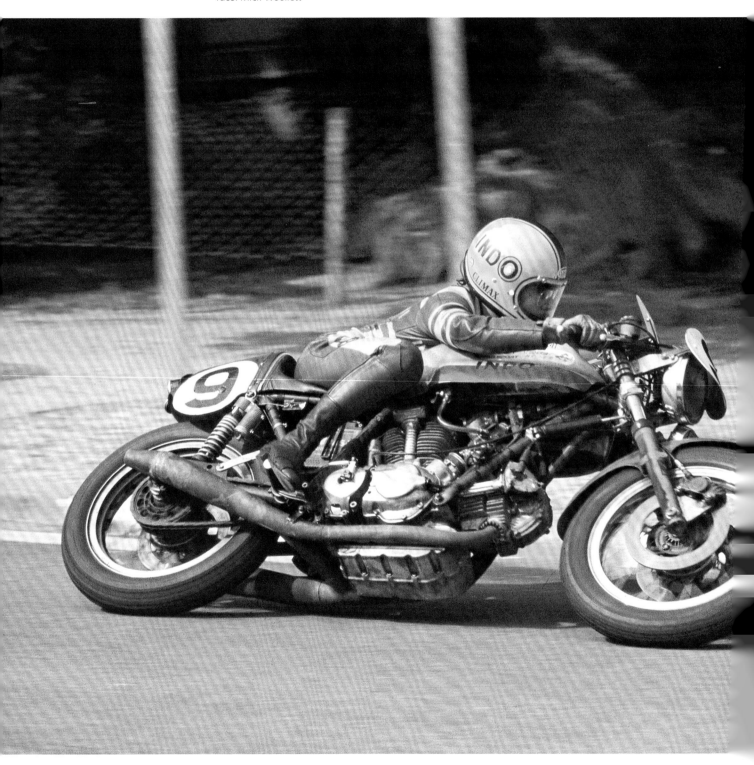

Benjamin Grau on his way to
victory on a 905 cc factory racer
in the 1975 Barcelona 24-Hour
race. *Mick Woollett*

9 THE ISLE OF MAN

AND THE MIKE HAILWOOD REPLICA

While Ducati had failed at the Montjuich 24-Hour race in 1974, this didn't deter the factory from becoming involved in a serious, and almost successful, attempt at the World Endurance Championship of 1975. Benjamin Grau was teamed with Canellas as usual, but also with the 23-year-old Virginio Ferrari, and Carlo Perugini when Canellas was unavailable due to car rally commitments. These factory bikes were still very much 750SS-based, right down to the front Marzocchi forks with Scarab calipers (except Grau used Lockheeds at Montjuich and Mugello). They also had 750SS-style bodywork, and looked liked race-kitted street bikes. For Montjuich and Mugello, they used the Borrani spoked wheels, later changing to the Campagnolo magnesium type. For long races, like the Bol d'Or, the bikes had a large fairing with twin headlamps. The 1975 series started well, with Canellas and Grau winning at Montjuich on a 905 cc (88 x 74.4 mm) bike, Grau following this with a win in the Mugello 1,000 km with Virginio Ferrari. At the Bol d'Or at Le Mans, Grau crashed out on the first lap, and though he restarted he was eventually sidelined by gearbox seizure. However, Grau still went into the final round at Thruxton with a slender one-point lead over the Japauto-Honda of Ruiz and Huguet. Unfortunately, a crash saw Grau with no points for this race and he ended up third in the championship. Ferrari and Perugini also won the non-championship 1,000 km race at Misano, and Ferrari the Italian 750 cc Championship that year on a factory-supported 750SS.

SCUDERIA NCR

With Ducati now under EFIM Group control and new management, economics were beginning to take precedence over prestige. Racing was deemed of secondary importance, and if it hadn't been for the persistence of an enthusiastic group of engineers and mechanics, particularly Fabio Taglioni and Franco Farnè, the endurance racers of 1975 may have been the very last racing Ducatis. Farnè had started racing Ducatis in 1956 and continued as racer, then tester, and finally chief racing mechanic. Until recently he was still involved with the World Superbike programme. So in 1976 Farnè, Mario Recchia, and Piero Cavazzi teamed up with the Scuderia NCR of ex-factory race mechanics

Below: Beautiful detail touches abounded on the NCR endurance racers, like this milled rear brake support. *Ducati Motor*

Right: The line-up of 1977 NCR endurance racers. They looked impressive but did not perform as well as expected. *Ducati Motor*

Giorgio Nepoti and Rino Caracchi, to create a semi-works, semi-independent racing shop. Nepoti and Caracchi had already prepared an entry of a 750 Super Sport in the 1973 Imola 200 and had raced under the NCR banner during 1975. Now, rather than compete against the two-strokes in Formula 750, they turned their efforts first to endurance racing, and later to a new Formula 1 class.

All had been involved throughout the 1960s and early 1970s with the Ducati racing team, so they collectively knew as much as anyone about the preparation of both singles and twins. NCR (or Nepoti, Caracchi Racing) now had limited access to the factory for special parts and they were conveniently located at Via Signorini 16, near to the factory at Borgo Panigale. So from 1976 until 1979 the factory racing Ducatis were built by Nepoti and Caracchi and officially titled the Ducati 900NCR. They were built to comply with either *Coupe d'Endurance* or Formula 1 regulations. What's more, F1 bikes were available for purchase (at the princely sum of L7,500,000 in 1978, or three times the price of a standard 900SS).

Of course the crowning glory for the 900NCR was Mike Hailwood's win at the Isle of Man in the Formula 1 race in 1978, but there had been many other notable victories at Montjuich, Mugello, and Misano in endurance races. No two of the endurance racers built between 1975 and 1979 were identical. They had completely different, lightweight frames of 25CrMo4 (made by Daspa of Bologna, not Verlicchi), special crankcases, dry clutch, spin-on oil filter, special Marzocchi suspension units, and magnesium Campagnolo wheels with a quick release system designed by Piero Cavazzi, allowing the rear wheel to be removed leaving the disc in place. Most of the engines utilized the 750 bevel-gear layout and round-cases, but were heavily modified. Many displaced 864 cc, but some used 88 mm pistons to give 905 cc, while others used a shorter stroke of 66.5 mm with 88 mm pistons to give a capacity of 808 cc. Desmodromic camshafts were more severe than the Imola race kit available as an option to Super Sport owners. Valve timing (inlet opening 69° before top dead centre and closing 103° after bottom dead centre, and exhaust opening 98°

before bottom dead centre and closing 73° after top dead centre) and lift (11–12 mm) was to endurance specification but still not the same as for the full racing Imola bikes of 1973. The cylinder heads used the 60° valve angle and valve sizes were generally 42 and 38 mm (44 mm inlet with the largest engines). Crankshafts, rods, primary gears, and gearboxes were all special. Claimed power for the 864 cc engine was 105 bhp at 8,800 rpm, and weight was down to 325 lb (148 kg) for the short stroke endurance versions. All bikes featured the marvellous styling of Mario Recchia, though the tail and seat shape was altered several times. The 900NCR endurance bikes were impressively presented, with spectacular attention to detail. These included the highly-machined rear disc caliper carrier, and brake and gear-shift levers deeply machined to save a few more grams. Even the brake discs were sometimes radially drilled, rather than cross drilled. Giorgio Nepoti did most of the engine work, while Rino Caracchi was the

master of the lathe responsible for most of the beautiful touches that adorned these racing bikes.

Three 900NCR bikes were built in 1976, and they were favoured to win the *Coupe d'Endurance*. However, it wasn't to be a good year as the bikes were too fragile, and the budget not big enough, to compete with the Hondas and Kawasakis. In endurance trim, claimed weight was only 344 lb (156 kg), with 96 bhp at 9,000 rpm from the 905 cc engine. There were no wins, the best results being a second at Mugello with Pentti Korhonen and Christian Estrosi, and a third at Montjuich for Jose Mallol and Alejandro Tejedo (who would have more success in a few years' time).

Despite five bikes built in 1977, this was an even leaner year for results in the *Coupe d'Endurance*, again with no wins, and only a fourth in the first round at Misano. A private 750SS ridden by Carlo Saltarelli and Arturo Venanzi finished third, beating the special 808 cc, 92 bhp, 325 lb (148 kg) NCR bike of Ermanno Giuliano

and Giovanni Mariannini. With Benjamin Grau
deserting Ducati for a Honda in 1977, there was no
success for Ducati at Montjuich Park either. NCR bikes
were still raced in endurance events throughout 1978
and 1979, but a new racing class had now appeared,
more suited to the Bologna twins – the TT Formula One
World Championship. Before considering this it's worth
first taking a look at some of the successes and details of
the final 900NCR endurance bikes.

With four bikes, results in 1978 were equally lean
except for Misano and Montjuich. Sauro Pazzaglia and
Giovanni Mariannini came third at Misano on their
864 cc NCR, while Benjamin Grau – now back with
Ducati after a poor year with Honda – teamed up with
Victor Palomo (1976 F750 World Championship
winner) to come sixth at Montjuich. Carlo Perugini,
and future 500 cc World Champion and Ducati team
manager Marco Lucchinelli, also rode the NCRs that
year. Some of the bikes had duplex chain final drive,
and others tried out the Campagnolo hydraulic conical
rear brake, as used by Walter Villa on his 250 and
350 cc AMF Harley-Davidson World Championship
winning machines of 1976. A significant result in 1978,
but almost completely overshadowed by Mike
Hailwood's Isle of Man success, was Canellas and
Grau's win in the Silhouette class at the 24-Hour race
at Le Mans, on an almost standard 900SS.

Results were much better in 1979. The five bikes,
now with 90 mm pistons giving 947 cc, had engines
that were more or less at the peak of their
development. These still used a highly-modified round-
case, with the electronic ignition mounted externally on

the right side of the engine, that had appeared on the
endurance bikes in 1978. The swing-arm was box
section, and there was a revised fairing and seat
arrangement. Victor Palomo and Mario Lega came
second at Assen and third at Nürburgring, while
Canellas and Grau came third at Montjuich.

Except for Montjuich 1979 was really the end of
regular factory involvement in the *Coupe d'Endurance*.
One of the most amazing results of all was the win by
Jose Mallol and Alejandro Tejedo in 1980 on a 900SS
modified for the Silhouette class. Entered by local
importer Ricardo Fargas, they only raced because the
event was also the final round of the Spanish
Endurance Championship. After all the big names
either crashed or broke down, the Spaniards took a
Ducati to victory for the first time in five years. They
had covered 757 laps at 74.12 mph (119.3 km/h), 26
more laps than Grau and Canellas in 1975. In 1981,
Mallol and Tejedo were slowed by breakages of their
Campagnolo wheels, but Benjamin Grau and Enrique
de Juan, on a 950 Ducati, covered 771 laps to take
second place. This bike was a factory-modified square-
case 900SS with a two-into-one exhaust and lacking
many of the special individual features of the NCR
bikes. Amazingly, with the addition of Carlos Cardus,
Grau came fourth at Montjuich in 1982, the 900
Ducati's final fling in endurance racing, for it was truly
outclassed by now. Fortunately, Ducati had a new
generation bike, and the next year saw Benjamin Grau
in the winners' circle again (see Chapter 11).

The TT Formula One Championship was created in
1976 in order to save the Isle of Man races that had
been boycotted by leading Grand Prix riders that year.
For 1977 there would be one event, the Isle of Man TT
only, and the rules suited Ducati. 1,000 examples of an
engine needed to have been manufactured and the
crankcases, cylinder heads, and barrels needed to have
a similar external appearance. Stroke must remain the
same, but there was no restriction on any engine
modifications. The regulations were much freer than
those of modern day World Superbike racing, as any
frame, brakes, wheels or suspension could be used.
Exhaust systems too could be anything, as long as they
were 115dB(A) measured at 11 metres.

In the production race at the Isle of Man in 1976,
Roger Nicholls and Steve Tonkin, on a modified Sports
Motorcycles-entered 750SS (with 860 pistons), had
given some indication of the Ducati's suitability to
the Island. Nicholls set a best lap of 103.13 mph

(165.96 km/h) before retiring. The following year Steve Wynne of Sports Motorcycles managed to obtain a used 900NCR endurance racer for Nicholls to ride, and he almost won the race from Phil Read on a Honda, but for a controversial shortening of the race that saw the Honda go without their final fuel stop. When Steve Wynne managed to persuade Mike Hailwood to race a Ducati as part of his Isle of Man return of 1978, Ducati agreed to supply new F1 900NCRs. In October 1977, a few months prior to the TT, Hailwood had ridden a square-case 750SS in the Australian Castrol Six-Hour production race at Amaroo Park, Sydney, where he and team-mate Jim Scaysbrook managed an impressive sixth overall.

The Formula One bikes, like that made for Mike Hailwood, used Daspa frames (weighing only 25 lb, and with extra bracing between the down-tubes and the steering head) and narrow crankcases with the spin-on oil filter. They lacked such detail touches of the endurance bikes as the quick release wheel, or even the special magnesium-bodied Marzocchi suspension. Eight complete F1 bikes, along with 20 engines displacing 864 cc, were built in 1978, and they continued to be built for several more years. According to Rino Caracchi a total of 18 customer bikes were made, and 70 of the special Daspa frames. While some of the later customer bikes used engines based on the square-case, for 1978 the engines were part 900SS and part 750SS,

using 900 heads and barrels on a 750 cam gear train. They even had the 750 ignition points, replaced by an electronic Lucas Rita by Wynne. The narrower sump allowed the use of low pipes rather than the high 'Imola' type, and a spin-on oil filter, and all these engines had a dry clutch and external oil-cooler mounted on the steering head. The NCR bikes came with the gearshift on the right side (via a 750 selector box) and the brake on the left, but Hailwood had a conversion, with the gearshift cross-over shaft going through the swing-arm pivot. (This was because he could no longer shift gears with his right foot as a result of injuries caused in a horrific Formula 2 car crash at the Nürburgring in 1974.) They also featured the one-piece tank/fairing unit of the endurance bikes.

Two NCR Formula One bikes were sold to Sports Motorcycles, and as soon as he got them, Steve Wynne completely stripped and reassembled the bikes. He installed US Venolia teflon-coated 11:1 pistons (as used by Cook Neilson at Daytona in 1977 – see next section), machining additional key-ways in the bevel-gears to fine tune the valve timing, and drilling most of the internal components to save weight. Girling shocks replaced the Marzocchis. An important modification was the replacement of the normal six-dog gearbox by one having only three engagement dogs, which was to become standard on all Ducatis four years later. In race trim for Hailwood, the bike weighed in at only 360 lb

Below: The 1978 NCR F1 bikes featured a different frame and the engine was based on the round-case 750. *Roy Kidney*

Bottom: The NCR F1 engine was quite different from production examples, with special narrow crankcases and a dry clutch. *Roy Kidney*

(163 kg). When *Motor Cycle Mechanics* put it on their dyno in October 1978, maximum power at the rear wheel was 80.5 bhp at 8,500 rpm. Sports Motorcycles entered three bikes at the TT. Besides Hailwood, Roger Nicholls rode one, and Mike's mate from Australia, Jim Scaysbrook, the other.

The TT F1 race itself, on 3 June 1978, was one of the greatest days ever for Ducati. 38-year-old Hailwood had not raced on the island for 11 years, but on a bike giving away at least 20 bhp to the Hondas and

Kawasakis he demonstrated not only his superiority, but also that of a tractable, good-handling two-cylinder motorcycle on a road circuit. In the process he demolished Phil Read's previous lap record by 9 mph, achieving 110.62 mph (178 km/h), and completed the race at an average speed of 108.51 mph (174.6 km/h). In his own words, it 'was the easiest TT I can remember'. His speed had been such that he would have finished fifth in the Classic TT against TZ750 Yamahas. If he had maintained his practice speed of 111 mph (178.6 km/h), he could have finished third. It had been a fairy-tale comeback, and Hailwood's success did a lot to ensure the continuation of the Isle of Man as a racing event. His success on a Ducati was to be of similar promotional benefit to the factory as the Imola victory of 1972 had been.

One week later, on 11 June, at the traditional Mallory Park post-TT event, Hailwood again won the F1 race on the Ducati, averaging 93.18 mph (150 km/h). Here he convincingly beat John Cowie (980 Kawasaki) and Phil Read (888 Honda) on a traditional British short circuit. The large crowd was spellbound. There were two more outings that year on the Sports Motorcycles Ducati, Donington and Silverstone. At Donington a broken piston ring caused Hailwood to ride harder than the Dunlop tyres would allow, to make up for a 500 rpm shortfall, and he crashed. For Silverstone a wider, 3.5-inch Campagnolo wheel was fitted to increase the tyre's effective radius, which, along with a front slick to replace the intermediate, caused some problems with the Marzocchi suspension. Out-powered by the Kawasakis and Hondas on the super-fast circuit, Hailwood still managed a 110 mph (177 km/h) lap and third place.

After these F1 races Hailwood returned to New Zealand, where he was living at that time. He teamed up with Jim Scaysbrook again in the Australian Castrol Six-Hour production race to ride a 750SS, but this time Scaysbrook crashed while they were in the lead of the 750 class. Scaysbrook took his 900NCR back to Australia, where it was campaigned for several years, most notably by future World 500 cc Champion Wayne Gardner in the inaugural Coca Cola Eight-Hour race at Oran Park in 1980.

As had happened after Imola, Ducati, elated with this success, promised Mike Hailwood Replicas. These were slow in appearing and, unlike the original 'Imola' replica 750SSs, bore only a superficial resemblance to the genuine Mike Hailwood Ducati when they were

Below: Just to prove the 1978 Isle
of Man victory was no fluke, one
week later, Hailwood rode the F1
Ducati to victory at Mallory Park.
Mick Woollett

eventually put into production late in 1979. Hailwood also agreed to ride a Ducati at the 1979 TT, but this time Ducati were to provide the bikes themselves. Hailwood tested the new F1 and endurance bikes at Misano, but he crashed before any improvements could be tested. The bikes had the square section swing-arm and a re-routed exhaust pipe behind the rear sub-frame.

Problems with EFIM management almost meant that there would be no factory bike for Hailwood, but at the last moment Ducati agreed to provide the bikes and factory mechanics. When the factory F1 bikes eventually arrived in May 1979 they were only modified wet clutch square-case 900SSs. The Classic TT bike was the latest type NCR endurance racer with the square section swing-arm and revised exhaust system. The factory also sent Franco Farnè, Rino Caracchi, and Nani Nero along with the 860 cc F1 and 950 cc Classic TT machines. Initial testing at Oulton Park showed both bikes to be inferior to the previous year, so Steve Wynne replaced the swing-arms with an earlier type, and even tried the 1978 frame. The 950 cc bike handled so poorly that Hailwood elected to ride a Suzuki in the Classic. Even his F1 bike was no match for the previous year, his best practice lap being only 105.88 mph (170.4 km/h). The production-based 900SS engine didn't produce enough power, but unfortunately the special narrow sump NCR crankcases were no longer legal for F1, and the best he could manage was fifth, with a loose battery and cracked exhaust pipe. In the Classic TT, George Fogarty crashed his 950 cc bike badly at Signpost Corner, but he still finished seventh on an 860 in the F1 race.

It was an unfortunate follow up to the magnificent 1978 result, and Hailwood declined to ride the F1 Ducati in the post-TT events of 1979. George Fogarty and others campaigned Sports Motorcycles 900s in F1 events for a couple more years, and Fogarty's son, Carl, went on to achieve greater things for Ducati 15 years later.

Ducati continued to make Formula One bikes in 1980, but primarily for the Italian series. Vanes Francini won the 1980 Italian Regions Trophy Championship on this final version, that now had fully floating discs, new wheels, and a revised exhaust system. The bevel-gear bikes were, by now, quite outclassed in international events. However, in 1981 Carlo Perugini and Mauro Ricci won the Italian Endurance Championship on a 900NCR. To celebrate this victory a 1982-version 900 TT1/*Coupe d'Endurance* bike was displayed at the Milan Show at

Below: Vanes Francini on his way to winning the 1980 Italian Regions Trophy. *Ducati Motor*

Right: George Fogarty rode the 950 cc racer at the Isle of Man in 1979, but crashed. *Ducati Motor*

the end of 1981 alongside the new TT2 600. With the square-case engine and electric start, it had the twin-filler caps of so many NCR bikes but was little changed externally.

THE 'CALIFORNIA HOT ROD'

Before looking at the production bikes that resulted from Mike Hailwood's magnificent success at the Isle of Man, it is important to outline one more significant victory for Ducati that had occurred over 12 months

prior to the Isle of Man of 1978. This was Cook Neilson's victory at the 1977 Daytona Superbike race on a privately prepared 750SS, with no factory support.

Cook Neilson was then editor of the now defunct *Cycle* magazine, and along with fellow journalist and Ducati enthusiast Phil Schilling had been racing a 750SS throughout 1975. For 1976 they decided to attempt the newly-created AMA Superbike series against factory-supported BMWs and Kawasakis. The bike had been very successful as a 750 throughout the

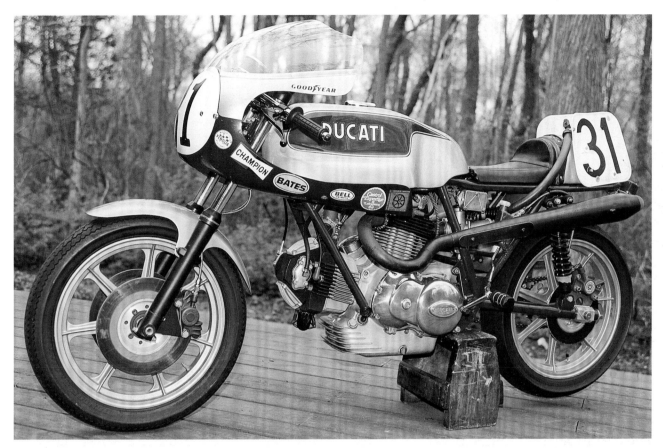

1975 season running 'Imola' race kit camshafts and high-rise Conti mufflers, so the next step was to fit 87 mm Venolia pistons (with Yamaha XT500 rings) for a capacity of 883 cc, Harley-Davidson 42 mm inlet valves, BMW exhausts, Toyota gudgeon pins, and K-Mart ignition coils. They called it the 'California Hot Rod'. Weight was paired off significantly using a magnesium Fontana rear brake caliper and mounting plate, along with Harry Hunt plasma-coated aluminium front discs and Morris magnesium wheels, to get the weight down to 398 lb (180 kg). Neilson only managed third at Daytona in 1976, but still set the fastest trap speed of 145.2 mph (233.7 km/h). Wherever they raced, Schilling always took a picture of Fabio Taglioni, poor results occurring only when they forgot Doctor T's picture!

For the next year they had a new gearbox made by Marvin Webster, and a re-worked Jerry Branch cylinder head, now with 44 mm Harley-Davidson XR inlet valves. Standard Ducati 750SS crankshafts were used, but replaced regularly, and the 883 cc engine put out 90.4 bhp at 8,300 rpm. At Daytona, Neilson won

the 1977 Superbike race at an average speed of 100.982 mph (162.51 km/h), with a timed trap speed of 149.50 mph (240.6 km/h).

Other Americans subsequently prepared and raced Ducatis in AMA Superbike events. Reno Leoni imported a 900NCR racer for Mike Baldwin in 1978, but he was disqualified after finishing a close second to Wes Cooley's Yoshimura Suzuki at Pocono; the AMA didn't consider the NCR a genuine production bike. Paul Ritter raced a 905 cc Ducati to success at Sears Point, and then bought the Cook Neilson bike. Others who rode for Reno Leoni included Richard Schlachter (who won several AMA Superbike races), Freddie Spencer (who almost won the Daytona 200 in 1979), and Jimmy Adamo (tragically killed at Daytona in 1993). However, by 1981 Ducatis were no longer contenders for the AMA Superbike Championship, being relegated to the Battle of the Twins class. Here they were virtually unbeatable, Jimmy Adamo, on Reno Leoni's bike, winning the US Battle of the Twins class three years in a row in 1981–83. Even in AMA Superbike events Adamo, on Reno Leoni's 947 cc

Below: The 1979 Mike Hailwood
Replica had a one-piece fairing
and was styled to replicate the
NCR bikes.

110 bhp bevel-gear twin, was a top ten finisher right through until 1984, and one of the fastest bevel-gear twins ever with a recorded trap speed of 161.7 mph (260.2 km/h) at Daytona in 1982. For 1985 Leoni and Adamo campaigned a Pantah-based Cagiva Alazzurra before reverting to a Mille-based racer in 1986.

THE MIKE HAILWOOD REPLICA

It was more than a year after Hailwood's victory at the Isle of Man before the first production Mike Hailwood Replica appeared on display at the London Show. The styling was based on the unsuccessful 1979 bike, and was very much a cosmetic alteration of a 900SS. They had a one-piece fibreglass fairing and a fibreglass cover over the ordinary steel SS petrol tank to appease British regulations. There were no side-covers, so the rear 40 mm Dell'Orto carburettor and battery were clearly visible. While the tank and seat design was modelled on

the 900NCR – the colours being the red/white/green of Hailwood's winning bike over a red frame – there was provision for a pillion with a removable cowling over the seat. Along with Darmah Nippon Denso instruments and switch-gear, these first models of MHR also had Conti exhausts, Campagnolo or Speedline magnesium wheels, and Brembo Gold-Line 08 brake calipers front and rear. They also differed from the 900SS in having a closer-fitting left-side exhaust pipe, 330 mm long Marzocchi rear shock absorbers, and polished alloy Marzocchi forks rather than black-painted ones. In addition performance was restored due to the fitting of 40 mm carburettors and Contis, and these first MHRs were excellent-performing machines, just like the first 900SSs. Despite a weight increase to 444 lb (201 kg), *Motor Cycle Weekly* reached 129 mph (208 km/h) in their test of October 1979.

It wasn't long before two of the problems of these very first models were rectified. In 1980 the petrol tank became a sculptured steel one, and the wheels FPS aluminium. With the release of the revised 900SS in 1981, the MHR also came in for an update, with a two-piece fairing, and side-covers (now covering the battery and rear carburettor). The two-piece fairing made maintenance tasks, like oil changes, much simpler, but the MHR was even closer to the standard 900SS with black-painted forks, regular Brembo brake calipers, and Silentium mufflers.

The MHR featured the same engine specifications as the 900SS, but with only 40 mm PHM Dell'Ortos. Still with 9.3:1 compression, power was a claimed to be 63 bhp at 7,400 rpm, whereas the 900SS with 32 mm carburettors produced a claimed 57 bhp at the same rpm, both with Silentium silencers. The MHR had higher final drive gearing with 15/33 teeth sprockets giving 2.2:1 (900SSs at this time had 16/38, or 2.375:1). Weight was up again to 463 lb (210 kg) dry. Instruments were still Nippon Denso, whereas the 900SS had Veglia. An important modification that occurred in 1982, from engine 2919 (and to all 900 SS and S2 engines), was the replacement of the six-dog gearbox with one using only three dogs, as used on the original Hailwood bike of 1978. This dramatically improved the reliability of the gearbox and reduced any tendency to jump out of gear.

During 1983 the Mike Hailwood Replica went through a major redesign, coinciding with the end of the 900SS and its replacement with the 900S2. The Replica now used the inferior S2 frame to accommodate an electric start, and this caused some problems, as mentioned in the previous chapter. Wheels were Oscam type to enable the use of tubeless tyres, there was a new, narrower two-piece fairing, and a new instrument panel with revised warning lights. Other styling changes included different, slotted side-covers, and new graphics. The Brembo brake calipers were mounted behind the 38 mm Marzocchi fork legs and the clip-on bars offset, as with the S2. A first for Ducati were electromagnetic fuel taps, and air caps on the fork legs. Some of these MHRs came with a Conti two-into-one exhaust system; however, most had the usual Silentiums and air cleaners. New Marzocchi gas rear shock absorbers, indicators and tail-light, and a larger 120/90V18 rear Michelin M48 tyre completed the specifications.

While some of the 1983 MHR 900s retained the old square-case engine, this year also saw a new engine introduced, which incorporated the first major revisions since the Darmah of 1977. The engine-case

was completely restyled to accommodate a much more compact Nippon Denso starter motor, a new alternator, and a hydraulically operated, dry clutch. A spin-on oil filter replaced the previous cartridge type, and now an oil-level sight glass appeared in the left-side crankcase. The kickstart had completely disappeared and couldn't even be retro-fitted, but fortunately the new electric start was very reliable – at least on the 900. Within the engine, everything was as before, except for Cermetal – the Italian equivalent of Nikasil – lined bores. The crankshaft was still the pressed-up roller bearing type and all internal gear ratios were as before. There was a slight reduction in ignition advance from the Bosch W7B electronic ignition system, now a maximum 28°, from 32° the previous year. (Ignition advance had gradually been reduced over the years from the 38° of the original 750GT.)

While not the final development of the bevel-gear engine, in some ways these 1983–84 MHR900 engines were the best of all. Smoothness approached 750 levels, and they were very tractable over a wide power band,

The final Mike Hailwood Replica was the Mille, which was to last until 1986.

more so than the later Mille MHR with its altered gear ratios. They were fast, particularly in top speed, but ground clearance with the fairing fitted was very poor. *Motor Cycle News* ran their test bike to 129 mph (208 km/h) in October 1983, with Silentium mufflers. The basic problem with this model was that while the engine was an improvement, the use of S2 frame and chassis components was a retrograde step. The higher-mounted engine contributed to a top heavy feel, and the bike was physically much larger than before. The dry weight was up yet again, to 467 lb (212 kg). I bought one of these bikes in 1984, but sold it two years later, continually frustrated with its handling when compared to the older Ducatis.

The 1983 900MHR was really only a stop-gap prior to the appearance of the final version of the bevel-gear engine, the Mille, and as soon as it was released there was talk of an even newer, V4, engine. When the development of a the V4 was dropped, Taglioni and Bordi turned their attention to the bevel-gear twin. The first change was to the crankshaft, now a Pantah-style forged one-piece item with plain big-end bearings. Crankpin diameter went up from 38 to 45 mm, with a huge increase in rigidity. Like the Pantah, but unlike the parallel twins, the high-speed angular ball-bearings for the mains were still retained, but with extra webbing in the cases to cope with extra stress. Along with this new crankshaft, the stroke was lengthened to 80 mm. However, to keep the engine the same height as the 900, the new pistons had their gudgeons closer to the top of the piston and the standard 860 con-rod length was maintained. Thus the rod to stroke ratio was lowered even more to 1.81:1. This had the effect of increasing low-speed torque, but at the cost of higher piston acceleration and more side-thrust, not really a problem on a street engine with an 8,000 rpm limit. Rather than use the 90 mm pistons of the last 950 cc NCR racers, the 88 mm pistons of the earlier 905 cc bikes were used to give a capacity of 972 cc.

The oil filtration was modified to provide a full-flow filter (a larger filter in the same location) and larger capacity oil pump. All the developments of the final 900 were also included, notably the revised engine covers, Nippon Denso starter motor, and dry clutch. Unfortunately the larger engine taxed the starter motor to the limit and cold-starting was a significant problem, even with a fully-charged battery. The extra friction of the plain big-end bearings coupled with 108 cc meant that many a Mille MHR or S2 had to be push-started on a cold morning. The cylinder heads still didn't utilize the 60° cylinder heads of the Pantah, but the 80° heads had larger valves, now 42 mm inlet and 38 mm exhaust. All the gear ratios were altered for this larger engine. The primary drive was raised yet again to 39/69, or 1.769:1, and the internal ratios were different, with much wider ratios between first and fifth. While fourth and fifth gears remained unchanged, first was now 2.720:1 rather than 2.237:1, second was 1.761:1 as opposed to 1.562:1, and third was now 1.250:1, where previously it was 1.204:1. With a very low 15/41 final drive ratio, a Mille would easily run to its 8,000 rpm red-line in top gear. Claimed power for the Mille was up slightly from the 900, to 76 bhp at 7,500 rpm.

This Mille engine was placed in the identical 900 MHR running gear. The earlier bikes had black-painted forks, but these were painted red on final examples, along with a red front guard. As it had the S2 frame and suspension it suffered from the same deficiencies. The first examples appeared in mid-1984, and when tested by *Motorrad* in November they achieved 214 km/h (133 mph). The bike also weighed in at 240 kg (529 lb) wet. When compared to their test of the 1974 750SS, which achieved 216.7 km/h (135 mph) and weighed 202 kg (445 lb) wet, one must wonder at the progress over ten years.

With the Cagiva take-over, the days of expensive bevel-gear engines were numbered, and by the end of 1985 the Mille was finished. This year saw a prototype built using a 16-inch front wheel and M1R Marzocchi forks, and Massimo Tamburini, formerly of Bimota, developed a new frame of square-section tubing, with a single shock rear end and 16-inch wheels, for the Mille engine. However, nothing ever came of these. I saw a Mille MHR with the new Cagiva-inspired Ducati lettering at the factory at the end of 1985, but by now production had ended. It was unfortunate, because, with development, this engine had potential. All it really needed was more up-to-date running gear, but economics had forced its hand. It was a difficult time for Ducati with Cagiva taking control, and production was at an all-time low. Some remained unsold into 1986, and they were to be the last of the illustrious line of bevel-gear Ducatis.

Arguably the most attractive
Pantah: the first 600SL Pantah
of 1981.

10 THE PANTAH: 500SL AND 600SL

The story goes that in 1976, when the management of Ducati finally realized that the parallel twins were a commercial disaster, Ing. Taglioni smiled, reached into his bottom drawer, and presented them with the full technical drawings for a 500 cc V-twin engine. The origins of the Pantah went back to the Armaroli 500 cc Grand Prix racer of 1973, and many of the features tried on this racing engine were incorporated in the first production models of 1979. The Pantah could have gone into production much earlier, but the EFIM management was in turmoil. During 1977–78 motorcycle production at Borgo Panigale was at an all-time low, partly due to the decline in the US market, but also because of the unsatisfactory model range, and in July 1978 control of Ducati passed to another conglomerate, the VM Group. VM were heavily involved in diesel engines, so they used the Ducati plant in Bologna for their production and development of industrial diesels. Under the control of the company in Rome, industrial diesel engine production was increased, while that of motorcycles was decreased. Finally, in 1979, after a two-year delay, Fabio Taglioni was allowed to put his new engine and motorcycle into production, an engine so successful that it continues to form the basis of the entire range of modern Ducatis.

While the range of production bevel-gear twins remained strongly influenced by the singles throughout their lifespan, the Pantah was a combination of the past and present. The prototype 500 cc Pantah had its roots very much in the 1971–73 racers. It used the same bore and stroke of 74 mm and 58 mm, and, like the final 500 racer of 1973, used toothed belts to drive the double overhead camshafts. When asked in 1977, by Dennis Noyes of *Motor Cycle*, why he chose to change to toothed belts over bevel-gears and shafts, Taglioni replied: 'It is no more precise but it lowers mechanical noise and will cut assembly costs. Our big V-twins are expensive to build because of the materials, and they have to be built with great care because of shimming and setting up clearances. With the belt drive we get the same accuracy without the complexity'. Taglioni also went on to say that several aspects of the design of the Pantah were compromised by the necessity to use many components from the parallel twin.

While not actually built by Ducati, the 1973 500 cc double overhead camshaft, eight-valve racing engine

Below: The Armaroli 500 cc racer
of 1973, with belt-driven double
overhead camshafts.

pioneered quite a few features that would eventually
find their way to the production engines. The engine
came from another Bolognese company, Armaroli, and
was based on the 500 cc bevel-gear crankcases. It still
had the gearshift on the right side, and primary drive
and dry multi-plate clutch on the left. The exposed
toothed belts were driven from the crankshaft inside
the primary gears, so the drive moved from the right
side of the engine to the left. Ignition was by a set of
contact breakers mounted on the external reduction
gear. In a move pre-empting the Paso 13 years later, the
rear cylinder head was reversed so that both Dell'Orto
carburettors faced forward between the cylinders, with
a rear exiting exhaust pipe. Unlike the bevel-gear 500
racing engine, the front cylinder had radial finning,
similar to the Moto Guzzi racing singles of the 1950s.
Power was 74 bhp at 12,000 rpm, not up significantly
from the bevel-gear engines. Mounted in one of the
Seeley frames with triple Lockheed discs and leading
axle Marzocchis, it was raced occasionally by Spaggiari
in 1973 without success.

Initial development versions of the new Pantah
engine still used needle roller big-end bearings, Ing.
Taglioni being reluctant to accept plain bearings.
However, experience with the parallel twins had some
effect on his thinking. By the time the first prototype
was displayed at the Milan Show of November 1977, it
had full-flow oil filtration, with a spin-on oil filter, and
a one-piece forged crankshaft. This show model also
featured a full fairing in the style of the race-kit
750/900SS fairing, and Campagnolo hydroconical
brakes. Belt-covers on these early engines mimicked the
cylinder head finning. Not much development
happened throughout 1978, and for the Cologne Show
in October another version was exhibited, now with
polished aluminium cam belt covers. One month later,
at Milan, the Pantah had the Speedlines replaced by
six-spoke FPS wheels. Production was announced to
begin in March the following year, but it would be
several months after that before the first series was
built. The pre-production bikes were painted two-tone
blue and white, but the first series of 250 bikes, when

they finally appeared after the summer break of 1979, were red and silver.

The Pantah deviated considerably in design from the 750/860 bevel-gear twins. It was intended for desmodromic valves only, and was much more compact. While using the 90° twin cylinder layout with vertically split crankcases, the swing-arm was also pivoted on bearings within the gearbox casing. This was done to bring the pivot as close as possible to the countershaft sprocket, reducing chain snatch. In many ways the Pantah was a mirror image of the bigger twin and earlier 500 racers. The crankshaft was still supported by axial thrust ball main bearings, Taglioni being wary of the plain main bearings as fitted to the parallel twin, with the helical primary drive gears on the right side, and the alternator on the left. Whereas the cylinders were offset with the horizontal cylinder to the left on the 750/860, in the interests of keeping the exhaust pipes more compact, this was also reversed on the Pantah. Also, unlike the big twin, the flywheel with ignition trigger sat inside the 200 watt alternator. The Bosch BTZ ignition system was new, and was adapted from the same system used on the Darmah SD900. As it was designed to be electric start only, the starter motor was neatly fitted under the front cylinder and drove through reduction gearing to a sprag clutch screwed to the back of the flywheel. The toothed belts and valve gear were driven off a jackshaft running between the cylinders and geared from the crankshaft on the left side. This enabled the engine to be kept much narrower (at only 14.8 inches or 376 mm) than the bigger engines that needed to fit the geared camshaft drive inside the alternator rotor.

The primary drive, with a ratio of 31/69 or 2.226:1, drove a standard Ducati-style wet multi-plate clutch, something which has been under continued refinement by the factory. It is beyond the scope of this book to detail every modification to Ducati clutches over the years, but generally they occur at almost annual intervals. If there has been an Achilles heel to Ducati engines over the years, it has been the clutch, and as the engines get successively more powerful, the clutch slipping problem is exacerbated. The Pantah clutch too was the reverse of the 860, in that the six springs clamped the driving and driven plates from the inside outward of the alloy clutch drum and hub. The forged one-piece crankshaft necessitated the change to two-piece connecting rods with plain bearing big-ends, and a corresponding increase in oil pressure. Whereas the

The Pantah engine was such an advanced design that it is still in production. *Ducati Motor*

old engines, with all their ball and roller bearings, could run with only 15 psi from its geared pump, the Pantah flow rate was regulated to 70 psi. The geared oil pump resided in the same location as the earlier engines, but was now driven by the helical primary drive gear.

Unlike the larger twin, maintaining a short wheelbase wasn't such a problem, so the gearbox was the indirect type, with separate input and output shafts. Consequently the engine rotated forward, not backward as the 750/860. As with the 860, though, the first engines (to engine number 3245), used gearboxes with six engagement dogs. Following racing 860 practice, these became the stronger three-dog type in 1982. Much of the reason for making the Pantah a mirror image of the earlier twin was so that the gearshift could be properly incorporated on the left side. The cylinder barrels were also Gilnisil (an Italian Nikasil), a plating incorporating silicon and carbon particles that was much harder than iron, lighter, harder-wearing, and offered better heat transfer. The only down side was that the cylinders couldn't be rebored. The two-valve cylinder heads used the 60° included valve angle of the 1973 racing bikes and parallel twins, with 37.5 mm inlet and 33.5 mm exhaust valves. The desmodromic valve actuation system mirrored Taglioni's design for the parallel twin 500 Sport, but with the different timing figures of inlet opening 50° before top dead centre and closing 80°

The 600SL was painted in MHR
colours for 1984. *Rolf im Brahm*

after bottom dead centre. The exhaust opened 75°
before bottom dead centre, closing 45° after top dead
centre. Feeding these cylinder heads were 36 mm
Dell'Orto PHF carburettors, restricted by a large air-
filter on top of the engine, under the fuel tank.
Compression ratio was 9.5:1, and claimed power was
52 bhp at 9,050 rpm.

Supporting this engine was a trellis-type frame, also
designed by Taglioni. Two pairs of parallel tubes
running from the rear cylinder to the steering head met
another pair of tubes running up from the rear of the
crankcases. This was braced for extra rigidity. The
engine hung below the trellis and was bolted to it at six
points. It wasn't the most compact frame, as the
wheelbase was still 57 inches (1,450 mm), but it was
considerably shorter than the larger twins. Suspension
was by Marzocchi front and rear, with 35 mm diameter
forks and 310 mm shock absorbers. With clip-on

handlebars, and a half-fairing, the 180 kg (396 lb)
Pantah 500SL was still very much a sporting
motorcycle. The Nippon Denso instruments and the
switch-gear were the same as on the Darmah.

When the first production models finally appeared
during 1980 they were painted a pale blue, with red
and dark blue stripes. The styling didn't meet with
universal acclaim, and the first 500SLs were unlike
other V-twin Ducatis in that they had very little bottom
end and mid-range power. As delivered, the Pantah was
an extremely quiet bike with its toothed belt camshaft
drive, rubber plugs in between the cylinder fins, and
quiet Contis. The engine liked to rev, but unfortunately
the gearing was so high at 2.533:1 that performance
was limited, and the bike wouldn't run near to its
power peak in top gear. *Motor Cycle Weekly* managed
114.34 mph (184 km/h) in October 1980, running to
only 8,500 rpm in top gear. Contemporary tests were

A Pantah Ice Trophy racer in
action during 1982.
Ducati Motor

extremely complimentary about the handling of the
Pantah. With a 30.5° steering-head angle, the Pantah
was a stable motorcycle, and the frame more than
sufficient for the modest weight and power of the
500 cc engine. My experience with 500 Pantahs was
that they handled well enough, and steered slowly and
predictably, yet did exhibit signs of looseness
somewhere between the rear wheel and steering head
over bumpy roads. The 35 mm forks were lacking in
rigidity too, especially by modern standards. The
engines, though, while lacking in torque compared to
an 860, were thoroughly reliable and oil-tight.
However, a small practical problem with Pantahs was
the slow discharge of the 12-volt 14Ah battery if they
weren't used regularly.

In line with past Ducati practice, it was obvious that
a simple overbore would be the first step in the
development of the Pantah. Already, early in 1980, a
600 Pantah with a Mike Hailwood Replica-style full
fairing had been seen at the factory, and a factory
racing kit that included larger pistons was marketed for
the 500, just as the first production bikes became
available. The new 600SL was displayed late in 1980
along with a prototype turbocharged Pantah engine.
Nothing came of the turbocharged version, but the
600SL became available in early 1981, with silver
paintwork, a new fairing, and a hydraulically-actuated
wet clutch with stronger springs. Paioli 35 mm forks
were fitted on the earliest versions, and throughout
1981 and 1982 either Marzocchi or Paioli forks and
shock absorbers appeared on the production bikes.
These also had larger 08 Brembo front brake calipers,
mounted behind the fork legs, and a larger 400H18
rear tyre. The 600SL was unchanged throughout 1982
except for a black plastic front guard. Claimed dry
weight was up to 187 kg (411 lb).

The 500 Pantah continued alongside the 600, and in
1981 received the 600-style fairing, but not the
hydraulic clutch. The engine cases were standardized as
they had been with the square-case 750/900SS in 1975,
so that, in effect, from number 1654 the 500 was a
sleeved-down 600 (for some reason 290 engines after
this had the earlier cases). The extra capacity for the
600 was gained in exactly the same way as the 750 had
become an 860, by a 6 mm cylinder bore increase. With
an 80 mm bore and the 58 mm stroke, capacity was
583 cc, with compression still 9.5:1. Valve sizes, valve
timing, and carburettors were shared by both models.
Claimed power was 58 bhp at 8,500, but by 1982 it

had risen to 61 bhp at 9,100 rpm, with compression
now 10.4:1. For the 500 the power went down to
45 bhp in 1982, with no change in specification. There
were many aberrations between claimed power and
weight figures for various models at this time, but it is
difficult to believe that a simple 17% capacity increase
would equate to a 35% power boost. The 600SL was
even more highly-geared than the 500 at 2.4:1, and
also wouldn't run to the red-line in top gear. The
English *Motor Cycle News* in April 1982 could only
manage 117.29 mph (188.8 km/h), in fourth gear. It
was five mph slower in top!

Both the 500 and 600SL Pantahs were listed through
to 1984, by which time the 600 was painted in the
Mike Hailwood Replica colours of red, with green and
white stripes, with a red frame. These last 600s had
also reverted to a cable-operated clutch and now had a
larger, steel clutch basket. The last 500SLs were white

The 1982 600TL was over styled, and as such was not one of Ducati's design successes.

same chassis and desmo engine as the 600SL, but with a small fairing, square headlight, new tank and seat, and a new instrument panel incorporating a fuel gauge. Other features that distinguished it from the SLs were electromagnetic fuel taps, a side stand, and smaller, Brembo 05 brake calipers. The production version was released in April the following year, along with the 350XL for the Italian market. Both these bikes were touring orientated, with higher handlebars than the 600SL. The 350 was a more appealingly-styled bike in black and red, but the 600TL was one of those unfortunate styling exercises that Ducati have tried from time to time. It was a bike that rivalled the 860GT for ugliness, but under the bodywork was a competent motorcycle. The 350 engine of the XL was the same as the later 350SL detailed in the previous section, but whereas the 600TL had the foot-rests mounted on large alloy plates, the 350XL still had the rear-set controls. For the German market and their specific insurance categories, a 27 PS version of the 350XL was also built. Claimed weight for these models was less than that of the SLs, both being 177 kg (390 lb). *Motociclismo* tested a 350XL in February 1983 and achieved a top speed of 165.2 km/h (102.6 mph) from their 187 kg (412 lb) test bike.

Also displayed at the 1981 Milan Show was an unusual bike called the 500 Pantah Speedway. A joint Ducati/Alfa Romeo project, this bike was intended for 'Ice Trophy' racing, and was fitted with spiked tyres and no brakes. There were 190 spikes on the front and 235 on the rear, and the basis of the bike was a 500SL Pantah. It was raced in 1982 by the Austrian rider Hans Maier but was not a hugely successful project. Only ten bikes were built.

The 1982 600TL was white with red and yellow stripes, but was a poor seller, due to its styling. Like the SL, a combination of either Paioli or Marzocchi suspension was used. Production continued through 1983, now painted metallic grey, and fitted with the Oscam wheels of other models of that time and Silentium silencers. There was also a 350TL version available for the Italian market during 1983, and by 1984 the 600TL was being heavily discounted on the UK market. Cagiva, who had just taken over Ducati, already had their 650 Alazurra as a replacement and there was no longer any need for the TL. My own experience with these later 600TLs confirmed that they were underrated bikes, condemned by their styling. The 58 bhp 600 engine was smooth, and torquier than the

with red stripes. For the Italian market, a 350SL appeared in 1983, also in the MHR colours, but with silver FPS wheels. The 349 cc engine, with a 66 x 51 mm bore and stroke, 10.3:1 compression, and 30 mm Dell'Orto carburettors, produced 40 bhp at 9,600 rpm.

PANTAH 600TL AND 350XL

To complement the sporting 500/600SLs, the 600TL debuted at the Milan Show of 1981. The TL had the

The final Pantah was the 650SL.
Two Wheels

500, but the bikes were still very overgeared, limiting top end performance.

When *Motociclismo* tested a 600TL in September 1983, they achieved 179.85 km/h (111.8 mph). Producing 52.7 bhp at 8,500 rpm, and weighing 188 kg (414 lb), the 600TL's performance data was surprisingly similar to that of the earlier 750GT. A blue and white police version was also built, with a number being sold to the Bologna police department. Called the 600 Polizia Urbana, claimed top speed was 165 km/h (102.5 mph) with full police specification that included a radio and loud-hailer. Ultimately the TL failed because, as in the past, Ducati didn't understand that their traditional market wanted good-looking, sporting motorcycles.

PANTAH 650SL

To homologate the 750TT1, Ducati needed to stroke the Pantah engine, and as an interim way of getting this stroke homologated the 650SL was created. While most aspects of the motorcycle and engine could be altered for the TT Formula racing classes, the road-going crankcases, cylinder-head castings, and stroke of the engine had to remain unchanged. By boring and stroking the 600, the 650 emerged, but it could easily have been a full 750. Also, for 1984 the World Endurance Championship saw a drop in the capacity limit from 1,000 cc to 750, so a 750 cc Pantah-based racer could once again mean that Ducati could be competitive in this class. By lengthening the stroke 3.5 mm to 61.5 mm, a moderate 2 mm overbore, to 82 mm, created the 649 cc engine. Valve sizes remained as for the 500 and 600, 37.5 mm inlet and 33.5 mm exhaust. Compression ratio was down slightly to 10:1, and power only up slightly to 62 bhp at 8,500 rpm. The most noticeable improvement with the 650 engine was some more mid-range torque.

Painted in the red/yellow colours of the factory F2 bikes, the 650SL was virtually identical to the final 600SL. They both shared the wheels, large indicators and tail-light of the 1983 MHR and 900S2, but the 650SL had the instrument panel of the 600TL with the large plastic surround, its electromagnetic fuel taps, and the new type of fuel cap that was notorious for allowing water, as well as petrol, into the tank. The 650SL continued in production after the Cagiva take-over, even though the same engine was sent to Varese

for the 650 Alazzurra. Despite being available through to 1986, they are a less common model than the earlier 500 and 600SL.

With the factory racing full 750 cc engines by the time the 650SL was available, it was overshadowed by the prospect of the street version of the 750TT1. When the 750F1 finally appeared in 1985, the 650SL was immediately superseded. It offered no real advance over the 500SL of 1979, yet the 750F1 was potentially a race replica in the very best Ducati tradition.

Unveiled for the 1981 season, the TT2 was one of the all-time classic racing Ducatis. Among the successful Italian riders was Massimo Broccoli. *Ducati Motor*

11 RACING PANTAHS AND THE 750F1

As the racing success of the 900NCR waned, the Pantah took over, and during 1980 two 600 cc race-kitted Pantahs were prepared by Franco Farnè. These were campaigned successfully in the Italian national junior championship by Vanes Francini, Paiolo Menchini, and Guido Del Piano, and were based on the standard SL frame but with Marzocchi racing suspension. The red and yellow bodywork was similar in style to that of the 900NCR, and power from the 583 cc engines was up to 70 bhp at 9,800 rpm. Then, for the 1981 season, Fabio Taglioni released his *tour de force*, the TT2.

The prototype TT2 was tested in Spain over the winter by Angel Nieto (14 times World 50 cc and 125 cc Champion) and successful Ducati endurance racer Salvador Canellas. So good was its design that, at its debut race meeting on 29 March 1981, the TT2, in the hands of Sauro Pazzaglia, won the opening round of the Italian TTF2 series at Misano. However, even as the TT2 was making its presence felt on Italian circuits, Sports Motorcycles' Steve Wynne and Pat Slinn had prepared a modified 500SL Pantah for Tony Rutter to race in the Isle of Man Formula 2 event in June 1981. Originally promised two factory bikes that didn't materialise, they had found an insurance write-off, installed a factory race kit, sent the frame off to Ron Williams of Maxton for some extra bracing, and signed up Isle of Man veteran Tony Rutter. Rutter won at an average of 101.91 mph (164 km/h), with a fastest lap of 103.51 mph (166.58 km/h). Ducati were pleased enough with this victory to offer Rutter a TT2 factory bike for the next round at Ulster on August 22. In atrocious conditions, Rutter finished second to secure the 1981 World Formula Two Championship.

The TT2 marked the return of the factory to official competition after an absence since 1975. By using an 81 mm bore capacity was increased to 597 cc, almost the class limit, and a completely new frame was designed by Taglioni and made by Verlicchi. Weighing only 7 kg (16 lb), rear suspension was by a cantilever and single Paioli shock absorber. This frame was exceedingly compact and strong, being heavily triangulated around the steering head, and comprising essentially straight tubes. It bolted to the engine in four places, still using the latter as a stressed member, with butt-fitted bosses rather than flat tabs as on the SL. The

The line-up of factory racing
Pantahs in 1980. *Ducati Motor*

18-litre fibreglass petrol tank was encased by this frame. Fitted with 35 mm Marzocchi racing forks with magnesium sliders and 280 mm Brembo front discs, the racer weighed in at a mere 270 lb (122 kg). It was also extremely compact, with only a 55-inch (1,395 mm) wheelbase. The 18-inch Campagnolo wheels were 2.15 inches wide on the front, and 3.00 inches on the rear.

In the engine department, the TT2 was pure factory racer. The 81 mm Borgo pistons only had moderate compression of 10:1, but valves were larger at 41 mm inlet and 35 mm exhaust. These valves were operated by desmodromic camshafts giving 12 mm of intake lift and 10 mm of exhaust. Italian regulations permitted the use of 40 mm Dell'Orto carburettors, but for the TT World Championship, standard 36 mm carburettors needed to be retained. Claimed power was 76 bhp at 10,750 rpm. There was much evidence of weight saving – exposed camshaft drive belts, a magnesium primary drive cover, and hydraulically operated dry clutch. A lightweight two-into-one

exhaust system was also used. Internally most gears were drilled for lightness and ignition was still by electronic Bosch BTZ, with the small battery mounted in the rear tailpiece. Because Italian regulations required an electric starter, both this and the 200 watt alternator were retained.

The TT2 was a very effective racing machine, in the best Taglioni tradition of achieving maximum results through a balance of power and weight. It was light, athletic, slim, had a wide power-band, and Taglioni was especially proud of the specific fuel consumption figures of 187 gr/HP/hr – less than a diesel! Just how effective it was as a racer was displayed by Massimo Broccoli in October 1981 at the final round of the Italian 500 series at Mugello. On a TT2 sleeved down to 500 cc, he finished seventh in a field of 500GP Suzukis and Yamahas. Broccoli had already secured the Italian TT2 championship ahead of the Kawasaki-powered Bimota KB2s. In its first full year the TT2 had won the two championship series that it had contested.

A triumph of form and function,
the TT2 was minimalist in
execution, and totally effective.
Roy Kidney

The TT2 was even more successful in 1982. In the Italian TT2 championship Walter Cussigh won every round on his factory TT2, and the now 40-year-old Tony Rutter again won the World TT2 Championship. For the Italian events power was up to 78 bhp at 10,500 rpm using 41 mm Malossi Dell'Orto carburettors, and Cussigh favoured a 16-inch Campagnolo front wheel with a 3.25–4.50 Michelin front tyre. Rutter still used the 18-inch wheels, preferring them to the 16-inch type on the bumpier street circuits. At the Isle of Man he was considerably faster than the previous year, winning the Formula 2 race on the factory bike at an average speed of 108.50 mph (174.61 km/h), with a fastest lap of 109.27 mph (175.85 km/h). He was timed at 144 mph (232 km/h) at a speed trap at the Highlander. With the World Championship now extended to three rounds, Rutter scored perfect points on his factory bike. He won at Vila Real in Portugal at an average speed of 86.69 mph (139.51 km/h), following it at Ulster with a win at 100.73 mph (162.1 kph).

During 1982 a limited number of production TT2 replicas were built for privateers. These were very close to the factory bikes but lacked items such as the magnesium primary drive cover and hydraulically-operated dry clutch. They still had the racing magnesium Marzocchi forks and 18-inch Campagnolo wheels. The engine had the same valve sizes as the factory racer, and valve timing figures of inlet opening 74° before top dead centre and closing 92° after bottom dead centre, and exhaust opening 100° before bottom dead centre and closing 64° after top dead centre. Still only using 36 mm Dell'Ortos, power was a claimed 76 bhp at 10,750 rpm. The TT2 also had straight cut primary gears, with a higher ratio than the street bikes. 36/70 teeth gave a ratio of 1.94:1. The five-speed gearbox had the same ratios as the street bike, except for fifth gear being moved closer to fourth. The final drive was considerably lower, at 3.15:1, with 13 and 41 teeth sprockets. Like the factory racer, an oil-cooler was mounted in the fairing, cooling oil to the

Tony Rutter was the TT2's most
successful exponent, winning
four successive World
Championships. *Mick Woollett*

750TT1

With the possibility of the World Championship TT2 class disappearing completely, Ducati hastened development of a 750 cc TT1 version of the Pantah for 1984. As previously mentioned, both TT1 and World Endurance were becoming limited to 750 cc, so a longer 61.5 mm stroked crankshaft was homologated with the 650SL Pantah. Even as far back as March 1982 a 750 cc version of the TT2 had been raced by Jimmy Adamo for Reno Leoni at the Daytona 200, finishing 13th overall. This bike had produced nearly 95 bhp at 10,250 rpm, with a top speed of almost 155 mph (250 km/h). The following year at Daytona, this time in the Battle of the Twins race, Tony Rutter took the 750 TT1 to third place. Then, in July 1983, at Ducati's happy hunting ground, Montjuich Park, a TT1 won the now non-championship 24-Hour race with Benjamin Grau, Enrique de Juan, and Luis Reyes. Prepared by Franco Farnè, the 135 kg (298 lb) racer produced 86 bhp at 9,000 rpm, but the riders limited this to 8,000 rpm during the race, and 83–84 bhp. In front of 250,000 spectators they completed 708 laps, compared to the second-place French Kawasaki's 690.

While Tony Rutter still raced the 600TT2 in 1984, and won the Formula 2 World Championship for the fourth successive year, he also campaigned a 750 cc version of the same bike in Formula 1. He failed to win the Isle of Man F2 race, coming second, but won at Vila Real (at 90.81 mph, or 146.14 km/h). Trevor Nation, also on a 600TT2, came second in the championship. In Formula 1, Rutter managed third overall on the new Ducati during the 1984 season, and the 750 had limited success in endurance racing. At the non-championship Le Mans 24-Hour race in April, a 750 TT1 ridden by Marc Granie, Philippe Guichon, and Didier Vuillemin finished fourth; there were only 18 finishers from a field of 54. They followed this up with a fourth at the Österreichring 1,000 km race, third in the Liège 24-Hours at Spa, and fourth at the Mugello Six-Hours. They finished fifth in the final placings. The works bike of Walter Villa and Walter Cussigh came fourth at the ADAC Eight-Hour race at the Nürburgring, but was plagued with problems throughout the season.

The TT1 differed slightly from the TT2. It still had the cantilever swing-arm, but this was wider to accommodate wider wheels, and was painted red and

cylinder heads in a similar system to that of the Imola racers a decade earlier. Because it still had the electric starting mechanism, weight was 130 kg (286 lb). Rear suspension was not Paioli as in 1981, but a Marzocchi PVS 1 remote reservoir gas shock absorber. Only about 20 of these bikes were made in 1982.

Racing results for the TT2 in 1983 weren't quite as spectacular as the previous year. Tony Rutter again won the World TT2 Championship, but not quite as convincingly. At the Isle of Man he headed a Ducati one–two with Graeme McGregor, at an average speed of 108.20 mph (174.13 km/h), with a fastest lap of 109.44 mph (176.12 km/h). At the other two rounds at Ulster and Assen he could only manage second, but it was enough to win the championship again. Another batch of TT2 replicas was built for 1983, virtually identical to the previous year, but now with a Campagnolo 3.50 x 16 inch front wheel to complement a rear 3.50 x 18 inch. Malossi modified 41 mm smooth bore Dell'Orto carburettors were fitted, and power was up to a claimed 78 bhp at 10,500 rpm.

blue, rather than red and yellow. The countershaft sprocket was offset for the larger section rear tyre, and the wheel now included a quick-change assembly in which the disc and caliper stayed in the swing-arm as the wheel and sprocket were removed. A 16-inch front wheel was specified, but most were raced with an 18-inch front. The 35 mm magnesium Marzocchi forks were retained. 88 mm pistons and the longer 61.5 mm stroke gave 748 cc. It no longer had the wet clutch, but a mechanically-operated dry clutch housed in an NCR primary drive cover. With the same valve sizes as the TT2, claimed power was only up to 80 bhp at the rear wheel.

The factory racer used by Walter Villa differed considerably from the customer TT1. The steering-head angle was reduced to 24°, and a rising rate suspension system was used, similar to the Suzuki full-floater, along with a box-section swing-arm. The bikes immediately suffered suspension problems, with retirement at Le Mans. During 1984, 41.7 mm Kayaba front forks with hydraulic anti-dive were tried, from a Suzuki RG500, before settling on new 42 mm aluminium slider Marzocchis. Brakes were the new type of quickly-detachable four piston Brembos with larger, 300 mm

discs, and a small, 230 mm disc at the rear. Marvic three-spoke 16-inch front wheels were used, along with 16-, 17- or 18-inch rears. Rim widths ranged from 3.5 inches on the front to 5.5 inches on the rear. By the end of the season a 16-inch front and 17-inch rear wheel were fitted, along with the new series of Michelin radial. The claimed dry weight was 287 lb (130 kg).

The engine was considerably developed from the TT2. Larger valves (44 mm and 38 mm) were operated by camshafts with intake lift of 11.45 mm and exhaust lift of 10.35 mm. Timing figures were inlet opening 75° before top dead centre, and closing 90° after bottom dead centre, and exhaust opening 102° before bottom dead centre, and closing 61° after top dead centre. Stronger, American-made Carillo con-rods were used on a standard, polished crankshaft. The 10.3:1 pistons were the cause of one failure during the season, as were problems with valve seats, but the engine still produced 94 bhp at 10,000 rpm with the 41 mm Dell'Orto-Malossi carburettors, reduced slightly to 90 bhp for 24-Hour events. The Bosch ignition rotor and alternator were now fitted in the magnesium left-side case, away from engine oil, and a mechanically-operated dry clutch replaced the previous hydraulic one. The factory

TT1 was by now significantly removed from the TT2, and ready for another assault on the World Endurance Championship, and Italian F1, in 1985.

Before detailing the F1 events, it must be mentioned that 1985 was also the final year for the TT2. Tony Rutter, riding a factory TT1 with the rising rate rear suspension, but fitted with a 600 cc engine, again won the Formula 2 race at the Isle of Man, but at the slower speed of 107.79 mph (173.47 km/h). He followed this with a second at Vila Real, and a third at Montjuich Park. Unfortunately a serious accident in the F1 race at Montjuich, on a Suzuki GSXR 750, tragically ended Rutter's career, and he was lucky to survive, having been initially pronounced dead. Despite not completing the season, Rutter still managed to finish second in the World TT F2 Championship that year. His record of four World Championships had been amongst the most significant racing results ever achieved by Ducati.

Despite all the development on the TT1 by Taglioni, Franco Farnè, and Walter Villa, the 1985 Endurance season was even less successful than the previous year. The only placings were a fifth and sixth at the opening round at Monza with Walter Cussigh/Oscar la Ferla, and Virginio Ferrari/Marco Lucchinelli. In the Formula 1 World Championship, Dieter Rechtenbach managed sixth overall, by virtue of finishing second at Montjuich, always Ducati's most successful venue. Another significant result for the TT1 was Marco Lucchinelli's sixth place in the Daytona Formula 1 race in March. It was a different story in the Italian Formula 1 Championship. Here TT1 Ducatis filled the first seven places, with Virginio Ferrari taking the title from Marco Lucchinelli.

The year started well in 1986, with Marco Lucchinelli winning the Battle of the Twins race at Daytona in March on an experimental 851 cc (92 x 64 mm) 750F1-based racer at just over 104 mph (167 km/h). Lucchinelli raced in both the Formula 1 and Battle of the Twins, and later went on to win the Battle of the Twins race at Laguna Seca. He also won the opening round of the World TT Formula 1 Championship at the Autodromo Santamonica, at Misano, on 6 April, at an average speed of 90.14 mph (145.06 km/h). Unfortunately he couldn't repeat this performance in other rounds. Graeme McGregor

Left: A few production TT1s were produced, still with cantilever rear suspension.

Below: For 1984 and 1985 the factory TT1 received rising-rate rear suspension. *Ducati Motor*

eventually came sixth overall in the championship on a non-factory TT1. There was no factory involvement in the Endurance World Championship until the debut of the new water-cooled eight-valve 748 at the Bol d'Or in September, but that is the beginning of a new generation, and belongs in Chapter 13. However, at the Jerez Eight-Hour race on 28 September, Juan Garriga and Marco Lucchinelli were teamed together on a four-valve 750TT1. They had pole position and initially led the race, eventually finishing second. Later, at the Barcelona 24-Hour race on 26 October 1986 (a non-championship event) Juan Garriga, Carlos Cardus, and the steadfast Benjamin Grau won using the 851 cc version of the TT1, proving the reliability of the larger engine. An 818 cc (92 x 61.5 mm) version of the engine was also tried during 1986, notably by Jimmy Adamo at the Battle of the Twins race at Daytona.

The final outing for the factory air-cooled racer was at the Pro Twins race at Laguna Seca in 1987. Marco Lucchinelli again rode, and his 851 cc bike featured revised inlet ports and ducting and metal shrouding around the rear cylinder to keep it cool. The standard TT1 chassis was fitted with a new type of upside-down White Power fork with a single, centrally-located spring damper unit. At the rear, a lightweight GSG Roma shock absorber was used. Wheels were Marvic 17-inch front and rear.

Besides the factory bikes, which were undoubtedly the most spectacular, TT1 replicas were widely raced with some success throughout the world. In Spain, Antonio Cobas built a frame for the F1, and Kenny Roberts tested this bike at Misano in August 1985 along with the Cagiva C10V 500 cc Grand Prix bike. Juan Garriga had raced it at the Montjuich round of the World Formula 1 Championship (the same race where Tony Rutter was injured), and had actually led at one stage before crashing. In Australia, future GP rider Kevin Magee rode local tuner Bob Brown's home-built 750 TT1 to some amazing results throughout 1984 and 1985 against 1,000 cc Hondas and Suzukis. Later the bike was enlarged to 850 cc and raced by Robert Holden and Aaron Slight with considerable success in the emerging Superbike class. In Battle of the Twins classes around the world, replicas of the TT1 took over where the bigger twins left off, but as a competitor to the Japanese head-on the TT1 was now

Left: Marco Lucchinelli after winning the 1986 Battle of the Twins race at Daytona. With him are Giuliano Pedretti (left) and Fabio Taglioni. *Ducati Motor*

Below: Virginio Ferrari rode the TT1 to victory in the 1985 Italian Formula 1 Championship. *Ducati Motor*

outdated. The two-valve Pantah heads had reached the limit of their development, and a new cylinder-head design was needed.

DUCATI 750F1

As expected, there were plans to produce a street version of the TT1 racing bike, and, typically, it took a while in coming. While replica frame kits made by Harris were available in England for the Pantah engine, at Ducati the original Pantah soldiered on. The TT2 and TT1 had brought them track success, but there was still a question over the reliability of the Pantah crankcases when the engine was enlarged to 750 cc. 1983 was also the time of negotiations regarding the Cagiva takeover, so both production and development were limited. Also, because a new oil-cooled V-four 1,000 cc engine was being developed at the same time, resources were stretched, and this delayed the introduction of the 750F1. However, the commencement of Cagiva control saw the V-four project cancelled, and by mid-1984 a prototype 750F1 was displayed. This bike used a replica of the Verlicchi racing TT2 frame with a steel cantilever swing-arm, and provision for a centre-stand. A square headlight was fitted in the full fairing, and it had 16-inch gold-painted Oscam wheels. Claimed power was 70 bhp at 9,000 rpm, with dry weight at 165 kg (364 lb). Other features were a hydraulic clutch and a two-into-one exhaust system. 36 or 40 mm Dell'Orto carburettors were specified, and the compression ratio was a high 10.4:1.

In mid-November 1984, photographs of mock production bikes appeared, now with an 18-inch rear wheel, and in February 1985 the 750F1 was premiered at the Sydney Motorcycle Exhibition. It still didn't have the fully-floating Brembo 280 mm front discs and 260 mm rear, but the engine was painted black and had a Conti two-into-one exhaust system, claimed to meet all noise regulations. The red frame, sourced from the TT2/TT1, had been widened to accommodate the camshaft belt covers and an adjustable steering damper fitted to complement the 16-inch front wheel. Even before the bike had gone into production there was controversy surrounding the fitting of a 16-inch front wheel.

When the first production models appeared during 1985 they were a confusing mixture of good and bad. The engine was only an over-bored 650 Pantah, still with the 37.5 and 33.5 mm valves of the 500. The oil-cooler lines were cheap rubber hoses crimped into place, yet the brake discs were full-floating iron Brembos. Basic air-assisted Marzocchi 38 mm suspension was used at the front and a Marzocchi adjustable shock absorber at the rear (which was still a cantilever rather than rising rate), yet an aluminium petrol tank was fitted. It was also the very last Ducati to feature the old Giugiaro graphics that had first appeared on the 860 in 1975. The rear seat and tail section was much larger and uglier than on the TT1 and TT2, designed to locate the 14Ah battery, and a dual seat at a later stage.

While still using the 36 mm PHF Dell'Orto carburettors of the Pantah, the 750F1 received new camshafts along with 9.3:1 88 mm pistons. Valve timing was now inlet opening 29° before top dead centre, closing 90° after bottom dead centre, and exhaust opening 70° before bottom dead centre, closing 48° after top dead centre, and power was only a claimed 62.5 bhp at 7,500 rpm. The primary drive ratio was altered, more in line to that of the TT2, to 36/71, or 1.97:1, and the 750F1 also received the fifth gear ratio of the TT2 at 0.97:1. A 300 watt alternator provided electrical power. Weight was up to 175 kg (386 lb), but

it was still a much more compact motor-cycle than the preceding Pantah. The wheelbase was only 1,400 mm (55 inches), and a far cry from the older bevel-gear bikes with their 60-inch wheelbase. Compared to the racer, steering rake was increased to 28°, with corresponding trail of 5.2 inches, making the F1 a relatively slow steerer in the traditional Ducati fashion. Performance wasn't particularly outstanding for its day, and didn't even match the 750SS of over ten years earlier. *Motorrad* tested the two bikes back to back in November 1985 and found the older bike accelerated faster and had a higher top speed. The 750F1 managed 206 km/h (128 mph) but was considerably punchier in the mid-range. I rode one of the first examples and, after the heavy feel of the last Mike Hailwood Replicas, was pleasantly surprised by the light weight and responsiveness of the F1. The F1 was a generation ahead when it came to steering and handling. Despite only a cantilever rear suspension system, the light weight and short wheelbase made the F1 a surprisingly quick road bike for its power output. Just like the magnificent TT1 and TT2 racers, it managed to match much more powerful bikes with its better balance and power characteristics. The only problem with the F1

Below: The author test riding the first production 750 F1 in 1985.

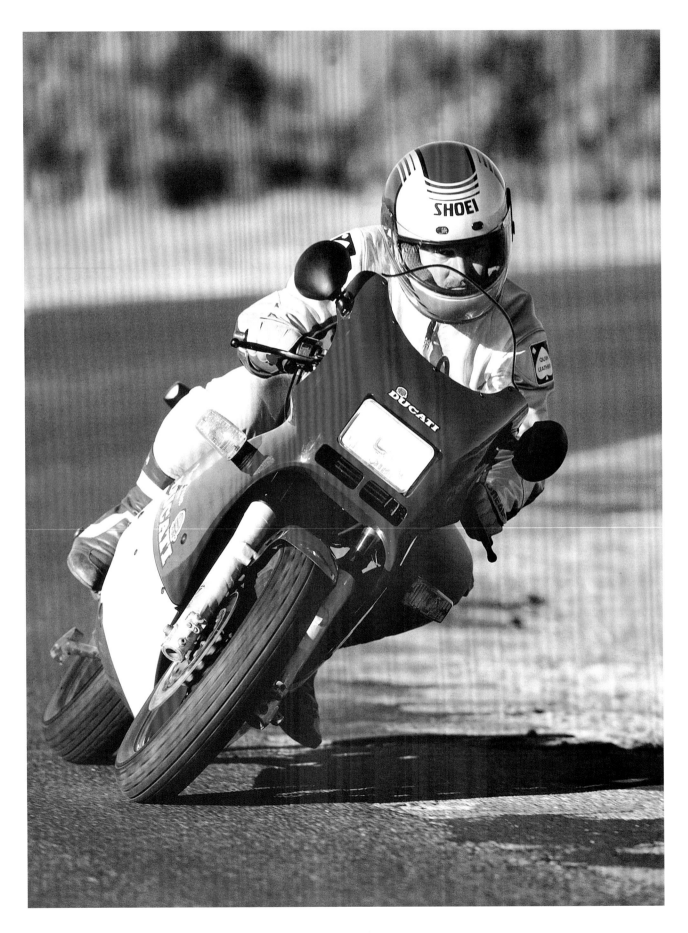

was that, because it was derived from the TT2, it was a very small motorcycle and the riding position was consequently cramped for larger riders.

By late-1985 F1s were being displayed with the new Cagiva graphics and logo. Some of these were silver and red, but they were all interim models before the arrival of the significantly improved 750F1 for 1986. Following racing experience with the TT1, the original 500 type crankcase, which had always cracked around the drive side main bearing under the stress of racing, was finally strengthened, with extra webbing between it and the gearbox mainshaft bearing. Straight cut primary gears now took power to a hydraulically-operated dry clutch and a new, stronger gearbox was fitted with 30° wider gears. The crankshaft was strengthened around the big-end journal with new connecting rods. The oil-cooling was now full-flow, rather than just a cylinder head bypass, and, in keeping with the larger capacity, valve sizes were increased to the 41 and 35 mm of the TT2, necessitating a move to smaller 12 mm spark-plugs. Along with slightly revised camshafts (about 8° retarded), and an increase in compression to 10:1 using higher-domed pistons, power went up to a claimed 75 bhp at 9,000 rpm. The new camshaft timing was, inlet opening 39° before top dead centre, and closing 80° after bottom dead centre, and exhaust opening 80° before bottom dead centre, and closing 38° after top dead centre. The same Dell'Orto PHF36 carburettors were used, with small foam air-filters.

The engine was certainly an improvement, and so was the front suspension. 40 mm Forcella-Italia forks, with provision for a wide range of adjustment in damping and preload, were vastly superior to the non-adjustable 38 mm Marzocchis. Also, the rear 260 mm disc was no longer the fully-floating type, and the 22-litre aluminium petrol tank became an 18-litre steel one. As has often been the case at Ducati, some things improve, but other details exhibit cost-cutting when models are revised. However, the instrument layout with the white-faced Veglias was a welcome relief from the Nippon Densos that had by now become dated, and still carries through to today on the Super Sport line. The styling of the rear seat was improved, but it still looked awkward from some angles, and the red Oscam wheels mirrored the racing TT1.

Cycle magazine summed up the 750F1 succinctly in February 1987 when it said 'the F1 allows a very competent street rider to understand how a race bike feels because the engine will help him rather than

intimidate him'. For the F1 still didn't possess exceptional horsepower. When *Cycle* tested an F1 in June 1988, it only achieved a standing quarter-mile time of 12.70 seconds at 103.1 mph (166 km/h). Perhaps the most disappointing aspect of the new 750 engine was the vibration, which after a long ride would leave you with numbed wrists. Somehow, the short-stroke 750 engine never managed to feel as smooth and relaxed as the earlier bevel-gear examples.

For 1987 and 1988 the 750F1 continued to be marketed in small numbers beside the new range of Cagiva-inspired Ducatis. From bike number 1505 the Japanese Kokusan ignition, that had first appeared on the limited edition 750 Montjuich, replaced the Bosch system. Also, the last versions had a locking fuel cap and a dual seat. However, by now the F1 was an anachronism within a Ducati range that was becoming increasingly Cagiva-influenced. To quote *Cycle* magazine again, the 750F1 was 'the last true fundamentalist Ducati'.

750 MONTJUICH, LAGUNA SECA AND SANTAMONICA

To celebrate the win by Grau, de Juan, and Reyes in the 24-Hour race at Montjuich Park in 1983, a limited edition race replica F1 in the finest Ducati tradition was announced at the end of 1985, and displayed at the Milan Show. As usual it had taken long enough to appear, but like the first 750SS of 1974 many thought it worth the wait. Though essentially a 750F1, the Montjuich was tuned considerably with hotter camshafts, Dell'Orto PHM40ND carburettors, and a less restrictive Verlicchi two-into-one *Riservato Competizione* exhaust system. Even though it still only had the cantilever rear end, the swing-arm was Verlicchi aluminium, and in a carry-over from the 750TT1 both front and rear wheels were 16-inch. The wheels were lightweight composite Marvic with magnesium hubs and spokes, and Akront aluminium rims. Rim sizes were much wider than the standard F1 at 3.50 x 16 and 4.25 x 16, and shod with Michelin 120/60V16 and 180/60V16 tyres. Other detail differences included a 22-litre aluminium fuel tank like the first 750F1, four-piston Brembo 'Gold Line' racing calipers with fully-floating discs all round (280 mm at the front and 260 mm rear), a vented dry clutch, and different front guard. While the prototype featured a

The 1986 750F1 Montjuich was a true race replica in the best Ducati tradition.

centre-stand, the production models saved a few kilos by only specifying a side-stand. The relationship between the Montjuich and F1 was similar to that which existed between the original 750SS and 750 Sport: a limited production bike that offered higher performance through engine modifications, better brakes, and less weight.

However, this is where the concept of the two bikes differs. The Montjuich was created and sold as a limited edition item, each of the 200 bikes having a numbered plaque on the petrol tank. It was only several years later that anyone realized how rare the original 750SS was, and by that stage many had been raced and ruined. Still, there were many detail differences to the Montjuich, and it was both lighter and significantly more powerful than the standard F1. Starting with the engine, the Montjuich received new camshafts with timing figures of inlet opening 67° before top dead centre, and closing 99° after bottom dead centre, and exhaust opening 93° before bottom dead centre and closing 70° after top dead centre. With 137° of valve overlap, these camshafts had more than the racing TT1, and inlet duration of 346° was also slightly more than the TT1. These were the fiercest camshafts ever fitted to a street Ducati, and as such the Montjuich was peakier than expected. Along with the larger carburettors and racing exhaust system, the camshafts lifted claimed power for the Montjuich to 95 bhp at 10,000 rpm. Unlike the earlier 750SS, the lower half of the engine was standard 750F1. There were no polished crankshafts or con-rods, and the 10:1 pistons and barrels were identical to the F1. The Montjuich had an aluminium clutch drum and slightly different gearbox internals, to accommodate the outboard countershaft sprocket. Rather than the Bosch ignition that had been used since 1977, a Kokusan system was used for the first time.

To compensate for the 16-inch rear wheel, the final-drive gearing was altered to 15/43, or 2.87:1, and a narrower, 5/8 x 1/4 inch chain was used. The Montjuich also used a better-quality Marzocchi rear shock absorber, but tests still criticized it for being underdamped. Claimed dry weight was a mere 155 kg (342 lb), but *Motorrad* weighed their test bike in at 178 kg (392 lb) fully wet, still much less than any other two-cylinder street Ducati. *Moto Sprint*, in April 1986, managed 221 km/h (137.3 mph), with 75 bhp at 10,000 rpm. *Cycle World* also put theirs through a standing quarter-mile in 11.87 seconds, at 113.52 mph (182.7 km/h).

Below: The 750 Laguna Seca of 1987 shared its wheels and brakes with the Paso.

Right: The final traditional Pantah was the Santamonica of 1988.

By now the Cagiva take-over was well in effect, and the new management was anxious to promote both Cagiva and Ducati in the US. It was this that led to Lucchinelli racing in and winning the Battle of the Twins at the Californian track of Laguna Seca. Though hardly as prestigious a win as that at Montjuich, it was considered momentous enough to name the 1987 series of F1 race replicas after it. Each of these 200 bikes had a replica Marco Lucchinelli signature on its petrol tank.

There were numerous differences between the Montjuich and Laguna Seca. Historically, Ducati have often lowered the specification of successive models. This was true of the 750/900SSs that in 1976 acquired indicators, smaller carburettors, and Lafranconi silencers, and a similar situation occurred in 1987 with the Laguna Seca. Most noticeable was the replacement of the lightweight Marvic wheels and fully-floating discs, with 16-inch Oscam wheels and 280 and 270 mm discs straight off the 750 Paso. Some Laguna Secas came with a dual seat option, detracting from its race replica status, and the alloy petrol tank became a standard steel F1 item. However, the engine specification was unchanged, and the Laguna Seca still offered significant performance gains over a standard

750F1, despite a noticeable weight increase. The exhaust system was either the Conti two-into-one of the 750F1, which hurt the power, or one with a less restrictive aluminium silencer. Claimed power was down slightly to 91 bhp at 10,000 rpm, and weight up to 165 kg (364 lb). The Laguna Seca came with a plastic mudguard over the rear wheel, attached to the aluminium swing-arm, and like the Montjuich it was painted red and silver.

Performance of the Laguna Seca was similar to that of the Montjuich. In October 1987, with the less restrictive exhaust, *La Moto* achieved a top speed of 221 km/h (137 mph), the same as the Montjuich. *Motorcyclist* in the US, testing a Laguna Seca with the Conti exhaust system, could only get a best standing quarter-mile time of 12.53 seconds at 105.7 mph (170 km/h). Their bike also weighed in at 418 lb (190 kg) wet, up considerably on the Montjuich.

Despite the factory's commitment to the Paso and the new 851, the limited edition 750F1 continued into 1988 with the Santamonica. Named after the circuit at Misano where Marco Lucchinelli won the Formula 1 World Championship race in 1986, this bike was a hybrid of the Montjuich and Laguna Seca. The composite Marvic wheels and fully-floating disc rotors returned, but with street-legal four-piston Brembo brake calipers, rather than the Gold Line racing versions (although the prototype was fitted with Gold Line brakes and a Verlicchi exhaust). The dual seat was standard, as was the Laguna Seca silencer with the aluminium can, along with the steel fuel tank. Colour was red and white. When *Moto Sprint* tested the Santamonica in August 1988 it went 219.715 km/h (136.5 mph) and weighed 173 kg (381 lb) wet. It also made 73.63 bhp at 9,250 rpm.

As such, the entire 750F1 line, and in particular the three models of limited edition replicas, represented the end of an era for Ducati. It started with one of the most successful Ducati racing bikes ever, the 600 TT2, and ended with a series of race replicas totally in keeping with the spirit and essence of Ducati. They were the last bikes with unfiltered 40 mm Dell'Orto carburettors breathing directly into the atmosphere, and, along with the smaller 350/400F3, the last Ducatis with symmetrical cylinder heads, those with both exhaust ports facing forwards.

350/400F3

The anomalies of both the Italian and Japanese markets have led to a range of smaller-engined Ducatis over the years. By the mid-1980s Japan was the largest market for Ducati, and their market requirements dictated a 400. The Italian market had always required a 350, and there had been 350 parallel twins such as the 350GTL,

350GTV, and 350 Desmo Sport, along with the 350XL Pantah especially for this. It seemed logical to capitalize on the success of the 750F1 by creating virtually identical bikes with smaller motors, and this is a practice that Ducati still continues today. Both the 350 and 400F3s of 1986 onwards were essentially 750F1s, but they continued in production until 1989, whereas the 750F1 was discontinued in 1988. The Italian market 350 had the engine of the 350XL. With a bore and stroke of 66 x 51 mm, and valve sizes of 33.5 mm and 30.5 mm, the 350 engine produced 42 bhp at 9,700 rpm. Carburation was by two Dell'Orto PHF30s and even the valve timing was different for the smaller engine, with the inlet opening 40° before top dead centre, and closing 80° after bottom dead centre, and the exhaust opening 57° before bottom dead centre, and closing 43° after top dead centre. The 400F3 was a bored 350, with engine dimensions of 70.5 x 51 mm to give 398 cc. Power was up slightly to 45 bhp at 10,000 rpm.

Much more basic suspension than the F1 was fitted, with 35 mm Marzocchi forks, and smaller, 260 mm dual discs were fitted along with 05 Brembo calipers. The paint scheme for both the 350 and 400 was a very attractive red and white. Instruments on some 400s were the Mille MHR Nippon Denso type, while the 350 had the white-faced Veglias of the 750F1. Claimed weight was only 165 kg (364 lb). As tested by *Motociclismo* in November 1986, the 350F3 went 178.3 km/h (110.8 mph). The final version of the 400F3 had a six-speed gearbox and a dual seat, and was still being shipped to Japan in early 1989.

Although an improvement over
the 750 Sport, the 1989 900SS
was still flawed. *Two Wheels*

12 THE CAGIVA TAKE-OVER

During the early 1980s, when Ducati was under the VM Group of industries, production levels were low and the plant was very unprofitable. Although 5,665 motorcycles were produced in 1982, these proved to be difficult to sell. By 1983, production had dropped further, to 3,909, and would reach an all-time low of 1,765 in 1984. The situation was so bad that the future of Ducati motorcycle production looked very bleak, then in a surprise move the managers of the VM Group started negotiations with the relatively unknown Cagiva company from Varese. On 1 June a press statement was released in Milan announcing a joint venture.

Cagiva had been built in 1978 out of the ashes of AMF-Harley Davidson (formerly Aermacchi) by the two Castiglioni brothers, Claudio and Gianfranco. Their move from manufacturing combination locks for briefcases and a wide range of fasteners and electrical hardware to motor-cycles was a brave one. However, within four years they were producing 40,000 motorcycles a year from their converted aircraft hangars on the foreshore of the Lago di Varese, north of Milan. These motorcycles were predominantly of small capacity (less than 350cc), so in order to expand their range into larger varieties it was easier to buy engines from outside than develop new ones. The initial agreement called for Ducati to supply engines for a range of Cagiva-badged motorcycles for seven years, with an option for automatic renewal. There were to be 6,000 engines for 1984, 10,000 in 1985, and 14,000 in the following years, with production of all Ducati motorcycles to cease by the end of 1984.

Production of the Cagiva range of Ducati-powered motorcycles was initially very slow, so Ducati persuaded their parent group, VM, to allow the continuation of motor-cycle production for another year. Then, during 1985, Cagiva bought Ducati, and with it pledged to maintain the Ducati name with a completely new range of bikes. Later they also bought Husqvarna and Moto Morini, and today the Cagiva group is the largest manufacturer of motorcycles in Italy.

750 AND 906 PASO

When Cagiva acquired Ducati in 1985, they also inherited a production line-up with an uncertain future. The Mille engine had reached the limit of its development, but there was still development life in the Pantah range of engines. The biggest problem facing Ducati at this time was that they were not profitable, and there was no new investment, a scenario similar to that which had afflicted the British motorcycle industry in the 1970s. Even before the Castiglionis bought Ducati, the bevel-gear engines had been considered too expensive to produce. Taglioni had indicated as much back in 1977, but the future seemed to be with smaller-capacity motorcycles at that stage, so the bevel-gear engine continued for a few more years. Cagiva immediately decided to concentrate on the Pantah, which by that time had only been developed to a maximum of 750cc. The initial contract had called for Ducati motors to be installed in Cagiva motorcycles, and several models appeared under this agreement, notably the 650 Alazzurra and the Elefant off-road bike. The 750 Pantah motor had made it to the F1, but the Castiglionis were determined to develop a completely new type of Ducati. The future of the Ducati marque lay in the radical Paso of 1986, not the traditional-style 750F1.

To the traditionalist, the announcement and display of the 750 Paso at the Milan Show of 1985 was a surprise – it was such a huge departure from the hard-edged, sporting F1 style. However, underneath all the bodywork was a vastly more modern motorcycle. It may not have been a race replica, but it promised to be the first Ducati that was a complete package. While the 750F1 was an excellent sporting motorcycle, as delivered from the factory it had poor rear suspension and inferior Michelin A48/M48 tyres, as was traditionally the case with Ducatis, even the race replicas, and the Paso was the first to break with this tradition.

The origins of the Paso only went back to 1984. When Cagiva entered into the agreement with Ducati, they also approached Bimota in Rimini to develop a new motorcycle around the Pantah engine. Massimo Tamburini (the 'ta' in 'Bimota') had broken with Giuseppe Morri (the 'mo' in the name) and set up on his own with Roberto Gallina, the former Italian racing champion and manager of the Suzuki HB Grand Prix team. He had been involved with the design of the TGA1 Suzuki Grand Prix with which both Marco Lucchinelli and Franco Uncini had won the 1981 and 1982 500 cc World Championships, and was approached by Cagiva to design a new chassis for the Mille (outlined in Chapter 9). Soon Tamburini was to

become head of the Cagiva research and development department, and when he considered the Bimota Pantah, later the DB1, too impractical for mass-production, he began work on a completely new frame for the Pantah engine (Bimota later put the DB1 into limited production). Tamburini called his new design the Paso, in memory of his friend and Grand Prix racer Renzo Pasolini, tragically killed in an accident at Monza in 1973.

Departing from more recent Ducati practice, Massimo Tamburini's cradle for the 750 Pantah engine did not use the engine as a stressed member. It was closely modelled on the frame that Bimota had designed for Yamaha, which had eventually become the FJ1100. Built from square-section tubing, but with an aluminium swing-arm with eccentric chain adjustment, both the wheelbase and steering geometry were altered from the 750F1. The swing-arm was lengthened by 60 mm, and the steering head angle pulled in to 25°, to give a wheelbase of 1,450 mm (57 inches). Trail was much less than the F1, at 103 mm (4 inches) rather than 133 mm (5.24 inches). The lower cradle unbolted to ease engine removal, but more importantly the new frame allowed access to the rear cylinder head to aid servicing of the desmodromic valve gear. There was no attempt to make the engine and frame visually appealing as they were to be completely covered by bodywork, but unclothed the Paso was one of the messiest looking Ducatis.

With the latest Marzocchi 42 mm M1R forks, and Öhlins CA 2508 rear shock absorber operating through a 'Soft Damp' rising rate linkage, the Paso had much more sophisticated suspension than any previous street Ducati. The Marzocchi forks were unusual in that the right fork leg controlled the rebound damping only, while the left fork leg looked after the compression stroke. Adjustment for rebound damping was provided by an external four-position knob on the right leg, which had initially appeared on the TT1 and TT2, and also on the Cagiva 500 cc Grand Prix bike. The rear Öhlins featured hydraulically adjustable spring preload. The wheel sizes were also a considerable break with tradition, with 3.75 x 16 and 5.00 x 16-inch Oscam wheels shod with the first new-generation low-profile Pirelli MP7 series radial tyres. The use of such wide tyres also required the engine to be offset to the left for the chain to clear the rear tyre.

There were also many changes to the engine. In a departure seen on the Cagiva Elefant a year earlier, the

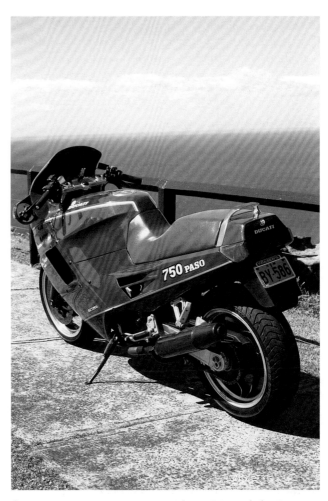

The 750 Paso, with its full-coverage bodywork, represented a significant departure from the traditional Ducati.

rear cylinder was rotated so that both inlet manifolds faced each other between the cylinders. The advantage of this was that both inlet tracts could now be of equal length, and straighter. They would also lend themselves to downdraught carburettors. Unfortunately, the choice of carburettors available for such a layout was limited, and Cagiva chose to adapt a Weber automotive type.

This 44DCNF 107 twin-barrel carburettor, 44 mm wide at the throttle and 36 mm at the venturi, was problematic and the cause of many complaints and factory jetting revisions. Despite problems with an off idle and mid-range flat spot, backfiring when hot, and throttle hesitations, the factory persevered with the Weber until 1991, seemingly oblivious to these problems. Finally they got the new engine right when they fitted the Mikuni carburettors for the 1991 season.

In other respects the engine was much the same as the 1986 750F1. It had the larger valves and slightly retarded valve timing (39/80/80/38), together with the stronger engine cases and gearbox, and a hydraulically operated dry clutch. All Pasos had the Kokusan ignition with the coils mounted on the left side of the frame, and there were two oil-coolers, one on each side of the fairing. Considering that the engine was now effectively silenced by the Silentium mufflers, the claimed power of 72.5 bhp at 7,900 rpm was very respectable. Where the Paso really did suffer in comparison with the F1 was in its weight. The claimed dry weight was 195 kg (430 lb), but *Cycle* weighed their test bike at 495 lb (224 kg) wet, a full 69 lb (31 kg) heavier than the F1.

The top speed achieved by *Motociclismo* in December 1986 was only 204.2 km/h (127 mph). However, sheer performance was not what the Paso was about. This was a refined sports tourer aimed at appealing to a broader range of riders than traditional Ducatis. The press loved it. *Motorcyclist* in the US in February 1987 said that 'the Paso represents a truly streetable version of the exotic Italian sport bike.'

There were many other changes incorporated in the Paso. A fuel pump kept the Weber supplied, and features like a fuel level gauge and much more modern switchgear put the Paso on a par with Japanese bikes. The styling, with totally enclosed bodywork and no clear fairing screen, was original, and eye-catching. However, while in many respects the Paso did bring Ducati up to date, as a sporting bike it still could not match a 750F1. I had the opportunity to test one of the first 750 Pasos in company with an F1, and the Paso was a disappointment. It understeered badly, and throttle response was vastly inferior to that provided by the 750F1's Dell'Orto PHM36s.

By 1987 the Öhlins rear shock absorber had been replaced by a much harsher Marzocchi unit, but in 1988 only small changes occurred. The triple clamps and handlebars were now painted black, and a fold-out handle was fitted to help in putting the bike on the centre-stand. In addition to red, there was now also the option of blue or white paintwork. The 750 Paso continued through until 1990, by which time it had the revised silencers from the new model 900SS, and the Weber had received numerous jetting modifications.

The importance of the Paso lay not in whether or not it was a superior motorcycle to the Ducatis of the past, but in the incorporation of new ideas within the traditional framework. For the first time since 1980, when the entire range had desmodromic valve gear,

The 906 Paso appeared in 1988 with different colours from the 750, but offered no real improvements.

Right: Another misguided marketing attempt was the 1986 Indiana, aimed at the US market. *Ducati Motor*

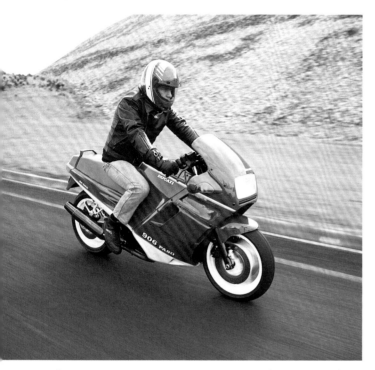

there was a genuine commitment to aid servicing. The new frame design not only aided access to the rear cylinder head for valve adjustment, but Massimo Bordi's assistant, Gianluigi Mengoli, also simplified the rocker layout by incorporating a spring clip on the opening rocker shaft so that the rocker could be moved sideways to allow shim removal. No longer did the opening rockers and pins need to be removed. Unfortunately the 750 Paso still did not appeal to the traditional Ducati buyer, and ultimately suffered a similar fate to that of the 600TL and 900 Darmah. It was sold off at heavily discounted prices in 1990, by which time it had been superseded. Still, it provided a strong basis for further development during 1988, and by 1989 had evolved into the 906 Paso.

Most of the changes between the 750 and the 906 occurred in the engine, which was now based on the new 851 'large crankcase' eight-valve engine detailed in the next chapter. With a six-speed gearbox rather than the 750's five-speed, the new bike was called the 906, the '6' indicating the six speeds. Actual capacity of the new engine was 904cc, for while the bore of 92 mm was shared with the 851, an extra 4 mm of stroke, to 68 mm, gave additional displacement. With an extra 6.5 mm of stroke over the 750, con-rod length also grew, from 124 mm to 130 mm. The con-rod length to stroke ratio was still 1.9:1, despite the necessity to keep

the cylinder and head as short as possible. Big-end bearing size increased to 42 mm from the 40 mm on the 750. In other respects, too, the 906 was a marriage of the 750 and 851: the water cooling for the cylinders and heads of the 851 was coupled with the two-valve desmodromic heads of the 750 and similar Weber 44DCNF 116 twin-choke downdraught carburettor with slightly revised jetting (160 rather than 150 main jet). The dual oil-coolers of the 750 went, to be replaced by a single radiator. Valve sizes were up to 43 mm inlet and 38 mm exhaust, and in the search for more performance there were new camshafts yet again. These featured steeper ramps and higher lift, but less overlap. Valve timing was now inlet opening 20° before top dead centre and closing 60° after bottom dead centre, and exhaust opening 58° before bottom dead centre and closing 20° after top dead centre. Valve lift was increased considerably from the 750, to 11.1 mm for the inlet (9.35 mm on the 750) and 10.56 mm for the exhaust (8.50 mm on the 750). Despite a slight reduction in the compression ratio to 9.2:1, the claimed power went up to 88 bhp at 8,000 rpm. The combustion chamber also came in for some redesign at this stage, to become the 'tri-spherical' type.

The 750's Kokusan ignition with progressive advance was replaced by a Marelli Digiplex inductive discharge type, powered by a new 350-watt alternator, up from the 750's 300-watt type. The clutch and all the gearbox and primary drive ratios were shared with the 851, as were the water pump, thermostat and radiator. Despite the very similar external appearance of the 750 and 906 Paso, there were a few changes to the frame and suspension. To prevent the front wheel hitting the longer front cylinder, a 20 mm-longer Marzocchi M1R 42 mm fork was fitted, with 15 mm less travel, and revised fork offset brought the trail back to 96 mm (3.8 inches). The rear suspension was identical to the later 750 Paso, with a Marzocchi shock absorber connected to the 'Soft Damp' rising rate system. The 16-inch Oscam wheels were the same as the 750, as were the Brembo brakes. Unfortunately, despite the power increase the downside to all this extra engine sophistication was in the claimed increased weight of 10 kg, to 205 kg (452 lb).

In many ways the 906 represented an even greater departure from the traditional Ducati philosophy of reducing power and weight to achieve a balanced motorcycle. This was demonstrated clearly in contemporary road tests of the 906, for while the new, larger engine produced more mid-range torque, overall performance was not improved on the 750 Paso. In November 1989 *Cycle* magazine managed 60.64 bhp at 7,000 rpm (only 6 bhp up on the 750), and the bike weighed in at a massive 235 kg (518 lb) wet. Drag strip performance was also slightly slower than the 750, at 12.79 seconds at 102 mph (164 km/h) for the standing quarter mile. On the other side of the Atlantic, performance of the 906 also failed to meet expectations. *Motorrad*, in January 1989, could only coax a maximum speed of 191 km/h (119 mph) from their test bike. However, testers welcomed the Cagiva influence on improved fit and finish, and though the Weber now carburetted better than it had two years earlier, it was still not perfect. The 906 lasted until 1990, by which time the new model 900SS had an oil-cooled version of the same motor, and the clutch actuation assembly had moved to the left-hand side of the engine. It was not one of the most memorable Ducatis, having less than a two-year production run, but it was to become one of their better sport-touring models when developed further for the 1991 season as the fuel-injected 907 IE.

INDIANA

As soon as Cagiva bought Ducati in 1985 they were looking for ways to use the production capabilities of the Bologna factory more effectively. By broadening the appeal of the range of Ducatis, especially for the US market, they hoped to expand production of the desmodromic Pantah engine. There had already been the Elefant enduro bike and the Cagiva Alazzurra of 1984, and in 1985 a prototype 900 bevel-gear-powered cruiser-style bike was built. This fortunately never made it out of Varese, but from it emerged the Indiana in 1986.

While based on the Alazzurra, the Indiana followed the Paso and Elefant lead in that it had the reversed rear cylinder head. There were two versions, a 350 for the Italian market and a 650 for elsewhere. A departure from other models was in the carburation. While the 350 Indiana had 30 mm Dell'Ortos, those of the 650 came fitted with 36 mm Bing constant vacuum carburettors. They had more conservative valve timing than the Elefant and Alazzurra, but still a high 10:1 compression ratio. Because of the vertical cylinder's rear-facing exhaust, the exhaust pipe snaked around the right side of the engine to maintain the symmetrical cruiser look. Claimed power for the 350 was 38 bhp at 9,250 rpm, and for the 650 53 bhp at 7,000 rpm, so for this type of motorcycle they were not sluggish performers. To finish the styling of the engine the cam-belt covers, dry hydraulic clutch cover (650), and left-side engine cover were chromed. The 350 had a cable-operated wet clutch.

The frame followed that of the Elefant rather than the Alazzurra. Built from square-section steel tubing, it was also a full cradle with a removable bolt on the right front down-tube to allow easy access to the camshaft belt covers. While the cast aluminium box-section swing-arm still pivoted in the rear of the engine crankcase, the engine itself was rigidly mounted at four points. However, because it was designed for a ladder-type frame, alloy arms from the engine to the frame bolted to the front engine mounts. A hollow pressed-steel backbone formed the basis of the structure, and also funnelled air into the airbox and filter beneath the seat. Generous 40 mm Marzocchi leading axle forks (a reminder of the early 750GT) were fitted. If it had not been for the cruiser-style rake of 33°, and the same wheelbase as the old 750GT (1,530 mm or 60.2 inches), the Indiana would probably have been quite a snappy handler. Twin Marzocchi shocks graced the rear end and braking was by a single 260 mm front disc and a larger, 280 mm, rear disc. The front brake caliper was one of the first four-piston Brembo types.

The Indiana did not receive particularly good press reports. *Cycle* wrote that the 'suspension compliance

and handling are areas where the Italians are clearly one, perhaps two generations behind the latest Japanese-style cruisers'. The model was not successful, and in many export markets not even sold at all. Like the 600TL, the Indiana grew into a police bike, and also into a 750 cc version with 55 bhp and 32 mm Bing carburettors. By 1988 it was no longer offered as a 650, but the 350 continued for the Italian market. Even though sales were poor, both the 750 and 350 continued until 1990. Of all the less successful Ducati models, the Indiana was possibly the one that most completely missed the target. In retrospect it seems ludicrous that Taglioni's magnificent engine, one that had won four World TT2 Championships, should end up in this style of bike. When its target market is considered, it is not surprising that buyers did not take to a cruiser with desmodromic valve gear.

While the Indiana was directed at the American market, it is worth noting too that the Cagiva Elefant enduro bike, in 900 cc Mikuni carburetted form, was marketed as a Ducati in the US from 1993. Called the Ducati E-900, this was just a re-badged Elefant in the hope that sales would benefit from the association with the Ducati name, rather than that of the lesser-known Cagiva. The racing versions had also had success in the Paris–Dakar race of 1994. Using the air-cooled engine from the 900SS, de-tuned to produce 68 bhp, in the Elefant full-cradle square-section frame, this was a large trail bike. Dry weight was 185 kg (408 lb), but the wet weight was 224 kg (494 lb) as tested by *Motorcyclist* in September 1993. The bike was fitted with 45 mm Showa inverted forks, and rear suspension was by a Boge shock absorber operating through the Cagiva 'Soft Damp' linkage. Braking was by two 282 mm front discs with single-action twin piston Brembo calipers, with a 240 mm disc at the rear. Not really a dirt bike because of its size, and not really a street bike, the Ducati E-900 was the two-wheeled Range Rover.

750 SPORT/900 SUPER SPORT (WEBER MODELS)

While the Paso, and to a lesser extent the Indiana, Alazzurra and Elefant, signified the path that Cagiva intended for Ducati, the 750F1 continued in production alongside them during 1986 and 1987. The 750F1, despite being an older design, continued to sell well, but was still an expensive motorcycle to produce, with its Forcella Italia forks and fully floating Brembo brakes. It was therefore decided to replace it with a similarly styled, Paso-derived model.

The Castiglionis were well aware of the historical significance of certain models of Ducati and also conscious of the importance of this to the Ducati enthusiast. With the release of the 750 Sport a deliberate attempt was made to appeal to those enthusiasts who could remember the superb 750 Sport of 1972–74. By combining ingredients from both the Paso and 750F1, Ducati hoped to recreate a classic, and lure back their traditional customers.

This *nuovo* 750 Sport was basically the engine of the Paso in the chassis of a modified 750F1. With the Paso there had been a new commitment to engines with reversed rear cylinder heads enabling the Weber 44DCNF 113 carburettor to be used. Consequently the F1 trellis frame, which was a descendant of the quadruple World Championship-winning Verlicchi F2 type, needed some modification so that the large air

filter could be fitted. The steel swing-arm of the F1 and F2 made way for an aluminium item (still a cantilever), similar in type to that on the limited edition Montjuich and Laguna Seca 750 F1s, but the 16-inch Oscam wheels and Brembo brakes were straight off the Paso. The aluminium swing-arm would be a constant problem, suffering from cracks and breakages, and warranty replacement in some countries.

The engine, including the intake and exhaust system, was identical to the 750 Paso but for the use of one oil-cooler rather than two. While the wheels and brakes were also the same, much more basic suspension was used to keep costs down. Non-adjustable 40 mm Marzocchi M1BB forks, and a Marzocchi PBS1R rear shock, were fitted. Like the F1, 28° of rake was used. Combined with 4.5 inches (114 mm) of trail, the steering of the 750 Sport was slow, more like a traditional Ducati. The wheelbase, at 1,450 mm (57 inches), was up slightly on the short 750F1, and the weight was a claimed 180 kg (397 lb).

As far as performance went, the 750 Sport was similar to the F1. *Motor Cycle News*, in September 1988, achieved a creditable best top speed of 132.6 mph (213.4 km/h), and in December 1989 *Cycle World* put their test bike through a standing quarter mile at 12.44 seconds at 107.27 mph (172.6 km/h). Most test reports were guarded in their praise for the bike. In many respects it was a step backwards from the Paso, which handled better, and it did not possess the symmetry and breeding of the 750F1. There were still carburettor problems with the Weber, and, being so obviously a cost-conscious entry-level Ducati, it lacked identity.

Released in mid-1988, these new Sports were initially painted bright red and blue. It was not the most attractive styling, and only a few months later, at the IFMA Cologne Show, the 1989 model was displayed in red and silver. The motor was also now air- and oil-cooled, with jackets around the bore liners circulating oil and supplementing normal airflow around the finned cylinders. An alternative colour scheme of silver and black was also offered at this time, but there were far fewer made in these colours. The 750 Sport failed to recreate the legend of its earlier namesake. With its 16-inch wheels the proportions were wrong, and it lacked the character of the older bike. By 1990 it had finished, but was already being developed into a superior design.

With the introduction of the water-cooled 906 Paso during 1989, it seemed logical to put this larger engine in the 750 Sport chassis, and in the process hopefully resurrect another classic Ducati, the 900SS. Instead of Super Sport, the generic title became Supersport. However, wanting to maintain the light and functional concept that set the 750 Sport apart from the Paso, the 904 cc engine that was installed in this traditional Ducati-style space frame eschewed the water cooling of the 906 Paso. Following an example set by the Paris–Dakar Cagiva Elefants of 1988 and 1989, and incorporated in the 750 Sport, the new engine used oil-cooled cylinders and heads. As with the 906, the crankcases and six-speed gearbox were shared with the 851, but the 900SS had the longer-stroked 68 mm crankshaft of the 906. It also used the same two-valve cylinder head with the 'tri-spherical' combustion chamber, the 43 mm and 38 mm valves, and 9.2:1 compression. The camshafts were similar to those of the 906, the valve overlap of only 40° being very moderate by Ducati standards. The valve lift was more

like that of the older 'Imola' camshafts, 11.76 mm for the inlet valve, and 10.56 mm for the exhaust. New camshaft belt covers appeared on these larger engines, allowing for belt tension adjustment without removing the entire cover.

Carburation was still by the Weber 44DCNF carburettor, and ignition by the Marelli Digiplex of the 906, but power was down slightly from the 906 to 83 bhp at 8,400 rpm. This would not be a handicap because the 900SS was considerably lighter than the 906 (180 kg versus 205 kg). The frame was that of the 750 Sport, but for some extra bracing around the steering head, and slightly less steering head angle at 27°, giving 122 mm (4.8 inches) of trail. The wheelbase was the same 1,450 mm (57 inches). However, the wheels, brakes and suspension were considerably upgraded from the smaller model. Instead of the 16-inch Oscams from the Paso, the white-painted 17-inch wheels came off the 1989 model 851, and their rim widths were a thoroughly modern 3.50 x 17, and 5.50 x 17. New 40 mm Marzocchi forks were fitted with the normal Marzocchi shock absorber operated by the aluminium swing-arm, still with no linkage. The brakes, too, were now from the 851, with four-piston 32 mm Brembo brake calipers, but operating slightly smaller 300 mm steel discs. At the rear was a 245 mm disc and Brembo twin-piston caliper. While the styling drew very much on the 750 Sport, the exhaust system mirrored that of the 851.

In grafting the larger wheels on to the 750 Sport, Ducati had created a much taller motorcycle, and with weight distribution heavily biased towards the rear, handling was less than perfect. They seemed to have made the same mistake as when they built the second generation of Mike Hailwood Replicas in 1983. By raising the centre of gravity and putting the rider too high, they took away the agility of the earlier model. The steering was still very slow and there was too much trail, so the bike was unwilling to turn quickly. Also, despite four years of development, the Weber carburettor was still not right. In October 1989 *Performance Bikes* complained of the 'imperfect carburation … when you really whack the throttle open at 4,000 rpm'. However, the bike performed considerably more strongly than previous two-valve twins. The Italian magazine *Moto Sprint* in November 1989 ran their test bike, weighing in at a modest wet weight of 192.9 kg (425 lb), to 219.369 km/h (136 mph).

Comparisons were inevitably drawn between the old and new 900SS. On paper the new bike was lighter, shorter, had vastly superior brakes and tyres, and, but for the Weber carburettor, was easier to live with. Like the 750 Sport, there were still problems with cracking of the aluminium swing-arm. Performance was up on the older model, but not dramatically so. The styling lacked the raw good looks of the earlier bike, and sales were not as good as expected. This would all be changed for the 1991 season when the 900SS came in for a dramatic revision, and in the process Ducati built a real successor to its earlier namesake.

907IE

At the Cologne Motorcycle Show in September 1990, not only was the revised 900SS displayed, but the Paso was also updated and considerably improved. This final version of the Paso was called the 907IE. The Paso name went, and so did many of the peculiarities that had afflicted it. After years of complaints, the

Below: The 907IE addressed many of the criticisms of the earlier Paso.

Weber carburettor was finally laid to rest, and replaced on the 907 with the Weber Marelli electronic fuel injection system from the 851, hence the initials 'IE', *iniezione elettronica*. The fitting of 17-inch wheels also eliminated the idiosyncratic handling of the Pasos. For 1991 the entire range of 851 and 900 engines featured stronger crankcases. After a series of crankcase cracking problems experienced by the factory while racing, and winning, the World Superbike Championship during 1990, the new crankcases had more extensive webbing and ribbing around the cylinder support base.

While the engine was essentially the water-cooled 904 cc two-valve unit of the 906, power was up to a claimed 90 bhp at 8,500 rpm. Sharing the same throttle sensors and computer with the 851, the 907 used smaller 42 mm throttle bodies rather than the 851's 50 mm examples. The camshafts of the 1989 900SS, together with the injection system and the higher-volume black-chromed cylindrical mufflers, translated into vastly improved engine performance over the 906.

On *Cycle* magazine's dyno in February 1991 the 907 made 70.0 bhp at 8,500 rpm, nearly 10 more than the 906. On the road this produced a standing quarter mile time of 11.74 seconds at 112.24 mph (180.6 km/h). Top speed was up too, with *Cycle World*, in their test of June 1991, managing a measured top speed of 136 mph (219 km/h).

The chassis also came in for revision. Tamburini's box-section, full-cradle frame was retained, along with the Marzocchi Duo-Shock and 41.7 mm M1R fork. As with the 900SS of the previous year, the same 17-inch wheels were fitted. The new front wheel was about 40 mm taller than that of the original Paso, and this necessitated reducing the fork travel slightly to 125 mm (4.9 inches), and lengthening the fork legs by 10 mm. Still with a steep 25° fork rake, trail went up to 107 mm (4.2 inches), and with a new 851-style swing-arm, wheelbase grew to 1,490 mm (58.7 inches). Claimed dry weight was 215 kg (474 lb), but the bike actually weighed around 230 kg (507 lb) wet, still a few pounds less than its predecessor. The brakes were also an upgrade from the 906, with the same 300 mm steel discs and four-piston Brembo P4.32d calipers that had been fitted to the 1989 900SS.

The fairing was slightly revised from the earlier Pasos, with a NACA duct incorporated on the solid windscreen in an effort to reduce turbulence at the rider's helmet. Ducati also wanted the 907 to appeal to a wider range of riders by having the valve adjustment intervals extended to 6,000 miles (10,000 km). This was an attempt to compete head-on with Honda's VFR750, a sport touring motorcycle with a similar concept. For the first time Ducati had a machine that could actually meet the Japanese, not only in performance terms but also in practicality. Only in terms of price did the 907IE suffer in comparison with the Honda, but then it did offer electronic fuel injection. *Cycle* magazine successfully summed up the 907 by saying that 'the 907 has an engine that responds crisply straight from the box, and has handling on par with some of the best sport bikes – yet it's still comfortable and civil, and hasn't lost any Latin character.'

Surprisingly, the 907IE failed to sell as well as expected. Offered again in 1992, with the option of metallic black paint, it finished that year, although unsold stock continued to be sold in the US in 1993. The front brake disc size went up to 320 mm along with the new type of gold Brembo P4.30-34 calipers.

The 907 had finally become the bike that the Paso should have been originally. Reliability and finish were much improved, it was a superb sports touring motorcycle, and once again Ducati buyers had demonstrated their preference for sporting motorcycles. But those looking for a 907 replacement had to wait until the release of the Sport Touring ST2 in 1997.

350/400/600/750/900 SUPERSPORT

Just as the 750F1 had existed in both 350 and 400 versions for the Italian and Japanese markets, the superseded 750 Sport was transformed into a unique Japanese market 400 Supersport Junior for the 1990 season. First displayed at the Tokyo Show in late 1989, this bike was essentially a 900 Supersport with the smaller 400 cc engine of the 400F3, but with the rear cylinder head reversed, as was the pattern now throughout the range. However, there were a number of interesting features that were peculiar to this particular model. In many ways it seemed to be a way to use up superseded spare parts, and in others to try out new ones. Thus it had the 16-inch composite Marvics that had been fitted to the 750 Montjuich, Santamonica and 1988 851 Strada, together with the same 280 mm fully floating Brembo front discs, and 260 mm rear disc. The bodywork, frame (with the 27° steering head angle) and aluminium swing-arm were 900 Supersport, but this bike did not have the troublesome Weber carburettor, which was replaced by a pair of Mikuni CVK V36 constant-velocity type, and these worked so well that Mikunis found their way into the entire range of Supersports within a year.

Like the final 400F3, the Supersport Junior had a six-speed gearbox and cable-operated wet clutch. The exhaust system, with cylindrical mufflers, was from the 1989 900SS. Weight was less, at 174 kg (384 lb), and the bikes were painted red over a white frame. Claimed power was 50 bhp at 11,000 rpm for the 398 cc engine. This unusual bike continued until 1991, by which time a new 400SS Junior had appeared, based on the new model Supersport. The older models were still being advertised in Japan as late as August 1991, alongside the new one.

In 1989 Massimo Bordi took the deliberate step of creating two distinct but complementary Ducati production lines. On one side there was the new-technology 851 series backed up with a successful racing programme in World Superbike, and on the other was the development and refinement of the F2 Pantah racing bike that had first appeared in 1981. As there was no longer any use for a racing version of the two-valve Pantah, the air-cooled line was to remain a street bike with all the racing duties going to the water-cooled eight-valve series, which was marketed to appeal to the traditional Ducati owner who wanted a less complex motorcycle than the water-cooled and electronically fuel-injected eight-valve 851.

The 1989 900SS had shown promise but was still a flawed motorcycle. The revision that occurred during 1990 was not major, but was enough to create one of Ducati's modern classics. The desmodromic 904 cc air- and oil-cooled engine remained essentially the same but for the stronger crankcases that were standardized throughout the range that year. The biggest change was in the use of Mikuni 38 mm B67 (B73 for the US) constant-velocity carburettors, matched to equal-length inlet manifolds, a first for carburetted Ducatis. While not vastly improving the power output, throttle response almost matched that of the fuel-injected 907IE. The new 900SS also saw the return of the Kokusan ignition rather than the Marelli Digiplex.

While the frame was still similar, in order to quicken the steering the rake was reduced from 27° to 25°, with

much less trail at 103 mm (4.1 inches). A new aluminium swing-arm reduced the wheelbase to 1,410 mm (55.5 inches) and was attached to a slightly longer Showa GD 022-007-OX shock absorber that raised the rear end and provided 65 mm (2.56 inches) of travel, still without any linkage. The Marzocchi M1R front forks went, and were replaced by a set of multi-adjustable 41 mm Showa GD 011 upside-down forks. The 17-inch Brembo wheels were same as the previous year, but larger 320 mm front disc brakes were now fitted, together with the 245 mm rear disc. In a further concession towards ease of maintenance, the newly styled steel fuel tank flipped up to allow access to the battery and air-cleaner. The oil-cooler was no longer mounted in the fairing, but on a bracket cast into the front cylinder head exhaust valve rocker cover; this was a very vulnerable position, right behind the front wheel. While the new aluminium swing-arm did not resolve all the previous cracking problems, the chain adjustment bolt also proved to be a weak point on the new model and was modified the following year.

The riding position was also completely revised, with higher clip-on handlebars and lower footpegs. A newly styled petrol tank, fairing and seat completed the redesign, which was first exhibited at the Cologne Show in September 1990. Two versions were offered, one with a half fairing clearly showing the engine and exposed oil-cooler, and one with full fairing. While the 900SS still had basically a traditional air-cooled engine, this engine was not the aesthetic delight that the earlier engines had been. However, it was a Ducati that carried on the tradition of the earlier 900SS by generating impressive performance through low weight and high torque. It lacked the high horsepower and technological complexity of even the 851, let alone Japanese four-cylinder motorcycles, but on the road it almost matched them and was easier to ride.

From 1991, power was now stated as at the rear wheel, rather than the crankshaft, so the claimed power for the 900SS was 73 bhp at 7,000 rpm. The claimed weight for the half-faired version was 180 kg (397 lb), but the on-the-road weight was about 200 kg (440 lb). The fully faired version weighed slightly more, at 183 kg (403 lb). Performance was similar to the 1989 900SS. In January 1991 *Motociclismo* put their test bike through the speed trap at 219.0 km/h (136 mph), and *Cycle*, in September 1991, managed a standing quarter mile time of 11.64 seconds at 114.72 mph (184.6 km/h), faster than a 907IE and not too far short of the 851. *Cycle* summed up the 900SS with the comment, '... this is the superlative sport bike that the Ducati faithful knew was at the heart of the original Pantah, the TT2, and the F1'. So good was the 1991 900SS that it continued as the mainstay of the Ducati range, virtually unchanged, until the end of 1997.

For 1992 only minor graphics changes, a passenger rear seat cowling, black-painted wheels, revised footrests brackets, and gold Brembo P4.30-34 front brake calipers (though these were fitted to 1991 bikes from No 1601) differentiated the two models. For the US, a black option with white wheels was available. There were even fewer changes for 1993. The frame was now bronze, and there was a new set of graphics, with a gold rather than black-bordered Ducati logo, and 'Desmodue' being termed for the Supersport line. In 1994 the wheels also became bronze, the fork was an uprated Showa, also fitted to the Superlight, and the clutch and brake reservoirs were remotely mounted. A larger-diameter front axle stiffened up the front end, and the foot controls and supports were now black. These changes lifted the claimed dry weight to 186 kg (410 lb). The 1995 model had an oil temperature gauge added to the instrument panel, the rear brake caliper was underslung, and there was a new windshield. These minimal differences from year to year show that the basic motorcycle was right when it was released in

1991. During 1995 7,195 Supersports were manufactured, down slightly on the 7,597 of 1994, and considerably less than the peak year of 1992, when 8,545 Supersports were built.

In November 1990 at the Bologna Show, two months after the new 900SS was displayed at Cologne, a smaller 750SS was shown, to be released during 1991. Using the five-speed 750 engine of the 750 Sport, it also featured a hydraulically operated dry clutch with the actuating system of the earlier 750, rather than the 900 type that operated from the left-side crankcase. While still using the Mikuni carburettor, they were the slightly different 38-B70 type. The 750SS used what Massimo Bordi termed the 'small crankcase', or the Pantah crankcase. This was used for all engines of 750 cc and less, and thus could not accommodate the six-speed gearbox of the newer 'big crankcase' family unless it was for the 350 cc or 400 cc versions that used narrower gears. The 750SS did not have the external oil-cooler of the 900, and had completely different valve timing. These new desmodromic camshafts would be standardized throughout the entire small crankcase family, including the 350, 400 and 600 Super Sport, as well as the later 600 Monster. The inlet valve opened at 31° before top dead centre, and closed 88° after bottom dead centre, while the exhaust valve opened at 72° before bottom dead centre and closed at 46° after top dead centre. Valve overlap, at 77°, was more like the Ducatis of the past, and the valve lift for the 41 mm and 35 mm valves much less than the 900, at 9.35 mm and 8.50 mm. Claimed power was 60 bhp at 8,500 rpm (at the rear wheel).

The 1991 750SS was only fitted with a single front 320 mm disc brake, and was the first Ducati to use the new gold Brembo P4 30/34 caliper. Following the practice of the racing Brembos, the new caliper used four pistons, but with the leading piston being of a smaller (30 mm) diameter than the trailing one (34 mm). The 750SS also used a smaller Brembo rear wheel, at 4.50 x 17. The front forks were still 41 mm upside-down Showas, but the non-adjustable GD 031 type. Weight was down to 173 kg (381 lb) and, like the 900, the 750 was offered with a choice of full or half fairings. With the full fairing, weight went up to 176 kg (388 lb), while the on-the-road weight (half-faired) was still a very light 417 lb (189 kg) as tested by *Motorcyclist* in April 1992, making the 750SS easily the lightest 750 cc bike on the market. A month earlier, in March 1992, *Cycle World* had put their test 750SS

Joining the 900 Supersport was
the similar 750 Supersport. This
1992 version has a half fairing.
Two Wheels

through the standing quarter mile at 12.10 seconds and 108.17 mph (174 km/h), noticeably faster than both the 750 Sport and earlier 750F1 that shared a similar engine. In the US the half-faired 750SS was sold as an entry level Ducati for a bargain $7,350 in 1992, but was less attractively priced in other markets. Top speed was, however, down on the 900SS, with *Moto Sprint* managing 208 km/h (129 mph).

The next year saw the 750SS receive the oil-cooler of the 900SS, together with the black-painted wheels; as with the 900SS, there was also the option of metallic black and white wheels. The engine was unchanged but for the clutch, which now became a hydraulically operated wet type, a modification that would find its way to all the small crankcase models. 1993 saw that year's revised colours and graphics of the 900SS, and for 1994 the 750SS received double 320 mm front discs, a steel swing-arm instead of the 900SS's aluminium type, along with the bronze wheels and larger-diameter front axle. The 750SS continued largely unchanged for 1995, but for the replacement of the Showa GD 031 forks by a new type of upside-down

Marzocchi. There was no 750SS for the US market after 1994, and a hybrid model was marketed; called the 900CR, it was essentially a 900SS engine mounted in the more basic running gear of the 750SS.

Alongside the 750SS in 1991 there was a new model 400 Supersport Junior, replacing the unusual 1990 Japanese market version. There was also a 350 Sport for the Italian market. These bikes used identical running gear to the 750, and also came with the option of half or full fairing. The 66 x 51 mm 350 had 10.7:1 compression and produced 36 bhp at 10,500 rpm, while the 70.5 x 51 mm 400 with 10:1 compression made 46 bhp, also at 10,500 rpm. Both engines still used the large 38 mm Mikuni carburettors of the larger bikes, but they produced flat spots under full throttle, not unlike the Weber-carburetted models. The exhaust system was a two-into-one, exiting on the right side, and, unlike the previous 400SS, the wet clutch was now hydraulically operated. The colour scheme of the SS Junior seemed to be a year behind the larger bikes, with the black-painted wheels coming in 1993, together with the bronze frame and steel swing-arm.

The 1992 900 Superlight, while not especially fast, was still a magnificent riding machine. *Rolf im Brahm*

For 1994 the 350 was discontinued and replaced by a 27 bhp version of the 400 for the German market. The various changes to the 750SS that year also appeared on the Junior, and the almost identical 600SS was added to the range, in 33 and 53 bhp versions. While building the SS Junior was undoubtedly a useful method for the factory to increase sales, the physical proportions of the bike were that of the 750SS, so it really ended up being a considerably underpowered motorcycle. *MO* magazine in Germany, testing a 1993 400 cc model in March of that year, still managed a respectable top speed of 175 km/h (108.7 mph), but the bike weighed in at 190 kg (419 lb). Coupled with the general lack of mid-range power that the small engine provided, testers were not over-enthusiastic about the Junior. Also, by this time the Japanese market was becoming less important for Ducati, being overtaken by Germany, and the sales of the 400 slowed. For 1995 the 400SS Junior was no longer offered, but reappeared in 1996 and 1997 for the Italian market.

The last 600 Ducati had been the 600SL of 1984, and the 600SS released for the 1994 season resurrected the same 80 x 58 mm, 583cc, five-speed engine. With the valve timing and Mikuni carburettors of the 350/400/750SS, the new 600 made 53 bhp at 8,250 rpm (at the rear wheel). While it seemed that the 600SS was merely an update of a ten-year-old design, it was actually a significant improvement, reflecting ten years of subsequent development of the Pantah engine. Also offered as a 33 bhp for some markets, in 53 bhp form it was a superior model to the asthmatic 350 and 400SSs from which it was derived. This was shown in the performance. *MO* magazine, in December 1994, managed 197 km/h (122.4 mph) from their 182 kg (401 lb) wet test bike. The 600SS continued virtually unchanged in 1995, but for the use of new 41 mm upside-down Marzocchi forks, the right leg no longer having the provision to mount an additional brake caliper.

900 SUPERLIGHT

Following the success of the numbered series of 851 (888) Sport Production bikes in 1990 and 1991, a numbered series of 900 Supersports was planned for 1992. To be called the 900SL, or 900 Superlight, originally 500 bikes were to be made, but this eventually became 1,317, with 300 bright yellow ones going to the USA. However, unlike the 888SPs, the

Superlight had the standard 73 bhp 900SS engine, frame and suspension. The lightweight parts on the bike took the form of carbon-fibre mudguards, vented clutch cover, and 17-inch Marvic composite wheels of the type fitted to the 750 Montjuich, Santamonica, 851 Strada of 1988, and Japanese market 400SS of 1989. Other main differences were a single seat (with minimal padding), high-rise exhausts, and fully floating 320 mm Brembo front discs. The Superlight was only offered with a full fairing, and with a claimed weight of 176 kg (388 lb) it was indeed a light bike, being significantly lighter than any comparable bike in its class.

Performance was similar to the regular 900SS. However, *Motorrad*, testing Superlight No 537 in June 1992, only managed a top speed of 204 km/h (126.7 mph). *Cycle World*, in August 1992, put their test bike No 253 through a standing quarter mile at 11.74 seconds and 113.78 mph (183.1 km/h), almost identical to their 1991-test 900SS. On the scales the Superlight failed to match the factory claim of being 7 kg less than the 900SS. *Cycle World*'s example weighed in at just 5 lb (2.3 kg) less, 409 lb (185 kg) dry, or 436 lb (198 kg) wet. Also, despite the presence of a numbered plate on the triple clamp, too many Superlights were built for them to benefit from any rarity value. They also offered few advantages over a standard 900SS except for the wheels and carbon-fibre guards.

The next year saw the release of Superlight II, but this model was unfortunately a step backwards. Repeating a scenario so often typical of Ducati, the first model was the best, with subsequent versions losing many of the special detail touches. First to go were the Marvic wheels, replaced by the regular Brembo type, now painted bronze to match the frame. There was no longer a vented clutch cover, and even the fully floating Brembo front discs were replaced by the normal steel variety. The only concession made to differentiate the Superlight II from the normal 900SS was the use of a fully floating rear brake linkage, with a carbon-fibre torque arm; breakages of this on some early models of both the Superlight II and 888SP5 saw its replacement by an alloy item. All these changes pushed the claimed weight up to 179 kg (395 lb), though *PS* weighed in their 1993 test bike at 200.5 kg (442 lb) wet, only 3 kg up on the 1992 model. Massimo Bordi admitted to me in 1993 that the Superlight of that year had been a mistake, and many details were rectified for 1994.

While cosmetically the 1994 Superlight III was very similar to the Superlight II, there were quite a few changes. First, the fully floating Brembo front discs returned and, instead of the regular clutch cover, a carbon-fibre one appeared. There was a new, stronger swing-arm, and the suspension was uprated through the use of the 41 mm higher-specification upside-down Showa forks that had appeared on the 1993 888SP5. The brake and clutch fluid reservoirs were remotely mounted, and the colours were now red or yellow. Weight was up yet again, to 182 kg (401 lb) dry, but the Superlight III was a more attractive proposition than the II had been. The Superlight IV of 1995 was almost identical, but for the addition of an oil temperature gauge and the new windshield, both shared with the 900SS. Each year production was reduced, and only 578 Superlights were produced in 1995.

The Superlight was no longer offered for the US market in 1994. In its place was the 900SS Sport Production, a Superlight III with a dual seat and low exhaust pipes. These 175 bikes also came with a serialised plate, and they were again offered in 1995. The lack of any passenger accommodation was one of the limitations of the Superlight, and in many markets they had to be discounted. While the sporting purist preferred the single seat, most buyers required a pillion, and for that reason the regular 900SS consistently outsold its more expensive and glamorous partner. If the Superlight had been a genuine limited edition bike, like the 888 Sport Production series, offering improved engine performance with better-quality suspension, it might have been more successful. As it was, for most buyers there were few benefits over a standard Supersport to justify the additional cost.

M600/900 MONSTER

By the end of 1992, with the end of the 907IE, the entire Ducati range was one of sporting motorcycles. These were the successful lines of the Supersport Desmodue, and Desmoquattro, so there was some surprise when a completely different Ducati was released at the Cologne Show in October 1992. Called the M900, and nicknamed *Il Mostro* ('the Monster'), it was the brainchild of Miguel Galluzzi, and was neither a sporting nor touring motorcycle. Neither was it a cruiser like the unsuccessful Indiana, but underneath its minimalist styling lay a truly competent sporting motorcycle in the best Ducati tradition. The Monster was probably the first successor to the original 750GT, a light motorcycle with a race-bred frame, torquey engine, and an upright riding position. It was also released at exactly the right time, and was immediately successful, though production was delayed until mid-1993 because of component supply problems. The Monster became a fashion statement, even being bought by such notables as Barry Sheene and Damon Hill.

The Monster seemed to be a 'parts bin special'. The engine was the identical 73 bhp air/oil-cooled unit of the 900SS, but the oil cooler was now mounted above the front cylinder. The frame was a modified 851/888 with 24° of fork rake and 104 mm (4 inches) of trail, and the same rear suspension linkage (without ride height adjustment). As this was the same frame that had been used to win three consecutive World Superbike Championships, it was obviously understressed by the 900SS motor. The non-adjustable 41 mm inverted Showa forks of the 750SS and a Boge rear unit were fitted, but the front brakes were the same dual 320 mm Brembos of the 900SS, as were the 17-inch Brembo wheels. The M900 was a curious mixture. There was no tachometer on the basic instrument panel, but parts of the bodywork (like the side panels) were carbon-fibre. The low weight of 184 kg (406 lb), and the low seat height of 770 mm (30.3 inches), contributed to a compact and manoeuvrable package. The US magazine *Motorcyclist*, testing a Monster in October 1993, put their example through a standing quarter mile in 11.78 seconds, at 112.0 mph (180 km/h). Their measured top speed, despite the poor aerodynamics, was 128 mph (206 km/h). This was with the same (15/37) final drive gearing as the 900SS, but there was also the option of a 39-tooth rear wheel sprocket. Even fully wet, the Monster only weighed 199 kg (439 lb), and certainly performed much more strongly than the old 750GT or any of its derivatives such as the 860GT, GTS or 900SD Darmah. Despite limited ground clearance due to the low mufflers, it also handled considerably more adeptly on its shorter, 1,430 mm (56.3-inch) wheelbase.

The M900 continued unchanged through 1994 except for the addition of black as well as red paintwork. For 1995 it mirrored the rest of the range by gaining the bronze frame and wheels, together with grey timing belt covers and rear sprocket cover. The mufflers now featured a chamfer to increase ground clearance.

During 1995 a small number (30) of special M900s, called the 'Club Italia', were manufactured for members of this exclusive club at the instigation of the

Launched in 1993, the iconic 900M Monster has become Ducati's most successful motorcycle.

Castiglioni brothers. Members included Piero Ferrari, Michele Alboreto and Clay Regazzoni. Not for sale, they were fitted with many higher-specification components such as an Öhlins rear shock absorber, fully floating iron Brembo discs, a leather seat, and fully adjustable Showa forks.

So successful was the Monster concept that in 1994 a 600 version, in red or yellow, was released. Using the same motor as the 600SS, but with the 900M two-into-two exhaust system, and the same single 320 mm disc front brake, the 600M was also made in 33 bhp as well as 53 bhp versions. Dry weight was 174 kg (384 lb), and the 600M tested by *Motociclismo* in September 1994 managed a top speed of 176.0 km/h (109.4 mph). With a standing 400-metre time of 13.592 seconds, at 156.36 km/h (97 mph), the 600M performed very similarly to the 750GT of more than 20 years earlier. In 1995 the 600M received the minor changes of the 900M, and at the 1995 Milan Show the only new Ducati model displayed was the 750 Monster, identical to the 600 but for the larger engine and an oil-cooler.

The Monster soon established itself as a particularly important model in the Ducati line-up, and with demand for naked motorcycles increasing it continues to be so.

Marco Lucchinelli on his way to
victory on the 851 prototype in
the Daytona Battle of the Twins
race of 1987.

13 THE 851

FOUR VALVES AND WATER COOLING

At Daytona in March 1987 the Desmoquattro Ducati 851 created a sensation by matching the speed of the four-cylinder Japanese bikes. It would have qualified sixth in the field for the Daytona 200, had it been eligible for the Superbike class, and recorded a trap speed of 165.44 mph (266 km/h). A few months earlier the 748 cc prototype, at its debut outing at the Bol d'Or 24-Hour endurance race, had also impressed with its speed, if not its reliability. For the first time a 750 cc twin had the speed to match a 750 cc four. The Desmoquattro and its descendants rewrote the rules for two-cylinder motorcycles, dominating the World Superbike Championship with 241 race wins and 13 manufacturers' titles, from 1988 until the end of 2005.

Following the positive reception for the Paso after the Milan Show of 1985, the Castiglionis were enthusiastic to develop a more modern, new four-valve engine, and Ing. Massimo Bordi was given the task of developing it. Bordi was an excellent choice, having completed his degree in mechanical engineering with a thesis on a four-valve cylinder head with desmodromically actuated valves. Over a period of six months many designs were investigated, including regular valve spring, four-valve heads, heads with five and even six valves, and desmodromic four-valve heads. The British firm Cosworth was consulted regarding the design of a four-valve cylinder head, but they wanted nothing to do with desmodromics. A partnership of Mike Costin and Keith Duckworth, Cosworth had created one of the most successful Formula 1 car engines ever in the Ford DFV V8. However, their brief flirtation with desmodromics had not been successful. As the Castiglionis wanted the new engine to be desmodromic, Bordi therefore had to do much of the development himself.

As with Taglioni's first design, the Gran Sport, the new engine was not to be compromised by the limitations of production engineering, and from the outset was designed for maximum performance. Water-cooling enabled full advantage to be taken of four-valve heads with a narrower included valve angle. Previous experimentation with four-valve heads on the air-cooled 500 twin in 1971–73 had yielded little benefit because it was impossible to get a sufficiently shallow combustion chamber. This new cylinder head was closely modelled on the Cosworth FVA Formula 2 car

Below: The Desmoquattro development team during 1987. Massimo Bordi is second from the left and the current technical director Gianluigi Mengoli is behind the bike. Long-term Ducati tester Franco Farnè is on the right. *Ducati Motor*

engine with an included valve angle of 40°, and was effectively a full race system to start with. While an even narrower valve angle may have been desirable in terms of thermal efficiency (more recent Cosworth designs such as the DVF and DFY had included valve angles of 38° and 22°), this was not possible with the mechanical layout of the head. The benefits of the desmodromic layout would have been diminished through compromising the working angle of the rockers on the valve stems. As it was, the inlet ports were very straight, and the compression ratio could still be kept at a high 11:1. The desmodromic layout used two belt-driven overhead camshafts per cylinder. These four-lobed camshafts slipped through tunnels in the heads, supported by ball bearings on the right side, and bushings on the left. Two lobes opened the inlet valves through straight rockers, while the other two closed the valves with 'L'-shaped rockers.

Six months of thought and discussion were followed by only a week of drawing, and in April 1986 blueprints appeared in order for new engine parts to be manufactured. Using modified Pantah crankcases, but

with more widely spaced cylinder studs, the prototype engine shared the dimensions of the 750F1 at 88 x 61.5 mm, giving 748 cc. This enabled it to be run in the World Endurance Championship, but with the air-cooled Pantah being raced concurrently in 851 cc form, it was obvious that development of the new engine would include a larger capacity. The prototype had 34 mm and 30 mm valves, and besides the water-cooling was the first Ducati to use open-loop computerized electronic fuel injection. Derived from experience in Ferrari Formula 1 racing cars, the Weber-Marelli IAW fuel injection system used sensors to monitor coolant temperature, engine revs, throttle position, air temperature and barometric pressure. These sensors were common components used on a range of Lancia and Fiat cars, and were sometimes of dubious quality. The computer memory contained a number of maps and, depending on the information from the sensors, plotted the timing of the two injectors together with the ignition advance. These EPROMs (erasable programmable read-only memory) were loaded into the computer with fixed instructions

Below: The first 748 was not
beautiful but its speed was
impressive. *Ducati Motor*

regarding specific fuel and ignition requirements derived from actual dyno tests. Known as an 'alpha/N' system, the computer responded to information from 'alpha' (throttle position), and 'N' (number of rpm). Ignition signals originated with a magnetic reluctor in the left engine case, triggering four tabs spaced at 90° on an alternator flywheel splined to the crankshaft. A second reluctor read a pulse from the camshaft drive pinion, allowing the computer to distinguish which piston was at top dead centre. The fuel was supplied by an electric pump at a pressure of 43.5psi (3 bar) to two injectors inside 50 mm intakes narrowing to 46 mm at the cylinder inlet. Originally designed for cars with multi-point injection, the same basic system with a 'P8' central processor unit was used until the final 996 SPS of 2000.

The adoption of water-cooled cylinders and heads required a water pump to be fitted on the left side of the engine, driven off the left end of the camshaft belt drive shaft running between the cylinders. There was also a radiator, and part of the frame was used as a coolant pipe. Water from the pump surrounded the

cylinders first, cooling the cylinder heads. At 10,000 rpm the pump circulated coolant at a modest 26 litres per minute.

By 13 September 1986, five months after the initial drawings appeared, an engine had been tested and installed in a modified 750F1 frame. Amazingly, five days later, on 18 September, the bike was racing at the Paul Ricard circuit in the South of France at the Bol d'Or 24-Hour endurance race. Ridden by Marco Lucchinelli, Juan Garriga and Virginio Ferrari, after 15 hours the new 748 was in seventh place before retiring with a broken con-rod. Still, it had been an impressive debut, especially as at 170 kg (375 lb) it was considerably overweight.

The next meeting for the new motorcycle was at the Daytona Battle of the Twins race in March 1987. Now in 851 cc form, it produced a claimed 120 bhp at 11,500 rpm at the rear wheel, and Marco Lucchinelli won easily. The larger engine used 92 mm three-ring pistons with a 64 mm stroke. The titanium Carillo-style con-rods were made by the Austrian firm of Pankl, and were the same 124 mm eye-to-eye length as the 750,

The prototype street version of the 851 of 1987 was almost a racer with lights. *Ducati Motor*

giving a still respectable rod-to-stroke ratio of 1.93:1. The prototype of 1986 had 40 mm con-rod big-end bearings, but these were increased to 42 mm for the larger engine. Now with a six-speed gearbox fitted into larger crankcases, 1987 was a time of constant development. Initially valve timing mirrored the long duration and wide overlap that had been Ducati's trademark over the years with their two-valve engines. The Daytona 851 cc bike used camshafts with the inlet valve opening 69° before top dead centre and closing 97° after bottom dead centre, and the exhaust valve opening 100° before bottom dead centre and closing 64° after top dead centre. With 346° of inlet valve duration and 133° of valve overlap, they were not yet of the shorter-duration, high-valve-lift type that was generally used in four-valve engines. The valve lift was 10 mm on the inlet, and 9 mm on the exhaust, for an inlet valve lift of 0.32 times the valve-head diameter. Other racing four-valve engines were using camshafts with lifts of up to 0.45 times the valve-head diameter. The valve sizes were down to 32 mm and 28 mm on the 851 prototype.

The chassis was based on the 750TT1-style multi-tube steel space frame with a braced aluminium swing-arm and a similar full-floater-type rising rate rear suspension. Like the Pantah, the swing-arm pivoted on the rear of the crankcases. While the engine was technologically advanced, the use of the steel frame was a link with the past, as were some of the dimensions. The steering head angle of 27½° was similar to past Ducatis, but in other respects the 851 was state of the art. The Marvic wheels were 3.50 x 17 and 5.50 x 17, and the front brakes dual 320 mm Brembos with four-piston calipers. The rear brake was a tiny 230 mm item. Front forks were Marzocchi 41.7 mm M1R and the rear shock absorber the same GSG Roma type that was being used on the final version of the TT1 air-cooled racer, also being raced in 1987. Wheelbase was a moderate 1,430 mm (56 inches), but the main problem with the bike was its weight. At around 150 kg (330 lb), the 851 cc racer was a long way from the minimum 140 kg (309 lb) allowed by European Superbike regulations.

This early 851 still had room for development. The engine looked messy with pipes everywhere and the computer just strapped on the right-hand side. Twenty-five replica racers were promised by mid-1987, and a prototype street version displayed by June, but it would be well into 1988 before these became a reality. That was also to be the first year of the World Superbike Championship, and Ducati needed to build 200 bikes in order for the 851 to be homologated for that series. It could race because the regulations allowed for 1,000 cc two-cylinder bikes to compete against 750 cc fours.

1988

The factory racing 851 had a dream debut when Marco Lucchinelli won the opening round of the new World Superbike Championship at Donington, England, on 3 April. However, he only managed to win one more race that year, the first leg at Zeltweg, Austria, in July. The bike was plagued with a series of crankcase and electrical problems and in order to prepare for the 1989 season Ducati decided not to contest the final two rounds in Australia and New Zealand. In retrospect this was a mistake, because series leader Davide Tardozzi and his Bimota suffered a loss of form, allowing Fred Merkel to win the title. If Ducati had raced, Lucchinelli could well have won the inaugural series, but he ended up fifth.

Throughout 1988 the racing 851 was constantly developed. Initially 851 cc, soon it had grown to 888 cc

by a 2 mm overbore to 94 mm. There were claims from competitors that the engine was even bigger, so fast was it for a twin. With the slightly larger valve sizes of 33 mm and 29 mm, along with a revised EPROM chip and airbox, the power was up to 125 bhp at 11,000 rpm at the rear wheel. The original Marzocchi M1R forks were replaced by a new Marzocchi upside-down type, and the swing-arm more heavily braced by the end of the season. The engine was tidied cosmetically with neater coolant plumbing, and the computer was now mounted behind the seat. It was still a heavy bike, though, at 148 kg (326 lb) dry, or 162 kg (357 lb) wet.

Three versions were offered to prospective customers, comprising 20 Lucchinelli Replicas, 200 851 Superbikes, and 300 851 Stradas. The Stradas were the *tricolore* models, and they were largely hand-built because full-scale production had not yet been implemented. The all-red Lucchinelli Replica was 888 cc, just like the factory racer, and with its 11.2:1 compression claimed power (at the crankshaft) of 130 bhp at 10,500 rpm. The frame, with 27½° rake and 105 mm (4.1 inches) of trail, 17-inch Marvic wheels, and Marzocchi 41.7 mm M1R forks and rear Supermono shocks, was the same as the 851 Superbike.

Below: The 1988 851 Strada, or
'Tricolore', in company with a
1989 851 Strada.

The front brake discs were in between the factory racer and the Superbike at 300 mm, with street-type Brembo four-piston calipers. These 888s were the first in an annual series of factory replicas sold to selected customers to race in Superbike events, but initially most privateer bikes failed to achieve significant results. The bikes were too slow and heavy as they came from the factory, and the new technology of the Weber-Marelli fuel injection limited the ease of tuning until alternative EPROM chips became available from non-factory sources.

Most of those who wanted to race an 851 had no access to the Lucchinelli Replica, but could purchase an 851 Superbike. Purely a homologation special, these were an unusual mixture of street and racing bike. In red, white and green, with a silver frame, they came with Michelin 12/60V17 and 18/67V17 racing slicks mounted on magnesium 3.50 x 17 and 5.50 x 17 Marvic wheels, electric starter, a side stand, and head and tail-lights. The engine was 851 cc (92 x 64 mm) with the 32 mm and 28 mm valves of the 1987 prototype racer. Valve timing, however, was different, with the inlet opening at 44° before top dead centre, closing 73° after bottom dead centre, and the exhaust

opening 77° before bottom dead centre and closing 42° after top dead centre. These camshafts still opened the nimonic valves 10 mm and 9 mm. With a modest 10.6:1 compression ratio, claimed power was 120 bhp at 10,000 rpm at the crankshaft.

The brakes were two 280 mm fully floating Brembo discs on the front, and a 260 mm on the rear, with street-type Brembo P4.32B and P2.T08N calipers. In other respects the 851 Superbike was the same as the Lucchinelli Replica, and also had the braced aluminium swing-arm. Wheelbase was up slightly to 1,460 mm (57.5 inches) and claimed weight was 165 kg (364 lb) dry, but this was very optimistic. *Cycle World*, testing an 851 Superbike in April 1988, weighed their bike at 417 lb (189 kg) dry, and 445 lb (202 kg) wet – too much for a racing bike. Still, they managed a top speed of 154 mph (249 km/h).

Alongside the 851 Superbike was the 851 Strada. Using the same frame (without the reinforced swing-arm) and similar bodywork (with Paso-style mirrors), the Strada differed in the use of the 16-inch Marvic/Akront composite wheels, and a de-tuned engine. With the same 32 mm and 28 mm valve sizes, camshaft timing used less duration and overlap, and

Below: Raymond Roche rode for
Marco Lucchinelli's team on the
factory 851 during 1989.

there was less valve lift. The inlet valve opened 11° before top dead centre, closing 70° after bottom dead centre, and the exhaust valve opened 62° before bottom dead centre, closing 18° after top dead centre. Inlet valve lift was 9.60 mm and exhaust valve lift 8.74 mm. With slightly less compression than the 851 Superbike at 10.4:1, the Strada produced a claimed 102 bhp at 9,000 rpm at the crankshaft. It also had the twin injectors per cylinder, and the same Pankl con-rods as fitted to the racing bikes. The Strada's six-speed gearbox also had more widely spaced ratios, with only first and second being the same. The hydraulically operated dry clutch did not get the vented clutch cover of the Superbike. Another difference between the two models was in the use of the Paso exhaust system and 16-inch Marvic composite wheels, as fitted to the 750 Montjuich and Santamonica. The brakes were identical to the 851 Superbike, and the claimed dry weight was 185 kg (408 lb).

The Stradas were criticized for uncertain handling due to the 16-inch wheels, and had some problems with fuel vaporization on hot days. According to *Motorrad*, in September 1988, the Strada tipped the scales wet at 215 kg (474 lb), and top speed was a disappointing 212 km/h (132 mph). Because they were very expensive, they were not a particularly successful model, and they were sold at discount prices during 1989; today the 1988 851 Strada is not particularly sought after. Their performance was not as spectacular as it was claimed to be, but it was probably the idiosyncratic handling characteristics that condemned it. However, these first available street versions of the *ottovalvole* featured many individual and hand-crafted pieces, like the rear shock absorber rocker linkage, and used high-quality components such as fully floating discs front and rear and braided steel brake lines.

1989

Marco Lucchinelli assumed the role of team manager for the World Superbike series (though he still raced at occasional rounds), with former 500 cc Grand Prix rider and 1981 World Endurance Champion Raymond Roche taking his place in the team alongside Baldassare Monti. With the 888 cc bike now having new upper outer tube Öhlins forks, Roche was immediately impressive, claiming pole position and setting fastest lap at the opening race at Donington. Electrical problems saw his retirement, however, and it was not until the fourth round, at Brainerd in the US, that Roche had a victory. Further wins at Hockenheim and Pergusa, Sicily, saw him finish third in the Championship, despite seven retirements. He still won more races than any other rider, but there was some way to go before the Ducati was reliable enough to win the Championship. Ducati also tried a larger displacement 919 cc (95.6 x 64 mm) engine towards the end of the season, and Lockheed brake calipers instead of Brembo. However, the extra capacity somehow did not translate into faster lap times, and was at the expense of reliability.

The factory bike was now making 128 bhp, and was lighter than the previous year at 158 kg (348 lb). It proved to be the fastest of all the Superbikes at the ultimate horsepower track, Hockenheim, where Roche knocked nearly four seconds off the lap record, set only the previous year. Displayed at the Cologne Show in 1988, an 888 cc Lucchinelli Replica continued to be offered, unchanged, and 30 were made in 1989. In place of the 851 Superbike with its confused identity, there appeared a new model called the 851 Sport Production, designed for the Italian Sport Production racing series for street-based motorcycles.

The 851 Sport Production used a similar engine to the 1988 851 Superbike in the revised running gear of the 1989 851 Strada. With a higher compression ratio of 11.5:1, it was still 851 cc, had larger 33 mm and 29 mm valves and used the same camshafts as the 851 Superbike. It produced 122 bhp at 10,000 rpm at the crankshaft. However, it did not have the twin injectors per cylinder, or the close-ratio gearbox of the 1988 Superbike, instead having the regular Strada ratios. Fuel was now supplied at a higher pressure of 5 bar (72.5psi), and the claimed dry weight of the SP was 180 kg (397 lb).

The SP shared its frame, wheels, brakes, suspension and bodywork with the revised 851 Strada of 1989. Thus, apart from a small badge on the top triple clamp, the 1989 SP was virtually indistinguishable from the 1989 Strada, which addressed many of the criticisms of the 1988 Strada. Production of the Strada was increased to 1,500, and these greater numbers, together with a dramatic price reduction, inevitably led to some economizing. While the engine remained largely unchanged from 1988, like the 851 Sport Production there was now only a single injector per cylinder, and the compression ratio was increased to 11:1. Power

was up slightly to 105 bhp at 9,000 rpm at the crankshaft. The crankshaft still used the Pankl connecting-rods, and the clutch actuation system changed to the left side of the engine with a rod passing through the gearbox main shaft. Suspension continued to be the Marzocchi 41.7 mm M1R forks and the Marzocchi Duo shock, most of the changes occurring to the frame, wheels and brakes.

The most important change to the frame (now painted white) was directly related to experience in World Superbike. To quicken the steering, the steering head angle was reduced by 3° to 24½°, with a corresponding reduction in trail to 95 mm (3.7 inches). The wheelbase was also reduced slightly to 1,430 mm (56.3 inches). Coupled with the use of new white-painted Brembo 17-inch wheels in the Superbike sizes of 3.50 x 17 and 5.50 x 17, the 1989 Strada was a considerably better-handling motorcycle than its predecessor, despite a rise in the claimed dry weight to 190 kg (419 lb). To improve weight distribution, and following racing practice, the battery was now mounted on a bracket alongside the front cylinder on the right-hand side of the engine.

While the front brake disc rotor size was increased to 320 mm, they changed from the fully floating iron to rotors in stainless steel. Brake calipers were unchanged and there was a smaller 245 mm rear disc. Now with totally red paintwork like Lucchinelli's factory bike, the 1989 Strada tested by *Motorrad* in June 1989 weighed the same as in 1988, at 215 kg (474 lb). Top speed was up to 228 km/h (142 mph). *Cycle* tested the 1989 Strada in September and found it to be the fastest two-cylinder bike they had ever tested, posting a standing quarter mile time of 11.61 seconds at 116.28 mph (187 km/h). They went on to say, 'The 851's handling is so good it's almost mystical'. The 1989 851, in either SP or Strada form, demonstrated what Ducati was learning on the track through their World Superbike racing programme and incorporating into the production line. The slightly quicker steering geometry along with the use of 17-inch rather than 16-inch wheels, absolutely transformed the 851. While it was still not an effortless machine to ride in the style of Japanese bikes, the 1989 851 was a rewarding bike in the best Ducati tradition, and it also offered comparable outright performance to Japanese 750s. If ever there was any truth in the notion that 'racing improves the breed', it was being reflected in the 851, and was even more so in 1990.

Below: Roche won the 1990
World Superbike Championship
on the 888 cc factory bike.

1990

Reverting to the 888 (from the larger 919), the factory bikes were sufficiently well developed for Raymond Roche to win the World Superbike Championship. With more power (130–134 bhp at 11,000 rpm) and less weight, at 147 kg (324 lb), by the end of the season it was also the improvement in reliability that clinched the Championship. Additionally, there was an improvement in tractability, with more mid-range power due to revised camshafts. Significantly, the 1990 engine made a useful 110 bhp at 8,000 rpm, which was reflected in the results, with Roche winning eight and team mate Giancarlo Falappa one, before he crashed heavily during qualifying at the Österreichring. They still suffered crankcase failures, but most of the electrical problems had been eliminated. It had been found that a faulty rpm sensor had been the cause of most of the electronic failures.

Visually, the 1990 bike was little changed from the previous year. It still used Öhlins suspension, with a revised rear linkage, and by the end of the year had more upswept exhausts with carbon-fibre mufflers. Other carbon-fibre parts appeared, such as a seat/tail section and front guard, in order to get the bike closer to the class minimum weight of 140 kg (309 lb). Starting the season at 157 kg (346 lb) with oil and water, by Monza in October the bike weighed a significant 10 kg (22 lb) less. A smaller, curved radiator raised the cooling temperature to 70–75°C because it had been found that sometimes the bikes had been running as cool as 40°C. An electronic tachometer was also used occasionally, and would appear again in 1991.

A limited number of 888 Corsa Roche Replica (formerly Lucchinelli Replica) racers were again available to selected dealer teams. These incorporated many of the developments that had occurred during 1989, setting a pattern that was to follow in subsequent years, and meant that the privateer bikes would always be one year behind the factory. The Roche Replica of 1990 had the upper outer tube Öhlins forks, Marvic magnesium wheels, and lightweight parts such as an aluminium sub-frame and magnesium

Below: The 1990 Sport
Production 2, the first of many
higher performing race replica
Desmoquattros, and a close
replica of Roche's factory racer.

primary drive cover. As with the factory bikes, the computer was housed in a bracket off the steering head. The claimed weight was 158 kg (348 lb), and the engine used larger (34 mm and 30 mm) valves, and a new inlet camshaft. Developed from the previous racing season, this opened the inlet valve at 53° before top dead centre, closing 71° after bottom dead centre. Intake valve lift was up 1 mm to 11 mm. The exhaust camshaft was the same as before, and was shared with the Sport Production series. Compression ratio was up to 12:1. The Roche Replica also used a completely different gearbox, with different ratios.

Alongside the Roche Replica of 1990, Ducati released possibly their most significant street bike since the 750SS of 1974, and certainly the most significant new street Ducati since the Cagiva take-over in 1985. Called the 851 Sport Production 2, this motorcycle was considerably removed from the 1989 Sport Production, and was the closest street bike to a factory racer available. In essence, it was a Roche Replica with lights and treaded tyres. Primarily aimed at the Japanese market, then Ducati's prime export destination and a market obsessed with race replicas, the SP2 was displayed at the Tokyo Show at the end of 1989.

Still called an 851, the SP2 was similar to the 1989 Sport Production but with an overbore to 94 mm to take the displacement up to 888 cc, as with the racing bikes. With the same 33 mm and 29 mm valves, and the same camshafts, power was up to 109 bhp (at the rear wheel). In the engine department there were still the Pankl con-rods, a polished and lightened crankshaft, polished rockers, oil cooler and vented dry clutch. Both the inlet and exhaust systems were considerably less restrictive, with no inlet air box and larger-diameter exhausts. The gearbox had the same ratios as the 1988 851 Superbike (lower third, fourth and fifth than the Strada), and there was a return to twin injectors per cylinder. However, while the frame was identical to that of 1989, this bike had the same suspension as the works racers, the Öhlins FG9050 42 mm upside-down forks and an Öhlins DU8070 rear unit. The quality of these components alone justified the price differential between the SP and the Strada, but there were many other differences besides the extra power. Like the 888 Corsa, the rear sub-frame was lightweight aluminium, there were fully floating iron 320 mm Brembo discs, and a carbon-fibre rear guard. The SP2 had moved further away from the Strada to become a true limited-edition race replica. Styling was very similar to the Strada, and apart from the suspension the most visible distinguishing marks were Agip and Michelin stickers on the fairing, and a numbered plaque on the top fork yoke. Dry weight was up from the SP1, largely due to the forks, at 188 kg (414.5 lb) from 180 kg (397 lb).

Performance of the SP2 dramatically eclipsed any previous street Ducati, even the 851 Strada. *Motociclismo*, in April 1990, managed an impressive top speed of 255 km/h (158 mph) from SP2 No 74. *Cycle* magazine also found the SP2 a strong performer, making 96.4 bhp at 9,000 rpm on their dyno in December 1990. *Motorcyclist*, testing the same SP2 No 50 in July 1991, powered through the standing quarter mile in an impressive 10.72 seconds at 128 mph (206 km/h). The SP2 was barely street legal in many countries, and the larger-capacity exhaust system with minimal muffling produced sounds reminiscent of the older Super Sports with their Contis, or the 750 Montjuich with its Verlicchi competition system. The racing-specification Öhlins forks transformed the handling of the 851 Strada, and the SP2 was one of the most confidence-inspiring motorcycles to ride at high speeds. *Cycle* thought it a fantastic motorcycle, claiming it to be 'perhaps the best production race bike money can buy'. To put the SP2 into perspective, they hailed it as 'one of the most desirable sporting motorcycles since the original Ducati 750SS', a statement with which I whole-heartedly agree.

In rather typical Ducati fashion, the Strada was softened slightly for 1990 with the addition of a dual seat. As the Strada and Sport Production 851 lines developed they diverged, and the performance gap between them increased. By 1990 the relationship was similar to that which existed in 1974 between the 750 Sport and 750SS, and also in 1986 between the 750F1 and 750 Montjuich. The higher-performance versions were made in more limited numbers (about 500 SP2s), and sold at a price almost 50% higher. However, in the case of the 851 series the performance difference was far more considerable between the SP and the Strada, as there was a genuine 20% power difference, and the SP had better-quality suspension, less weight, and improved weight distribution.

The 1990 Strada continued essentially unchanged in the engine department, but the Pankl con-rods were replaced by the standard Pantah style. The addition of the dual seat with a stronger sub-frame increased the

weight to 506 lb (230 kg) as tested by *Cycle World* in June 1990. Performance, however, had not suffered, and their test bike posted a standing quarter mile time of 11.26 seconds at 121.29 mph (195 km/h), with a measured top speed of 150 mph (241 km/h).

1991

An indication of the outcome of the 1991 World Superbike Championship was demonstrated at an international Superbike race in Mexico in December 1990. Doug Polen and Raymond Roche were on factory 888s, and Polen won both legs. Recently having left the Yoshimura Suzuki team, Polen had only tested the Fast by Ferracci Ducati at Daytona a week before the Mexico race.

For 1991 there would still be the two factory bikes, for Raymond Roche and Giancarlo Falappa, but also support for Polen and Stéphane Mertens. Polen was racing for Eraldo Ferracci, an Italian who had spent 25 years building racing bikes in the US, and who had enjoyed moderate success with Ducati 888s in 1990 in the AMA series with rider Jamie James. In comparison to the factory effort, Ferracci operated on a much smaller budget, and Polen was contracted to Dunlop rather than Michelin tyres. He also teamed up with the legendary veteran Ducati tuners, Giorgio Nepoti and Rino Caracchi of NCR.

Both the factory and two supported riders had bikes close to the class minimum of 140 kg (309 lb). Through the considerable use of carbon-fibre for radiator, exhaust and fairing brackets, as well as the airbox and air ducts, rear-brake torque-arm and fuel tank, the works machines weighed 143 kg (315 lb). Other modifications such as a smaller rear disc (190 mm in carbon or steel from 216 mm in steel), smaller calipers, titanium exhausts and Termignoni carbon-fibre mufflers, also contributed to the weight reduction. An important by-product was the improvement in weight distribution, with more front weight bias. In January 1992 the Japanese magazine *Bikers Station* put the Fast by Ferracci 888 on the scales: total weight was 146.5 kg (323 lb), and weight distribution was 51/49% front to rear.

By getting close to the allowable minimum weight, Ducati were now making the most of the regulations that gave two-cylinder motorcycles a 25 kg (55 lb) advantage over their four-cylinder opposition. These regulations came in for increasing criticism from the

Below: Doug Polen
demonstrating the style that took
him to two World Superbike
Championships.

Right: The 1991 SP3 was similar
to the SP2 but for a carbon-fibre
front guard and upswept
exhausts. This is the author's
example.

Japanese teams, but the credit still had to be given to Ducati for designing and developing a twin-cylinder motorcycle capable of competing with 750 cc four-cylinder bikes. When the regulations were drafted in 1987, it had appeared inconceivable that a twin could become as dominant as the Ducati did during the 1991 season. So good had the 888 racer become that Ducati won 23 World Superbike races, and they were only beaten once. Doug Polen himself was so dominant on the Fast by Ferracci Ducati that he won 17 races. He even held the outright lap record for a while at Jarama, Spain, during 1991. To emphasize the superiority of the Ducati 888, Davide Tardozzi on his Team Grottini bike won the European Superbike Championship, with four wins from six starts.

The Fast by Ferracci bike used the 888 cc engine with 36 mm and 31 mm valves, and with 11.8:1 compression produced 133 bhp at 11,500 rpm. The camshafts used by Ferracci had more lift, but less duration than even the SP, with the inlet opening 48° before top dead centre, closing 68° after bottom dead centre, and the exhaust valve opening 68° before bottom dead centre and closing 40° after top dead centre. A new crossover exhaust system contributed to the extra 3 bhp, and more upswept exhausts, homologated on the SP3, together with some changes to the front fairing, improved aerodynamics. Roche's

bike sometimes featured different specifications, but all the racing engines now used modified crankcases that solved the crankcase cracking problem of 1990. There was now more extensive webbing and ribbing around the base of the cylinder. Engine problems early in the season were solved by drilling an oilway up the Pankl con-rod to the gudgeon pin. Whereas the FBF bike still used the Öhlins upside-down forks as fitted the previous year and to the 1991 Corsa and SP, Roche had a new type of Öhlins fork. Braking was usually by a combination 320 mm steel and carbon disc with Brembo calipers, and wheels a Marchesini 3.50 x 17 front, and 6.25 x 17 rear. With slightly less steering head angle, at 23.5°, the wheelbase was shortened slightly to 1,420 mm (55.9 inches).

The 50 Corsas made in 1991 included many of the modifications of the factory bikes. Using a carbon-fibre seat-tail unit together with a carbon-fibre petrol tank, the weight was down to 155 kg (342 lb). The computer was now housed in a carbon-fibre bracket incorporating the air intake and supporting the electronic tachometer. The engine was largely unchanged from 1990 (but for the stronger crankcases), and the claimed power (at the rear wheel) was 128 bhp. Wheel sizes were up to 3.75 x 17 front, and 6.00 x 17 rear. The frame, brakes and suspension were identical to 1990.

The SP3 was slightly restyled for 1991. Even though it was still called an 851, the 888 cc SP3 now had upswept mufflers, carbon-fibre front mudguard and black wheels, a revised air intake system and, like the SP2, was also made in small numbers (about 500), with a numbered plaque on the top triple clamp celebrating the winning of the 1990 World Superbike Championship. With the Agip and Michelin stickers and the white racing plate on the rear seat, it was the closest replica yet and really looked like a street version of the 1991 factory racers. The claimed power of the SP3 was slightly up on the SP2, now 128 bhp at 10,500 rpm at the crankshaft, or 111 bhp at the rear wheel. All 1991 models received the stronger crankcases, and the SP3 a specially machined and polished crankshaft. While most of the engine and gearbox specifications were unchanged, one area where the SP3 was improved over the SP2 was the clutch, a notorious area of weakness; it now had eight driving plates, and could also be retrofitted to the rest of the 851 range. Still with the Öhlins FG9050 upside-down forks, the SP3 was fitted with a slightly different Öhlins DU0060 rear unit. Front brakes were the same fully floating 320 mm iron Brembo with four-piston calipers, but the front master cylinder diameter was increased from 15 mm to 16 mm. Other minor changes from the SP2 included a degasser in the aluminium fuel tank (reducing the

capacity to 17 litres from 20 litres), and remote location of the front brake and clutch reservoirs. Claimed dry weight was still 188 kg (414.5 lb) and essentially the two models were identical.

As expected, the performance of the SP3 was similar to that of the SP2. *Moto Sprint* achieved a top speed of 261.1 km/h (162.2 mph) with a 0–400-metre time of 10.78 seconds at 207.664 km/h (129 mph). *Motociclismo* managed 106.82 bhp at 10,250 rpm, at the rear wheel, so just like the SP2, the SP3 was a powerful motorcycle. Wet weight for the SP3, as measured by *Moto Sprint*, was 202.1 kg (445 lb). Being fortunate enough to have some experience of riding an SP3, I can confirm that these motorcycles were superb sporting bikes. Despite being a modern, computerized device, there was still a lot of the rawness of previous race replica Ducatis in the SP3.

The 851 Strada for 1991 gained Showa GD011 upside-down front forks, but also the Öhlins DU0060 rear unit of the SP3. Engine specifications remained unchanged but for a slightly lower compression ratio of 10.5:1, with the claimed power being 91 bhp at 9,000 rpm at the rear wheel. Dry weight went up to 199 kg (439 lb). Visually it was little changed from the dual-seat 1990 bike, and was still red with white wheels. The front brake and clutch reservoir were now remotely located, as with the SP3, and the diameter of the front brake master cylinder was also increased to 16 mm. The eccentric adjustment for the ride height was also deleted from the Strada, though it remained on the SP. The machined rear suspension rocker arm was also replaced by a forged item. As tested by *Cycle* in September 1991, the 851 covered the standing quarter mile in 11.23 seconds at 120.80 mph (194.4 km/h). *Motorcyclist*, in November 1991, weighed the 851 Strada at 220 kg (485 lb) wet, and managed a top speed of 149 mph (240 km/h).

1992

Although Ing. Bordi had talked during 1991 of a new bike with a longer-stroked engine in a Massimo Tamburini-designed frame with a single-sided swing-arm, the 888 had proved so competitive that it continued virtually unchanged from the previous year. Whereas the street 851 and 888SP4 had a revised frame, footpeg brackets and styling, the factory racers and 888 Corsa still used the 1991 frame and bodywork.

Doug Polen was now riding for the official Ducati team, alongside Giancarlo Falappa. With sponsorship from Italian sunglasses manufacturer Police, the team was managed by another former Italian World Champion, Franco Uncini; he replaced Marco Luchinelli, who had been arrested and imprisoned for drug offences during 1991. Unfortunately, due to the bad publicity, this resulted in considerable lost sponsorship. Uncini had a long association with Ducati, having raced a 750SS during 1975 and 1976 for Bruno Spaggiari's team in the Italian Championship. Raymond Roche now found himself a privateer, electing not to become part of the Police team, but still with a factory bike, and tuned by ace tuner Rolando Simonetti. More often than not, Roche's bike was the fastest of all the Ducatis and allowed him to come from the back to win the race after one of his traditional poor starts. Other factory machines were supplied to Stéphane Mertens, Davide Tardozzi and Daniel Amatriain.

There were very few changes to the all-conquering 1991 888. With yet another new clutch and a new exhaust camshaft design, the power was up slightly to 135 bhp at 11,800 rpm. The new exhaust camshaft allowed safe revs to 12,000 rpm, and different valve sizes of 35 mm and 30 mm were tried, along with variable-length inlet tracts on Roche's bike. The biggest changes came in weight saving, not just in carbon-fibre parts, but also now within the engine. Narrower

gearbox gears (6 mm to the Corsa's 10 mm), hollow camshafts and more titanium and magnesium helped to get the weight down to 142 kg (313 lb), and the shape of the Pankl con-rods was slightly altered to eliminate some of the breakages of the past. All bikes now used the new type of 42 mm Öhlins fork that Roche had used the previous year. The type of disc rotors varied, Polen generally using US-made C-CAT carbon discs, and Roche the regular 320 mm steel Brembo type.

Due to some difficulties within the team, Doug Polen had a slow start to the season, and the Ducatis were nowhere near as dominant as they had been in 1991. Polen won nine, Roche six, and Falappa four races (out of a total of 26), but the most impressive was probably Carl Fogarty's win in the second leg at Donington on one of the production Corsas. However, Polen again won the World Championship, with Raymond Roche second, but it was obvious now that the 888 was nearing the end of its competitive life.

The weight-saving programme of the factory racers passed down to the 888 Superbike Racing (Corsa) for 1992. Still using the 1991 frame and bodywork, but with more carbon-fibre, the weight was reduced to 150 kg (330 lb). The engine now had magnesium primary drive, ignition, and camshaft covers, and, while power was still quoted at 128 bhp at 11,000 rpm, the Superbike Racer received the revised exhaust camshaft, still with 9 mm of valve lift, but with the valve opening at 71° before bottom dead centre, and closing 45° after top dead centre.

The suspension was the new type of 41 mm Öhlins forks with magnesium triple clamps, as used on the factory bikes, together with an Öhlins shock absorber as before. The 320 mm front brakes were also uprated to the latest Brembo racing type with a 19 mm PS13B master cylinder and P2105N 30 and 34 mm calipers. The rear disc was now a smaller 190 mm unit (from 210 mm). All the frame dimensions remained unchanged from 1989, but for a slight increase in trail to 98 mm (3.86 inches). The limited number of 1992 Superbike Racers made (30) were much more competitive bikes than in previous years, as witnessed by Fogarty's consistently good results on his privateer Corsa. While they were no more powerful, they were much lighter, even if there was 7 kg (15.4 lb) between the Superbike Racer and the factory bikes.

In 1992 the first signs of cost effectiveness became evident, even with the SP series. While the factory racers and Corsas still used the old frame with individually welded sections around the steering head, the 851 Strada and SP4 now utilized a single bent tube. Following the 1991 900SS, they also now had a flip-up steel petrol tank instead of the aluminium one. There was also an improved cooling system with a curved radiator. The fairing, tank and seat were redesigned, as were the footrest brackets that had a tendency to break on the previous model if the bike fell over. The engine of the SP4 was identical to that of the SP3, but for 1992 an even more special model was provided, the 120 bhp SPS, or Sport Production Special. The SPS had a carbon-fibre petrol tank, seat and silencers. The racing cooling radiator was fitted, without a fan, so the weight was down to 185 kg (408 lb). The engine was virtually that of the 1991 Corsa, the power being up due again to 1 mm larger valves (34 mm and 30 mm), together with a Corsa inlet cam. There were other minor engine differences between the SPS and the SP4, these being different Pankl connecting-rod bolts, and a double-roller main bearing rather than an oblique single type. As usual there was yet another clutch modification this year, with an additional driven plate.

Visually the SP4 and SPS were very similar. Now '888s', they shared the Öhlins suspension with the SP3, but had the new type of gold series Brembo P4 30/34 front brake calipers (also shared with the 851 Strada and Supersport range). Both the SP4 and SPS also used the same series of numbered plaque on the top triple clamp. As with the SP3, these bikes were loud with their open airbox and exhausts, so for some markets (such as Germany) the SP4 came with a normal 851 airbox and clutch cover. The SP4 used the vented clutch cover of the SP2 and SP3, but the SPS had the more open Superbike Racing type.

The SPS was the strongest performing of all 888SPs, and *Moto Sprint* achieved 268.1 km/h (166.59 mph) with a 0–400-metre time of 10.39 seconds at 212.015 km/h (131.7 mph). The SP4, with the same engine as the SP3, performed very similarly to that model. Tested by *Moto Sprint* in March 1992, SP4 No 69 was slightly slower and heavier than the SP3, managing 256.76 km/h (159.5 mph) and weighing 205 kg (452 lb). The SPS really eclipsed the SP4 with its lighter weight and higher-performing engine; it was the consummate race replica Ducati, and is still a highly desirable motorcycle. However, any of the Sport Production 888s with Öhlins forks have to be considered among the best street bikes ever produced by the factory. They were produced in limited numbers with the most expensive proprietary

Doug Polen (left) carried the number 1 plate in 1992, and while now in the official factory squad, retained Eraldo Ferracci (right) as crew chief.

components, and even though they were very expensive to buy, they offered exceptional value.

The divergence of the Strada and SP lines continued further as the 851 Strada gained more weight (now 202 kg, or 445 lb) with the steel tank instead of aluminium, and lost the Öhlins rear shock absorber for a Showa GD012. The front brakes were now the same Brembo P4 30/34 calipers as the SP, but still with the 320 mm steel discs. With the new bodywork came a revised passenger seat, with flip-out grab rails. The 1992 Strada also inherited the larger SP valves (33 and 29 mm), and with 10.5:1 compression, and a redesigned cylinder head, the power was increased to 95 bhp at 9,000 rpm. It was a case of slightly increasing the power to maintain the same performance level of the earlier bikes, and to compensate for the increase in weight. The cooling system was also revised, with the curved radiator of the SP4 and the new cooling circuit.

Moto Sprint managed a top speed of 239.5 km/h (149 mph), the same as the 1991 Strada, and *Cycle World*, in August 1992, a standing quarter mile time of 11.53 seconds at 122.61 mph (197.3 km/h). These figures were on a par with the 1991 model, even though the power was measured at 90.9 bhp at 8,750 rpm, at the rear wheel. It was the increase in weight to 493 lb (223.6 kg) wet (*Cycle World*'s test) that hurt the performance.

1993

As the 888 replacement had been held over for one more year, the factory continued to race that highly developed model. Competition was now much stronger, from Kawasaki in particular, but with Honda delaying the introduction of its fuel-injected RC45 until the 1994 season, Massimo Bordi decided to do the same with the 916. The weight limit for twins was increased slightly, to 145 kg (320 lb), with the fours remaining at 165 kg (364 lb).

Following his excellent performances on a privateer bike the previous year, Carl Fogarty now took over from Doug Polen who decided to race in the US AMA Superbike series on the Fast by Ferracci-prepared bike. Thus Fogarty was teamed with Falappa, and now managed by Raymond Roche. Other factory support went to Davide Tardozzi's Team Grottini with riders Stéphane Mertens and ex-Grand Prix and endurance rider Juan Garriga. The tuner for Grottini was Pietro Gianesin, from GPM of Vicenza, who had a long association with Ducati. Later in the season Garriga was replaced by Mauro Lucchiari.

The Roche team used Rolando Simonetti as tuner, and the bikes were a little different from the previous year. Using the 1992 production frame with the bent, rather than individually welded, tubes, and carbon-fibre footrest brackets, they also had the revised fairing and seat that had appeared on the SP4 and SPS. The extra weight of these pushed the weight above the minimum, to 147 kg. The engine was overbored 2 mm, to 96 mm, to make 926 cc, and 1 mm larger valves (37 mm and 31 mm) were used. Power was not noticeably up from the 888 (142–144 bhp at 11,500 rpm), and the engine was less responsive due to the heavier, 11.9:1, pistons. It was nicknamed *il pompone* ('big pump'), and had a second crankcase breather located next to the normal one. Other detail differences included a sprag-type anti-lock clutch, a sealed airbox, and a revised computer that allowed for the separate mapping of each cylinder. They also used an electronic quick-shifter that cut the engine between gearshifts.

Despite winning 19 races out of 26, Ducati's victories were spread between Fogarty, Falappa and privateer Andreas Meklau, so they lost the title to Scott Russell on the Kawasaki. However, in the US AMA Series, Doug Polen easily won the Championship, and Edwin Weibel won the German Superbike Championship. While the 888/926 may well have been approaching the

end of its racing (and production) life, it was still a highly competent motorcycle. This was put into perspective by Carl Fogarty in 1993: at Donington during October he set a new lap record for Superbikes on his factory 926 racer at 1 min 35.22 sec, or 152.11 km/h (94.517 mph). Only two months earlier, having a one-off ride on the Cagiva 500 cc Grand Prix bike in the British Grand Prix (where he finished fourth, and very nearly third), his fastest lap had been 1 min 35.332 sec. Not bad at all for basically a seven-year-old design.

The 888 Racing for 1993 also shared the revised frame and bodywork with the factory bikes, and through the use of more carbon-fibre (such as the footrest brackets) the claimed dry weight was down to 145 kg (320 lb). While still 888 cc, larger valve sizes of 36 mm and 31 mm, together with an increase in exhaust valve lift to 10.5 mm, raised the power to 135 bhp at 11,500 rpm at the rear wheel. There was also a completely new six-speed gearbox, with closer ratios, and an improved clutch. The Marchesini wheels, Öhlins suspension and Brembo brakes were similar to before. The 1993 Corsa also had revised mapping to optimize the individual cylinders, and the one-piece, larger-capacity airbox.

While waiting one more year for the 916, the street bikes were now all 888 cc, and there was an SP5, an SPO (for the US market), and the 888 Strada. While the Strada was developed into a better motorcycle, as had so often happened in the past, the SP5 suffered from economizing. The most noticeable loss was the replacement of the expensive racing Öhlins front forks with Showa 41 mm GD061, but the Öhlins rear unit remained, now a DU8071. The SP5 did get the higher performance SPS engine (without the racing radiator), but with slightly less power at 118 bhp at 10,500 rpm. Thus it had the 34 mm and 30 mm valves, together with the Corsa inlet camshaft, still twin injectors per cylinder, and the same main bearings and con-rods as the SPS. All the 1993 bikes featured improved electronics, with reprogrammable EPROMs, and an external trimmer for adjusting the carbon monoxide level through a small hole in the rear of the seat unit. The SP5 also received the carbon-fibre mufflers of the SPS, but lost the carbon-fibre fuel tank for a regular steel item. The rear brake was also different, now with a torque-arm, initially in carbon-fibre but later in alloy because of some breakages in the carbon-fibre versions, and the clutch cover was no longer the vented type. There were no clutch modifications this year, and as

The SP5 had Showa forks and
carbon-fibre mufflers, but was
more powerful than the SP3 and
SP4. *Rolf im Brahm*

before the SP5 had a smaller, lighter, 300-watt
alternator than the Strada's and SPO's 350 watts. The
limited number of SP5s (still about 500) also carried
the plaque on the top triple clamp celebrating the
winning of the 1992 World Superbike Championship.
As with the 1993 900 Superlight, the Brembo wheels
were now painted bronze to match the frame. Apart
from the use of braided steel lines for the front brakes,
these too were unchanged from the SP4 and SPS. While
the claimed weight was still 188 kg (414.5 lb) dry,
actual wet weight, as tested by *Cycle World* in
November 1993, was 468 lb (212 kg) wet.

While not quite up to the performance level set by
the SPS, *Moto Sprint* still managed an impressive top
speed from their SP5 of 260.3 km/h (161.7 mph), and a
0–400-metre time of 10.57 seconds at 210.226 km/h
(130.6 mph). *Cycle World*'s test bike put out 110 bhp
at 10,250 rpm at the rear wheel.

For the US market a special model was produced
called the SPO, or Sport Production *Omolagato*. This
was an 888 Strada with the single seat, upswept
exhaust pipes and Öhlins shock absorber (together

with eccentric ride height adjustment) of the SP5. The
engine was essentially an overbored 1992 851 Strada,
and produced a claimed 100 bhp at 9,000 rpm at the
rear wheel. The single fuel injector per cylinder, valve
sizes and camshaft profiles were all the same as the
1992 851. Claimed weight was the same as the SP5,
but when tested by *Motorcyclist* in October 1993 the
SPO weighed 482 lb (219 kg) wet, despite not having
the oil-cooler of the SP5. On *Cycle World*'s dyno in
July 1993 the SPO made 94.0 bhp at 8,750 rpm at the
rear wheel, and turned the standing quarter mile in
11.25 seconds, at 123.45 mph (198.7 km/h).

For other markets the 888 Strada replaced the 851
Strada, and was an improved motorcycle. While still
heavy, at 202 kg (445 lb) dry, the extra capacity,
together with some changes to the mapping of the fuel
injection, now compensated for the increase in weight.
The bodywork was identical to the 1992 Strada, but
for revised graphics (with the new gold Ducati logo)
and the bronze-painted frame. For 1993 the Strada still
had black-painted wheels. *Moto Sprint* achieved
245.9 km/h (153 mph) on their test bike, and *PS*, in

March 1993, weighed their test machine at 224 kg (494 lb). While the weight had increased significantly since its inception in 1988, the Strada had now evolved into a thoroughly sophisticated motorcycle, and was arguably the most practical of the entire series. With the basic engine, frame, wheels and suspension unchanged since 1989, and the concept from 1987, the 888 Strada was at the pinnacle of its development as a street bike. The excellence of the original design had been well and truly vindicated, both on the street and the race track, by a system of continuous refinement over seven years.

1994

Towards the end of 1993 Ducati finally exhibited to the press a prototype of the 888 replacement. This had actually been ready some time earlier, so by the time it was put into production the 916 was a well-developed second-generation Desmoquattro. A product of the Cagiva Research Centre headed by Massimo Tamburini (who had designed the Paso), the 916 was one of their first major designs since moving from Rimini to the nearby Republic of San Marino. It still used essentially the same engine, but in a new tubular steel frame, and was clothed in bodywork inspired by the Supermono (of which more later in this chapter). The lower part of the fuel tank was designed to be incorporated into the upper part of the airbox. The basic change to the engine was to lengthen the stroke by 2 mm, to 66 mm,

so that it could be homologated for the World Superbike series. Other changes were also designed to improve the potential of the bike as a racing machine. To allow for ease of removal of the rear wheel in endurance racing, a Honda-style single-sided swing-arm was used. A criticism of the 888/926, especially towards the end of its racing life, had been a lack of weight on the front wheel, so weight distribution was improved by canting the engine forward 1.5°, and shortening the bike by reducing the wheelbase to 1,410 mm (55.5 inches). The frame was made of thicker, 28 mm, tubing, with the swing-arm pivot now being supported by the frame as well as the engine cases. There was also provision to alter the steering head angle from 23½° to 24½°, without altering the wheelbase. The 916 was displayed at the Milan Show in October 1993, where it caused a sensation, and was soon being developed for the 1994 World Superbike Championship.

In 1994 the 750 cc four-cylinder bikes received a weight reduction of 5 kg, to 160 kg (353 lb), so the gap between the fours and the twins was now only 15 kg (33 lb). With the prospect of increased competition from Honda's new fuel-injected RC45, the 916 was bored 2 mm to create a 955 cc version. As the racing department was limited in its ability to build a large number of these, only selected riders were to get the new 955. Virginio Ferrari (another ex-GP rider with a long association with Ducati) was now the team manager for

Carl Fogarty and Giancarlo Falappa, and Fabrizio Pirovano was Davide Tardozzi's new rider. Other factory 955s went to James Whitham, riding for the British Moto Cinelli team, and occasional World Superbike rides to Troy Corser, the Australian 1993 Superbike Champion, now riding for Eraldo Ferracci in the US AMA Superbike series (on a 955 cc-engined 1994 Corsa). After Falappa injured himself badly while testing, Mauro Lucchiari replaced him in the Ferrari team.

A new type of 46 mm Öhlins upside-down fork was used, together with an Öhlins rear unit. The new airbox, with 58 mm intakes and larger valves of 37 mm and 31 mm, allowed the 955 engine to develop 150 bhp at 11,000 rpm. Titanium valves were tried, but were the cause of several engine failures throughout the season. The 955s also used titanium Pankl con-rods, and Omega 11.6:1 pistons. The weight was right on the minimum 145 kg, and 290 mm carbon front brakes were gripped by the latest type of Brembo racing caliper.

It was a lot to expect the new bike to be totally competitive immediately, and there were some initial problems in the handling department. Race results confirmed that the 955 still needed some development;

winning just 12 out of the 22 World Superbike Championship races, it was nowhere near as dominant as in the past. However, some of this was probably due to injuries to Carl Fogarty and, more seriously, Giancarlo Falappa. By the end of the season most of the factory 955s had a 25 mm longer swing-arm, together with a different rear shock leverage ratio to improve rear-end traction. Fogarty received a special swing-arm, while lesser teams such as Moto Cinelli had to fabricate their own. Fogarty eventually came back from breaking his wrist at Hockenheim to win the World Superbike Championship with 10 victories. It had been an impressive debut season for the new 955.

Rather than using the new 916 as a basis, the 30 1994 Corsas owed much to the 1993 926 cc factory racer. As a thoroughly developed machine, this was still a surprisingly competitive piece of equipment, as was so ably demonstrated by Austrian rider Andreas Meklau with his two second place finishes at the Austrian round at Zeltweg. There were quite a few differences from the previous version, most noticeably the use of a 96 mm piston to give 926 cc. With a claimed 142 bhp at 11,500 rpm, the 926 used the lighter titanium Pankl con-rods,

While the trademark trellis frame continued on the 916, there was a single-sided swingarm, and spectacular attention to detail. *Rolf im Brahm*

Right: The 916 rewrote the rules for styling and twin-cylinder performance, and became the most important model ever in Ducati's history. *Rolf im Brahm*

1 mm larger inlet valve (37 mm), and new, stronger crankcases. The use of lighter Omega pistons and crankshaft assembly improved the response of the larger engine, overcoming criticisms of the past. The frame was altered too, with the steering head angle now 22½°, and the trail 102 mm (4.02 inches), and there were new Brembo P4.32-36 front brake calipers, with a 19 mm master cylinder, together with thinner discs. At the rear no torque-arm was now fitted, and other changes mirrored those of the factory 926 of 1993, including a new airbox and larger-bored exhaust, 42 mm Öhlins suspension and steering damper, a new crankcase breather and tank, and five-spoke Marchesini wheels with rim sizes of 3.50 x 17 and 6.00 x 17. The final version of the old design may have been overshadowed in 1994 by the 916 and 955, but it was still a very impressive racing motorcycle, and one that could be purchased by privateers.

When the 916 was released in early 1994, it received incredibly favourable press reports and, as in the past, a Sport Production version was made available. By 1992, with the 888/851, the Strada and SP lines had

become quite diverged, but in 1993 the gap had closed again as the SP5 had not received the racing Öhlins front forks. With the 916 the gap closed even more: there was virtually no difference in weight, and while the SP made higher rpm horsepower, at the expense of the lower end, the performance differential was nowhere near as great as it had been between 1990 and 1992. The 916SP had the same higher-specification engine of the SP5, still with twin injectors per cylinder, and the same valve sizes of 34 mm and 30 mm, together with the titanium Pankl con-rods of the Corsa. With 11.2:1 compression, the claimed power was up to 131 bhp at 10,500 rpm (at the crankshaft). The titanium con-rods (still with a length of 124 mm) allowed the maximum engine rpm to be increased to an impressive 11,500. Unlike the previous SP, the 916 version used the 350-watt alternator of the Strada, and no longer had the close-ratio gearbox.

The chassis was also identical to the 916 Strada, except for the use of an Öhlins DU3420 rear shock absorber. All the bodywork, together with wheels and front suspension, was the same, and there was no carbon-fibre airbox as was initially indicated, the carbon-fibre parts being limited to the front and rear guards, chainguard, and the Termignoni mufflers. The SP had adjustable brake and clutch levers, but the frame was identical to the Strada, down to the aluminium sub-frame, an item previously reserved for the SP series only. While the claimed dry weight was 192 kg (423 lb), the German magazine *PS*, in their test of August 1994, weighed their bike at 207 kg (456 lb). Their 916SP also reached 259 km/h (161 mph). As with previous SPs, the 916SP had the fully floating iron 320 mm front discs, and a white number patch on the seat.

The 916 Strada, released at the Milan Show in October 1993, was the most significant new model Ducati since the 851 (even more so than the Supermono a year earlier). While the engine was not very different from previous versions, the 916 was designed as a total package, with, for perhaps the first time at Ducati, an attempt to make the bike easy to service. The front forks were 43 mm Showa GD051, supported in a massive 80 mm steering head, with especially sturdy triple clamps. Everywhere there was

the most spectacular attention to detail, from the machining of the top triple clamp with its steering damper, to the levers and controls. The wheels, shared with the SP, were three-spoke Brembo in sizes of 3.50 x 17 and 5.50 x 17, mounted with either Pirelli or Michelin tyres, the rear a larger 190/50-ZR17. Perhaps the weakest aspect in the 916 Strada specification was its Showa GD052-007-02 rear shock absorber, which was criticized for being under-damped.

In the engine department the 916 Strada was a combination of the 888 Strada and SP, having the external oil-cooler and the Pankl (non-titanium) con-rods. The clutch was the 15-plate 888 Strada type, as was the six-speed gearbox, and the camshafts were also the milder Strada, still with 33 mm and 29 mm valves. With a single injector per cylinder, claimed power was 109 bhp at 9,000 rpm (or 114 bhp depending on the source), at the crankshaft. However, in reality the 916 was a considerably faster bike than its power figures would suggest. Improved aerodynamics over the 888, and a claimed dry weight of 198 kg (436 lb), saw the 916 Strada approach the performance of the much

Carl Fogarty totally dominated
the 1995 World Superbike
Championship on the 955 of
Ferrari's Ducati Corse.

more highly tuned 888SP models: *PS*, in July 1994, saw
256 km/h (159 mph). The wet weight was 211 kg
(465 lb). For an engine not that different from the 888
Strada, the 916 Strada produced considerably more
power, 104.3 bhp at 9,000 rpm on *Cycle World*'s dyno
in July 1994. They also managed a standing quarter
mile time of 10.72 seconds at 130.62 mph (210 km/h),
figures approaching that of the 888 Sport Production.
The 916 won every 'Bike of the Year' award in 1994,
but *Motorcyclist* magazine in the US summed it up in
their test of September 1994: 'The essence of the new
916 is its intoxicating blend of sound, looks, feel and
the way it turns street riding into an almost religious
experience.'

While most of the attention was centred on the 916,
the 888 Strada also continued to be offered as a 1994
model, alongside the 888LTD for the US market. The
100 examples of the 888LTD were built in September
1993, prior to the commencement of the production of
the 916, and each was fitted with an identification
plaque, like the earlier Sport Production series. While
they had carbon-fibre mudguards, much of the LTD
was the same as the 888 Strada, including the engine,
bronze-painted wheels, larger-diameter (25 mm) front
axle, and black anodized footpeg brackets and
controls. The LTD retained the SPO's Öhlins rear shock
absorber with eccentric ride height adjustment, and
made 95.8 bhp at 9,000 rpm, at the rear wheel, on
Cycle World's dyno in June 1994. This was enough to
propel it to a top speed of 157 mph (252.6 km/h), and
through a standing quarter mile in 10.81 seconds at
128.02 mph (206 km/h). The 888LTD also

convincingly won *Cycle World*'s comparison with its
four-cylinder Japanese opposition.

The final 888 Strada also received the bronze wheels
and larger-diameter front axle, together with braided
steel front brake lines. Some testers claimed that this
final version was the best of all the Stradas, but it was
overshadowed by the 916.

1995

For the 1995 season the minimum weight was
increased by 2 kg (4.4 lb) to 147 kg (323 lb) for twin-
cylinder and 162 kg (356 lb) for four-cylinder bikes,
still maintaining the 15 kg differential. However, with
more development of the 955 cc factory racers over the
winter, they immediately started to dominate the 1995
World Superbike Championship, so dominant in the
first three rounds that the FIM increased the weights
for twins for the fourth round at Monza to 155 kg
(341 lb), and reduced the fours to 160 kg (352 lb).
With Carl Fogarty and Mauro Lucchiari riding for
Virginio Ferrari's Ducati Corse, there was also Alfred
Inzinger's Austrian Promotor Team of Troy Corser and
Andreas Meklau, managed by Davide Tardozzi.
Additionally there was Fabrizio Pirovano (Taurus
Ducati), and ex-GP rider Pierfrancesco Chili riding the
Team Gattalone's customer 955 Corsa. In the US
former World 500 cc Champion Freddie Spencer rode
the Fast by Ferracci 955 in the AMA series.

One of the most significant changes for 1995 was
the controversial banning of carbon discs, so all the
factory bikes now used 320 mm iron front Brembo
discs. Winning 13 of the 24 races, Carl Fogarty
dominated in a style reminiscent of Doug Polen in
1991, and he easily won the Championship from Troy
Corser with four wins.

The 955 cc engine remained virtually unchanged
apart from new valves, rockers, camshafts, and the
occasional use of a 996 cc engine with 98 mm pistons.
With more emphasis on reliability, the horsepower,
according to Virginio Ferrari, was 141–145 at the rear
wheel at 12,000 rpm. There were detail modifications
to the rear suspension linkages and steering head angle,
but generally the increase in weight hurt the lap times
compared to the previous year. Ducati's big advantage
was in their use of telemetry so that they could fine the
suspension very quickly.

The customer 916 Racing was essentially the 955 cc
bike that Fogarty had raced the previous year, and even

Below: The 916 Senna I of 1995
was ostensibly a 916 Strada.

as they came from the factory they were competitive machines. With a total of 62 constructed, they even had to take over the new 748/916 production line to be completed. They had the 96 x 66 mm 955 cc engine that now produced a claimed 155 bhp at 11,500 rpm at the crankshaft. Though still using 37 mm and 31 mm valves, a new inlet camshaft, with 12 mm of valve lift, was fitted. The timing figures were inlet opening 31° before top dead centre, and closing 78° after bottom dead centre. Now based on the 916, the weight was up considerably from the 1994 888 Racing at 154 kg (340 lb). The Öhlins forks were now the 46 mm upside-down type as used by the works bikes in 1994, together with an Öhlins DU3360 rear shock absorber. Compared to the street bikes the swing-arm was lengthened 10 mm, to make the wheelbase 1,420 mm (55.9 inches), only 10 mm shorter than the 888 Racing. The brakes were of similar specification to the previous year, but for a smaller (24 mm) rear brake caliper.

The 916SP was largely unchanged for 1995, but for a strengthened frame, modified wiring, steel braided brake lines, and an extended carbon-fibre chain cover. As to be expected, the performance, too, was similar to

1994, with *PS* achieving 262 km/h (163 mph) from their test bike in August 1995. Two distinct models took the place of the Strada. Following what had happened in 1990, the Strada gained a dual seat, and lost the Pankl connecting-rods for the regular forged items. This new model was called the Biposto ('twin seat'), and with a steel rear sub-frame, dry weight was up to a claimed 204 kg (450 lb). Other changes with the Biposto included a revised Showa GD052-007-02 rear shock absorber, to allow for the extra weight of a passenger. As tested by *PS* in April 1995, the 916 Biposto was faster than the 1994 Strada, at 258 km/h (160 mph), but the wet weight was up to 217 kg (478 lb).

The 916 Senna was created in memory of the great Formula 1 racing driver Ayrton Senna, killed at Imola shortly after approving the new bike on 7 March 1994. Using the 1994 Strada engine with the Pankl con-rods, together with SP bodywork, Öhlins rear shock absorber, brakes and carbon-fibre mufflers and clutch cover, each of the 300 Sennas came with a plaque on the top triple clamp, and they were painted grey with red wheels. They also came with a certification document, and, like all the Desmoquattros for 1995, had a revised CPU management system, the '1.6', adapted from an automotive single-point injection system.

The new model for 1995 was the 748. The Desmoquattro had started life in 1986 at the Bol d'Or as a 748, and this same size engine was used to make a new motorcycle eligible for the 600 Supersport class, where 750 cc twins were now allowed to compete against 600 cc fours. There were two versions of the 748, an SP and a Biposto, the SP being very similar to the 916SP, and the 88 x 61.5 mm engine produced 104 bhp at 11,000 rpm at the crankshaft. The cylinder heads were very similar to the 888 SP2 and 3, with the same camshafts and 33 mm and 29 mm valves. The throttle size was reduced from 50 mm to 44 mm, and unlike the 916SP the 748 used the close-ratio gearbox of the 888SP. The claimed dry weight for the 748SP was 200 kg (440 lb), and in many respects it shared components with the 916SP, such as the 320 mm fully floating iron Brembo front discs, steel brake lines, Öhlins rear shock absorber, and adjustable brake and clutch levers, but there were no carbon-fibre body parts and the con-rods were the regular forged type. There was also only a single fuel injector per cylinder, the 748SP using the Weber Marelli '1.6' CPU.

Only available in yellow, kits for three stages of racing uprating were available for the 748SP, but even in standard form it was an impressive performer for its displacement. Weighing in at 210 kg (463 lb) wet, *Motorrad* tested one in April 1995 and managed a top speed of 248 km/h (154 mph). In Supersport 600, the class for which the 748SP was intended, Michael Paquay was totally dominant and easily won this World Superbike supporting series. Serafino Foti rode another 748SP to second in the Championship.

The 748 Biposto was a derivative of the 916 Biposto. The engine and gearbox were similar to the 748SP, but with the Strada camshafts, so the power was slightly less – 98 bhp at 11,000 rpm at the crankshaft. There was no oil-cooler, but because of the dual seat dry weight was up to 200 kg (440 lb), and all the frame, wheels and brakes were shared with the 916 Biposto. As tested by *PS* in July 1995, the 748 Biposto achieved 243 km/h (151 mph).

SUPERMONO

When Ing. Fabio Taglioni drew his sketches for the 750 V twin Ducati in 1970, he basically formed the 90° twin out of two singles on a common crankcase. The

single-cylinder engine had been the basis of most Ducatis, and virtually all their production bikes, from the time he joined Ducati in 1952, and it was easier to create the twin from existing designs. What happened then was quite unexpected. The twin completely took over from the single and within four years the overhead-camshaft bevel-gear Ducati single was dead. The era of the large-capacity bike was here and, despite the oil crisis of 1974, there was no longer any demand for the economical four-stroke single.

There had been a brief flirtation with a belt-driven overhead-camshaft single in the late 1970s with the Utah and Rollah, both based on the Pantah twin, but it was not until 20 years after Taglioni designed the 750 twin that Ing. Massimo Bordi drew up his idea of a modern single-cylinder engine. Whereas the twin had emerged from two singles, now the single emanated from the 90° twin. In essence the new engine was a twin without one cylinder. History had come full circle.

Fabio Taglioni made his 90° twin with the crank counterweights set at 100% of reciprocating and rotating weight, giving perfect primary balance, but with a secondary vibration at right angles balanced by the other piston. This was not possible with a normal single, as the heavier crankshaft counterweights would cause an imbalance when at right angles to the cylinder axis. So, when Massimo Bordi designed his single, he used the same balancing principle as in a 90° twin. The imbalance at right angles to the cylinder axis was thus balanced by a dummy piston, as in a twin. While this effectively reduced vibration, there was also considerable friction generated by this piston, limiting power, so in its place Bordi fitted a lever pivoting on a pin fixed in the crankcase. This lever was then attached to the small end of the second con-rod. As unique as Taglioni's desmodromic valve gear, the phrase *doppia bielletta*, 'double con-rod', was coined to describe this balance system.

In much the same way that the 750 Twin owed much to the overhead-camshaft bevel-gear singles, the Supermono was closely related to the 851/888/916 Twin. Together with water-cooling, and the double-overhead camshaft four-valve desmodromic cylinder head, the same Weber IAW Alfa/N fuel injection system was used, with twin injectors and 'P8' CPU as in the SP and Corsas.

By late 1990 the first engine had been tested. Using the lower half of an 851, and the 95.6 mm pistons from the 919 cc racer, together with a stroke of

New for 1995 was the bright
yellow 748SP. *Rolf im Brahm*

68 mm, the displacement was 487 cc. Later prototypes used a slightly longer, 70 mm, stroke for 502 cc. There were several departures from the 851, the most important being the use of two plain main bearings, rather than the four-roller type. The main journal was 45 mm in diameter, allowing a more rigid crankshaft, and the water pump was driven off the exhaust camshaft, rather than the camshaft drive shaft. This tidied the water plumbing, allowing the cylinder to sit more deeply into the crankcase, and with only the exposed portion water-cooled. The width of the engine could now be reduced, and there was a dry 180-watt alternator, incorporating the ignition pick-ups, on the left side of the engine. The intention was to use the Supermono as a test bed for improvements that would eventually find their way into the next generation of twins.

During 1991 development of the Supermono continued under the guidance of Claudio Domenicali and Luigi Mengoli, and by mid-1992 a Sounds of Singles racing version had been tested by Davide Tardozzi at Misano. The claimed power of this 502 cc prototype was 70 bhp at 10,500 rpm, and it had bodywork similar to the 1992 SP4. However, when the

Supermono was finally displayed at the Cologne Show late in September 1992, it had stunning new bodywork by designer Pierre Terblanche. He had only received the bare chassis in July, and the result was unique, and would strongly influence the 916 a year later. The Supermono was the sensation of the IFMA Cologne Show of 1992.

When it finally went into limited production during 1993, the Supermono was a Sounds of Singles racer only with an individually numbered plaque, and constructed by the racing department. Like the 888 Corsas, only the highest-quality proprietary components were used. A lightweight (6 kg) tubular steel space-frame, not dissimilar to that of the 888, was used, constructed from ALS500, not 25 CrMo4 as with the 888. The swing-arm pivoted directly on the crankcases, and operated an Öhlins DU2041 shock absorber without any rising rate linkage, to reduce weight. The Öhlins shock was adjustable for ride height via an eccentric mounted on the chassis end, and was mounted horizontally for mass centralization. The forks were 42 mm Öhlins, with magnesium triple clamps, almost identical to the 888 Corsa, with a steering head angle of 23°, giving 92 mm (3.62 inches)

The Supermono engine incorporated a number of technical updates over the Desmoquattro, including the water pump drive from the horizontal cylinder. Only 67 Supermonos were produced between 1993 and 1995. *Rolf im Brahm*

of trail. The Supermono was incredibly compact with its 1,360 mm (53.5-inch) wheelbase and 760 mm (29.9-inch) seat height, the wheelbase being 20 mm less than Bordi originally anticipated. More importantly, the weight distribution placed 54.5% on the front wheel. Marchesini three-spoke magnesium wheels in sizes of 3.50 x 17 and 5.00 x 17 were fitted, together with Brembo 280 mm fully floating iron front discs, and racing P4.30-34 calipers. At the rear was a 190 mm Brembo disc with a torque-arm attached to a carbon-fibre bracket. In order to keep the weight down to 122 kg (269 lb), every body part was made of carbon-fibre, including the computer housing, located, as with other Corsas, in front of the instruments. There was no rear sub-frame, the carbon-fibre seat fulfilling this function. The Supermono was a work of art, and looked just as good with the bodywork off.

When it finally went into production, the engine displaced 549 cc by using a 100 mm piston, still with the 70 mm stroke. Because of the *doppia bielletta*, two Pankl con-rods needed to be used, certainly adding to

the cost and making the design less attractive for later mass-production. The more compact injector body had a single 50 mm venturi tapering to 47 mm at the throttle butterfly. The valve sizes were 37 mm and 31 mm, but the camshafts had much more radical valve timing than even the 888 Corsa. With the inlet valve opening at 53° before top dead centre, and closing 71° after bottom dead centre, and the exhaust valve opening 66° before bottom dead centre and closing 48° after top dead centre, valve overlap was a massive 137°. This was reflected in the running characteristics of the engine, which was unhappy under 4,000 rpm and best above 8,000 rpm, demonstrating the advantages of the *doppia bielletta* in allowing the engine to rev to 10,500 rpm without vibration. Intake valve lift was 11 mm, and exhaust lift 10.5 mm, and with 11.8:1 compression the power was 78 bhp at 10,000 rpm at the crankshaft.

For 1995, with a 102 mm piston giving 572 cc, the power was up to 81 bhp at 10,000 rpm and there were also new suspension and brakes. With the use of plain main bearings, oil pump flow was increased on the Supermono to 3.3 litres/minute every 1,000 rpm, from 2.6 litres/minute/1,000 rpm on the twin, and as with the larger Corsas the engine side covers were magnesium, and the clutch cover carbon-fibre. The six-speed gearbox was unique to the Supermono, with closer ratios than any of the twins.

Because Bordi adopted the horizontal cylinder of the V twin, making the *doppia bielletta* out of the vertical cylinder, he rediscovered the benefits of a low engine pioneered by Moto Guzzi as long ago as 1921, and developed to its ultimate fruition by Ing. Giulio Carcano with his racing single-cylinder Guzzis. The 250s and 350s in particular were incredibly successful against larger, more powerful bikes by virtue of their superior agility, lighter weight, and better weight distribution. These bikes won eight 250 and 350 cc World Championships between 1949 and 1958, demonstrating the advantages of balance and finesse over sheer horsepower.

The Supermono also confirmed these benefits convincingly. At race tracks around the world Supermonos, with more like 62 bhp at the rear wheel (as on *Cycle World*'s dyno), consistently turn in lap times similar to 100-plus bhp 600 Supersports. They have also proven to be exceptionally reliable, with brilliant handling. *Cycle World*, testing a Supermono in September 1993, managed a standing quarter mile in 11.44 seconds at 122.11 mph (196.5 km/h) with the single-exit Termignoni exhaust. Using the optional twin-exit with a revised EPROM as supplied with each bike would have undoubtedly produced even more performance. Fully wet, their test bike weighed 301 lb (136.5 kg), and *Sport Rider* achieved a top speed of 144 mph (232 km/h) in April 1994.

In 1995 a Supermono followed earlier Ducati singles by winning the Single Cylinder TT on the Isle of Man. After finishing a close second in 1994, New Zealander Robert Holden took his Supermono to an easy victory with a fastest lap of 111.66 mph (179.7 km/h). Set to repeat the feat in 1996 on a 572 cc 1995-spec Supermono, Holden was tragically killed during TT Formula 1 practice on a 916 Corsa. In practice for the Singles TT he had set a time 6 mph faster than his nearest competitor. Holden's death resulted in immediate abandonment of Steve Wynne's Sports Motorcycles team for which he rode, a team that had enjoyed an association with racing Ducatis for many years, including Hailwood's 1978 TT Formula 1 victory.

While the few racing bikes that were built were initially meant to herald a range of Supermono street bikes, nothing has transpired, although Massimo Bordi has indicated to me on several occasions that he would still like to see it in production, particularly in Supersport form. I saw prototype air-cooled four-valve cylinder heads lying around the factory in 1993, but these have now been consigned to the museum. Looking closely at the engine, it is obvious that provision was made for an electric starter, and the cases are even drilled and tapped for a clutch cable. Still, there was no provision for the mounting of a sidestand on the engine cases and these will be redesigned if the bike does go into production. It also seems likely that the plain main bearings will return to the previous ball type. For now, the Supermono lives only as the racing bike, leaving the handful built as rare examples of a superb and fascinating motorcycle. With production only reaching about 50 bikes by mid-1995 (although about 80 engines had been built), another series of 20 was constructed at the end of that year. These had new numbered plaques indicating that they were from the 1995 series. As a finite item, the Supermono is the rarest of all current Ducatis.

In every respect, the Supermono represents the pinnacle of the Ducati philosophy created by Ing. Taglioni with the first desmodromic singles way back in 1956. Not content with mainstream solutions to solve a problem, Ducati have continued to be different, this time with the adoption of its unique balance system. In a manner reminiscent of earlier Ducatis, superior racetrack performance is achieved, not through sheer power, but through a more balanced overall package.

There is no doubt that without Cagiva, Ducati would have disappeared entirely, swallowed up within an Italian Government conglomerate. Unfortunately, ominous signs that not all was well started to appear during 1994 and 1995. Partially constructed bikes were to be seen at the factory waiting for delivery of components from outside suppliers. By 1996 there were waiting lists for all models all around the world. Fortunately, even though Ing. Taglioni had now retired, the management was still dominated by engineers. Massimo Bordi was General Manager of Cagiva Motorcycles, and his protégé, Claudio Domenicali, operated the racing department. These three engineers represented the past, present and future of Ducati, and it was to be the engineers that would keep the company alive through its next crisis.

The 1996 World Superbike
Championship went to the
final round and was won by
Troy Corser on the 996 cc
Promotor Ducati.

14 AMERICAN BUY-OUT

To anyone wishing to purchase a new Ducati during 1996 it was obvious that there were some serious production problems at Bologna. Rather than an expected increase in production, it went down from 20,989 in 1995 to 12,509 in 1996. There was no doubt that Cagiva was in financial difficulties. Suppliers were not being paid and by 1996 Ducati were finding it difficult enough to maintain, let alone increase, production. There were waiting lists for all models, particularly the Desmoquattro.

1996

Production difficulties aside, the World Superbike racing programme continued to be well supported and given high priority. Fortunately the racing team operated as if the company's financial problems were of little consequence. The cost of running a racing team, even with high riders' salaries, was still far less than that of developing a new production motorcycle, and it was important for Ducati's profile to continue at the forefront of World Superbike. Following the dominance of the 955 during 1995, the FIM again increased the minimum weights for twins to the same as fours, at 162 kg (357 lb). After Fogarty had tested a prototype 996 cc engine at the first and final rounds of 1995, Claudio Domenicali and his racing department decided to use the full capacity limit allowed by the regulations. With 98 mm pistons, all engines would displace 995.8 cc. Again there were two factory-supported teams in World Superbike, Virginio Ferrari's Ducati Corse, and Alfred Inzinger's Promotor. With Carl Fogarty moving to Honda, former 250 cc World Champion John Kocinski was signed by Ferrari as his replacement; partnering him would be GP privateer Neil Hodgson. Troy Corser again rode for Promotor, his team-mate being the American Mike Hale, and as before the team was managed by Davide Tardozzi.

The season started extraordinarily well for Kocinski and Ducati Corse with Kocinski taking a double win at Misano. Troy Corser soon matched this with a double at Donington to create some rivalry between the two factory teams. To add further spice, Pierfrancesco Chili on the Pietro di Gianesin-tuned Gattalone 955 was often faster than the factory bikes and won two races. However, there were problems within the Ferrari team.

The relationship between Ferrari and Kocinski soured and by mid-season they were barely talking to each other. Unfortunately this affected the team's results and Kocinski did not dominate the series as many had initially expected. While still taking five victories, it was Corser with seven wins who eventually took the title. As they had for every year since 1990, Ducati won the Manufacturers' Championship.

The 996 cc bike still produced similar power to the previous 955, 157 bhp at 11,800 rpm, but had about 12 bhp more at 8,500 rpm. Valve sizes were also unchanged at 37 and 31 mm, and as always there were new camshafts with revised rocker ratios. It translated to superior track performance, but at the expense of reliability. The problem now lay with the larger cylinders, which stretched the 916 engine cases to the limit. What had started with 92 mm pistons had been progressively enlarged to accept the new 98 mm Omega pistons. Not only did the bottom of the cylinder liner have a tendency to crack then break as it was too thin (only 1 mm), the engines were prone to failure after wheel-stands because of the sudden loss of oil pressure. This was a particular problem for Troy Corser, noted for both his wheel-stands and engine failures during 1996.

The throttle bodies increased in size to 54 mm with the larger engine (up from 50 mm in 1995), together with a larger airbox and radiator, and 54 mm diameter exhaust pipes. Elsewhere, because of the 7 kg weight increase, there was less need for religious weight saving, weight distribution being more important. The engine covers were no longer magnesium, and many of the fasteners were also steel rather than magnesium. The fuel pressure was increased from 4.5 to 5.0 bar with a new regulator. There was a new primary drive ratio of 32/59 (1.84:1), creating a hunting tooth to spread the load more evenly.

On the track, so good was the 1996 factory 996 racer that it could turn in lap times comparable to those of 500 cc Grand Prix bikes, despite a weight penalty of 32 kg and considerably less horsepower. At Donington in April, Troy Corser set an outright lap record of 1 min 33.470 sec, at an average speed of 154.950 km/h (96.281 mph). Lap times on other circuits were also similar to that of the 500s, a tribute to the development and balance of the factory 996. As usual Ducati contested the AMA Championship, this time with 1992 125 cc World Champion Alessandro Gramigni on the Fast by Ferracci bike; although he

won two races, he did not figure in the final AMA Championship results. Ducati achieved similar results in the *Motor Cycle News* British Superbike Championship, Terry Rymer winning two races at Brands Hatch on the Old Spice Ducati 955, and ending up third in the title. It was a different story in Germany. Now the company's premier market, Ducati took the German Pro Superbike title with the Swede Christer Lindholm.

In the World Superbike support series, Supersport World Cup, the Ducati 748 once again exhibited its superiority. With increasing participation from both Italian and Japanese manufacturers, the status of this series was elevated. There were ten races, and former Yamaha World Superbike rider Fabrizio Pirovano on the Team Alstare Corona 748SP easily won with six victories.

The 916 Racing for 1996 featured few changes. As the weight had to be increased to 162 kg, the suspension was re-calibrated and thicker front discs fitted. The 46 mm Öhlins forks featured a top-out spring, and the Öhlins shock absorber had an aluminium casing with fast preload adjuster; shock travel was 65 mm. There were only some detail changes to the engine, and capacity was still 955 cc. The inlet camshaft was now from the factory 1995 racing bikes, and with 12 mm of inlet valve lift the 37 mm inlet valve opened 36° before top dead centre, closing 72° after bottom dead centre. Claimed power was 153 bhp at 11,000 rpm. A free-wheel clutch was fitted, together with a new exhaust system with 52 mm exhaust headers. Other revisions included an oil pump with an enclosed relief valve, and new timing belts. Larger front Brembo brake calipers, with 32 and 36 mm pistons, featured on the 916 Racing. Externally the only way to distinguish the Corsa from the previous year was the seat unit, now without an air intake to improve the visibility of the white number plate.

Despite some inside the factory wanting to discontinue it, the 916SP was again offered, now titled the SP3. While sold at a somewhat higher price than the regular 916, the Sport Production series always had a much higher engine specification and was considerably more expensive to manufacture. It was not only the Pankl con-rods and special main bearings that set the SP apart from the Strada; it also received Corsa-style cylinder heads. To keep the cost down, there were fewer carbon-fibre body parts for 1996; neither the clutch cover nor exhaust pipe insulating

Still available with a half-fairing
in 1996, the 900SS was a classic
design.

panel were carbon-fibre. As with the earlier SP888s, a numbered plaque was now fitted to the top triple clamp. It was initially also intended to produce the Senna II during 1996, also with fewer carbon-fibre parts, and with yellow wheels to distinguish it from the Senna I. However, no Sennas were manufactured in 1996, probably as a result of that year's general production problems. The Senna would make a return during 1997.

The engine of the SP3 carried over from the previous year, still using the inlet camshaft and 34 and 30 mm valves developed on Raymond Roche's World Superbike racer of 1990. Unlike the other production Desmoquattros, the SP3 used twin injectors per cylinder and thus kept with the Weber Marelli 'P8' 1.8 CPU. As before the tubular steel frames were supplied by Cagiva Telaio, and constructed in ALS450, a similar material to that used on the Supermono.

To homologate the 955 Corsa for AMA Superbike racing, 50 955SPs were also constructed during 1996 for the United States only. Regulations required that racers and production bikes must share the same engine capacity, so these SPs came with a 955 cc engine (with

96 mm pistons) and a special numbered plaque. While essentially similar to the 916SP3, they were easily recognizable by the white front number plate and 955 fairing decals. With so few constructed it could have been a collector's item, but was soon superseded by the 996SPS.

The 916 and 748SP and Biposto were virtually identical to 1995. They received the quieter clutch with sound-absorbing clutch cover, shared with the Supersport and Monster, and also adjustable-ratio clutch and brake master cylinders. With the total production pre-sold there was really no reason to change what had become a thoroughly well-developed product. As with the Supersport, US 916s differed from those for the rest of the world. There was no Biposto for America, the solo-seat 916 Strada also receiving the Öhlins rear shock absorber of the SP3. Only in Australia were there problems with the unique 916 headlights; difficulties with compliance with Australian Design Rules saw all 916s and 748s fitted with exceptionally ugly square headlights. There was no easy solution to this, and these revised upper fairings were still being fitted two years later in 1998.

Other models also continued into 1996 virtually unchanged: the 600 Supersports in 33 and 53 bhp versions, the 750 Supersport, and the 900 Supersport and Superlight. They all looked visually identical, although the 600 Supersport received a stainless steel two-into-one exhaust system, the 750 sound-absorbing panels, and the 900 a sound-deadening clutch cover. The 400 Supersport also made a return, but only for the domestic market, and 200 were manufactured. As before, the 900CR and 900SS SP were still produced for the United States, and a limited number of Superlights made. Every year there were fewer Superlights, with only 300 in 1996, considerably down on the massive 1,317 constructed during 1992. Undoubtedly the limited edition concept had been over-used by Ducati with the Superlight; unlike the 916SP it offered no performance advantages over the standard bike and consequently was difficult to sell against the standard 900SS. The unchanged nature of the Supersport line for 1996 indicated that it was nearing the end of its life, and total production was considerably reduced from 1995, with only 2,791 Supersports built during 1996. Not all this decreased production was due to reduced demand, overall production being considerably reduced that year.

For 1996 the M900 finally received fully adjustable forks, now Marzocchi rather than Showa. All Monsters also had the choke mounted on the handlebar, a vacuum-operated fuel tap, rubber footrests, and the sound-deadening timing belt covers. As the M900 shared its engine with the 900SS, it also featured a sound-absorbing clutch cover. Colours were as before: red, black and yellow. The 750 Monster that had been displayed at the Milan Show at the end of 1995 was the only additional model for 1996. It was essentially a single-disc-brake 600M with non-adjustable front forks fitted with an air/oil-cooled 64 bhp 750 Supersport engine. As with the 600, the rear wheel was an MT 4.50 x 17. Performance of the M750 was increased significantly over the 600, *Motor Cycle News* managing a top speed of 124.8 mph (201 km/h) in their test during June 1996. As the weight for the silver M750 was only increased marginally to 176 kg (388 lb), it was possibly the best balanced of all the Monsters. Though only possessing a five-speed box, the 750 cc engine was also less snatchy than the 900. The M600 continued as before in 33 and 55 bhp versions, the only changes being those that appeared on all the Monsters for 1996.

There had also been plans to produce a Special Edition Monster 900 during 1996, but production problems meant that this did not emerge. Virtually identical to the 30 'Club Italias' of 1995, the Special Edition was displayed at the Milan Show of 1995 and also featured on the 1996 Monster brochure. Special parts included fully floating cast-iron front discs and rear brake arm, leather seat, remote reservoir master cylinders, and a small fairing. Also available were a special Police M600 and M900.

Early in 1996 there were many rumours of a buy-out of Ducati. Sam Zell, a Chicago financier and enthusiast, was linked with one take-over bid through the Zell Chilmark Fund. This foundered, and eventually a new company was created through a joint venture between the Texas Pacific Group, a group of investors led by Abel Halpern, and the Castiglioni brothers. A press release of 30 September 1996 stated that 'a company called Ducati Motor S.p.A. has acquired all the assets of Ducati motorcycles from the Cagiva Group'. The final terms were that the Castiglioni brothers maintained a 49% interest in the company, TPG another 49%, with 2% held in trust in an Italian bank. Claudio Castiglioni was still chairman of the new company. What also happened was that Ducati Motor was now independent of Cagiva, and that required Ducati to set up its own commercial and research and development departments.

The transaction was facilitated by Deutsche Morgan Grenfell, who engaged Bain & Company as consultants to assess Ducati and its potential for investment. Bain then sent Federico Minoli and a team of ten experts to study the company. Minoli was an inspired choice, as he was an Italian based in America. Hailing from Varese where Cagiva were located, he also possessed more than a passing interest in motorcycles. In his youth he had owned a Ducati Scrambler, then a Moto Guzzi before crashing it and retiring from bikes for a few years. So impressed was he with Ducati that in April 1997 Minoli accepted the position as CEO of Ducati Motor.

Although TPG had no previous association with motorcycles, they had a strong background in rebuilding under-capitalized companies, their purchase and subsequent turnaround of the Texas-based Continental Airlines being a particular success story. With TPG's stated intention of listing Ducati Motor on the New York Stock Exchange, there was some apprehension among traditional Ducati enthusiasts.

What the TPG interest initially meant was that there was an immediate increase in production as suppliers could be paid. However, it also signified a change in direction of the company, one aimed at creating a specialized niche market. The only way to make Ducati more profitable was to increase production to a projected 40,000 by the turn of the century, so to sell considerably more than the projected 1997 figure of 27,000 motorcycles an even larger market needed to be created. While many enthusiasts were initially sceptical about American involvement in a traditional Italian company, at least the company survived. More importantly, to expand the customer base TPG began to recognize the significance of racing and racing history as a marketing tool. What had always been a secret jewel for a limited number of enthusiasts worldwide was about to be unleashed on a wider market.

1997

While the company was in the middle of a managerial upheaval, the World Superbike racing programme continued largely unabated during 1997.

Virginio Ferrari very enthusiastically welcomed Carl Fogarty back into his ADVF Team, still with Neil Hodgson. Ferrari no longer had outside sponsorship from Kremlyovskaya vodka, the Ducati factory now funding the team. Alfred Inzinger decided to take his Promotor team, and World Champion Troy Corser, off to the world of 500 cc Grand Prix racing, so Pierfrancesco Chili and the Gattalone team inherited the spare factory-supported bike. Chili's tuner from the previous year, Pietro di Gianesin, had often produced embarrassingly fast bikes, so he was offered 748SPs to prepare for the World Supersport series.

In terms of racing results, 1997 was an indifferent year for Ducati. Now the stronger 996SPS crankcases had been homologated it was expected that the bikes would not only be totally reliable, but also fast. The wider SPS cylinder head studs meant thicker barrels, and 2 mm liners could now be used. The result was vastly improved reliability, but less satisfactory performance overall. For the first time in eight years Ducati failed to win the Manufacturers' Championship. Too many crashes by Fogarty also saw him lose

Below: Paolo Casoli took the
Gio.Ca.Moto 748SP to victory in
the 1997 Supersport World Cup.

the title to Kocinski, but he still won six races. Chili suffered some bad luck during the season, often being taken out by other riders, but managed to triumph in three races, including a brilliant ride in the wet at Misano.

The bike itself came under some particularly vocal criticism from Fogarty, who claimed that he 'could win if he had his 1995 bike'. Unfortunately, the solution was less easy to find. The increase in weight to 162 kg had affected the weight distribution on the Ducati. New crankcases and frame were homologated with the 916SPS, and in the process the balance of the bike was altered. As Virginio Ferrari said, 'We lost the harmony between the engine and chassis.' The throttle bodies increased in size to a massive 60 mm, certainly creating a noticeable power increase but giving problems with the smoothness of the delivery. On the track it translated into lap times that were no better than in 1995, the problem being that the increase in weight had not been easy to incorporate into the 916 design.

Other changes for 1997 included a redesigned carbon-fibre fuel tank, increased in size from 23 to 24 litres, and new first and second gears; these had a slightly lower ratio than before, first at 1.88:1 and second at 1.57:1, giving the gearbox a wider spread to suit the larger engine. The 46 mm Öhlins forks had 5 mm more wheel travel (125 mm) with wider spacing to help cool the thicker brake discs. These were sometimes reduced in size to 290 mm, the smaller discs helping the bike to turn more quickly. Rear rim size decreased slightly from 6.00 x 17 to 5.75 x 17.

In the AMA Championship the former Cagiva 500 cc rider, Australian Matthew Mladin, rode the Fast by Ferracci 996, winning four races. However, this was not enough to win the Championship and Mladin finished third. Former champion Thomas Stevens rode for the newly formed Vance & Hines team. Again the *Motor Cycle News* British Superbike Championship was disappointing for Ducati; although taking two victories, John Reynolds on the Reve Red Bull 996 finished fourth. Ian Simpson, also on a Red Bull 996, won one race, as did Sean Emmett on the Groundwork South East Ducati. Only in the Supersport World Cup was the Desmoquattro victorious. Now with television coverage, this series continued to grow. Eleven races were held in 1997, nine in Europe and two in Asia (Japan and Indonesia). As with World Superbike, the Ducatis were no longer as dominant, and the overall result was not decided until the final race. This time Paolo Casoli on the Gio.Ca.Moto. 748SP, with three race wins, was triumphant by 1 point over the Yamaha-mounted Vittoriano Guareschi. So competitive was this class of racing during 1997 that these were the only two riders to win more than one race.

As expected, the 916 Racing for 1997 incorporated many of the improvements that had appeared on the factory racers during 1996. Within the engine there was an increase in displacement to 996, and the new crankcases with wider cylinder head studs homologated with the 916SPS. Compression with the 98 mm pistons was increased slightly from 11.8:1 to 12:1, and claimed power was also marginally higher at 155 bhp at 11,000 rpm. While the valve sizes were unchanged, as was the inlet camshaft, there was a new exhaust camshaft. The timing figures were now exhaust opening 69° before bottom dead centre and closing 47° after top dead centre; valve lift was still 10.5 mm. In line with the 1996 factory bikes there were now 54 mm exhaust pipes, and an increase in fuel pressure to 5.0 bar via a pressure regulator. The primary drive was also changed to the 32/59 of the 1996 racers.

Other changes also reflected the continual development of the factory bikes. The airbox had a greater capacity and was fed by a larger air intake in the fairing. Smaller changes were evident throughout the motorcycle: a larger oil radiator, thicker front brake discs, a new rear wheel hub assembly, and new attachments for the handlebars. While 46 mm Öhlins front forks were still used, the triple clamps now had adjustable offset. Thus, while the trail was previously 97 mm, this could now be adjusted within a range of 96.6–109.2 mm. With a new Öhlins rear shock absorber, rear shock travel was increased from 65 to 74 mm, translating into 136 mm of rear wheel travel.

Perhaps the most important new model for 1997 was the 916SPS. This was intended as a very limited production motorcycle alongside the 916SP, purely to homologate the new crankcases for World Superbike and FMI Sport Production. However, there was more to the SPS than merely new crankcases and larger pistons, as 36 mm inlet valves (up from 34 mm) were used, together with new inlet and exhaust camshafts. With 10.8 mm of inlet valve lift, the valve opened 14° before top dead centre and closed 73° after bottom dead centre. The exhaust valve now opened 57° before bottom dead centre, closing at 23° after top dead centre with 9.8 mm of valve lift. The compression ratio was

marginally increased to 11.5:1 and claimed power was up to 134 bhp at 10,000 rpm. The gearbox ratios for third, fourth, fifth and sixth gears were also altered for the SPS, being shared with the 748BP and SP. The SPS also received the new primary drive gears (32/59) of the 916 Racing and the same titanium con-rods. Unlike the single-injector Desmoquattros, the SPS continued with the Weber Marelli 'P8' CPU, but the throttle bodies remained at 50 mm.

Visually similar to the 916SP, and sharing the chassis and running gear, the 916SPS had all the performance equipment associated with limited-edition Sport Production Ducatis: cast-iron fully floating 320 mm front brake discs with steel brake lines, Öhlins shock absorber, and larger-diameter exhaust pipes with carbon-fibre leg-shields. All 916SPSs came with carbon-fibre Termignoni mufflers and an alternative chip. Continuing a trend started back in 1974 with the 750 Super Sport, the 916SPS was the standard by which all sporting motorcycles were judged. It was also the fastest Ducati to date, the Italian magazine *Motociclismo* in April 1996 managing a top speed of 270.1 km/h (168 mph) in standard form, or 275.4 km/h (171 mph) with the performance kit that included the Termignoni mufflers and revised computer chip. Horsepower, too, was impressive: 122.59 bhp at 9,500 rpm, increasing to 124.35 bhp at 9,500 rpm with the performance kit. In production racing the 916SPS was immediately competitive, winning the production race at the North West 200 and coming second on the Isle of Man. Unanimously named 'Bike of the Year' by magazines around the world, it was initially intended to continue the 916SP alongside the SPS, but demand for the latter was so strong that it soon replaced the smaller bike. Rather than a proposed production series of only 200, nearly 800 916SPSs were built during 1997. With the injection of capital from TPG, overall production was significantly increased during the year, 8,500 Hypersport 916/748s being constructed.

After a hiatus during 1996, the 916 Senna was again produced as a limited edition of 350 during 1997. As in 1995, the Senna had red wheels and steel grey bodywork, although this time a lighter colour than before. No Sennas were produced with the yellow wheels intended for the 1996 version. Although it had the Öhlins shock absorber, fully floating cast-iron brake rotors and a carbon-fibre front mudguard, the Senna retained the standard 916 engine of the Biposto and Strada. All Sennas came with a numbered plaque

The 916SPS was built specifically to homologate the crankcases for the 996 racer.

on the top triple clamp, but suffered in much the same way as the 900 Superlight. For a premium price they offered no performance advantage over a standard bike and too many were built for them to qualify as a very limited edition.

The 916 Strada and Biposto continued essentially unchanged – why alter something that was so successful and desirable? Even with an increase in production there were insufficient to satisfy demand. The US still received a solo-seat 916 with an Öhlins shock absorber, but it was otherwise identical to the European Biposto. There were also no changes to the 748SP and 748 Biposto. Only available in yellow, the former was manufactured in similar numbers to the 916SPS, but with fewer special parts. At the Cologne Show of 1996 a hybrid 748S was displayed. This red solo-seat 748 used the standard 748 Biposto engine (without oil-cooler) in a 748SP chassis. It never made it to the production line.

Now into its seventh year of production, the Supersport was starting to look a little dated. For several years there had been talk of a replacement, but the financial difficulties of 1995 and 1996 had meant further delays to this project. With a new commitment to the Supersport line, the specification was upgraded for 1997 in order to maintain sales. Overall Supersport sales had been falling from a high of 8,545 in 1992, and while 3,741 were built in 1997 (plus 500 1998-model Final Editions), numbers were well down on those of the Hypersport and Monster. The Superlight was no longer offered, and most of its special features made their way to the 900 Supersport.

Although now at the end of its production run, the Supersport for 1997 was a thoroughly developed machine. In 900 guise especially it offered a number of more appealing features over the earlier models. The engine specifications of all Supersports were unchanged except for bimetallic inlet and exhaust valves to better suit unleaded fuel. The oil radiator on 750s and 900s was now mounted above the front cylinder, similar to that of the Monster, and a heating kit was installed on all front carburettors to minimize icing in cold weather, which had always been a problem on Mikuni-carburetted models because of their long inlet tracts.

As there was no Superlight offered for 1997, the 900 Supersport received the fully floating rear brake and carbon-fibre front mudguard. There were also steel brake and clutch lines for Europe, and adjustable brake

and clutch levers. The clutch cover was grey, and standard equipment included Michelin Hi-Sport tyres. Offered in red or yellow, the 900 Supersport shared its new bodywork with the 750 and 600 Supersport; the fairing had revised graphics, with an air intake and internal sound-absorbing panels. Other improvements for 1997 were the increased steering lock to 28° either side, and a more comfortable seat. Cosmetic changes included anodized aluminium footrest plates.

With unchanged specifications, the 900 Supersport continued to offer a balanced package with the less extreme riding position of the Hypersports 916/748, and for many it still offered enough performance. The Italian magazine *Super Wheels* of March 1997 managed 220.856 km/h (137 mph) with a standing 400 metres at 11.777 seconds at 182.426 km/h (113 mph). Significantly, however, the measured dry weight was 189.8 kg (418 lb). The gradual development of the Supersport over a seven-year period had also seen it become a thoroughly refined sporting motorcycle, without the demands placed on the rider by the race replica Hypersports. It still appealed to those who wanted a simpler, lighter sports bike, without a racetrack orientation. Unfortunately the market also perceived the Supersport to be old-fashioned; just as had happened with the earlier bevel-gear Supersport, Ducati had let what was once their most successful model run too long and sales were suffering as a result. It was not really a case of the motorcycle being obsolete, but more the continual emphasis placed by the press on new products. Also the Supersport was coming under increasing pressure in the marketplace from the Honda VTR1000F and Suzuki TL1000S 90° V twins. These new bikes were priced in Supersport territory but offered more performance, albeit without the character and breeding of the Ducati model.

For the United States there was once again the 900 Supersport SP and CR. As the regular Supersport for Europe incorporated most of the previous Superlight features, the SP now only differed in the use of the fully floating Brembo cast-iron front brake discs, carbon-fibre rear mudguard, and numbered plaque. US bikes did not receive the steel brake lines. The 900CR continued as before, still essentially a 900 engine in a 750 Supersport chassis. Although only 60 750 Supersports had been manufactured during 1996, production was back to reasonable levels in 1997, and 1,146 were built. As with the 900, the oil-cooler was mounted in an upper position, and all the alterations to the steering lock, valves, carburettor heating kit, fairing, seat, and graphics also made it to the 750. The 600 Supersport also continued, again incorporating these changes, and all Supersports were available in yellow or red.

Of all the existing models, the M900 Monster came in for the most modifications during 1997. Previous 900 Monsters had shared engines with the Supersport, but now the 900M received a de-tuned engine to improve low-down power, better suiting its role as a city bike. The 900 engine had always been slightly unhappy running below 3,000 rpm, so to help cure this the cylinder head received smaller valves, now 41 and 35 mm, and there were new camshafts. New and much more sophisticated computer programs that came with the TPG involvement now enabled the development department to design desmodromic camshafts much more quickly. Whereas in the past there had only been a few desmodromic camshaft profiles, 1997 saw a range of camshafts for different models. The M900 in this lower state of tune now had a camshaft that opened the inlet valve 12° before top dead centre, closing it 70° after bottom dead centre. The exhaust valve opened 56° before bottom dead centre, closing 25° after top dead centre. Valve lift was unchanged at 11.76 mm and 10.56 mm respectively. Claimed power was reduced to 77 bhp at 7,000 rpm, but more significantly the lobe centres of the camshaft were retarded for better low-down power characteristics.

Other engine changes from the Supersport were carried through to the new M900 engine: sintered steel valve seats and bimetallic inlet and exhaust valves for better compatibility with unleaded fuel, and the carburettor heating kit to prevent icing.

Complementing the lower state of tune on the M900 was a new Kokusan ignition system and revised jetting for the Mikuni 38 mm carburettors. Elsewhere the specifications were unchanged, except for the small front fairing that had featured on the projected Special Edition Monster of 1996. Colours for the M900 of 1997 were black or red. As expected, ultimate performance was reduced with the lower-tuned engine, the 1997 M900 managing a top speed of 196.3 km/h (122 mph) in a test by *Motociclismo* in April 1997; earlier M900s had achieved around 206 km/h (128 mph). *Cycle World*, when testing an M900 in November 1997, found it also to be slightly slower over a standing quarter mile at 11.98 seconds at 108.53 mph (175 km/h).

An M900 Solo with front cast-iron disc brake rotors and a single seat was also intended for 1997. Displayed at the Cologne Show in 1996, as with the Special Edition of a year earlier it was not put into production due to negative dealer response. This M900 Solo was almost identical to the M900 Police, which also had a solo seat. The silver M750 and red and yellow M600s continued as before.

Below: The first sport-touring Ducati since the 907IE, the ST2 was the first new model introduced after the TPG takeover.

To help promote the Monster in Italy, Ducati supported the 'Ducati Monster Cup 97'. Organized by Techna Racing in Rome, six races were held, with identical Gio.Ca.Moto. M900s being allocated by lot for the series. The yellow racing Monsters had a solo seat, belly-pan, and 916-style Gianelli exhausts. Monsters had always been particularly popular in Italy, and the strength of the local market saw Monster production outstripping both the Hypersport and Supersport, with 10,000 units in 1997.

Although it was originally intended to release it during 1996, the ST2 was also delayed due to the production difficulties experienced by the company that year. First displayed at the Cologne Show at the end of 1996, the ST2 was Ducati's first exploration of the sport-touring category since the 907IE of 1991–92. Historically this had not been the most successful area for Ducati as it meant competing directly with the Japanese. The company's past was littered with some rather dismal forays into this area, the 860GT and Paso in particular. While some other examples were excellent motorcycles, notably the 750GT, Darmah and 907IE,

after initial success they never achieved the sales that were expected. Many of the earlier attempts at sport-touring motorcycles had suffered particularly from poor reliability and incomplete development. Early reports suggested that the ST2 was a finely developed machine, but still had considerable competition.

One of TPG's objectives was to expand into wider market segments, and the ST2 fitted this bill comfortably. With progress already well advanced by the time of the merger with Cagiva, it took only a short time to construct another assembly line for the ST2. Production began in April 1997, and during that year 4,300 ST2s were manufactured.

Development of the ST2 was facilitated by utilizing as many existing parts as possible. Thus the basic frame was from the Monster (originally 851/888) constructed of ALS450, in concert with a swing-arm with a 916-style linkage. The 43 mm Showa front forks were also similar to the 916, but with more fork travel (130 mm), as was the new-generation Brembo front wheel. With 24° of fork rake and 102 mm of trail, steering was quicker than the earlier 907. Latest-specification

Brembo brake calipers were also employed, with revised internal fluid passages and wider bolt spacing to increase rigidity. These brake calipers would find their way to other models during 1998.

Styled by Miguel Galluzzi (who was also responsible for the Monster) at Cagiva Morizzone, the ST2 incorporated many features expected of sport-touring motorcycles of the late 1990s. Notable features were the aspherical rear-view mirrors, and an instrument panel that incorporated a digital display for fuel consumption, fuel reserve, time, and water temperature. The entire layout of the cockpit, with the ignition key on the fuel tank and cast handlebars, gave the ST2 a look of integrated design that was new to Ducati in the sport-touring segment. Complementing its status as a long-distance machine, the ST2 came with matching panniers from Nonfango, and exhaust pipes that could be adjusted for increased ground clearance. During 1997 the ST2 came in red, silver and black.

In the engine department the ST2 took over where the 907IE had left off. The basic six-speed, two-valve, water-cooled engine was inherited from the 907, but a 2 mm bore increase to 94 mm took the displacement out to 944 cc. Compression, too, was increased on air-cooled 900s to 10.2:1. The ST2 also received new camshafts, not only with different timing, but also increased valve lift. The inlet valve opened 26° before top dead centre, closing 72° after bottom dead centre, with 11.8 mm of valve lift. The exhaust valve opened 61° before bottom dead centre, closing 34° after top dead centre, with 11.4 mm of maximum valve lift. The six-speed gearbox was carried over, but the ST2 had the revised primary gears of the Corsa and SPS (32/59). The Weber Marelli electronic fuel injection used a 40 mm throttle body and the '1.6' CPU of other single-injector Ducatis.

Although no lightweight at a claimed 212 kg (467 lb), the measured wet weight was closer to 234 kg (515 lb) as tested by Cycle World in December 1997. However, the ST2 was a surprisingly strong performer for this type of motorcycle. Although power was only 83 bhp at 8,500 rpm, Cycle World achieved a standing quarter mile in 11.81 seconds at 113.10 mph (182 km/h). Top speed was 136 mph (219 km/h). These were very similar figures to the significantly lighter 900 Supersport, indicating that the ST2 was not only more powerful, but possessed excellent aerodynamics.

Undoubtedly a highly competent long-distance motorcycle in the best European tradition, there is still a question mark over how successful Ducati will be with this new attempt at the Sport Touring market. History tells us that it is an area where the company has always struggled. This was vinidicated by 2005 as sales of the ST range plummeted by 55% compared with those of the previous year.

1998

The affect of the TPG buy-out really became noticeable during 1998. The workforce increased to 714 employees, 434 in production and the remaining 280 in sales, research and administration. During 1997 the personnel had numbered 550, with 280 in production. Increased investment (30 billion lire by 1998) had seen new CNC machines installed and 30 CAD stations in the engineering department, as production moved from labour-intensive to capital-intensive. More components were sourced outside, leaving heat-treatment, finishing and engine assembly the primary processes now undertaken within the factory. While the existing motorcycles continued with only minor developments, there was a new emphasis on marketing and expanding the customer base. Thus not only were there more variations on the four themes, but TPG wanted to create a sport performance experience for Ducati owners in a manner similar to that of the Harley-Davidson lifestyle. Reflecting the increase in production was a huge increase in turnover, from 200 billion lire in 1996 to an estimated (by early 1998) 400 billion lire in 1997.

Central to TPG's plan was also a new logo and corporate identity. The previous logo had come with Cagiva in 1986 and TPG needed to create a fresh image. Ducati approached Massimo Vignelli, a leading American graphic designer responsible for corporate logos for Bloomingdales and American Airlines. Vignelli delved into the past to create a new logo that recalled the clean lines of the graphics on the 1972 Imola racers. A new symbol was also created alongside the logo; suggesting a spinning bike wheel, this came directly from the classic eagle logo of the overhead camshaft singles of the early 1960s. This interest in an association with past success would play an important role in TPG's vision for the future of Ducati, and to celebrate this further, the last-surviving Ducati brother, Bruno Cavalieri, was made honorary chairman of the company.

While other great Italian marques, notably MV Agusta and Moto Guzzi, were well known for their museums and maintaining their history, Ducati itself did not have a museum, and until Cagiva bought the company in 1985 all important racing machines had either been sold or destroyed. Thus the factory had lost the racing heritage of the 1950s, '60s and '70s. Many of the most significant bikes had survived in private hands, but many more were lost. Part of TPG's plan was to create a 10,000 sq ft museum on the first floor of the factory at Borgo Panigale, but the difficulty was in reclaiming some of the earlier bikes. It was not only racing machines either – there were also few examples of street bikes from the pre-Cagiva era. Fortunately most of the prototypes that had not made the production line had not been destroyed.

Charged with creating primarily a racing museum, Marco Montemaggi worked hard at persuading collectors in Italy to lend significant racing machines to the museum for its opening in June 1998. Noted restorer Primo Forasassi was also employed to restore some of the important exhibits. The museum was eventually to be linked with the Ferrari museum at nearby Maranello, emphasizing not only an underlying connection with Ferrari, but also the strong Emilia Romagna engineering tradition. Coinciding with the opening of the museum was the first World Ducati Weekend, held from 12–14 June 1998 at Misano, Rimini and Bologna.

It was obvious that TPG was now committed to raising the profile of Ducati beyond its previous boundaries. One way of doing this was by creating a special-edition silver 748L (with carbon-fibre front mudguard and chainguard) to be sold through the prestigious Neiman Marcus catalogue for men in the United States. Only 100 were available, and with a Donna Karan New York leather jacket and Dainese gloves provided, this became the first mail-order Ducati. Complementing this new marketing move was the opening of monofranchised flagship Ducati Stores, the first, along 'Gasoline Alley' in Manhattan, opening in March 1998. These 300 sq m superstores were designed by the US-based architectural studio Gensler in conjunction with Bologna architect Michele Zacchiroli. Offering accessories and an Internet site, they certainly represented a totally new direction for Ducati, and one that was not entirely welcomed by the traditional enthusiast. Other stores soon opened in various Italian cities – Bologna, Florence, Rome, Milan, Genoa, Savona, Treviso and Turin – followed by an Australian flagship store in Sydney.

One of the strongest product lines in the new Ducati Store was Ducati Performance. Formed in December 1996 as a joint venture between Gio.Ca.Moto. and Ducati Motor, it was established by September 1997. With the intention of developing new performance products with Ducati and using the same suppliers as that of original equipment, Ducati now hoped to also capture a large slice of the lucrative performance market. The Ducati Performance catalogues covered all models in the line-up, and included chassis as well as engine parts. Another new product line was that of official apparel; an agreement with the Vicenza-based Dainese company provided a range of high-quality leather racing clothing, and also available was a limited range of other lifestyle sportswear. Future developments in the accessory and performance sphere lay in specialized performance shops where customers could have their motorcycles modified with factory back-up.

Having lost the World Superbike Championship in 1997, a concerted effort was made in 1998 to win again. While out to make a profitable company, TPG realized the importance of racing, not only for product development, but also as a means of promotion. At the end of 1997 there had been some upheaval within the factory teams for World Superbike. Carl Fogarty wanted his own team and initially organized a one-rider team with a factory bike through Alstare with Corona sponsorship. In the meantime Troy Corser was welcomed back by Ducati after a disappointing year in the 500 cc Grands Prix. After two poor seasons, Neil Hodgson lost his place in the Virginio Ferrari team, Pierfrancesco Chili inheriting that berth. When Fogarty's team failed to materialize, Ducati was left with a difficult situation. Both Corser and Fogarty were past World Champions, and to have them both in the same team would be undesirable. Another team needed to be formed for one of them. Fortunately a solution was found with the formation of Ducati Performance with Gio.Ca.Moto. Having just won the Supersport World Cup, Daniele Casolari's team was expanded to run a one-rider World Superbike factory bike alongside the Supersport 748SPS. With Davide Tardozzi as team manager, it was expected that Troy Corser would go with Gio.Ca.Moto., but surprisingly Carl Fogarty left the Virginio Ferrari camp to a team where he was to be the sole rider.

Carl Fogarty was the only rider in
the Ducati Performance team,
and he won the 1998 World
Superbike Championship.

There were some considerable changes to the factory racers for 1998. Ducati Corse produced 18 machines this year with a new frame homologated through the SPS. There were upgraded forks, brakes and rear suspension, and a completely revised Weber Marelli engine management system developed for Formula 3 car racing. This MF3 type was reputed to operate 20 times faster than previously, with full connection to the telemetry system on the motorcycle. All the modifications were done to address the criticisms of the previous year, particularly in throttle response and handling. These developments resulted in Ducati again triumphing in the

World Superbike Championship, Carl Fogarty taking his third World Superbike crown. Ducati once again won the Manufacturers' Championship with ten race victories (Chili five, Fogarty three and Corser two).

As an American company, TPG was determined to win the AMA Series for 1998. Thus two teams of two riders were supplied with World Superbike-specification factory bikes. The Fast by Ferracci team fielded Mike Hale and Tom Kipp, while the West Coast-based Vance & Hines had wild Australian Anthony Gobert joining Thomas Stevens. Although Gobert won three races, success in this series still eluded Ducati. After winning

Below: The third and final 916
Senna of 1998 was most
distinctive.

the Supersport World Cup three years running, Ducati
again supported Paolo Casoli on the Ducati
Performance 748R, managed by Stefano Caracchi.
Casoli could not repeat his success, finishing fourth in
the 1998 World Supersport Championship.

Many of the detail improvements of the 1997
factory bikes made their way to the 916 Racing for
1998. Only 24 were built, the most significant changes
being a new frame (shared with the 1998 factory bikes)
and a magnesium swing-arm that lengthened the
wheelbase 10 mm to 1,430 mm. The frame was TIG-
welded in 25CrMo4, and while it looked identical
externally, the tubes were thinner at 1.5 mm. There was
also a new, lighter rear sub-frame. The front forks were
similar to the 1997 factory bike and had the same axle
lugs, and there was hydraulic adjustment for the
preload for the rear Öhlins shock absorber. The shape
of the carbon-fibre fuel tank was altered to mirror the
factory racers and capacity increased by 1 litre to 24
litres. While the thicker 320 mm front brake discs were
still fitted, alternative 290 mm discs of the type used on

the factory racers during 1997 were also supplied.

Only detail improvements were made to the engine,
primarily in the use of 60 mm throttle bodies and new
intake manifolds. Lighter pistons and con-rods, a new
crankshaft, and changes to the primary drive spline
couplings also featured on the 916R for 1998. There
was a new gearshift selector drum to smooth out the
gearshift, a new crankshaft inlet oil seal, and timing
belt rollers with bigger rims. Completing the alterations
was a bigger water radiator and a waterproof cover for
the 'P8' injection control unit. With all 916Rs allocated
to various distributors, and so many new developments
featured, it indicated that the factory was very serious
about winning the many domestic Superbike
Championships around the world. While the factory
bikes had been supremely victorious on the world
stage, Ducati was still waiting for those wins in
England, Australia and the United States.

New for 1998 was the 748R, primarily constructed
for the Supersport World Cup. The tight regulations
forbade any alteration to pistons, camshafts, valve sizes

or crankshaft, so most of the special parts of the 748R were confined to weight saving. Only 20 of these 170 kg 748Rs were constructed for 1998. However, other engine parts were considerably uprated. The 748R received the 916R gearbox and sintered clutch plates with stiffer springs, as well as nimonic valves and the same water and oil radiators. As with the 916R, only a 180-watt alternator was used and the wiring system located the '1.6' CPU in the front fairing. All the bodywork, sump guard, clutch cover, dashboard, chainguard, exhaust guards, mufflers and intake manifolds were in carbon-fibre. With its racing rev counter the 748R was very much a 916R with a 108 bhp engine and standard wheels, brakes and front forks. When prepared by Gio.Ca.Moto. for Paolo Casoli, power was increased to 117 bhp at the rear wheel.

So successful had the 916SPS been during 1997 that production was increased for 1998, indicated by the four-digit numbered plaque; 958 were produced for Europe, plus another 100 916SPs for the United States. As happened every year with the race-derived Desmoquattro, there were many more developments appearing on the 916/748 than on the Super Sport or Monster line. The 916SPS for 1998 received not only the new graphics, but the lighter frame of the Corsa (thinner tubing and no longer constructed in ALS450) and also new Showa forks to accept the revised front brake calipers. An Öhlins steering damper was fitted as well as new titanium con-rods; these were still Pankl but not the racing type that had been used on the 1997 SPS. There was also a new regulator, and a carbon-fibre airbox and heat shields. Other engine specifications remained unchanged. It was really difficult to see how the 916SPS could be improved.

There was one more series of 916 Sennas for 1998 of which 300 were constructed, with few updates to differentiate them from earlier versions. Though still with an Öhlins shock absorber, carbon-fibre guards, and fully floating cast-iron front discs, the Senna with its standard 916 engine was now painted black with red wheels. Other changes were a carbon-fibre airbox and heat shield. The 916 Biposto continued very much as before, except for a new regulator, braided steel brake and clutch lines and new graphics. These small changes were also shared with the Senna. For the United States the Biposto was also offered alongside the earlier solo version. 916s for the US were red or yellow.

With the small number of modifications allowed by World Supersport regulations, the 748SP was upgraded to the 748SPS for 1998. Still in yellow, it was closer to the 916SPS than the earlier SP in the use of the new 25CrMo4 frame, titanium con-rods, and new brake calipers. The rear brake and clutch lines were now braided steel, and the engine had bronze valve guides. Other alterations were to the ignition pick-ups and regulator, but general engine specifications were unchanged from the 748SP. The 748SPS still used single injectors and the '1.6' CPU. As tested by *Moto Sprint* in January 1998, the 748SPS achieved 249.4 km/h (155 mph) and produced 97.68 bhp at 10,800 rpm at the rear wheel; this was very little different from the 250.778 km/h the Italian magazine *Super Wheels* had managed from a 748SP in April 1997.

Although under the shadow of the 916, the 748 Biposto continued to account for approximately 50% of Desmoquattro production. This was not really all that surprising because the bikes looked externally identical, and engine performance on the 748 was amazingly strong given its capacity. It was only about 5 mph (8 km/h) down on top speed on a 916 Biposto, but won out with superior handling and a smaller price-tag. The only changes for 1998 were the generic ones of new graphics, new regulator, and no battery charge light on the dashboard. For the United States the 748 came in both Biposto and solo-seat versions, either yellow or red. With one production line designated to producing Hypersports, output was limited by the number of engines that could be built, and total production of 916s and 748s for 1998 was similar to that of the previous year, at 8,744.

To celebrate the end of the distinguished production run of one of the classic modern Ducatis, the 900 Supersport, a limited Final Edition was produced, 500 for Europe and 300 for the United States. More a continuation of the Superlight concept, the Final Edition was designed to appeal to collectors, or those with strong memories of the earlier classic silver 900 Super Sports of 1975–78. Just like the earlier bikes, the 900SS FE had silver bodywork, but with new graphics, accentuated by black wheels. As with the Superlight, there was only a single seat, upswept Termignoni exhausts, cast-iron floating front brake discs, and carbon-fibre mudguards. Carbon-fibre extended to the chainguard and simplified dashboard (without a battery warning light). The two versions differed slightly in specification: the European FEs used 1997 engines with silver engine covers and Mondial pistons and cylinders with external cylinder oil lines, and also had a carbon-fibre clutch cover and steel brake lines, while the US 900 FEs were produced later, in January 1998, and used 1998-specification engines with grey engine covers and clutch cover. The new Tecnol cylinders were neater looking as the oil lines were now incorporated internally. As usual for the United States, these bikes had rubber brake lines. The FE would be the last Supersport with carburettors and was a fitting end to the line that had started back in 1990 for the 1991 season – a line that cemented the position of the Supersport alongside the Desmoquattro as the Ducati for traditionalists, with emphasis on the street rather than the racetrack.

In late 1997 and early 1998, a final run of 900CRs was manufactured, these (together with the US-spec Final Edition) being the last bikes of this Supersport series. Still with the earlier Cagiva graphics, 200 red and 200 yellow of these final 900CRs were produced, and they were unusual in that, unlike other 750s and 900s, the oil cooler was still mounted underneath the front cylinder. The 1998-specification 900 engine was also used, with Asso pistons and Tecnol cylinders, and without external oil lines.

The delayed production of the ST2 during 1997 saw it continue into 1998 with only a few changes. Following criticism, a longer gearshift lever was fitted and there was easier access to the spring preload adjuster on the rear shock absorber. In line with all models, it received new graphics. Always envisaged as a companion to the ST2, the ST4 was an easy amalgamation of the 916 Desmoquattro engine in the ST2 chassis. Although production was delayed until July 1998, this was purely done to enable the new Supersport to be established. The ST4 was actually ready to go into production earlier than the SS, and was visually similar to the ST2. The engines provided quite different characteristics, however, the smaller, more powerful ST4 having a stronger top-end at the expense of the mid-range.

Where the TPG influence became most noticeable was in the Monster line-up. No longer being available in a limited range of three capacities, the basic Monster was now offered in a variety of options, with three 900s and two 600s alongside the 750 and a 400 for the Italian market. While the Monster M900 continued as before in red, black or yellow, with limited alterations, more interest now lay in the two new Monsters, the 900S and 900 Cromo.

For 1997 the M900 had a number of modifications, notably the addition of a small fairing, and a de-tuned engine. Splitting the 1997 900 Monster idea in two resulted in the M900S and M900. The M900S used the more highly tuned Supersport engine and featured the handlebar fairing, and the M900 came without a fairing but retained the lower-tuned engine. Both 900s received fully adjustable 41 mm GD 021 Showa forks (the same as the 900SS Final Edition) rather than Marzocchi. Other features shared with the SS were the remote reservoir brake and clutch master cylinders, and the braided steel brake and clutch lines.

Unlike the European 900SS FE, however, the engine of the M900S was full 1998 specification, with Asso pistons and Tecnol cylinders. These engines also used the 520-watt alternator of the ST2. In other respects the M900S was very much like the limited-edition Supersport. Wheels were black and the front brakes fully floating cast iron, with a rear brake torque-arm. Mudguards, side panels and exhaust heat protector were carbon-fibre, and there was also a lower rear mudguard under the swing-arm. The black continued through to the frame, fuel tank and seat cover. Undoubtedly the M900S was the most appealing Monster since its first appearance in 1993 and showed that by broadening the concept there was still life left in the now ageing design.

Other 900 Monsters for 1998 fitted below the M900S in specification. The 900 Cromo, so called because of the chrome-plated tank, took the basic M900 with its 71 bhp engine but added the black frame and wheels, and carbon-fibre mudguards and side panels of the 900S. With its carbon-fibre seat cover, the Cromo certainly expanded the Monster idea to new boundaries. Whether factory customizing in such a way would be successful for a performance-oriented company like Ducati remained to be seen.

Because of the two new special 900 Monsters, the basic Monster 900 was downgraded slightly. It did receive the Showa forks, remote reservoir master cylinders and braided steel brake and clutch lines, but lost its exhaust heat shield and now had plastic side panels. This led to a converging of the basic 900 and 750 Monsters. The M750 now had dual front disc brakes and came in a choice of silver, red or yellow. In terms of equipment there was little to separate the 750 and 900 except for steel brake lines, remote reservoir master cylinders, a narrower rear wheel, and non-adjustable 40 mm Marzocchi forks. Even performance

Below: The 900 SS Final Edition
was ostensibly a Superlight,
retaining a solo seat and upswept
exhausts.

was quite similar, the lower power of the 750 engine being balanced by the lighter weight.

For the first time since 1991 the five-speed small crankcase 750 (and 600) engine came in for a small redesign. There was a new wet clutch with the actuation moved to the left side as with all the large-crankcase engines. This meant that the clutch could be disassembled without the need to bleed the hydraulic system. The camshaft belt covers were also like those on the 900, being split to allow for easier belt tension adjustment. The same changes were made to the 600 engine, but only the 750 received an oil-cooler.

Despite the release of the new Supersport, perhaps the most significant new model for 1998 was the Monster Dark. As an entry level Ducati sold at an extremely competitive price worldwide (but not in the United States), it was designed to attract younger buyers to the marque. Functionally identical to the regular 600 Monster with its single front disc brake, the slightly lower-priced Dark came in three colour combinations, all with a flat black fuel tank: bronze frame and rear shock U-bolt with black wheels; black frame and shock U-bolt with black wheels; and yellow frame, U-bolt and wheels. The Dark also came with an unpainted front mudguard, no footpeg rubbers, and no seat cover. The new engine provided slightly more sprightly performance than earlier 600 Monsters. *In Moto*, testing a Dark in February 1998, managed a top speed of 182.7 km/h (113.5 mph) with a standing 400 metres in 13.1 seconds at 158 km/h (98 mph). Early reports suggested that the Dark was a bold marketing move, proving particularly successful in Italy. As a long-term strategy, models like the Dark would prove to be important for the company to sell the proposed 40,000 motorcycles a year.

With the demise of the 400 Supersport, there was an even more basic specification Monster for 1998. However, unlike the 400 Supersport that had a six-speed gearbox, the M400 used the five-speed 1997 600 engine as a basis, but with smaller pistons and shorter stroke. The clutch modifications that had appeared on the 600 and 750 Monsters did not make it to the 400, this now being the only Ducati with the clutch actuation on the right-hand side of the engine.

The big news at the 1997 Milan Show was the long-awaited 900 Supersport replacement. It was a tribute to the excellence of the design that the current Supersport had lasted so long, having existed largely unchanged since 1991. However, the style was now becoming

dated, and the suspension and brakes were an older generation to that fitted to the ST2. Also continual noise and emission requirements would eventually see the end of all carburetted engines, and the new Supersport was the first of the traditional models to incorporate fuel injection. It would also be the first new model conceived after the TPG buy-out.

On 15 December 1996 Massimo Bordi had approached Pierre Terblanche and asked him to co-ordinate the design of the new Supersport. Terblanche, responsible for the Supermono, was at that stage working in nearby San Marino at the Cagiva Research Centre with Massimo Tamburini. He immediately resigned from CRC to concentrate fully on this project.

Terblanche's brief was quite specific, and much of the existing motorcycle needed to be carried over. This was not only to minimize cost, but also to maintain links with the Supersport concept because the SS customer was considered very traditional. Thus water-cooling was eschewed, the engine remaining at 904 cc as with the previous version. This was primarily because the extra heat generated from the larger

Below: Pierre Terblanche's new Supersport was strongly derived from his earlier Supermono. It was a clever combination of modern components and style within a traditional framework.

capacity made the cooling marginal for the rear cylinder with an air/oil cooling system. Later plans may call for a larger engine with water-cooling, but in the meantime the venerable Pantah engine continued.

Another carry-over part was the frame, although with a new rear section and a steering head angle 1° steeper at 24°. To facilitate easier development and early production, many components were shared with other models in the range. The instruments and footpegs came from the 916, and the front forks and brakes from the ST2. The 43 mm Showa forks were new generation, as were the Brembo brakes. The caliper mounts were wider apart to improve rigidity, and the brake calipers had increased internal fluid capacity. Both the clutch and front brake master cylinders were also a new generation, with revised lever ratios. The Brembo front wheel was from the 916, and

the rear from the ST2. A by-product of the heavier forks and bigger silencers was a slight increase in dry weight to 188 kg (414 lb).

The new Supersport was the first Ducati designed in-house, and the first to use three-dimensional computers and mathematical surfaces. As Ducati had no design studio in Bologna, Terblanche initially went to Futura Design in Birmingham, England, to produce the clay mock-ups. For a Ducati it all happened very quickly, and only 15 months separated the first drawings and the eventual production motorcycle.

There were a number of significant alterations to the engine, notably the use of Weber Marelli electronic fuel injection. To complement the injection there were also new camshafts, with new valve timing. The inlet valve opened 25° before top dead centre, closing 75° after bottom dead centre, and the exhaust valve opened 66°

before bottom dead centre, closing 28° after top dead centre. Valve lift was slightly different, and the same as the ST2, the inlet opening 11.8 mm and the exhaust 11.4 mm. While peak power was only marginally increased to 80 bhp at 7,500 rpm, the engine ran more cleanly, particularly at under 3,000 rpm. The new camshafts and injection system meant that there was no need for a high inertia flywheel and a lighter flywheel could be used. The Weber Marelli fuel injection ECU, the '1.5', was the third generation to be used by Ducati, and the first Marelli processor designed specifically for a motorcycle application. Not only was it cheaper and smaller than earlier units, but it could also be adapted for multi-point systems and would eventually be used on those models with twin injectors. Incorporating the absolute air pressure sensor inside the ECU, it also promised better reliability. With the injection system was a new 10-litre airbox.

Other engine changes for 1998 were new cylinders (Tecnol), pistons (Asso), and piston rings (NPR). There were also new intake manifolds and the ST2 520-watt alternator. Finally the troublesome 31/62 primary drive became the 32/59 (1.84:1) of the ST2 and 916SPS.

Many observers were surprised to see the new Supersport retain a similar frame and the cantilever swing-arm of the earlier bike. However, factory testers believed that for 90% of road use the cantilever rear suspension was a good compromise. It was lighter and simpler than linkage suspension, which was not seen as so critical on a sports bike that would see its use on the street rather than the track. The stroke on the Showa GD132-007-00 shock absorber was increased to 71 mm (up from 65 mm). Also, by retaining the cantilever swing-arm the historical link with the TT2 was retained.

Although his design came in for some criticism, Pierre Terblanche had tried to incorporate many of the features that had made the Supermono an outstanding design in 1992. As he said to me in early 1998, 'It is much more difficult designing a Supersport than a Hypersport because there are many compromises in the style. It cannot be a total racing look with a low front and high rear. A Supersport is by definition a less extreme motorcycle than a 916, more like a Honda CBR600. Though I found this a challenging project I am very pleased with it.'

One of the problems faced by the new Supersport in the marketplace was the typical reaction to something different, and with the Supersport customer being traditional and conservative, this effect was exaggerated. There was a similar reaction to the new logo at the end of 1997. However, with the new bike offering undoubted advantages in the areas of power delivery and handling, it was certain to gain acceptance over time. The new Supersport had no seat cover, but a single-seat version was planned for a later date using a redesigned seat unit. Beginning in March, production was scheduled for 4,403 units for 1998.

Following on from the success of the 'Ducati Monster Cup' held during 1997, the 1998 Supersport took to the Italian circuits in the 'Supersport Cup'. As with the Monsters, these were prepared by Techna Racing in Rome, the solo-seat Supersports being allocated by lot over a six-race series.

The 916 was still successful, but thought had to be given to its replacement. By 1998 Ducati was still working on the layout, but the trademark desmodromic 90° V twin in a tubular steel frame would undoubtedly be retained. The intention was to develop the engine and frame together to create a unified structure. Other plans looked at combining Massimo Bordi's 1975-thesis four-valve desmodromic cylinder head rocker layout with fuel injection to narrow the included valve angle. In the meantime, all Monsters would become fuel injected.

1999

On 31 July 1998, the Texas Pacific Group (TPG) and Deutsche Morgan Grenfell announced they had purchased the remaining 49% of Ducati Motor S.p.A. from Claudio and Gianfranco Castiglioni. This was also the most successful year to date for the company, with net sales of 465.1 billion lire and production up to 28,011 motorcycles. This success would pave the way for a global public offering of shares in March 1999.

1998 again saw Ducati triumph in World Superbike with Carl Fogarty taking his third World Superbike crown. Ducati once again won the Constructors' Championship with 10 race victories (Chili 5; Fogarty 3; and Corser 2). During the season there had been some problems with Virginio Ferrari, and after five years his contract was not renewed. In 2005, Ferrari sued Ducati Motor for damages of €6,714,000, for the alleged loss of income for three years of sponsorship as originally agreed. So for 1999, there was only one officially supported factory team, that of Ducati Performance, managed by Davide Tardozzi. The racing department was reorganized with the formation of a separate company, Ducati Corse headed by Claudio Domenicali, supplying teams for four different championships: World Superbike, AMA, Supersport, and the Italian Championship. The two riders for World Superbike were Fogarty and Corser, with the 996 racer little changed from the previous year. Thus it incorporated the revised injection system with three injectors, and the new frame and airbox that had been introduced at Kyalami, mid-way through the 1998 season. There were a few changes to the brakes and suspension, most notably the use of smaller diameter (42mm) Öhlins front forks and Grand Prix-style radial brake calipers.

Thicker cylinder head castings provided increased rigidity, along with improved porting and re-angled valves. There was a new airbox and intake tracts, and the same triple injector MF3-S injection system with differential mapping between the cylinders. During the season the stainless-steel exhaust system was increased to 57 mm. With 168 bhp at 11,500 rpm the greatest improvements for 1999 were less power drop off throughout the range and a noticeable increase in engine reliability.

Fogarty still wanted to replicate the balance of the 1995 955 racer and to improve front tyre feel there were two smaller, 42 mm, diameter Öhlins front forks. While not as stiff they reduced unsprung weight and provided mounts for the new generation of Brembo radial four-piston brake calipers. These improved braking action as the calipers were more rigidly located

on the fork slider. The smaller, 290 mm discs also contributed to improved steering response. There was also a new Öhlins TT44 shock absorber and a revised rear suspension linkage.

Right from the outset, the combination of Fogarty and the 996 dominated the 1999 World Superbike Championship. Finally, the fine balance of the 1995 version was replicated and Fogarty won eleven races during the season. Corser's three race wins and victories at Laguna Seca by Anthony Gobert and Ben Bostrom further emphasized the superiority of the 996 this year. Undoubtedly much of this was due to the continual evolution of the design. Paolo Casoli was the official Ducati Corse testing and development rider, and on the 996 Factory Evolution racer he won every round of the Italian Superbike Championship. As a test bed for World Superbike continual improvements filtered through, although the single injector fuel-injection system, with the throttle butterfly even closer to the valves, was held over for 2000.

After finishing fourth in the World Supersport Championship of 1998, once again Paolo Casoli also rode the Ducati Performance 748 SPS in the World Supersport Championship. Casoli was also the chief development and test rider for Ducati Corse in the five-round Italian Superbike Championship. Here new developments were tested on an Evoluzione 996 before they made their way to the World Superbike machines. Though dominant in World Superbike, Ducati still failed to win any of the other national championships during 1998. Thus factory support continued,

Left: One of the most successful
racing Ducatis was the 1999
Superbike. Fogarty dominated
the World Superbike
Championship this year.

Below: The ST4 continued the
style of the ST2, but with the
Desmoquattro motor. This is the
author testing the new ST4 in
Italy.

particularly in the U.S. For the AMA Superbike
Championship two teams received factory 996s for
1999. Anthony Gobert and Ben Bostrom for the Vance
& HinesTeam, and Matt Wait for Fast by Ferracci.
Bostrom performed well, only narrowly losing the
championship. Additionally, several teams received
support with the new customer 996 Racing Special.
These included Lucio Pedercini and Doriano Romboni
in World Superbike, and Neil Hodgson and Troy
Bayliss for the GSE Racing team in British Superbike.
Other 996 RSs went to Sean Emmett and John
Reynolds of the Reve Red Bull team for the British
Championship, Craig Connell and Steve Martin for the
Australian Superbike Championship, and Andreas
Meklau in the German Superbike Championship. As it
featured 60 mm throttles inside the airbox, 39 and
32 mm valves, and a 13 mm lift inlet camshaft, the
996RS was considerably more competitive than early
Corsas. Bayliss won the British Championship and
Steve Martin the Australian title.

The 996SPS continued as for 1998 but for minor
changes. These included a three-phase 520-watt
alternator, five-spoke black Marchesini wheels, and
320 x 5 mm semi-floating stainless steel front discs on
aluminium carriers. Production of the 1999 model
996SPS was only 808. There were more changes to the
916. Now nearly five years old, this was updated for
1999 by growing to 996 cc, the stronger crankcases
and 98 mm pistons shared with the SPS. The 996 now
featured twin injectors, although still with the Marelli
1.6 CPU. Thus the two injectors operated
simultaneously and not sequentially as with the P8
system of the 996SPS. The 996 also featured the 36 and
30 mm valves of the SPS, but retained the 916
camshafts. For the 996 the exhaust system was a larger
diameter (45 mm), with a 120 x 420 mm silencer.
Other features shared with the 996SPS were the three-
phase alternator, 32/59-tooth primary drive gears,
revised brake calipers with wider lug spacing, and the
new front discs. The wheels of the 996 were as before,
but were now lighter, being constructed of a higher
silicon alloy (GA/Si7). Many of these features were
shared with the 748 for 1999, although the front discs
were 320 x 4 mm and the 31/62-tooth primary gears
were retained. The 748SPS became more of a
homologation model for World Supersport racing, now
the only model to retain the lighter 350-watt alternator.

Released in October 1998, the ST4 was the most
significant new model for 1999. Basically the 916

engine of before was installed in an ST2 rolling chassis,
creating one of the best performing sport touring
motorcycles available. To retain the same weight
distribution as the ST2, the cylinder heads were shorter,
with the exhaust camshaft moved 10 mm closer to the
centre of the engine. Other improvements were shared
with the ST2, noticeably the revised sidestand, and
34 mm rear brake caliper. Both models now had lighter
wheels, and the three-phase alternator.

As the main new model of 1998, the 900 Supersport
continued unchanged, but was joined by a 750 and
half-faired varieties. The 750 Supersport used the five-
speed 750 Monster engine, but with Weber Marelli
electronic fuel injection with a 1.5 CPU. If anything
characterized 1999, it was the proliferation of
Monsters. This included the expansion of the highly
successful 600 Dark to 750 and 900 cc, along with the
creation of the City. As before there were two types of
900 engine, both with Mikuni 38 mm carburettors.
The Monster 900, 900 Dark, 900S, 900 Cromo, and

The top-of-the-line Monster for 1999: the M900S.

900 California received the 74 bhp version, while the Monster 900 City and 900 City Dark used the small valve 71 bhp engine. The 900S was the highest specification Monster, with an Öhlins shock absorber, steering damper, and numerous carbon fibre parts. The Dark represented the austere Monster with its black frame and matt black tank and guards. In between were the Cromo with a chrome-plated fuel tank, and the City with its windshield, more comfortable seat, higher handlebars and Mandarina Duck bags. Along the lines of the 900 was the Monster 750 Dark, 750 City, and 750 City Dark. These were also supplemented by the Monster 600 City and 600 City Dark. Along with the regular 600 and 750 Monster there were now 15 Monsters in the line-up.

Future production Ducatis would undoubtedly follow the pattern set by Pierre Terblanche's Mike Hailwood Evoluzione, first shown at the Munich Intermot in September 1998. Terblanche went to AKA design in Hitchin, north of London, where he developed this project in a mere 11 weeks, working with a three-dimensional computer model. Terblanche always had an affinity for the NCR Ducatis of the late 1970s. He admired their elemental simplicity. Thus he used an air-cooled 904 cc two-valve fuel injected 900 Supersport engine as the basis. 'I have a horror for all those ugly wires and tubes everywhere,' says Terblanche, 'that's why I have created sump covers to hide the oil cooler and lines, and placed the ignition coils on the camshaft bearing supports on the cylinder heads. It was my intention to visually clean up the engine.' Special components abounded on the bike including the lightweight diaphragm clutch, 305 mm Selcom (carbon-silesium) front disc, nylon polymer integrated fairing and fuel tank, 80 mm Valeo headlight, television rear view mirror and voice recognition locking system. The frame was specially constructed by the Dutch company Troll, placing the engine as far forward in the frame as possible, with a 23½° steering head angle, and 1,420 mm wheelbase.

On 4 March 1999, an initial public offering of 90,200,000 shares of common stock was issued in the form of shares or American Depository Shares, each representing ten shares. The initial price was 2.90 Euros or US$31.67 per ADS, with the public ownership expected to be 66.1%. There were 900,000 shares reserved for Ducati employees. This public offering coincided with an overall increase in production and sales, with motorcycle production totalling 8,110 units through until September 30, an increase of 16.6% over 1998. Twelve new Ducati stores were opened, bringing the total to 32 outlets worldwide.

As for the future of Ducati, much has changed at Ducati since the TPG buy out. Most of the management was replaced almost immediately, and there was considerable expansion of the marketing and communications divisions. Worldwide marketing was coordinated through joint venture distribution in major markets, particularly Germany, France, Japan, and the UK. Ducati Motor also increased its stake in performance accessory company Gio.Ca.Moto to 99.9%. No longer will Ducati be only for the cognoscenti, and more investment and increased profitability will only add to the quality and competitiveness of the product. With exciting developments on the horizon Ducati should be able to stay at the forefront of motorcycle technological supremacy. After four changes of ownership since 1926, and several more managerial upheavals, this new era for the company offered a promising scenario for the future. With many more innovative projects under consideration Ducati looked to the future with confident anticipation.

Carl Fogarty rode only briefly in the 2000 World Superbike Championship before a crash ended his racing career.

15 A NEW AGE

By the year 2000 it was evident a lot had happened at Ducati since TPG had acquired an interest in the company back in 1996. Although still a small manufacturer in world terms, Ducati was now known as a premier producer of high-quality sporting motorcycles, with a high international profile. Investment in plant and machinery resulted in motorcycle production increasing from 12,509 in 1996 to 34,657 in 1999. While racing continued as an essential element, the marketing programme was much broader than in the past. Ducati was taken beyond the closeted realm of the motorcycle enthusiast into the wider community. As the Western world became more affluent and there was increased demand for leisure products, emulating the success of the Harley-Davidson 'lifestyle' experience was working for Ducati.

2000

The new millennium began dramatically in Bologna when, on 1 January 2000, at 00.01 GMT, Ducati began selling the production MH900 Evoluzione on the Internet. This was the first motorcycle sold through E-commerce, with the same pricing (€15,000) throughout the world. The production version of the MH900e was similar to Terblanche's 1998 concept version, and remained based on the two-valve fuel-injected 900 Supersport. Production was initially scheduled to be undertaken at the Bimota factory in Rimini, but with the collapse of Bimota, the MH900e was delayed. The first three production machines were delivered at the World Ducati Weekend in June 2000, and only 21 were produced during 2000.

In the World Superbike Championship Ducati replaced Troy Corser with former AMA champion, 25-year-old Ben Bostrom, to ride alongside Carl Fogarty in the official Team Ducati Infostrada. However, Fogarty crashed at Phillip Island, the injuries ending his career. After test rider Luca Cadalora failed, Troy Bayliss took Fogarty's position. Bostrom had difficulty adapting to the factory machine and its Michelin tyres, and was soon relegated to the satellite NCR team on Corser's 1999 racer. Juan Borja replaced Bostrom in the Infostrada line-up.

The factory 996 received new cylinder heads, with more material around the studs and ports, and new

The final limited-edition 996SPS
was the 'Pista', or 'Circuit', of
2000.

camshafts with less overlap. The titanium valves were still 39 and 32 mm. The compression ratio was now over 13:1, and the Marelli MF3-S injection system, while retaining 60 mm throttle bodies included a single injector positioned above the throttle valve. Shorter or longer bell mouths altered the power requirements for individual tracks and there were 50–60 mm shorter intakes, with the throttle bodies closer to the cylinder head. The power was 173 bhp at 12,000 rpm, Ducati's evolutionary development yielding an increase of 15 bhp over the previous three years. The chassis and Pierobon frame were similar to the 1999 version, but there were revisions to the internal cartridge of the 42 mm Öhlins fork. The weight was right on the minimum 162 kg. Pre-season testing also saw experimentation with a double-sided swingarm, with high exiting exhausts similar to the earlier 888. These experiments proved inconclusive, but the twin-sided swingarm would reappear in 2002 on the next-generation 999.

The 996 factory racer was still a formidable machine, but the team was ill-prepared for Fogarty's withdrawal from the championship. Bayliss went on to win two races, Neil Hodgson two, and John Reynolds one. Apart from the official factory machines a further ten 996 Racing Specials were produced for selected teams in World Superbike and national championships. The specification included the revised single-injector MF3-S Marelli injection system and a 57 mm stainless-steel exhaust system with the engine producing 162 bhp. Niall McKenzie joined Hodgson in the INS/GSE team, with James Haydon teaming with Reynolds on the Reve Red Bull 996RS. The Ducatis dominated, Hodgson winning the British Superbike Championship.

Bayliss was originally signed alongside Steve Rapp in the Vance & Hines team for the AMA Superbike Championship, and was replaced by veteran John Kocinski when Bayliss moved to World Superbike. Larry Pegram rode a 996RS for Competition Accessories, but Ducati's results were again disappointing.

For the 2000 World Supersport season Ducati Corse produced a considerably higher specification 748RS (Racing Special). Based on the new production 748R, this featured a newly homologated frame and airbox, and an injection system similar to that of the 996 Factory racer. A single Marelli injector was placed above the throttle valve, with the throttle body inside the airbox and very short intake ducts. The injection system was the production Marelli 1.6M, but with 54 mm throttle bodies. There were also a number of engine developments, including new camshafts, a 12:1 compression ratio, 36 mm and 30 mm valves, a closer ratio gearbox, and lighter flywheel. There were also wider, 19 mm, exposed cam belts and with a 54 mm racing titanium exhaust system the power was an impressive 124 bhp at 12,000 rpm. The chassis was ostensibly the same as the 748R, and Team Ducati Infostrada ran two 748RSs, prepared by veteran tuner Pietro di Gianesin. Paolo Casoli was joined by Ruben Xaus, and Casoli finished a close second in the championship with two victories.

The Production 996SPS was upgraded yet again for 2000. The engine specifications were as before, but the chassis received some development. Most significant was the Öhlins front fork with TiN-coated fork legs. The final series of 996SPS Factory Replicas was also produced for 2000, the 996 Factory Replica 2, or 'Pista' (circuit), while for the USA the 996S was

The first production model to feature the larger capacity airbox and shower injector of the racing bikes was the 2000 model 748R.

available. The 996S was essentially a 996SPS with a stock 996 motor. Upgrades to the 996 included Marchesini five-spoke wheels.

There were three versions of the 748 this year. Replacing the 748SPS was the 748R, which was the highest specification production Ducati to date. The engine included CNC-machine cylinder heads, titanium con-rods, new high lift (12.5 mm and 10.5 mm) short duration camshafts, and 36 mm and 30 mm valves. Apart from closer cam phasing and less overlap to reduce exhaust emissions, the valve timing was similar to that used in the racing 996. Also racing inspired was the injection system, with 54 mm throttle bodies with shower injectors and short manifolds enclosed within the larger capacity airbox. The power was increased to 106 bhp at 11,000 rpm, and an upgrade kit was available to boost the power to 112 bhp.

The 748R frame was the modified type of the Fogarty Replica, and the wheels 5-spoke Marchesini. In some respects the 748R was downgraded, as the

suspension was identical to the lower specification 748S; Showa front and rear, although the fork did include low-friction TiN-coated fork tubes. The claimed top speed for the 192 kg 748R was over 255 km/h.

Both other 748s featured the earlier 97 bhp engine, with the entry-level 748 having a more basic chassis specification. The steering head was non-adjustable, there were no quick-release body fasteners, and the rear shock absorber was Boge. The wheels remained the earlier three-spoke type. The Monoposto or Biposto 748S was similar to the 1999 model 748, but for the five-spoke Marchesini wheels and TiN-coated fork tubes.

Apart from cosmetics, there were few changes to the Sport Touring models for 2000. The ST4's brakes were upgraded to differentiate it from the ST2, with thicker (5 mm) disc rotors, and it received a larger 180V55/17 rear tyre. There were also only minimal updates to the Supersport this year. The two capacities (750 and

Below: The new engine for 2001,
the Testastretta. The camshafts
ran in plain bearings and there
was a deep sump. *Ducati Motor*

900 cc) were as before, and both were available with
either half or full fairing. To improve rider comfort the
handlebars were raised by 12 mm, and the Plexiglas
windscreen was higher. The braking system was now
shared with the 748, and included a new Brembo
PSC16 radial master cylinder.

For the first time since it appeared at the end of
1992, the Monster was revised. Monsters were
important to Ducati, comprising 43% of sales during
1999, and the company embarked on a programme of
model variety that would later expand to other
families. For 2000 there was an almost bewildering
range of Monsters available, in 900, 750, and 600 cc
forms. There was the Monster Dark, City, Metallic,
and Special, and all versions received a 43 mm Showa
front fork, restyled tail-light, fuel tank, wheels and
mudguards, and upgraded front brakes. The air-cooled
Monster 900 was now fuel injected, with a 900SS
camshaft, 45 mm throttle bodies, larger oil cooler, and
748 six-speed close-ratio gearbox. The power was
78 bhp at 6,750 rpm. The Monster 900 also received a
new dashboard (with tachometer), while the top-of-the-
line Monster 900S featured carbon-fibre mudguards
and an Öhlins rear shock absorber. The 600 and 750

remained with Mikuni carburettors, but these now
included heated float chambers for cold starting.

Several important changes in management and
company structure occurred during 2000. In July,
Federico Minoli stepped down as CEO of Ducati
Motor, his position taken by Carlo Di Biagio, the
former finance director. Minoli remained Chairman
and Massimo Bordi resigned as General Manager in
December. In September, Carl Fogarty announced his
retirement from racing, but would continue as an
ambassador for Ducati. From November 2000, Ducati
Motor S.p.A. was merged into Ducati Motor Holding
S.p.A. Motorcycle sales increased by 18% during 2000,
to 39,087, with the Superbike and Supersport sector
strongest, up 21% to 16,347. Although motorcycles
sales were healthy, the biggest growth was now in
apparel and accessories, this rising by 49.7%.

2001

At the Munich Intermot in September 2000 the second-
generation Desmoquattro, Testastretta or 'narrow
head', was finally unveiled. Development of this new
engine began during 1998 when Massimo Bordi
approached retired Formula One Ferrari engineer Ing.
Angiolino Marchetti to assist in the design. Marchetti
worked closely with Bordi, but died during 1999
without seeing the project come to fruition. The cylinder
head design featured a narrower, 25° included valve
angle, requiring a redesign of the Desmoquattro rocker
layout. Marchetti's solution was to relocate the opening
rocker arms outwards, keeping the closing rockers
inside. To support the closing arms inside the head while
maintaining a central spark plug, there was a central
cast steel sleeve inserted for the spark plug. The hollow
camshafts rotated in plain bearings, contributing to the
more compact cylinder head. With a 100 mm bore and
63.5 mm stroke the new engine displaced 998 cc, and
provided room for larger valves. In line with racing
engines since 1998 the sand-cast crankcases also
featured a *coppa bossa*, or bottom cup, placing the oil
pickup lower. The cylinders were rotated backwards 10°
to assist gravity oil scavenging from the front cylinder.

Unlike many earlier designs that were production
models before the racers, the Testastretta was
immediately adapted for World Superbike racing. The
MF3S Magneti Marelli electronic injection system was
similar to that on the 996R00 factory racers, with 60 mm
throttle bodies and a single Marelli IWF1 injector per

Below: After substituting for
Fogarty in 2000, Troy Bayliss rode
the 998 to victory in the 2001
World Superbike Championship.

cylinder. The more compact cylinder heads allowed for a larger capacity airbox and the exhaust headers were increased to 60 mm. The valve sizes were 42 and 36 mm. Extensive use of titanium saw the racing engine weight reduced to 66 kg, 5 kg less than the production 998, and the factory racers produced a claimed 176 bhp at 12,000 rpm, with a maximum of 12,500 rpm.

The frame was made by Verlicchi, and there was revised Öhlins suspension, the 42 mm pressurized front fork featuring a sealed hydraulic cartridge, and a low friction spring as the fork was now pressurized. Brembo now supplied vented steel discs (290–320 mm on the front and 218 mm on the rear), while the wheels were standardized to 16.5-inch front and rear, with the rear rim width either a 6.00 or 6.25 inch. Homologated through the production 996R was also a new fairing, without the upper side air scoops, improving the drag coefficient by 1%, and the factory racer was close to the minimum weight limit of 162 kg.

Ducati Corse supported two teams in World Superbike. In the Team Ducati Infostrada Bayliss was joined by Ruben Xaus while Ben Bostrom resumed full works status, but in a separate L&M-sponsored team, on Dunlop tyres. Both teams were run under the direction of Tardozzi, and they were the only teams with the Testastretta engine for 2001.

Bayliss was immediately happier with the 998, and with six wins he took the riders' championship. After a slow start Bostrom won five races in succession and Ducati gained their tenth manufacturers' title, with 15 wins. At the final round at Imola Bayliss fronted with a silver paint scheme replicating the Imola 200 Formula 750 racers of nearly 30 years earlier.

As was usual practice, the customer 996RS was similar to the previous year's factory bike, retaining the earlier, 98 x 64 mm 996 cc Desmoquattro engine. With the shorter intake system of the 2000 factory racers the power was increased to 168 bhp at 12,000 rpm. The forks were 42 mm Öhlins, with radial caliper Brembo front brakes. Hodgson proved surprisingly competitive against the new-generation factory machines in the World Superbike Championship, and in Britain, John Reynolds, Sean Emmett, and Steve Hislop were unbeatable. Veterans, Hislop and Reynolds fought for the championship all year, Reynolds eventually prevailing.

For the first time in North America, the AMA Superbike racing effort was brought in-house. Ducati sponsored two dealer race teams, Competition

Although it looked similar to the 996SPS, the 2001 996R was powered by the first-generation Testastretta motor.

Accessories and Hansen Motorcycles (HMC), increasing the number of factory-supported riders to three. HMC signed Superbike legend Scott Russell alongside Steve Rapp, but Russell's season came to a premature end in a horrific start-line crash at Daytona. Andreas Meklau was drafted to replace Russell but he struggled with the circuits. Larry Pegram rode the Competition Accessories 996RS, but despite the huge factory effort results were not forthcoming. Ducati was absent from the rostrum all season, and this was a year to forget for Ducati North America.

The Testastretta was homologated for World Superbike with the limited-production 996R, initially also only offered for sale on the Internet. This replaced the 996SPS as the top-of-the-range production model. The larger bore and shallower valve angle allowed for larger intake valves than on the 996, with 40 mm valves inclined at 12° and 33 mm exhaust valves inclined at 13°. There were also new camshafts, with the inlet valve opening 16° before top-dead-centre and closing 60° after bottom-dead-centre. The exhaust valve opened 60°

before bottom dead centre, closing 18° after top dead centre. The valves also opened more than on the 996 SPS, the inlet opening 11.7 mm and the exhaust 10.1 mm.

Another advantage of the Testastretta cylinder head design was steeper, more downdraft porting to give the mixture a straighter path to the valves. While retaining a toothed-belt drive to the four overhead camshafts, this was also improved on the Testastretta. One of the design weaknesses of the earlier Desmoquattro was the extreme angle between the upper timing belt pulleys and so the new system used lower-positioned pulleys with a revised belt tensioning system. The keyed pulleys on the camshafts were divided in two, enabling the belt to turn without pulling the camshaft during tensioning adjustment.

The 996R featured 100 mm Asso pistons, providing a compression ratio of 11.4:1, while the con-rods were Pankl titanium. The crankshaft also had racing-type spline, nut and lock washer coupling for the primary drive, rather than the taper and key set-up of the Desmoquattro. Also new was the lighter and more

Sport Touring became more
performance orientated with the
996 cc ST4S of 2001.

compact 5.9M Marelli electronic ignition and injection control unit. Unlike the P8 system that used a separate rpm sensor and injection timing sensor, the 5.9M was similar in design to the 1.6M with a single inductive pick-up. The throttle bodies were increased to 54 mm, with a single spray-type injector per cylinder. The power was 135 bhp at 10,200 rpm, and each 996R came with an optional power kit that included Termignoni mufflers and ECU remapping, providing an additional six bhp.

The 996R frame was a modified Fogarty-type, constructed of 2 mm diameter chrome-molybdenum tubing, with an aluminium rear subframe and larger, 12 mm engine mounting bolts as were all Superbike models that year. While the Öhlins suspension and Marchesini wheels were similar to those of the 996SPS, the front brakes included thinner discs, and four-pad Brembo front brake calipers with four 34 mm pistons. The carbon-fibre fairing no longer incorporated side vents, while the weight was down to 185 kg.

Built as a limited production of 500 units, 350 996Rs were sold immediately over the Internet on its

release on 12 September 2000. The other 150 were retained for racing homologation, but these did not feature an individually numbered plaque. Also, because of difficulties regarding street homologation, all US examples came without lights and stands, although the wiring remained in place.

With the 996R a limited-edition model, the previous 123 bhp 996SPS engine powered the 996S, filling the line-up between the 996R and basic 996. While the engine specifications were similar to the SPS, the con-rods were not titanium, and the electronic injection system was the 1.6M instead of the P8. The Monoposto or Biposto chassis included an Öhlins shock absorber, and a Showa front fork. The 996 also received an Öhlins shock, but retained the earlier 112 bhp engine. There was also a specific US 996S, with an Öhlins front fork and Ducati Corse decals. All US examples retained the lower bhp motor.

As for 2000, there were three versions of the 748, with the 748R receiving several updates. Inside the engine was a lighter flywheel, tungsten inserts to

Below: The first limited-edition
retro model was the MH900e,
but it was more a styling than a
functional exercise.

balance the crankshaft, titanium valve cotters, and a
vacuum precision-cast gear selector drum. The power
was unchanged at 106 bhp. The chassis included a
1.5 mm thick chrome-moly tubular steel frame, lighter
996R-type Brembo braking system, an Öhlins TiN-
coated 43 mm upside-down fork, and Öhlins racing
rear shock absorber. Apart from small updates shared
with all Supersport models (such as the sealed-for-life
battery), the 748 and 748S were as before.

The ST4S joined the Sport Touring line-up alongside
the ST2 and ST4. Powered by a 117 bhp (at 8,750 rpm)
Desmoquattro 996 motor, this featured similar cylinder
heads to the 916 cc ST4, with a lowered exhaust
camshaft. The intake valves were 36 mm with 8.74 mm
lift, and the exhaust valves 30 mm with 9.7 mm lift. The
injection system was the new 5.9M, while the gearbox
ratios were the same as the other STs. Also new for the
ST4S was Asahi-Denso switchgear, an Öhlins rear shock
absorber, aluminium swingarm, and Brembo five-spoke
wheels. The ST4 now had a Sachs rear shock absorber,
while the ST2 included new timing belt rollers with
stepless hub adjustment for more accurate valve timing.
These were used with all two-valve models this year, as
were the gunmetal grey frame and wheels.

As only a few examples of the limited-edition
MH900e were produced during 2000, general
production commenced the following year. Powered by
the 75 bhp fuel-injected 900 cc engine of the 900

Supersport, several components were changed from the
prototype in the transition to production. The 43 mm
Showa front fork was now the non-adjustable type of
the 750 SS, and the round headlight was more
conventional. The tubular steel trellis frame was
specific to the MH900e, as was the 60 mm steel single-
sided swingarm. Like the earlier prototype, the engine
featured styled sump covers, and the graphics were the
earlier Giugiaro style. Not only was the MH900e
technical specification disappointing, it was not the
rare limited-edition model that was originally
envisaged. Total MH900e production was 2,010, with
most produced after September 2001, as 2002 models.

The Supersport range was expanded to include three
models for 2001, an entry-level 750 Sport joining the
750 and 900 Supersports. There was also a 34 bhp 750
for European age-related licence restrictions. The matt
black 750 Sport came with a single front disc brake,
and all Supersports featured a Sachs rear shock
absorber. Updates included an improved lubrication
system, allowing the 900 to use air-cooled cylinders as
on the 750 instead of the previous air-oil cooling
system. Oil jets at the base of the cylinder cooled the
piston and con-rod small-end. Brembo five-spoke
wheels set the 900 apart from the 750 this year.

While there were only limited updates to the
Supersport, the Monster range was expanded to include
the long-awaited Desmoquattro Monster S4. This was
not a variant of the existing two-valve versions, but an
adaptation of the ST4, sharing its basic engine and
frame architecture with the sport-touring model. From
the ST4, came the 916 cc Desmoquattro engine with
lowered exhaust camshafts, enabling the engine to be
positioned further forward for optimum weight
distribution. There was a new Weber Marelli 5.9M
electronic engine management system, with a single
injector positioned inside the 50 mm throttle bodies.
The only different engine specification from the ST4
was the inlet camshaft, closing the inlet valve earlier
(61° degrees after bottom-dead-centre). With an 11:1
compression ratio the power of the Monster S4 was
lower than that of other 916s, at 101 bhp at 8,750 rpm.
To improve the engine aesthetics the battery was moved
to behind the airbox and above the rear cylinder, and
there was a new water pump housing and engine cover.
The Desmoquattro engine was still not exactly
beautiful, but these changes were an improvement.

Although the Monster S4 styling followed that of the
two-valve Monsters, the frame was based on that of the

The S4 Monster Foggy, which was
only available over the Internet,
was very much an expensive
Monster S4. *Ducati Motor*

ST4, with thicker, 28 x 2 mm, tubing and a 24° steering head angle. The engine was positioned 20 mm higher than the 900 IE Monster, and the wheelbase lengthened to 1,440 mm. The 43 mm Showa front forks and Brembo brakes were similar to those on the ST4, and there was a Sachs rear shock absorber. With a dry weight of 193 kg Monster S4 promised exciting and lively performance.

In honour of their most successful ever racer, Carl Fogarty, Ducati offered the limited-edition Monster S4 Fogarty for sale over the Internet in June 2001. Ostensibly a standard Monster S4, there were a number of updates to justify the €18,000 price. The impetus came from Daniele Casolari of Ducati Performance in October 2000. Casolari asked the stylist, Aldo Drudi, to create new colour-coded bodywork, reshaping the fuel tank and incorporating additional carbon-fibre body parts. The Foggy S4 received upgraded Showa 43 mm forks with TiN-coated fork legs, and the weight was reduced to 189 kg. The optional high level exhaust system with oval carbon-fibre Termignoni mufflers, saw the power climb to 110 bhp at 9,750 rpm. Within the first 24 hours of release 142 of the 300 Fogarty S4s offered

were sold over the Internet on 20 June 2001.

After the restyle of the Monster range for 2000 there were only minor updates to the air-cooled Monsters for 2001. The engine sizes were unchanged, at 400 cc (exclusively for the Japanese market), 600, 750 and 900 cc. All but the 900 featured carburettors. There were four versions of the Monster 900 and three of the Monster 600 and 750, including the Dark; Metallic (a Dark variant with metallic paint), the Cromo, and the 900 Special. For America there was a Monster 600 USA, with a 35 mm lower seat. All versions now included a tachometer.

Motorcycle sales increased by 2% in 2001, and were noticeably stronger in Japan (up 51%) and the UK (up 10%) with total motorcycle production being 40,016. While it was a significant year for new designs, the year also marked the end of two earlier eras. On 14 May, the sole-surviving Ducati brother, Bruno, died at the age of 96, and on 19 July the great engineer Fabio Taglioni died at the age of 80. But already a new age had begun when Ducati announced in May, that Ducati Corse was developing a four-stroke Grand Prix motorcycle to compete in the forthcoming MotoGP class.

Below: Bayliss only narrowly failed to retain the World Superbike Championship in 2002 on the Infostrada F02.

Right: Gérard Rancinan produced a series of 'Genesis Speed Art' for Ducati Corse to celebrate the creation of Desmosedici. The riders are Troy Bayliss (left) and Loris Capirossi, with the main proponents of the project looking on: Preziosi, Domenicali and Cecchinelli. *Ducati Corse*

2002

Alongside the development of the MotoGP racer, Ducati Corse continued to update the Factory Superbike. The 998 was to be an interim model until the advent of the new 999, but received a second-generation Testastretta engine. Chief Engineer Filippo Preziosi enlarged the engine slightly to 999 cc, with a 104 mm bore and 58.8 mm stroke. All the engine castings were new, the throttle bodies were non-cylindrical (still with a single injector per cylinder), and with a revised exhaust system the output of the 998F02 went up to 188 bhp at 12,500 rpm. Braking updates saw metallic brake pads, allowing 290 mm front discs to be used all season. During the year other improvements included the installation of a cooling duct from the right side of the radiator to the rear cam belt and pulley.

There were new minimum weight regulations this year. The 1,000 cc twin's weight was now 164 kg with the 750 cc fours at 159 kg, a reversal of the original regulations that were drafted when fours were dominant. The change reflected the success of Ducati's process of on-going evolution that had seen them continue to dominate the World Superbike Championship.

There was no change to the official factory Superbike team line-up for 2002, and this year Ducati narrowly failed in their quest for another World Superbike Championship. In one of the most exciting racing seasons ever Bayliss set the stage with 14 victories, before Colin Edwards countered on the Honda SP-2 to win the final eight races, and the championship by nine points. The HM Plant Team with riders Hodgson and James Toseland ran the 2001-spec 998F01s, with a claimed 179 bhp at 12,000 rpm, and weighing in at 165 kg. The customer 998RS was powered by a Testastretta this year, and this was also competitive in the hands of Lucio Pedercini and Juan Borja.

Ducati was also back in force contesting the British and AMA Superbike championships. This year Steve Hislop, riding for Paul Bird's MonsterMob, was equipped with a customer 998 Testastretta, as were the Renegade duo of Michael Rutter and Shane Byrne. The British Championship was also one of the most exciting seasons to date, the Ducatis totally dominating with Hislop winning the title. The season was again less satisfactory in the USA, however HMC was the only sponsored team, and began the season at Daytona with Canadian rider Pascal Picotte. Political machinations saw Picotte fired, replaced by ex-Kawasaki veteran

THE DUCATI STORY

Superbike Champion Doug Chandler. Chandler brought along tuner Gary Medley and immediately provided Ducati with improved results. They did not win any races but at least Chandler saw the podium three times, and finished eighth overall in the standings.

Nine months after the MotoGP project began the design stage of the Desmosedici (16-valve Desmo) was complete. After considering a twin-cylinder oval piston engine, Ducati Corse decided the best solution was a 'twin-pulse' 90° V-four with round pistons and a simultaneous two-by-two firing order to reproduce the working cycle of a twin and generate a 'big bang' effect. Ducati Corse Technical Director Filippo Preziosi designed a desmodromic valve timing system capable of exceeding 18,000 rpm. In keeping with tradition the Desmosedici used a tubular trestle frame, and the prototype was officially unveiled at the *Autodromo Internazionale del Mugello* on 30 May.

For 2002, the 998 cc Testastretta engine powered all the large displacement Superbikes, now with the generic title 998. Only the 998R featured the short-stroke 999 cc motor, while the 748 range was unchanged but for colours. All fairings were the improved aerodynamic type of the previous 996R. There were three versions of the Testastretta this year,

the 998 featuring a high sump die-cast crankcase and the 998S and 998R the sand-cast low sump. Previously only available on the 996R, all 998s included the Marelli 5.9 CPU. They also had a larger capacity airbox, and throttle body with a single injector positioned above the throttle. Other updates shared by all 998s included the racing type frame.

Heading the range was the spectacular 998R. Displacing 999 cc, with a 104 mm bore and 58.8 mm stroke, and a higher 12.3:1 compression ratio, the power was increased to 139 bhp at 10,000 rpm. Chassis updates included a carbon-fibre seat (without air intakes), 4.5 mm offset front brake discs, lighter Marchesini wheels (-400 grams at the front, and -800 grams at the rear), and Öhlins suspension. Many small engine improvements were incorporated this year and as the final example of the 916-derived limited edition homologation models the 998R was arguably the finest. While the later 999R was an improved motorcycle, the 998R best combined the timeless 916 style with the newer generation Testastretta engine.

Somewhat down the scale in specification below the 998R, the 998S was essentially the earlier 136 bhp 998 cc motor of the 996R, in the 998 chassis, with a Showa fork. The base 998 for 2002 included a high

217

The Bostrom 998S was a limited-edition model in colours replicating the American racer's machine, but it was not as technically exotic as the 998R. *Ducati Motor*

Right: The Bayliss 998S was identical in specification to the Bostrom 998S.

sump crankcase and produced 123 bhp at 9,750 rpm. Because the higher bhp engine was not street legal in America, US 998Ss also received the lower-powered 998 engine, but included an Öhlins front fork. Later in 2001, Ducati announced two limited-edition 998S, the Bayliss 998S and Bostrom 998S. Both included an Öhlins front fork and special graphics with numberplates and signatures, but were otherwise identical to the regular 998S. They were certainly not as special as the short-stroke 998R, but 300 998S Bayliss sold in less than two days when it was released on the Internet. US versions had the 123 bhp 998 engine, and more carbon-fibre bodywork to compensate for the lower power. The Bostrom 998S was similar to the Bayliss, with three batches of 155 produced; one for the USA (with the 123 bhp motor), another for the rest of the world, and the other for Europe, with the 136 bhp motor.

The Sport Touring range was much as before, as was the Supersport line-up except for an additional model, the 900 Sport bringing the range up to four models, all available with a half or full fairing. To differentiate it from the 900 Sport, the 900 Supersport received a height-adjustable Öhlins rear shock absorber, and a new aluminium swingarm, 40% stronger than before.

By the end of 2001, the Monster had become the most successful model in Ducati's history, with sales topping 100,000 – even more than the classic 916-998, the Monster had come to typify Ducati. Already a cult motorcycle, the Monster range was expanded to

include five different displacement versions for 2002. Apart from the base 600 Dark, the entire family was redesigned along the lines of the S4. This included 5.9M electronic fuel injection, immobilizer, electronic instrument panel, new airbox, exhaust system, new suspension with Sachs shock absorber, and the S4 frame.

New for 2002 were the 620 I.E. and 620 S I.E. Monster. Although the engine of the 620 was derived from the 600 (the additional capacity coming from the 750's 61.5 mm stroke), there were a number of updates. The valves were larger, 41 mm intake and 35 mm exhaust, and there was a shorter camshaft, supported by only two ball bearings (instead of three). The lubrication was updated with an internal duct, rather than an external pipe, from the left casing to the clutch located in the right casing. Further updates included a rubber damper at the front sprocket to reduce drive chain noise, and the output was 60 bhp. The rev range was increased 1,500 rpm over the 600, with maximum revs at 9,500 rpm, but the gearbox was still five-speed. Both 620s featured dual front disc brakes and the 620S included a headlight fairing, different mufflers, carbon-fibre side covers and heat shields, ride height adjustment, and a taller seat. The swingarm was steel on the 620 I.E., and aluminium on the 620S I.E. The 750 I.E. Monster was also introduced this year, with a 750S I.E. available in the USA. Apart from the larger capacity these two models were similar in specification to the two 620s. The 900 I.E. replaced the 900S.

At the Milan Show at the end of 2001, a new concept motorcycle, the Multistrada, was unveiled. Created by Pierre Terblanche, Multistrada signified 'many roads', and was designed as a real world street bike that would excel in all conditions. In particular this meant the mountain passes, like the famous Futa Pass in the Apennines near Bologna, where a combination of sports bike performance and an enduro-like riding position were considered ideal. As usual, the direction of the style of the Multistrada was handled by prototype testing chief, Andrea Forni who looked at the bikes commonly found carving the mountain roads and city streets. 'Most sports bikes, with their pinpoint handling, high bhp and firm suspension work well on the race track,' noted Forni, 'but when conditions deteriorate and surfaces degrade, handling and stability often suffer. Big dual-purpose models have the comfort, but also low quality suspension and brakes, and unimpressive sporting abilities.' Project Multistrada's design brief called for a compact, lightweight, versatile and comfortable motorcycle with striking styling; equally at home on mountain roads, highways, city streets, or a day at a race track.

In designing the Multistrada Terblanche used the facilities at Idea Institute, an automotive design firm in Turin. Many features were new for motorcycles. The 1,100 mm single-piece tank-seat assembly allowed a 20-litre tank with the fuel distributed between the main tank chamber and a second chamber under the seat. A valve between the two tank chambers ensured a progressive reduction in fuel level.

A new engine was also developed to power the Multistrada, the 1000DS (dual spark). An evolution of the long-serving two-valve air-cooled engine, Gianluigi Mengoli's Research and Development Department created new cylinder heads, with a narrower included valve angle of 56°, twin spark plugs per cylinder, and the single overhead camshaft running in plain bearings. The valves were also larger (45 and 40 mm), with thinner, 7 mm stems, while the timing pulley diameter was increased (with 20 teeth) to allow the belt to follow a more direct route.

At the same time, the crankshaft was redesigned, with more centralized mass and repositioned oil delivery ports. The lubrication system was uprated with higher volume and oil pressure because of the plain

camshaft bearings. The clutch basket, and driven plates were aluminium, and the transmission output shaft was supported by a double row bearing on the drive side. To improve cooling an additional fin was added to the cylinders. A gasket was now fitted between the cylinder head and cylinder, and the exhaust pipe shortened to improve heat transmission. With a bore and stroke of 94 x 71.5 mm the displacement was 992 cc, Ducati's largest capacity air-cooled twin since the Mille nearly 20 years earlier.

The chassis was also new for the Multistrada. The frame was the usual Ducati steel trellis design of ALS 450 tubing, incorporating the engine as a stressed member and with a single-sided swingarm. As on the 998, the frame included additional lower support for the swingarm pivot. The Showa fork, with TiN-treated tubes, included an additional 25 mm of travel, for a total of 160 mm. The rear suspension was Öhlins, adjustable for ride height independent of spring preload. The brakes included the usual Brembo 'Serie Oro' calipers, with 320 mm front discs and a 245 mm rear disc. The front discs were mounted directly to oversized hubs, eliminating the disc carriers. The Multistrada was another bold concept from a company endeavouring to establish another niche market, and production was scheduled for 2003. Also scheduled for 2003 was the new-generation Superbike, the 999, officially released in July 2002 with the term 'Redvolution'. In the meantime, motorcycle sales were

First displayed at the end of 2001, the Multistrada was a successful attempt at creating a new niche market.

desmodromic valves and a tubular steel frame, with the engine as a stressed member. The rear suspension attached an aluminium swingarm directly to the engine, with the only chassis as such a tubular steel bracket connecting the engine and the steering head and supporting the 42 mm Öhlins front fork. True to form the Desmosedici combined the best of modern design with links to the past. The all-enveloping bodywork was designed by noted British F1 car aerodynamicist Alan Jenkins.

The liquid-cooled 16-valve 86 x 42.6 mm engine produced over 220 bhp at 16,000 rpm. The engine layout was pure racing; a train of spur gears driving twin overhead camshafts from a two-crankpin, 360° crank, chosen in preference to the 180° twin-pulse type that had resulted in crankshaft failure. Power was transferred via a six-speed cassette-type gearbox, and multiplate slipper clutch. The weight was only 145 kg and riding the Desmosedici were Loris Capirossi and Troy Bayliss. Corrado Cecchinelli moved across from World Superbike to act as technical director.

From the outset the Desmosedici was competitive, Capirossi astonishing the pundits in pre-season testing with the fastest lap times and a top speed of 328.19 km/h (203.93 mph). Capirossi finished on the rostrum in the Desmosedici's first race and it was soon evident the Ducati was the only real threat to Honda domination. Capirossi won Ducati's first Grand Prix since 1959 at Cataluyna, and turned up at Brno mid-season with a new chassis, with a 50 mm Öhlins fork, and new bodywork. This featured a re-profiled nose with additional air intakes to improve cooling. Capirossi finished fourth in the championship, with Bayliss sixth. Ducati ended second in the Manufacturers' Championship; a phenomenal effort first time out for such a small manufacturer.

With all the other manufacturers deciding to concentrate on MotoGP, Ducati was left as the only factory supporting a team in the World Superbike Championship. Sponsorship was by Fila, and while many technicians departed to the MotoGP team, the team was still overseen by Tardozzi with Ernesto Marinelli as technical director. Paolo Ciabatti continued as director, successfully ensuring adequate sponsorship. Although overshadowed by the Desmosedici project the new 999 racers were impressively presented and formidable racers. This year regulations allowed four-cylinder 1000s for the first time, with 32.5 mm inlet restrictors, but it did not seem

still strong, topping 39,607 during 2002 and with 19,600 Monsters sold this range still predominated. The total production of 39,534 was only slightly less than in 2001.

2003

The year 2003 was a milestone in the history of Ducati. Not only did this see the release of the 999 and Multistrada, but also Ducati's successful venture into motorcycle racing at the highest level, the world of MotoGP. With a budget of €30 million, and only 16 engineers, Ducati Corse produced a 989 cc racer that took the racing world by surprise. Typical of Ducati, the 90° V-four used established technology, such as

Below: Claudio Domenicali
headed Ducati Corse and
coordinated the Desmosedici
development.

Bottom: Loris Capirossi
astounded everyone with his
exploits on the D16 during 2003.

to handicap the Ducatis. After an absence of six years Neil Hodgson was back with the team, joined by Ruben Xaus. Hodgson easily won the World Superbike Championship with 13 victories, and with Ducatis taking every round of the championship it was no surprise to see it nicknamed 'The Ducati Cup'.

With a single injector IWF1, 60 mm throttle bodies, and a Marelli MF5 processor shared with the Desmosedici, the 999 cc Testastretta motor in the 999F03 produced a claimed 189 bhp at 12,500 rpm. New camshafts were designed to reduce timing belt wear, and the 65 mm (up from 60 mm) 2-1-2-1 Termignoni exhaust system was 50% lighter. The large radiator incorporated a big triangular oil cooler at the bottom, as well as an air duct to the rear upper cam drive. The new chassis, with a 20 mm longer swingarm than the stock 999 and a 1,440 mm wheelbase, required some refinement before Hodgson was totally happy with it, the low rear/high front set-up differing to the 998. The frame was originally too stiff, and was modified mid-season to provide more flex, and hence more feel, and the swingarm was heavily braced underneath. Front braking was by 305 mm ventilated discs on Hodgson's bike, and 320 mm unventilated discs on Xaus's. The 42 mm front fork was a pressurized

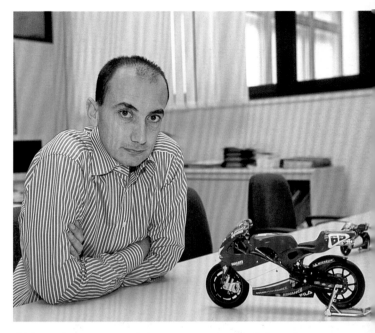

Below: Claudio Domenicali
headed Ducati Corse and
coordinated the Desmosedici
development.

Öhlins, the same as on the Desmosedici, and the Fila team was fortunate to have access to the best 16.5-inch Michelin tyres available. As on the Desmosedici, aerodynamic development of the production 999 bodywork was entrusted to Alan Jenkins.

Bottom: Loris Capirossi
astounded everyone with his
exploits on the D16 during 2003.

Neil Hodgson was back on a
factory Ducati Superbike in 2003,
and won the World Superbike
Championship.

The 2002 F02 bikes were run by the GSE Team under Colin Wright, with James Toseland and Chris Walker, Toseland winning one race. There was also a large number of private 998RS machines on the grid, and Chili and Laconi regularly finished on the podium.

The Ducati 998 continued to dominate the British Superbike Championship, but this year it was Shane 'Shakey' Byrne who took the series on the MonsterMob Ducati, with 12 victories. Replacing Hislop, who was dumped by the team over the winter, Byrne had two new F02 Superbikes at his disposal. Michael Rutter, riding for the Renegade Team, had two well-used F02 bikes, but lacked the spares and backup to consistently battle at the front.

Ducati's woes in the AMA Championship continued during 2003. Two teams started the season, Ducati Austin with Anthony Gobert, and the Dream Team with Larry Pegram. After Gobert was sacked, again mid-season, replaced by Giovanni Bussei, the Dream Team quietly faded away altogether. At least Bussei made some amends, finishing second in the final race.

Heading the production line-up for 2003 was the 999, joined shortly afterwards by a similar 749. The 999 was available in three versions, the 999R, 999S and 999, with the 749 in two versions, the 749S and

749. All were powered by Testastretta motors, the 999R and 999S with sand-cast deep-sump crankcases, and the 999 and 749 with die-cast low-sump crankcases. The earlier 998 and 748 continued for another year, but only in standard guises.

As expected, the 999, another product by Pierre Terblanche retained Ducati's trademark features, but was purposefully long, low and narrow, to reduce frontal area. For the first time a sports bike was ergonomically designed with the rider an integral component, and included five-way adjustable footpegs and on Monoposto versions, a seat/tank unit that slid fore and aft 20 mm to adjust to the height of the rider. With 30% fewer parts simplification and ease of maintenance were primary considerations. Technical updates included an asymmetrical exhaust, the front pipe diameter increasing from 45 to 55 mm compared to the constant 45 mm diameter of the rear pipe, to simulate a symmetrical length system. The airbox was also larger, at 12.5 litres, and was no longer sealed by the bottom of the fuel tank. While retaining the signature steel trellis frame, the swingarm was now double-sided, and the chassis was designed to place more weight on the front wheel. As on the 998, the front fork rake was adjustable due to an eccentric in the steering head (23.5–24.5°), altering trail without affecting the 1,420 mm wheelbase. The 43 mm front fork and rear suspension on the 999R and 999S was Öhlins, with Showa on the 999 and 749. The front brake discs remained at 320 mm, but the rear disc was increased slightly over the 998, to 240 mm. The 999R included racing-style radial Brembo front brake calipers for the first time on a production Ducati.

As evidenced by its success in the World Superbike Championship, the 999 was an improvement over the 998. The attention to weight distribution and lowering the centre of gravity, and the longer swingarm and wheelbase, contributed to a machine with improved stability under braking and acceleration.

Powering the 999 were engines very similar to those of the 2002 998. The 999R retained the shorter stroke 999 cc, 139 bhp engine, while the 999S used the 136 bhp 998 motor, and the 999 the 124 bhp engine. New this year was the next evolution of the Testastretta, the 749. Displacing 748.14 cc, the bore and stroke were 90 x 58.8 mm. The included valve angle of 27° was slightly wider than the larger Testastretta, 12.5° for the intake and 14.5° for the exhaust. The valve sizes were 37 and 30.5 mm. New desmodromic camshafts included eight lightening holes, and the lubrication and cooling ducts in the cylinder head were redesigned. While the basic 749 chassis configuration was the same as the 999, the weight bias was more pronounced, with 101 kg on the front and 98 kg on the rear.

During 2003 a limited edition 999R Fila was released. Celebrating 200 World Superbike victories, this was produced in the livery of the Team Ducati Fila. Updates over the standard 999R included racing-type forged wheels, a titanium headlight assembly, a carbon-fibre fairing, and a racing exhaust with a remapped CPU.

The traditional Supersport line-up was re-engineered and repositioned in the marketplace. This featured an expansion to three capacities: 620, 800 and 1,000 cc. They included the 620 and 800 Sport, and 800 and 1000 Supersport. This year the 800 and 1,000 engines replaced the 750 and 900 throughout the Supersport and Monster line-up, while the 620 was the same engine introduced in 2002 on the Monster 620. All engines featured the Marelli 5.9 CPU, and lighter throttle bodies with Pico fuel-injectors. The 1000DS Supersport was powered by the same dual spark motor introduced for the Multistrada (described in the previous section). The power was 85.5 bhp at 7,750 rpm.

Below: The 999 presented a new face, and incorporated a number of important developments over the 998. The 999S had Öhlins suspension. *Ducati Motor*

Bottom: Heading the 999 range was the 999R, with radial front brake calipers.

New for 2003 was the 802 cc air-cooled engine, a development of the previous 750 that originated with the Pantah-derived 750 F1 back in 1985. The 800 shared its engine cases with the 620 and was termed 'mid-size' to distinguish it from the larger motors. As on the 620, the additional capacity for the 800 was achieved with a longer, 66 mm stroke, while retaining the 750's 88 mm bore, but with cast instead of forged pistons. While most design features were shared with the 620, the 800 received a six-speed transmission and a rubber cush drive with cylindrical springs for the primary drive. As on the 620, the camshafts rode in only two ball bearings, and the aluminium was wet. The power was 73 bhp at 8,250 rpm.

The range of chassis equipment reflected the status of each model, with the 620 and 800 Sport including a non-adjustable Marzocchi 43 mm front fork, Boge rear shock, steel swingarm, and three-spoke wheels. The Supersport 800 featured an adjustable Showa fork, an aluminium swingarm, and five spoke wheels. A 600 gram lighter Showa adjustable front fork graced the Supersport 1000DS, there was a height adjustable Öhlins rear shock, an aluminium swingarm, and five-spoke wheels. The 1000 Supersport also included lighter exhaust manifolds and footpeg brackets. Dual 320 mm front discs featured on the entire range this year, and the rear brake caliper piston was larger (34 mm). Other updates extended to a new instrument panel and headlight.

For 2003, the Sport Touring family was expanded to include the ST4S ABS, but apart from small updates there were few changes to the other models (ST4S, ST4,

and ST2). There was a redesigned gear selector drum, and the ST4S had a new starter safety system to allow the engine to run with the side stand down and the bike in neutral. The Bosch ABS was developed by Brembo in collaboration with Ducati and allowed separate ABS management of the front and rear braking systems, to have traditional feel.

The iconic Monster family was further expanded for 2003, and was now available in four engine capacities encompassing seven varieties of S and Dark. The Monster 620 i.e. and Monster S4, were joined by the Monster 800 and Monster 1000DS. The latter were powered by the same motors as for the Supersport, and previously detailed, although the 1000DS made slightly less power (84 bhp) in the Monster. The entire range now featured the S4-type frame, but with differing seat heights to appeal to a variety of riders.

During 2003 an additional Monster was released, the S4R. Expected for some time, this had a more sporting emphasis than other Monsters. Powered by a 113 bhp version of the 996 cc Desmoquattro, this was essentially the same motor as that of the ST4S, but with

Left: The 999R Fila was released during 2003 to celebrate 200 Ducati World Superbike victories. *Ducati Motor*

Below: The 1000DS motor also made it to the Supersport for 2003, bringing a new lease of life to this traditional family.

Bottom: More sporting than the standard Monster, the S4R featured a number of technical innovations, as well as a 996 cc motor.

a new airbox housing the 50 mm throttle bodies, and a wider ratio gearbox. Several styling and technical features differed from the S4. The exhaust was a high-rise two-into-one-into-two, and the tubular aluminium swingarm single sided. The handlebar was a variable section aluminium type, and new footpegs allowed for an increase in ground clearance. Quality suspension included a Showa fork with TiN-coated tubes, and a Showa rear shock absorber. The Multistrada also made it into production during the year, and was immediately successful, sales numbering 6,025 in 2003. In March, Carlo Di Biagio resigned as CEO, his position taken by Federico Minoli, and in May, Ducati announced it was teaming up with Warner Brothers to promote the movie *The Matrix Reloaded* that featured a road chase on a Ducati 998 Superbike. In October, three new concept bikes, the SportClassics were unveiled in Tokyo. Headed by the Paul Smart 1000, these replicated the famous 'round-case' 750 twins of 1971–74; the 750 Super Sport, 750 Sport, and 750GT. The PS1000 was inspired by Paul Smart's 1972 Imola race winner.

Below: The D16GP4 was almost all new, but the performance was disappointing. *Ducati Corse*

Despite the release of the 999 and Multistrada, motorcycle sales decreased in 2003, down 3.5%, to 38,128. Total motorcycle production was down 2.8%, to 38,417. Hardest hit were the Sport Touring (down 34.6% to 2,275) and the Superbike and Supersport (down 26.3% to 12,126).

2004

After surprising everyone with the Desmosedici in 2003, Ducati Corse produced an updated D16GP4 for the 2004 MotoGP season. Of the 915 individual components, 60% were new on this evolutionary model. Although the bodywork was outwardly similar, it was built of four parts to simplify maintenance, and was designed to improve cooling. Overheating had been a problem during 2003.

A new titanium exhaust was produced by Termignoni, with the vertical cylinders exiting under the tail and the horizontal cylinders on the right. This allowed the fuel tank to be redesigned, extending under the seat to improve mass centralization. The tubular steel frame was similar in design, with different engine mounts to allow easier engine removal, and the redesigned pressed-aluminium swingarm was lighter. The front fork went back to 42 mm, while the airbox was larger. Inside the engine was a new combustion chamber and new components to reduce weight and internal friction. This resulted in a 10 bhp increase, to 230 bhp at 16,500 rpm, and allowed the D16 to achieve a top speed of 347.4 km/h in pre-season testing (again the fastest MotoGP bike).

Unfortunately, the D16GP4 did not fulfil initial expectations. Power was not a problem, but alterations to the chassis affected stability and from the outset the riders struggled. Ballast was added to the front to improve the weight balance and 2003 models were built out of spares for a test comparison. After Cataluyna there was a new traction control. Eventually there was a new 'twin-pulse' engine, but with the cylinders decoupled by around 45°, staggering the power impulses to avoid the earlier reliability problems. After Phillip Island a new chassis and swingarm was tested, and there was an improved Öhlins TT25 fork. By the end of the season the bike was better, with some rostrum finishes, but the GP4 was a disappointment after 2003. Capirossi finished a lowly ninth in the World Championship, while Bayliss's frequent crashing saw him finish 14th, and lose his ride for 2005. The 2003 D16s were ridden by Hodgson and Xaus for the d'Antin team, occasionally beating the factory Marlboro team.

For the 2004 World Superbike Championship, Ducati signed 23-year-old James Toseland and Régis Laconi to ride the Fila 999F04s. The only official factory squad in the series, the 999s managed first and second in the championship, Toseland becoming the youngest ever champion. This year was much more hard fought as the Fila team no longer had the advantage of special tyres, all teams using Pirelli, while new regulations allowed the four-cylinder machines to displace 1,000 cc. Updates to the F04 racers included new two-ring Omega pistons and longer titanium Pankl connecting rods designed to reduce weight and friction. Valve sizes were 43.5 mm inlet and 34 mm exhaust. To improve reliability the rev limit was set 500 rpm lower

Below: James Toseland narrowly won the 2004 World Superbike Championship from Regis Laconi. *Ducati Corse*

Right: Compact and powerful, the V-four 990 cc Desmosedici motor. *Ducati Corse*

than in 2003, at 13,200 rpm. The compression ratio was up to 15.8:1, and with a titanium 2-1-2-1 63.5 mm exhaust system output was 189 bhp at 12,500 rpm. The carbon-fibre airbox and intake ducts were designed by Alan Jenkins, and the Verlicchi frame was as before. The 999 continued to be very sensitive to set up, and Toseland only narrowly won the championship from Laconi. The Fila bikes won ten races.

The factory also supplied customer teams (DFX, Renegade, NCR, and PGS-1) with close replicas of the F03 999. These RS04 racers were close in specification to the F04, except for the latest pressurized 42 mm Öhlins front fork, but didn't share the factory machines' reliability. On the track they were as fast, Haga winning six races and McCoy one. They also proved fickle to set up, and Chili openly criticized his 999, switching back to the older 998. Handling

The 749R was the highest specification production Ducati available in 2004, and was raced with some success in the World Supersport Championship by Lorenzo Lanzi. *Ducati Corse*

Right: The ST3 replaced the ST2 for 2004, all STs receiving a new headlight and fairing this year. *Ducati Motor*

problems were also evident in the British Superbike Championship, with Sean Emmett struggling on the pre-season favourite MonsterMob Ducati. Emmett could only manage two race wins, to finish fifth overall. In the AMA Superbike Championship Eric Bostrom was the sole Ducati factory entry on the Ducati Austin 999. Shod with Michelin tyres, Bostrom had a disappointing season but took one victory, at Pikes Peak.

After an absence of three years, Ducati Corse re-entered the World Supersport Championship. It was a tentative entry, with only one rider, Lorenzo Lanzi on the new 749R. The short-stroke 749R (detailed in the next section) was already the most advanced production bike offered by Ducati, and racing developments included a Magneti Marelli MR600 ECU, 57 mm Termignoni exhaust system, ported cylinder heads, and racing air filters. The power was an impressive 140 bhp at 13,000 rpm, and Lanzi was timed at an astonishing 292 km/h at Monza. Lorenzo Lanzi proved very competitive on the Breil 749R,

finishing the World Supersport Championship in fifth place. In other championships, David Muscat took the French Supersport Championship on a 749R, and Michael Laverty won one race in the British series on the MonsterMob 749 and ended second overall.

By 2004, the 999 and 749 range was firmly established and two final versions of the 998 were released, the 998 FE (Final Edition), and 998 Matrix. The 998 FE was similar to the earlier 998S, with an Öhlins front fork, while the 998 Matrix was a 998, painted dark green, as in the *Matrix Reloaded* film. This year there were three versions of the 999 and 749, standard, 'S' and 'R', with most updates centred on the 749. The 749S motor was uprated, the power increasing from 103 to 110 bhp, and the 749R was released for Supersport racing. There were only a few updates to the top-of-the-range 999R. All the bodywork was now carbon-fibre, including the heat dissipation partition, which was previously aluminium alloy. The headlight support was magnesium. As World Superbike Championship rules did not allow the removal of standard fixed chassis parts for racing, and the racing exhaust pipes were larger in diameter, the size of the foot peg mounting plates was reduced, limiting adjustment to two positions. The Brembo Marchesini wheels were new, weighing one kilo less than the 2003 999R. The short-stroke 999 cc engine was much as before, and included a Termignoni 102 Db exhaust, with horizontal rear half-manifold without catalytic converter and specific electronic control unit.

The 749R was the most exciting model released this year. A real racer for the street, this was the most technically advanced production bike ever offered by Ducati. Powering the 749R was a new short-stroke version of the Testastretta motor. The 94 x 54 mm motor displaced 749.5 cc, and with a 12.7:1 compression ratio produced 118 bhp at 10,250 rpm. The crankcases were deeper sump, but now pressure die-cast (shared with the 999S). The pistons were forged Asso, and the cylinder head ports were unmachined to allow modification for racing. Unlike the 999R, with special (Wills) cylinder head sealing rings, the 749R used a four-layer metal gasket. As the top-end assembly was identical to other 749s, the shorter stroke required longer titanium Pankl con-rods (128.5 mm). These also had the advantage of limiting piston lateral thrust against the cylinder. The camshafts were higher lift (13 mm intake and 11.5 mm exhaust), with extremely steep ramps, and valves 39.5 and 32 mm. The 749R was the first production Ducati with titanium valves (by Del West) as standard equipment, and because titanium has high surface abrasion, the valve seats and valve guides were Berilbronz.

While the included valve angle was unchanged at 27°, the closing valve stem adjuster set-up was the same as on the factory Superbike engines, with two titanium cotters instead of the usual half-rings. The desmodromic rocker arm acted on the adjuster to close the valve, its thickness determining the clearance. This clearance was critical, and could affect valve timing if incorrect. The valve stems were also narrower (6 mm) than on other Testastrettas. The crankshaft was also designed for racing, with smaller flywheels, their cross-section tapered and grooved. The profile was designed to reduce internal friction. To reduce timing belt failure due to excessive heat build up, a cooling duct was installed for the rear carbon-fibre belt cover. The clutch was a slipper clutch type, the pressure plate with cylindrical clutch springs and a composite drum with inclined surfaces activated during back torque. The valve covers were magnesium.

Unlike the 749 and 749S that used the gear teeth, a phonic wheel was machined on the outer rim of the camshaft drive gear, coupled to a magnetic induction sensor, to generate the rpm signal and phase for the engine management. This provided a clearer electronic signal at higher rpm. For racing, another sensor was installed for rpm, coupled to the flywheel with four teeth at 90° intervals. The single Magnetti Marelli IWPR2 injector per cylinder, mounted above the throttle inside the 54 mm throttle body, was not the single-hole injector found on other Testastrettas, but a 12-hole racing type. The ECU was an IAW 5AM.

The chassis included a new aluminium swingarm, a replica of that on the 999 F03 World Superbike racer. The pivot area was cast aluminium, while the arms were box sectioned, the left side featuring lower reinforcement. It also incorporated Superbike type chain adjustment sliders instead of a conventional cam mechanism. Also new was the rear suspension linkage, with FLAT progression, and a different spring and shorter stroke (from 71 to 56 mm) for the Öhlins shock absorber. The rocker arm was positioned above the shock absorber with a different push-rod mount. As on the 999R, the 43 mm Öhlins front fork allowed for radial brake calipers, and the forged aluminium wheels featured five 'Y' spokes with ten anchor points on the inside of the rim. For racing, the fork offset could also be altered via a pin. There were two settings, 30 and 36 mm, but this feature was disabled for street use.

Also new for 2004 was the 749S. This was similar to the base 749, but for more advanced suspension and an adjustable chassis. The engine received a modified crankshaft, with new journals and lighter flywheels. The intake valves were increased to 38 mm, with lighter opening rocker arms. A new connecting system between the valve stem and the closing rocker arm adjuster was adapted from the racers, allowing higher lift camshafts, 11.4 mm for the intake and 10.2 mm for the exhaust. The power went up to 110 bhp at 10,000 rpm.

As the Supersport family was considerably revised the previous year, there were minimal updates for

2004. After only one year the 620 and 800 Sports exited, leaving only two Supersports, the 800 and 1000, both fully faired. This reduction in models indicated the revamped Supersport was not attracting the sales expected, and this was evident in the production figures.

It was the Sport Touring range's turn to be revised for 2004, and this included an all-new model, the ST3. The 916 cc ST4 disappeared and while the ST4SABS, and ST4S, continued much as before, all STs included a restyled taller fairing and double curved headlight. There was a new instrument panel (similar to the Multistrada) and rider ergonomics were improved with adjustable handlebars (movable up or down 20 mm) and a new seat. The most significant update was the replacement of the ST2 two-valve engine with the ST3 three-valve motor. The dimensions and capacity of the Desmotre were the same as on the 1000DS, but the engine retained liquid cooling and featured two 34 mm intake valves and one 40 mm exhaust valve. Developed from the I.Mech.E. design thesis by Diego Mengoli, 29-year-old son of chief engineer Gigi Mengoli, the valves were inclined at 20°, reproducing the 40° included angle of the Desmoquattro. The valve stems were 7 mm. As a single overhead camshaft design, all six lobes were machined on one camshaft, and this was supported in plain bearings in the head.

The crankcases were derived from the 1000 DS, with the water pump being integrated into the alternator cover. The ST3 also featured dual-spark ignition. The compression ratio was 11.3:1 and output was similar to the 916 Desmoquattro at 102 bhp at 8,750 rpm, but with improved low and mid-range power. As an ST2 replacement, the ST3 was equipped with more basic suspension than the ST4S, the 43 mm Showa fork adjustable for pre-load only and there was a Sachs adjustable rear shock. The swingarm was also steel.

Celebrating ten years of production and 130,000 examples, the Monster family now included a new 620, with a six-speed gearbox and an ATPC clutch (Adler power torque plate clutch) to reduce back torque during deceleration. The clutch disc diameter was reduced from 150 to 140 mm, and the effort to compress the helical springs of the pressure plate was reduced from 860 to 560 N. The lighter springs reduced clutch lever effort. The 620 Dark retained the five-speed gearbox, and there was an additional Monster Matrix 620 I.E. and 620S Capirossi, in honour of the factory MotoGP rider.

There were few other changes to the continually evolving Monster line-up that now included seven versions with one of four engines. These were the 620, 800, 1000DS, and 996 Desmoquattro. Like the ST4, the S4 also made an exit this year, leaving the 996 as the only Desmoquattro. After ten years the venerable 916 cc Desmoquattro was no more. Only introduced in 2003, the Multistrada also continued unchanged and in May 2004 it was announced that Desmosedici Racing Replicas would be produced. Plans called for the first example to be delivered at WDW2006, and it would closely follow the technical specification of the factory D16, with sand-cast crankcases and plentiful titanium and carbon-fibre. Production was intended to be no more than one bike a day, or around 250 per year. Despite the promise of the exotic D16, and the imminent production of the Sport Classic series, the sales situation continued to decline in 2004. There was a particularly difficult time during December 2004

when the company briefly laid off the workforce. Total sales were down 5.2%, to 36,089, the only market showing an improvement being the US, up 14.7%. Motorcycle production also declined in the wake of the sales slump, to 36,560. The Supersport was particularly hard hit this year, production down 49.4%, to 1,426, while the Sport Touring and Multistrada also struggled in the marketplace.

2005

In January 2005, Claudio Domenicali assumed the position as head of product development for the street bikes, retaining control of Ducati Corse. This year was to be a difficult one for Ducati. While there was some success in MotoGP, results in World Superbike were extremely disappointing, and motorcycle sales continued to fall. During the first half of 2005 registrations were down by 6.7% on the same period in

Bridgestone tyres made a difference in 2005 and Capirossi had a much more successful season than the previous, winning two MotoGP races. *Ducati Corse*

2004, and in the UK they were down 25%. Only in the USA were sales improved, up 18.4% to 3,933. Total motorcycle production from January to June was also down 8.5%, from 21,878 to 20,028. Despite these disappointing figures the outlook was not all gloomy. Hopes now rested on the success of the forthcoming SportClassic range, of which 4,000 examples were pre-sold, and the limited production version of the Desmosedici MotoGP racer.

In MotoGP Carlos Checa joined the Ducati Marlboro team alongside Capirossi on the D16 GP5. Riding in the satellite D'Antin team on the GP3 was former 250 GP rider Roberto Rolfo. After the disappointment of trying to implement too many changes in the design of the D16 GP4, Ducati returned to their traditional philosophy of 'evolution not revolution'. Updates included a new Marelli engine management system, and a stiffer chassis and swingarm. The other significant development was a partnership with Japanese tyre manufacturer Bridgestone. The tyre testing team included Japanese rider Shinichi Ito. The bodywork was very similar to the GP4, with subtle updates to the nose and rear, and both riders had custom top cowlings to aid aerodynamics.

Again, Capirossi set the pace in pre-season tests, and an experimental engine braking system was tried. This dispensed with the traditional slipper clutch, using an electronically-triggered system to de-clutch on corner entry. Neither rider was happy with the system and did not race with it. Although the D16s were still consistently the fastest on the track (Checa clocked 340.5 km/h at Mugello), the season started indifferently. Bridgestone introduced a new tyre at Brno and there was a new, less rigid, chassis. Immediately, results improved, Capirossi winning two MotoGP races in succession (Japan and Malaysia). Although in contention for second in the championship at one stage, a crash in practice at Phillip Island ended his hopes and he ended sixth overall.

The World Superbike team was now sponsored by Xerox, and the riders were still Toseland and Laconi. Ducati Corse also supported Lorenzo Lanzi on an NCR 999RS prepared by Stefano Caracchi. Updates to the World Superbike Factory 05 racers were mainly centred around electronic devices. Effort was made to improve weight distribution by changing from a carbon-fibre fuel tank to aluminium and moving the electronic controls from the front to behind the

The 999F05 World Superbike
racer was little different to
2004, but not as successful.
Ducati Corse

The 999F05 World Superbike
racer was little different to
2004, but not as successful.
Ducati Corse

steering head. The oil breather tank was no longer incorporated in the fuel tank, but located on the right side of the bike. To compensate for the reduced grip of the Pirelli tyres compared to the Michelins of 2003, sophisticated electronic traction control made an appearance for the first time. This year the Factory 05 bikes had Magneti Marelli Marvel 4 electronics similar to those used on the Desmosedici GP5. Two new engine management strategies were adopted, one to improve the engine braking and the other to provide a more linear power delivery on the initial throttle opening. Engine braking was managed by the normal slipper clutch assisted by a throttle adjustment with a small electric motor. The initial power delivery was corrected by reducing ignition advance. The Marvel 4 also combined engine management and data logging functions in one unit. Engine updates included new pistons, con-rods, and crankshaft (similar to the GP5). With a new type of fuel and oil developed by Shell, the power was increased by around 5 bhp, to 194 bhp at 12,500 rpm.

Improved aerodynamics saw a new windscreen, while the Öhlins TT25 front fork featured the separation of low and high-compression damping with

improved internal pressure balance. Braking was radial Brembo, with 4 x 34 mm calipers on the front with either 320 mm or 290 mm discs, and a 4 x 24 mm or 2 x 34 mm caliper on the rear, with a 200 mm or 218 mm vented disc. For the first time starter motors featured on the F05 racers, necessary to meet the 162 kg weight limit. As was usual, a small number of customer racing 999RS was offered, but this was to be the final year. While similar in mechanical specification to the 2004 factory racer, the electronics were significantly less complex, and these machines were not as competitive as in the past.

After a disappointing start to the World Superbike season, a testing session at Mugello resulted in Laconi and Toseland finally winning a race each at Silverstone. Laconi doubled up at Misano. At Brno there were new triple clamps and a stiffer swingarm, externally identical but with internal bracing and additional welding. Lanzi substituted for an injured Laconi at Lausitzring, winning the second race and effectively sealing a berth for 2006. However, the 2005 season was the most disappointing for the factory Ducati squad since 1988, with Toseland finishing fourth and Laconi sixth.

Below: After only two years the
999 was considerably updated
for 2005. The engine was more
powerful and there was a new
fairing. *Ducati Motor*

In the British Superbike Championship Gregorio Lavilla, initially filling in for an injured James Haydon, rode the Airwaves Ducati. Lavilla impressed, and with seven race victories and 22 podiums from 26 starts, won the championship. Ducati also fielded two factory bikes in the AMA Championship for Neil Hodgson and Eric Bostrom, and it was one of Ducati's most successful seasons ever in America. The Ducati Austin bikes were ostensibly identical to the World Superbike machines, but the AMA bikes did not feature traction control because AMA rules forbid a front-wheel sensor. On Dunlop tyres instead of Michelin, Hodgson started the season well with a second place at Daytona. Early in the year, the 999 seemed to lack torque exiting the turns, but their fortunes improved with Bostrom winning at Pikes Peak, Laguna Seca and Mid-Ohio. Hodgson won at Elkhart Lake and finished sixth in the championship. During the year Hodgson's bike received new engine electronics, as used in World Superbike.

Ducati Corse decided not to contest the World Supersport Championship in 2005, but provided support to Gianluca Nanelli on the Team SC 749R. Nanelli provided the 749R its first World Supersport victory at Imola, his 749R painted in retro-750SS colours.

Heading the production Superbike line-up for 2005 was a new-generation 999 and 749. Particular emphasis was placed on the 999R, with the intention of homologating it for AMA racing. Updates to the range extended from styling to chassis and engine improvements. The basic 999 was more powerful, the 999S more exclusive, and the 999R the most powerful production bike ever produced by Ducati. For all 999s and 749s the fairing was redesigned, with a higher and wider cockpit without the two upper side air ducts, and higher screen. The lower fairing had more protective spoilers, as on the previous R models, and was constructed of a new high-strength polymer, Terblend. Other updates included a 500 gram lighter box-section swingarm and a black anodized aluminium exhaust protective heat shield.

The 999R engine now produced 150 bhp at 9,750 rpm, and was modified to conform with AMA rules

Below: Expansion of the Monster
SR line-up continued with the
800 cc S2R of 2005.
Ducati Motor

that required racing engines be almost identical to the corresponding production units. There was a new cylinder head to go with the 104 mm cylinders, with the distance between the valves and valve seat increased for the titanium valves with bigger heads but 6 mm stems. The valves were retained by conical collets as on the 749R. New rockers increased the valve lift. The con rods were new, and the crankshaft more rigid with improved lubrication channels. The injectors were the 12-hole type as on the 749R, and the compression ratio was increased to 12.45:1. The chassis was similar to before, with the highest quality Brembo brakes, Öhlins suspension, and Brembo/Marchesini wheels. The styling included the updates shared with other 999s, but the fairing was carbon fibre.

As before, the 999S slotted between the base 999 and limited-edition 999R. Although the 999 was upgraded this year, the 999S engine retained titanium con-rods and a lighter crankshaft, and produced slightly more bhp (143 bhp at 9,750 rpm). To differentiate it further the 999S also received a race kit as standard, and retained an Öhlins front fork, now with radial-mount brake calipers.

In response to more powerful competition, the base 999 motor was considerably upgraded, the power increasing from 124 to 140 bhp at 9,750 rpm. The die-cast crankcases were the low-sump type of the 999S, and there were new camshafts, and vented timing belt covers. The four 749 models (749 Dark, 749, 749S, and 749R) were similar in specification to those of 2004, but shared the new fairing with the 2005 999. This year the 749R produced 121 bhp at 10,500 rpm, the 749S 116 bhp at 10,500 rpm, and the 749 108 bhp at 10,000 rpm. Despite all the updates, 999 and 749 sales were down 29% in the first nine months of 2005. Particularly hard hit was the 749.

The Supersport's woes continued for 2005. Sales slid by 48% compared with 2004 and just 525 were sold worldwide in the first six months of the year, and only the 1000DS was offered. Now only with top-of-the-range chassis specification, and a full fairing, there

Below: Apart from the double-sided swingarm there was little to distinguish the smaller Multistrada 620 from the 1,000 cc version. *Ducati Motor*

were no updates from 2004. Now close to the end of its model cycle, the future for the Supersport looked ominous, especially with the prospect of the SportClassic on the horizon.

As the ST family had been significantly updated for 2004, there were only selected refinements to the ST3 and ST4S for 2005. All the clutches were now wet, and there were improved fairing fasteners in order to reduce maintenance time. The wet clutch was designed to reduce noise, last longer, and incorporated dampers to extend transmission life. As with the Supersport, the Sport Touring range struggled in the market this year. Sport Touring sales worldwide were down 55.4% in the first half of 2005, to only 855.

Again it was the Monster family that continued to sustain Ducati. Although more than a decade old, continual updates and range expansion ensured the Monster's popularity. For 2005 the Monster range doubled, with the S2R joining the S4R, heralding the birth of another Monster family. This year also saw the return of the limited-edition 1000 Cromo, with a

chrome-plated fuel tank. Both the 1000 and the 620 ranges consisted of three models, the 620 including the Dark *Monodisco*. All 620s were fitted with the APTC clutch this year. The S2R was immediately successful, selling more than 6,800 units through until September 2005.

The S2R and S2R Dark were powered by the air-cooled two-valve 803 cc twin introduced in 2003, but this year incorporated the APTC clutch. The style followed that of the S4R, with the right-side twin exhaust, small fairing, and single-sided aluminium swingarm. The S2R was slightly lower in specification, with a 43 mm Marzocchi front fork, Sachs rear shock absorber, and 300 mm front discs with twin floating piston calipers. The S2R Dark was lower again in specification, and came without the fairing and seat cover, and with a steel handlebar. The three 1,000 cc Monsters shared a higher specification chassis than the 620s. The ride height was adjustable, as was the Sachs shock absorber. As before, the front fork was an adjustable 43 mm Showa, and the M1000S swingarm

Below: For 2006 the 695 Monster
became the base model in the
line-up. *Ducati Motor*

was aluminium. The S4R was as before, but with the additional colours of red and black, both with white stripes. The power for the 2005 S4R was quoted at 117 bhp at 8,750 rpm.

While the importance of the Supersport and Sport Touring families waned during 2005, further emphasis was placed on expanding the Multistrada. This went in two directions; towards the more sporting with the Multistrada 1000S, and the budget, with the 620 and 620 Dark. This demonstrated the Multistrada idea of combining enduro and sports in a street-orientated motorcycle was one on which Ducati placed considerable emphasis, and it was well rewarded. Multistrada sales rose 111% in the first nine months of 2005, making this Ducati's second-most popular family after the Monster.

It was not difficult to see why the Multistrada was the new sales success story. In the wake of an ageing motorcycle clientele and increasing speed restrictions there was a general move away from racetrack-orientated sports bikes to real-world usable machines.

For many, including the author, the Multistrada was arguably the ideal street bike. For 2005, Multistrada updates included redesigned seats with a new anti-slide system for the passenger, a taller screen, new rear-vision mirrors, and more stable side stand. Options included panniers, rack, GPS navigator, and a racing exhaust.

Heading the Multistrada line-up was the 1000S DS, with variable section aluminium handlebars, carbon-fibre front mudguard and timing belt cover, and Öhlins suspension front and rear. The 43 mm front fork included TiN-coated fork tubes. The Multistrada 1000DS was similar to before, but there were two new entry-level 620 versions, the Multistrada 620 and 620 Dark. The 63 bhp 620 engine included the APTC clutch. While ostensibly identical to the 1,000 cc version, the 620s featured a smaller, 15-litre fuel tank, a Monster-style double-sided swingarm, and simplified instrument panel. The wheels were three-spoke, and suspension was a Marzocchi 43 mm front fork and a Sachs rear monoshock with adjustable preload and

Below: Troy Bayliss made a return to World Superbike on the factory Ducati in 2006.
Ducati Corse

Bottom: After an impressive showing in 2005, Lorenzo Lanzi also gained a factory World Superbike ride in 2006.
Ducati Corse

Below: Another limited-edition
999R replicating the World
Superbike racers was available
for 2006, the Xerox.
Ducati Motor

rebound. The front brakes were two 300 mm front discs with floating piston calipers, as on the S2R. The Dark featured a matt black colour scheme and a single front 320 mm disc brake.

As the public response to the SportClassic was extremely favourable, with the first series sold out by July 2004, it was announced this new retro family would go into production. The first Paul Smart 1000 would be available in November 2005 as a 2006 model, with the Sport 1000 and GT1000 to follow.

2006

The year 2006 was a significant one for Ducati as it marked the 80th anniversary of the foundation of the company, the 60th anniversary of the start of motorcycle production and the 50th anniversary of Taglioni's desmodromic valve system.

At the end of 2005, it was announced that Sete Gibernau would join Loris Capirossi in the Ducati Marlboro Team on the D16 GP6. The Desmosedici GP6 was an evolution of the GP5, developments including more power, a broader powerband, and

increased fuel efficiency due to a reduction in internal friction and a revised engine management system. A new frame, wheels and front fork also enabled the GP6 to be lighter and stiffer. Weight was 148 kg and the claimed power in excess of 235 bhp at 16,500 rpm, with maximum torque of approximately 100 Nm (10.2 kgm) at 14,000 rpm. Alongside the official Marlboro Team was the d'Antin Ducati satellite team, which included two riders for 2006 – Alex Hofmann and Jose Luis Cardoso. Their 2006 bike was termed the GP6-Sat, for satellite team, and was a mixture of the factory GP5 and GP6.

The MotoGP season started brilliantly for Capirossi with a victory in the opening race at Jerez, and at Mugello – Ducati's home circuit – the bikes were raced in special livery to celebrate the company's three anniversaries. At the time of writing, in mid-season, Capirossi was leading the championship. In May 2006 test rider Vittoriano Guareschi tested the 800cc D16 GP7 at Mugello in preparation for the change of regulations in 2007.

After a season on the Camel Honda in MotoGP, Troy Bayliss made a return to the factory Xerox

One of the most exciting models
ever offered by Ducati: the 998 cc
S4RS of 2006. *Ducati Motor*

Ducati in the World Superbike Championship. Lorenzo Lanzi partnered him on the Xerox 999F06. During 2005 Ducati also announced they would no longer provide a customer 999RS, citing the increasing cost of electronic systems. They would continue to supply engines, matched to standard electronic management systems, but for the first time in 15 years the World Superbike grid would not be filled with customer Ducati racers. This was of no concern to the factory Xerox team as Bayliss soon stamped his mark, winning seven races in succession in the first half of the season. Utilizing Magneti-Marelli Marvel 4 electronics, the 999F06 produced 194 bhp at 12,500 rpm. There was considerable crossover between the 999F06 and GP6, including electronic traction control, the Öhlins TTX20 42 mm front fork and the Öhlins TTX36 rear shock absorber.

After such a successful season in 2005, it was no surprise to see Lavilla again on the Airwaves F06 in the British Superbike Championship; Leon Haslam rode the second machine. Both were provided official Ducati Corse 999F06 bikes and Lavilla soon stamped his mark with a string of podium finishes. Ducati Corse was also officially involved in the AMA Championship for a

second year, providing factory 999s to the Parts Unlimited Ducati Austin team. Neil Hodgson was partnered by Ben Bostrom, who replaced his brother Eric, returning to Ducati after a three-year break.

With so many developments to the 999 and 749 having been made for 2005, there were only minor updates to this series for 2006. Heading the Superbike line-up was the 999R Xerox, with the colours and graphics of the World Superbike team. Also distinguishing the Xerox from the regular 999R were a black anodized steering head and footrests, as well as the red Brembo Racing logo on the radial brake calipers and mounts. The rear Öhlins shock absorber was a racing type, with adjustable compression damping for high and low speed, an aluminium body, hydraulic adjustment of spring preload, and a top-out spring.

The 999R, 999S, and 999 were much as before, the 999R engine still with specific cylinder heads, semi-cone valve adjusters, and stiffer con rods and a crankshaft featuring a racing-style lattice pattern. The three models of 749 – the 749R, 749S and 749 – were also ostensibly unchanged for 2006.

Although sales were virtually non-existent, the 1000DS Supersport continued, at least for one more

The limited-edition Paul Smart
1000 was a modern interpretation
of the style of the iconic 1974 750
Super Sport, seen here in the
background. *Ducati Motor*

year. It was only available in one colour for 2006, red bodywork and frame, with black wheels. The Sport Touring range was also rationalized for 2006, with the ST3S ABS replacing the ST4S ABS. All Sport Touring models were powered by the three-valve Desmotre this year. Evolution of the injection and ignition system saw a new automatic idle speed control system and compliance with 2007 emission limits. The ST3S ABS was virtually identical to the ST3, but for the ABS anti-lock braking system (inherited from the ST4S), five-spoke wheels, Showa fork with TiN-coated fork legs, and an Öhlins rear shock absorber with remote preload adjustment.

The Monster line-up focused on the expansion of the SR-series for 2006. Characterized by the single-sided swingarm, there was now a choice of two S2Rs, 800 and 1,000 cc, and a new model, the S4RS Testastretta. The most powerful Monster yet, the S4RS featured the 998 cc Testastretta motor, detuned slightly to 130 bhp at 9,500 rpm. This was a high-specification Monster, a Superbike without the bodywork, obviously aimed at countering the success of the Aprilia Touno Racing. Many of the visible engine components were redesigned, including the triangular-shaped oil cooler

and forged aluminium coolant pipes. There was also a new airbox and throttle body with IWP 189 injectors. The chassis included a stiffened red-painted frame, black swingarm, Y-spoke wheels, and an Öhlins front fork with radial front brake calipers. Carbon-fibre abounded, and included the front mudguard, timing belt covers and the exhaust pipe heat shield.

The 996 cc Monster S4R continued as before, and there was only one 1,000 cc air-cooled Monster for 2006, the S2R. This followed the style of the unchanged S2R, released a year earlier, but included carbon-fibre side panels, 320 mm front disc brakes with four-piston calipers, a PSC master cylinder with separate reservoir, and adjustable Showa 43 mm fork. The 1000DS engine was the same as on the Supersport and Multistrada 1000, but with a special twin exhaust and automatic choke instead of the earlier manual choke. But for new colours, the Monster 620 was initially unchanged, as was the four-model Multistrada family.

Early in 2006 a replacement for the Monster 620, the Monster 695, was announced as an early-release 2007 model. After nearly 15 years and 170,000 examples the Monster remained the backbone of

Ducati's sales, and the 695 was now the entry-level model. Engine updates included new dimensions (88 x 51.7 mm), allowing larger valves (43 and 38mm). The larger valves were matched to larger ports and featured 7 mm valve stems, as used in the Testastretta, instead of the previous 8 mm stems. The power increased to 73 bhp, providing the the highest specific output of any Ducati air-cooled engine. The chassis, including a Marzocchi 43 mm fork and Sachs rear shock absorber, was largely unchanged.

It was Ducati's new retro series, the SportClassic following from the earlier MH900e, that was the most anticipated for 2006. Headed by the limited-edition Paul Smart 1000, these were a modern interpretation of the great trio of 1970s 750 Ducatis covered in chapters 6 and 7. The Ducati 750 Sport and Super Sport of the 1970s were long and low, with curving lines and distinctive colours. Designer Pierre Terblanche sought to emulate this style, using an air-cooled 1000DS engine, exposed tubular steel frame, twin rear shocks and wire wheels laced to 17-inch Excel aluminium rims. Each wheel had 36 chrome-plated spokes, with a variable taper from 5 mm at the hub to 4.4 mm at the

rim. To maintain the traditional look, the wheels featured centre-spoke drilled rims, requiring tube tyres. The tyres were also the same pattern as the Pirelli Phantom on the early 1980s. The spoked wheels required a more compact brake caliper on the side facing the wheel so the front brake calipers were floating Brembo with thermally insulated 30 and 32 mm pistons which are thermally insulated. The semi-floating discs were 320 mm, 4 mm thick. Instead of the usual organic brake pads, the SportClassic pads were sintered. The rear brake was a floating single piston Brembo brake caliper and a 245 mm disc.

The exhaust system was a distinctive black chrome and stainless steel, with stacked mufflers on the right, while the 60 mm diameter tubular steel swingarm incorporated an elliptical right leg to accommodate the exhaust. The drive chain adjusting mechanism was also similar to the original Seeley-style 750. Other retro features included the rounded tail-light and chromed turn signals, and the battery housing with drilled base.

The 1000DS engine was the same as that powering the Multistrada, Supersport, and Monster S2R. A Magneti Marelli 5AM electronic control unit sat under

the rear of the seat and featured a reprogrammable
Flash EPROM. The clutch and timing inspection covers
were chromed, and the valve covers polished.

Only 2,000 Paul Smart 1000 Limited Editions were
produced, and as a contemporary interpretation of the
iconic 750 Supersport included the highest quality
components. Details included a polished Sachs steering
damper with chrome-plated rod. Unlike the 2003
prototype, the front fork was Öhlins, and there was a
single Öhlins shock absorber on the left. The colours
were Metallic Silver and Sea Green of the 1974 750
Super Sport. The 2003 prototype featured a blue frame,
painted to match Paul Smart's Imola racer, but the
eventual production version reverted to the blue/green
of the original 750 Super Sport. In 2003 the design
department was unaware that Paul Smart had
repainted the racing bike frame back in 1972 with
the only match he could find at the time, that of a
Hillman Imp.

The Sport 1000 was similar in style to the original
1973 750 Sport, an elemental sports bike without a
fairing. The large single round headlight and bar-end
rear vision mirrors were typical 1970s features. Initially

scheduled to be yellow only, like the original, three
colours were eventually offered for the Sport 1000:
yellow, black, and red. The suspension included a 43 mm
Marzocchi fork, and a Sachs shock absorber. Both the
Paul Smart and the Sport had clip-on handlebars, with
the Sport handlebars positioned 20 mm higher. To
emulate the long look of the 1970s bikes, the
wheelbase was longer than the Supersport 1000
(1,425 mm), and the fork legs offset by 25 mm.

Completing the SportClassic line-up was the
GT1000, entering production in the spring of 2006.
This model reflected the line and the shape of the 1971
750GT, a basic two-seater bike with exposed engine
and single headlight, much like a modern naked
motorcycle. Differences to the PS 1000 and Sport 1000
included high handlebars, mufflers on each side, and
twin shock absorbers. The Excel 17-inch wheel rims
were chrome-plated steel instead of light alloy.

Another concept motorcycle, the Hypermotard, was
unveiled at the Milan Show in November 2005. With
the success of the Supermotard-style motorcycle from
other European manufacturers (such as KTM), Ducati's
offering was not unexpected. The motorcycle market

was continually evolving, and like every manufacturer, Ducati needed to move with market trends. A Supermotard was light and narrow, a motorcycle pared to essentials, and designed for the ultimate performance in a real-world street environment, be it cities or canyons. What Ducati endeavoured to do with their Hypermotard was provide exceptional performance – a 100 bhp air-cooled motor in a 175 kg package. The 992 cc dual-spark motor on the prototype included a slipper clutch and magnesium engine covers. A high specification chassis saw a huge, 50 mm Marzocchi RAC fork, Öhlins shock absorber, and a single-sided swingarm. Forged and machined Marchesini racing wheels included a single radial mounted front Brembo four-piston, four-pad caliper with a 320 mm disc.

By the middle of 2005 there were more rumours of a company buyout, and it seemed inevitable that TPG, still controlling 33% of the company, would sell if a suitable buyer could be found. The operating loss for the year 2005 was €33.6 million, compared with a profit of €9.2 million the previous year. Motorcycle production in 2005 was 5.5% less than in the previous year, at 34,536, and registrations were down 3.5%, to

34,631. This continued a disturbing downward production and sales trend that began in 2002. Only in the USA was the outlook more promising, with registrations up 21%, but in most European countries sales were significantly down. In the UK they were down by 16.2%, in Germany by 15.2% and in Italy – the most important market of all – by 14.7%. Most product families suffered, in particular the Sport Touring (down 53.4%), and Superbike 999/749 (down 40.3%). This bleak sales and financial trend continued in to 2006, with revenue and production down despite a small increase in motorcycle registrations. In the first quarter of 2006 registrations were up 3.3%, but much of the sales were of existing stock as motorcycle production was reduced 18.2%, to 7,337. The Superbike series continued to slide, now down 45.9%.

On 2 December 2005, TPG agreed to the sale of their stake in Ducati to the Italian holding firm InvestIndustrial. The company was then back under Italian control and on the verge of a new era. While TPG had done much to raise the profile of Ducati since 1996, particularly the creation of an internationally acclaimed brand name, by 2006 it was apparent that

Left: Gregorio Lavilla won
the 2005 British Superbike
Championship and defended
it in 2006 on the Airwaves
Ducati. *Ducati Corse*

Below: For the 2006 Italian Grand Prix the
factory MotoGP bikes were painted a
special colour scheme to celebrate the
60th anniversary of Ducati. Capirossi rode
to second place. *Ducati Corse*

more was required than a marketing-led programme. For a small company Ducati was incredibly successful in competition. It was the only European manufacturer capable of taking on the juggernaut Japanese companies in the highest forms of motorcycle road racing, MotoGP and World Superbike. Ducati was acknowledged as a leader in the production of quality high-performance motorcycles, but the company was no longer unique. The most successful models of the past have stood alone, including iconic motorcycles such as the Marianna, Mach 1, 750 Super Sport, 916 and Monster. While continuing its traditional path of evolution, Ducati had neglected to create distinctively new and different products. Some opportunities had been lost, such as a production Supermono, while history told that the Sport Touring was always going to be a difficult sector for Ducati. And for all its excellence as a performance motorcycle, the 999 had not had the impact of the 916, as sales figures attest.

In an affluent fashion-conscious world, a high-end product like Ducati has to be seen to offer something new and better. During 2005, Federico Minoli indicated a restructure, and change in direction for Ducati, moving away from volume manufacture to smaller numbers of more expensive, high-profit models, predicting that the company would be back in profit by 2008. In the past Ducati has sometimes tried to exist by producing fewer motorcycles, but the years in which production dropped significantly (1976, 1984 and 1990) were characterized by motorcycles that were dictated by fashion rather than function. Each of these periods coincided with a crisis in the company, and in 1976 and 1984 Ducati almost ceased motorcycle production altogether.

The success of the SportClassic demonstrates the importance of history to Ducati, as the company has always relied on race replicas to spearhead its sales. Just as Ducati needed the 750 Supersport after Imola, the company now saw the need for a Desmosedici RR production replica. This was launched at the Italian Grand Prix at Mugello in June 2006.

The first road-going MotoGP replica, the RR was derived from the Desmosedici GP6, the body design and the aerodynamics following the same form. Scheduled for production by July 2007, with only 400 to be produced each year, the RR was only to be sold through the official Ducati dealer network, with Ducati 999R owners receiving priority.

After considering a full racing-specification engine, then a softer wet-clutch version, the final configuration was a sports engine based on the GP6. Similar to the MotoGP racer, the engine on the RR was a 16-valve desmodromic 989 cc V4, with an asymmetrical Twin Pulse firing configuration. The double overhead camshafts were gear-driven, and the six-speed gearbox was a cassette type. The clutch was a hydraulically actuated dry multi-plate slipper type. Due to the limited production numbers, the engine crankcases and cylinder heads were sand-cast aluminium, the connecting rods and valves titanium, and the engine covers sand-cast magnesium. Four 50 mm Magneti-Marelli throttle bodies, with 12-hole 'microjet' injectors fed the cylinders, and were controlled by a Magneti-Marelli 5SM ECU. A four-into-two-into-one exhaust, with vertical exit muffler in the tail, contributed to a claimed 200 bhp (with the 102 dB racing silencer and dedicated CPU). Despite this extrememly high power output, the Desmosedici RR was homologated for road use, with an exhaust catalytic oxygen sensor to comply with Euro3 emissions standards.

The red-painted welded tubular steel frame (ALS

450) shared its geometry with the Desmosedici GP6 and included a carbon-fibre seat and rear support. Also inspired by the GP6 was the long, cast, forged and pressed aluminium alloy swingarm, with the rear shock absorber attached above the swingarm to a rocker hinged to the crankcase. The 43 mm upside-down Öhlins FG353 pressurized forks (PFF), with TiN-coated fork tubes, were similar to the racing unit, as was the fully adjustable Öhlins rear shock absorber and Marchesini seven-spoke forged and machined magnesium alloy wheels. As suppliers for the GP6, Bridgestone also developed a special BT001R street tyre suitable for dealing with 200 bhp.

Further racing influences included a pair of Brembo radial 'monobloc' front brake calipers with four 34 mm pistons. The monobloc technology provided improved caliper stiffness and the semi-floating 320 x 6mm front brake discs, with a machined flange, were as for the wet-weather race GP6 set-up and also the F06 999 Superbike. At the rear was a 240 mm Brembo fixed disc and a twin 34 mm piston caliper.

Alan Jenkins was responsible for the style of the carbon-fibre bodywork and aluminium tank, and the colour schemes. Two versions were available: the

The first production MotoGP replica motorcycle was the Desmosedici RR, available in limited numbers during 2007. This promised to be the most exotic and best performing production motorcycle available. *Ducati Motor*

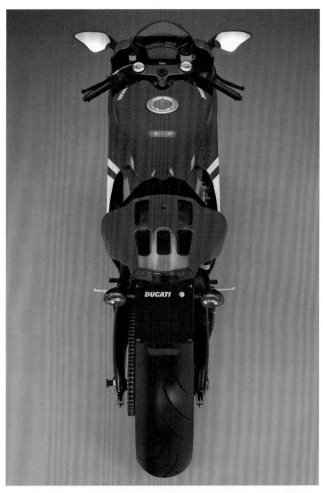

Rosso GP with a white number plate on the tail section and a white Ducati logo on the fairing, and the Team Version painted like factory Corse bikes, with a white stripe on the fairing. A team sponsor decal kit was provided with each bike. They also came with a new lightweight multi-function dashboard, with LCD graph tachometer, trip/odometer, anti-theft immobiliser, lap time measurement and readings for oil pressure, fuel reserve, clock and air temperature. This was the same as fitted to the 2007 Desmosedici GP7.

As the most expensive and exotic production motorcycle available, the Desmosedici RR created a huge impression and was soon sold out. Racing success is supposed to generate sales, but this had not been happening despite Ducati's success in MotoGP and World Superbike. The Desmosedici RR arrived just when Ducati desperately needed an exotic, range-topping motorcycle to ensure its status as Italy's premier manufacturer of sporting motorcycles. Such a technologically advanced, limited-edition motorcycle will surely spearhead a sales revival further down the range. With the next-generation Superbike twin set to be a more classically styled 1200, Ducati will be looking ahead with optimism.

DUCATI MOTORCYCLES 1952–2006

Model	Years	Engine	Bore (mm)	Stroke (mm)	Displ (cc)	Comp ratio	Cooling system	Fuel system	Transmission	Front suspension	Rear suspension	Front tyre	Rear tyre	Wheel base	Weight (kg)
65N, T, S TL, TS	1952–57	1 Cyl, OHV	44	43	65	8:1	Air	Weber carburettor	3-speed	Hydraulic fork	Twin shock swing-arm				55
98N, T, TS TL, Sport Bronco	1952–62	1 Cyl, OHV	49	52	98	7:1	Air	Dell'Orto carburettor 16mm	4-speed	Hydraulic fork	Twin shock swing-arm	2.50 X17	2.75 X17	1245	87
55/R/E	1954–56	1 Cyl, OHV	39	40	48	6.7:1	Air	Weber carburettor	2-speed	Leading link	Twin shock	2.00 X18	2.00 X18	1092	45
125TV, TS, Aurea, Bronco	1956–66	1 Cyl, OHV	55.2	52	124	6.8:1	Air	Dell'Orto carburettor 18mm	4-speed	Hydraulic fork	Twin shock swing-arm	2.50 X17	2.75 X17	1285	90
85T, S	1957–61	1 Cyl, OHV	45.5	52	85	9:1	Air	Dell'Orto carburettor 16mm	4-speed	Hydraulic fork	Twin shock swing-arm	2.50 X17	2.75 X17	1245	79
175T	1957	1 Cyl, SOHC	62	57.8	175	7:1	Air	Dell'Orto carburettor 22mm	4-speed	Hydraulic fork	Twin shock swing-arm	3.00 X17	3.00 X17	1320	103
175 Sport	1957–60	1 Cyl, SOHC	62	57.8	175	8:1	Air	Dell'Orto carburettor 22.5mm	4-speed	Hydraulic fork	Twin shock swing-arm	2.50 X18	2.75 X18	1320	106
48 Sport	1958–65	1 Cyl, 2 stroke	38	42	48	9.5:1	Air	Dell'Orto carburettor 15mm	3-speed	Hydraulic fork	Twin shock swing-arm	2.25 X19	2.25 X19	1180	54
100S	1958	1 Cyl, SOHC	49	52	98	9:1	Air	Dell'Orto carburettor 18mm	4-speed	Hydraulic fork	Twin shock swing-arm	2.50 X17	2.75 X17	1320	89
125S/T/TS	1958–65	1 Cyl, SOHC	55.2	52	124	8:1	Air	Dell'Orto carburettor 20mm	4-speed	Hydraulic fork	Twin shock swing-arm	2.50 X17	2.75 X17	1320	100
175TS Americano	1958–60	1 Cyl, SOHC	62	57.8	175	7:1	Air	Dell'Orto carburettor 22mm	4-speed	Hydraulic fork	Twin shock swing-arm	2.50 X18	2.75 X18	1320	108 (118)
200 Elite Americano TS	1959–65	1 Cyl, SOHC	67	57.8	204	8.5:1	Air	Dell'Orto carburettor 24mm	4-speed	Hydraulic fork	Twin shock swing-arm	2.75 X18	3.00 X18	1320	111
200 Motocross	1959–60	1 Cyl, SOHC	67	57.8	204	8.5:1	Air	Dell'Orto carburettor 27mm	4-speed	Hydraulic fork	Twin shock swing-arm	2.75 X21	3.00 X19	1380	124
250 Monza	1961–68	1 Cyl, SOHC	74	57.8	249	8:1	Air	Dell'Orto carburettor 24mm	4/5-speed	Hydraulic fork	Twin shock swing-arm	2.75 X18	3.00 X18	1320	125
250 Diana/ Daytona	1961–64	1 Cyl, SOHC	74	57.8	249	8:1	Air	Dell'Orto carburettor 24mm	4-speed	Hydraulic fork	Twin shock swing-arm	2.75 X18	3.00 X18	1320	120
250 Scrambler	1961–67	1 Cyl, SOHC	74	57.8	249	9.2:1	Air	Dell'Orto carburettor 27mm	4/5-speed	Hydraulic fork	Twin shock swing-arm	3.00 X19	3.50 (4.00) X19 (18)	1350	109 (120)
48 Brisk Piuma	1962–67	1 Cyl, 2 stroke	38	42	48	6.3:1	Air	Dell'Orto carburettor 12mm	1-speed 3-speed	Hydraulic fork	Twin shock swing-arm	2.00 X18 (X19)	2.00 X18 (X19)	1160 (1170)	45 (52)
80 Setter	1962–64	1 Cyl, 2 stroke	47	46	80	7.1:1	Air	Dell'Orto carburettor 15mm	3-speed	Hydraulic fork	Twin shock swing-arm	2.25 X18	2.50 X17		62

Model	Years	Engine	Bore (mm)	Stroke (mm)	Displ (cc)	Comp ratio	Cooling system	Fuel system	Transmission	Front suspension	Rear suspension	Front tyre	Rear tyre	Wheel base	Weight (kg)
48, 50 Piuma Sport	1962–66	1 Cyl, 2 stroke	38	42	48	6.3:1	Air/fan	Dell'Orto carburettor 15mm	3-speed	Hydraulic fork	Twin shock swing-arm	2.25 X18	2.25 X18	1160	49
250 Mark 3	1963–67	1 Cyl, SOHC	74	57.8	249	10:1	Air	Dell'Orto carburettor 27/29mm	4/5-speed	Hydraulic fork	Twin shock swing-arm	2.50 X18	2.75 X18	1320 (1350)	110 (112)
48/100 Brio	1964–68	1 Cyl, 2 stroke	38/51	42/46	48/94	7/10:1	Air/fan	Dell'Orto carburettor 12/16mm	3-speed	Leading link fork	Twin shock swing-arm	2.75x9 3.50x8	2.75x9 3.50x8		63.5/ 80
48/50 SL1/2	1964–69	1 Cyl, 2 stroke	38 (38.8)	42	48/50	7/11:1	Air/fan	Dell'Orto carburettor 15/18mm	3/4-speed	Hydraulic fork	Twin shock swing-arm	2.25 X19	2.25 X19	1150	58/61
100 Cadet, Falcon	1964–68	1 Cyl, 2 stroke	51 (52)	46	94/98	10:1	Air/fan	Dell'Orto carburettor 18 (24)mm	3/4-speed	Hydraulic fork	Twin shock swing-arm	2.25 X18	2.50 X18	1160	66
100 Mountaineer	1964–68	1 Cyl, 2 stroke	51 (52)	46	94/98	10:1	Air/fan	Dell'Orto carburettor 18 (24)mm	3/4-speed	Hydraulic fork	Twin shock swing-arm	2.50 X16	3.50 X16	1170	68
250GT	1964–66	1 Cyl, SOHC	74	57.8	249	8:1	Air	Dell'Orto carburettor 24mm	5-speed	Hydraulic fork	Twin shock swing-arm	2.75 X18	3.00 X18	1320	125
250 Mach 1	1964–66	1 Cyl, SOHC	74	57.8	249	10:1	Air	Dell'Orto carburettor 29mm	5-speed	Hydraulic fork	Twin shock swing-arm	2.50 X18	2.75 X18	1350	116
160 Monza Junior	1964–67	1 Cyl, SOHC	61	52	156	8.2:1	Air	Dell'Orto carburettor 22mm	4-speed	Hydraulic fork	Twin shock swing-arm	2.75 X16	3.25 X16	1330	106 (108)
350 Sebring	1965–67	1 Cyl, SOHC	76	75	340	8.5:1	Air	Dell'Orto carburettor 24mm	5-speed	Hydraulic fork	Twin shock swing-arm	2.75 X18	3.00 X18	1330	123
125 Cadet 4 Lusso Scrambler	1967	1 Cyl, OHV	53	55	121	8.4:1	Air	Dell'Orto carburettor 18mm	4-speed	Hydraulic fork	Twin shock swing-arm	2.50 (2.75) X18	2.75 (3.25) X18 (16)	1160	72 (75)
50 Rolly	1968	1 Cyl, 2 stroke	38	42	48	7:1	Air	Dell'Orto carburettor 12mm	1-speed	Hydraulic fork	Solid	2.00 X18	2.00 X18		42
250 Scrambler (wide-case)	1968–74	1 Cyl, SOHC	74	57.8	249	9:1	Air	Dell'Orto carburettor 24 (26)mm	5-speed	Hydraulic fork	Twin shock swing-arm	3.50 X19	4.00 X18	1380	132
250 Mark (wide-case)	1968–74	1 Cyl, SOHC	74	57.8	249	10:1	Air	Dell'Orto carburettor 29mm	5-speed	Hydraulic fork	Twin shock swing-arm	2.75 X18 (X19)	3.00 (3.50) X18	1360	127
250 Mark 3D, Desmo	1968–74	1 Cyl, Desmo, SOHC	74	57.8	249	10:1 (9.7:1)	Air	Dell'Orto carburettor 29mm	5-speed	Hydraulic fork	Twin shock swing-arm	2.75 (3.25) X18	3.00 (3.50) X18	1360	127
350 Scrambler	1968–74	1 Cyl, SOHC	76	75	436	9.5:1	Air	Dell'Orto carburettor 29mm	5-speed	Hydraulic fork	Twin shock swing-arm	3.50 X19	4.00 X18	1380	133
350 Mark 3	1968–74	1 Cyl, SOHC	76	75	340	10:1	Air	Dell'Orto carburettor 29mm	5-speed	Hydraulic fork	Twin shock swing-arm	2.75 X18 (X19)	3.00 (3.50) X18	1360	128 (127)
350 Mark 3D, Desmo	1968–74	1 Cyl, Desmo, SOHC	76	75	340	10:1	Air	Dell'Orto carburettor 29mm	5-speed	Hydraulic fork	Twin shock swing-arm	2.75 (3.25) X18	3.00 (3.50) X18	1360	127
50/100 Scrambler	1969–70	1 Cyl, 2 stroke	38.78/ 52	42/46	50/98	10.5/ 11.2	Air	Dell'Orto carburettor 18/24mm	4-speed	Hydraulic fork	Twin shock swing-arm	2.75 (2.50) X18	3.50x16 2.50x17	1150/ 1180	59/67
450 Scrambler	1969–74	1 Cyl, SOHC	86	75	436	9.3:1	Air	Dell'Orto carburettor 29mm	5-speed	Hydraulic fork	Twin shock swing-arm	3.50 X19	4.00 X18	1380	133

Model	Years	Engine	Bore (mm)	Stroke (mm)	Displ (cc)	Comp ratio	Cooling system	Fuel system	Transmission	Front suspension	Rear suspension	Front tyre	Rear tyre	Wheel base	Weight (kg)
450 Mark 3	1969–74	1 Cyl, SOHC	86	75	436	9.3:1	Air	Dell'Orto carburettor 29mm	5-speed	Hydraulic fork	Twin shock swing-arm	2.75 X19 (X18)	3.00 (3.50) X18	1360	130 (127)
450 Mark 3D, Desmo	1969–74	1 Cyl, Desmo, SOHC	86	75	436	9.3:1	Air	Dell'Orto carburettor 29mm	5-speed	Hydraulic fork	Twin shock swing-arm	2.75 (3.25) X18	3.50 X18	1360	130 (127)
125 Scrambler	1971	1 Cyl, SOHC	55.2	52	124	8.5:1	Air	Amal carburettor 20mm	5-speed	Hydraulic fork	Twin shock swing-arm	2.50 X19	3.50 X18	1340	105
450R/T	1971–73	1 Cyl, Desmo, SOHC	86	75	436	9.3:1	Air	Dell'Orto carburettor 29mm	5-speed	Marzocchi fork 35mm	Twin shock swing-arm	3.00 X21	4.00 X18	1450	128
750GT	1971–74	2 Cyl, SOHC	80	74.4	748	8.5:1	Air	2 Dell'Orto carburettors 30mm	5-speed	Hydraulic fork 38mm	Twin shock swing-arm	3.25 X19	3.50 X18	1530	185
750 Sport	1972–74	2 Cyl, SOHC	80	74.4	748	9.3:1	Air	2 Dell'Orto carburettors 32mm	5-speed	Hydraulic fork 38mm	Twin shock swing-arm	3.25 X19	3.50 X18	1530	185
750 Super Sport	1974–79	2 Cyl, Desmo, SOHC	80	74.4	748	9.65:1	Air	2 Dell'Orto carburettors 40mm	5-speed	Marzocchi fork 38mm	Twin shock swing-arm	3.50 X18	3.50 120/90 (1500) X18	1530 (1500)	180 (189)
860GT, GTE	1974–76	2 Cyl, SOHC	86	74.4	864	9:1	Air	2 Dell'Orto carburettors 32mm	5-speed	Ceriani fork 38mm	Twin shock swing-arm	3.50 X18	4.00 X18	1520	206 (217)
125 Six Days	1975–77	1 Cyl, 2 stroke	54	54	124	10.5:1 14.5:1	Air	30/32mm carburettor	6-speed	Hydraulic fork 35mm	Twin shock swing-arm	3.00 X21	3.75/ 4.00 X18	1420 (1430)	108 (97)
900 Super Sport	1975–82	2 Cyl, Desmo, SOHC	86	74.4	864	9.3:1	Air	2 Dell'Orto carburettors 40 or 32mm	5-speed	Marzocchi fork 38mm	Twin shock swing-arm	100/90 (3.50) X18	110/18 (3.50) X18	1500	205 (190)
860/900 GTS	1976–79	2 Cyl, SOHC	86	74.4	864	9.8:1	Air	2 Dell'Orto carburettors 32mm	5-speed	Hydraulic fork 38mm	Twin shock swing-arm	3.50 X18	120/90 X18	1520	217
350GTL	1976–78	2 Cyl, SOHC	71.8	43.2	350	9.6:1	Air	2 Dell'Orto carburettors 26mm	5-speed	Marzocchi fork 35mm	Twin shock swing-arm	3.25 X19	3.50 X18	1400	170
500GTL	1976–78	2 Cyl, SOHC	78	52	497	9.6:1	Air	2 Dell'Orto carburettors 30mm	5-speed	Marzocchi fork 35mm	Twin shock swing-arm	3.25 X18	3.50 X18	1400	170
350 Sport Desmo	1977–80	2 Cyl, Desmo, SOHC	71.8	43.2	350	9.6:1	Air	2 Dell'Orto carburettors 26mm	5-speed	Paioli fork 35mm	Twin shock swing-arm	3.25 X18	3.50 X18	1400	181
500 Sport Desmo	1977–80	2 Cyl, Desmo, SOHC	78	52	497	9.6:1	Air	2 Dell'Orto carburettors 30mm	5-speed	Paioli fork 35mm	Twin shock swing-arm	3.25 X18	3.50 X18	1400	185
350GTV	1978–80	2 Cyl, SOHC	71.8	43.2	350	9.6:1	Air	2 Dell'Orto carburettors 26mm	5-speed	Paioli fork 35mm	Twin shock swing-arm	3.25 X18	3.50 X18	1400	183
500GTV	1978–80	2 Cyl, SOHC	78	52	497	9.6:1	Air	2 Dell'Orto carburettors 30mm	5-speed	Paioli fork 35mm	Twin shock swing-arm	3.25 X18	3.50 X18	1400	181
900 Darmah	1978–84	2 Cyl, Desmo, SOHC	86	74.4	864	9.3:1	Air	2 Dell'Orto carburettors 32mm	5-speed	Hydraulic fork 38mm	Twin shock swing-arm	3.50 X18	120/90 X18	1550	216
900 Mike Hailwood Replica	1979–84	2 Cyl, Desmo, SOHC	86	74.4	864	9.3:1	Air	2 Dell'Orto carburettors 40mm	5-speed	Marzocchi fork 38mm	Twin shock swing-arm	100/90 X18	110/90 X18	1500	210.5
900SS Darmah	1979–80	2 Cyl, Desmo, SOHC	86	74.4	864	9.5:1	Air	2 Dell'Orto carburettors 32mm	5-speed	Marzocchi fork 38mm	Twin shock swing-arm	3.50 X18	120/90 X18	1550	216

Model	Years	Engine	Bore (mm)	Stroke (mm)	Displ (cc)	Comp ratio	Cooling system	Fuel system	Transmission	Front suspension	Rear suspension	Front tyre	Rear tyre	Wheel base	Weight (kg)
500SL	1980–84	2 Cyl, Desmo, SOHC	74	58	499	9.5:1	Air	2 Dell'Orto carburettors 36mm	5-speed	Hydraulic fork 35mm	Twin shock swing-arm	3.25 X18	3.50 X18	1450	180
600SL	1982–84	2 Cyl, Desmo, SOHC	80	58	583	10.4:1	Air	2 Dell'Orto carburettors 36mm	5-speed	Hydraulic fork 35mm	Twin shock swing-arm	3.25 X18	4.00 X18	1450	187
350XL	1982–84	2 Cyl, Desmo, SOHC	66	51	349	10.3:1	Air	2 Dell'Orto carburettors 30mm	5-speed	Hydraulic fork 35mm	Twin shock swing-arm	3.00 X18	3.50 X18	1450	177
600TL	1982–84	2 Cyl, Desmo, SOHC	80	58	583	10.4:1	Air	2 Dell'Orto carburettors 36mm	5-speed	Hydraulic fork 35mm	Twin shock swing-arm	100/90 X18	110/90 X18	1450	177
900S2	1982–84	2 Cyl, Desmo, SOHC	86	74.4	864	9.5:1	Air	2 Dell'Orto carburettors 40mm	5-speed	Marzocchi fork 35mm	Twin shock swing-arm	100/90 X18	110/90 X18	1500	190
650SL	1984–86	2 Cyl, Desmo, SOHC	82	61.5	650	10:1	Air	2 Dell'Orto carburettors 36mm	5-speed	Marzocchi fork 35mm	Twin shock swing-arm	100/90 X18	110/90 X18	1450	187
Mille MHR, S2	1984–85	2 Cyl, Desmo, SOHC	88	80	973	9.3:1	Air	2 Dell'Orto carburettors 40mm	5-speed	Marzocchi fork 38mm	Twin shock swing-arm	100/90 X18	130/80 X18	1500	198 (193)
750F1	1985–88	2 Cyl, Desmo, SOHC	88	61.5	748	9.3:1 (10:1)	Air & oil	2 Dell'Orto carburettors 36mm	5-speed	Hydraulic fork 38/40mm	Adjustable single shock	120/80 X16	130/80 X18	1400	175
350F3	1986–88	2 Cyl, Desmo, SOHC	66	51	349	10:1	Air	2 Dell'Orto carburettors 30mm	5-speed	Marzocchi fork 35mm	Adjustable single shock	100/90 X16	120/80 X18	1400	165
400F3	1986–89	2 Cyl, Desmo, SOHC	70.5	51	398	10.4:1	Air	2 Dell'Orto carburettors 30mm	6-speed	Marzocchi fork 35mm	Adjustable single shock	100/90 X16	120/80 X18	1400	165
Montjuich, Lag. Seca, S. Monica	1986–88	2 Cyl, Desmo, SOHC	88	61.5	748	10:1	Air	2 Dell'Orto carburettors 40mm	5-speed	Forc. Italia fork 40mm	Adjustable single shock	12/60 X16	18/67 X16	1400	155
750 Paso	1986–90	2 Cyl, Desmo, SOHC	88	61.5	748	10:1	Air	Weber twin choke carburettor	5-speed	Marzocchi M1R 42mm	Single shock rising rate	130/60 X16	160/60 X16	1450	195
Indiana 750/650/350	1986–90	2 Cyl, Desmo, SOHC	88 (82) (66)	61.5 (51)	748 (650) (349)	10:1	Air	2 Dell'Orto carburettors 36mm (30mm)	5-speed	Hydraulic fork 35mm	Twin shock swing-arm	110/90 X18	140/90 X15	1530	180
750 Sport	1988–90	2 Cyl, Desmo, SOHC	88	61.5	748	9.5:1	Air	Weber twin choke carburettor	5-speed	Marzocchi fork 40mm	Adjustable single shock	130/60 X16	160/60 X16	1450	180
851 Strada	1988	2 Cyl, Desmo, DOHC	92	64	851	10.4:1	Liquid	Marelli electronic fuel injection	6-speed	Marzocchi M1R 42mm	Single shock rising rate	130/60 X16	160/60 X16	1460	185
851 Strada	1989–90	2 Cyl, Desmo, DOHC	92	64	851	11:1	Liquid	Marelli electronic fuel injection	6-speed	Marzocchi M1R 42mm	Single shock rising rate	120/70 X17	180/55 X17	1430	190 (192)
888 Racing	1989–93	2 Cyl, Desmo, DOHC	94	64	888	12:1	Liquid	Marelli electronic fuel injection	6-speed	Upside down fork 42mm	Single shock rising rate	S1016	S1423	1430	155 (150) (145)
900 Super Sport	1989–90	2 Cyl, Desmo, SOHC	92	68	904	9.2:1	Air	Weber twin choke carburettor	6-speed	Marzocchi fork 40mm	Adjustable single shock	130/60 X17	170/60 X17	1450	180
906	1989–90	2 Cyl, Desmo, SOHC	92	68	904	9.2:1	Liquid	Weber twin choke carburettor	6-speed	Marzocchi M1R 42mm	Single shock rising rate	130/60 X16	160/60 X16	1450	180
851 (888) Sport Production	1990–93	2 Cyl, Desmo, DOHC	94	64	888	11:1	Liquid	Marelli electronic fuel injection	6-speed	Upside down fork 42mm	Single shock rising rate	120/70 X17	180/55 X17	1430	188

Model	Years	Engine	Bore (mm)	Stroke (mm)	Displ (cc)	Comp ratio	Cooling system	Fuel system	Transmission	Front suspension	Rear suspension	Front tyre	Rear tyre	Wheel base	Weight (kg)
350 Supersport	1991–93	2 Cyl, Desmo, SOHC	66	51	341	10.7:1	Air	2 Mikuni carburettors 38mm	5-speed	Upside down fork 41mm	Adjustable single shock	120/60 X17	160/60 X17	1410	173
400 Supersport	1991–97	2 Cyl, Desmo, SOHC	70.5	51	398	10:1	Air	2 Mikuni carburettors 38mm	5-speed	Upside down fork 41mm	Adjustable single shock	120/60 X17	160/60 X17	1410	172
750 Supersport	1991–97	2 Cyl, Desmo, SOHC	88	61.5	748	9:1	Air	2 Mikuni carburettors 38mm	5-speed	Upside down fork 41mm	Adjustable single shock	120/60 X17	160/60 X17	1410	173 (176)
851 Strada	1991–92	2 Cyl, Desmo, DOHC	92	64	851	10.5:1	Liquid	Marelli electronic fuel injection	6-speed	Upside down fork 41mm	Single shock rising rate	120/70 X17	180/55 X17	1430	199 (202)
900 Supersport	1991–97	2 Cyl, Desmo, SOHC	92	68	904	9.2:1	Air	2 Mikuni carburettors 38mm	6-speed	Upside down fork 41mm	Adjustable single shock	120/70 X17	170/60 X17	1410	183 (186)
907IE	1991–92	2 Cyl, Desmo, SOHC	92	68	904	9.2:1	Liquid	Marelli electronic fuel injection	6-speed	Marzocchi M1R 42mm	Single shock rising rate	120/70 X17	170/60 X17	1490	215
900 Superlight FE	1992–98	2 Cyl, Desmo, SOHC	92	68	904	9.2:1	Air	2 Mikuni carburettors 38mm	6-speed	Upside down fork 41mm	Adjustable single shock	120/70 X17	170/60 X17	1415	176 (179) (182)
Supermono	1993–95	1 Cyl, Desmo, DOHC	100 (102)	70	550 (572)	11.8:1	Liquid	Marelli electronic fuel injection	6-speed	Upside down fork 42mm	Adjustable single shock	310/480 R17	155/60 R17	1360	122
888 Strada	1993–94	2 Cyl, Desmo, DOHC	94	64	888	11:1	Liquid	Marelli electronic fuel injection	6-speed	Upside down fork 42mm	Single shock rising rate	120/70 X17	180/55 X17	1430	202
900M Monster	1993–99	2 Cyl, Desmo, SOHC	92	68	904	9.2:1	Air	2 Mikuni carburettors 38mm	6-speed	Upside down fork 41mm	Single shock rising rate	120/60 X17	170/60 X17	1430	185
600M Monster	1994–02	2 Cyl, Desmo, SOHC	80	58	583	10.7:1	Air	2 Mikuni carburettors 38mm	5-speed	Upside down fork 41mm	Single shock rising rate	120/60 X17	160/60 X17	1430	174
600 Supersport	1994–02	2 Cyl, Desmo, SOHC	80	58	583	10.7:1	Air	2 Mikuni carburettors 38mm	5-speed	Upside down fork 41mm	Adjustable single shock	120/60 X17	160/60 X17	1410	172
888 Racing	1994	2 Cyl, Desmo, DOHC	94	64	926	12:1	Liquid	Marelli electronic fuel injection	6-speed	Upside down fork 42mm	Single shock rising rate	120/60 X17	180/60 X17	1430	145
916 Strada	1994	2 Cyl, Desmo, DOHC	94	66	916	11:1	Liquid	Marelli electronic fuel injection	6-speed	Upside down fork 43mm	Single arm rising rate	120/70 X17	190/50 X17	1410	195
916 Sport Production	1994–96	2 Cyl, Desmo, DOHC	94	66	916	11.2:1	Liquid	Marelli electronic fuel injection	6-speed	Upside down fork 43mm	Single arm rising rate	120/70 X17	190/55 X17	1410	195
748 Biposto/S	1995–03	2 Cyl, Desmo, DOHC	88	61.5	748	11.5:1	Liquid	Marelli electronic fuel injection	6-speed	Upside down fork 43mm	Single arm rising rate	120/60 X17	180/55 X17	1410	202 (196)
748 SP/SPS	1995–98	2 Cyl, Desmo, DOHC	88	61.5	748	11.6:1	Liquid	Marelli electronic fuel injection	6-speed	Upside down fork 43mm	Single arm rising rate	120/60 X17	180/55 X17	1410	200
916 Biposto	1995–98	2 Cyl, Desmo, DOHC	94	66	916	11:1	Liquid	Marelli electronic fuel injection	6-speed	Upside down fork 43mm	Single arm rising rate	120/70 X17	190/50 X17	1410	204
916 Senna	1995–98	2 Cyl, Desmo, DOHC	94	66	916	11:1	Liquid	Marelli electronic fuel injection	6-speed	Upside down fork 43mm	Single arm rising rate	120/70 X17	190/50 X17	1410	201
916 Racing	1995–96	2 Cyl, Desmo, DOHC	94	66	955	12:1	Liquid	Marelli electronic fuel injection	6-speed	Upside down fork 46mm	Single arm rising rate	12/60 17SC	18/76 17SC	1420	154

Model	Years	Engine	Bore (mm)	Stroke (mm)	Displ (cc)	Comp ratio	Cooling system	Fuel system	Transmission	Front suspension	Rear suspension	Front tyre	Rear tyre	Wheel base	Weight (kg)
750M Monster	1996–01	2 Cyl, Desmo, SOHC	88	61.5	748	9:1	Air	2 Mikuni carburettors 38mm	5-speed	Upside down fork 41mm	Single shock rising rate	120/60 X17	160/60 X17	1430	178
916 Racing	1997–99	2 Cyl, Desmo, DOHC	98	66	996	12:1	Liquid	Marelli electronic fuel injection	6-speed	Upside down fork 46mm	Single arm rising rate	12/60 17SC	18/60 17SC	1430	162
916 SPS/ 996 SPS	1997–00	2 Cyl, Desmo, DOHC	98	66	996	12:1	Liquid	Marelli electronic fuel injection	6-speed	Upside down fork 43mm	Single arm rising rate	120/70 X17	190/50 X17	1410	190 (187)
ST2	1997–03	2 Cyl, Desmo, SOHC	94	68	944	10.2:1	Liquid	Marelli electronic fuel injection	6-speed	Upside down fork 43mm	Single shock rising rate	120/70 X17	170/60 X17	1430	212
900 Super Sport/Sport	1998–02	2 Cyl, Desmo, SOHC	92	68	904	9.2:1	Air	Marelli electronic fuel injection	6-speed	Upside down fork 43mm	Single shock rising rate	120/70 X17	170/60 X17	1395	188
400M Monster	1998–03	2 Cyl, Desmo, SOHC	70.5	51	398	10:1	Air	2 Mikuni carburettors 38mm	5-speed	Upside down fork 40mm (43mm)	Single shock rising rate	120/60 X17	160/60 X17	1430	174
ST4	1998–03	2 Cyl, Desmo, DOHC	94	66	916	11:1	Liquid	Marelli electronic fuel injection	6-speed	Upside down fork 43mm	Single arm rising rate	120/70 X17	180/55 X17	1430	215
750 Supersport/ Sport	1999–02	2 Cyl, Desmo, SOHC	88	61.5	748	9:1	Air	Marelli electronic fuel injection	5-speed	Upside down fork 43mm	Single shock rising rate	120/70 X17	160/60 X17	1405	183 (181)
996/ 996S	1999–02	2 Cyl, Desmo, DOHC	98	66	996	11.5:1	Liquid	Marelli electronic fuel injection	6-speed	Upside down fork 43mm	Single arm rising rate	120/70 X17	190/50 X17	1410	198
900M Monster	2000–02	2 Cyl, Desmo, SOHC	92	68	904	9.2:1	Air	Marelli electronic fuel injection	6-speed	Upside down fork 43mm	Single shock rising rate	120/70 X17	170/60 X17	1430	185
748R	2000–02	2 Cyl, Desmo, DOHC	88	61.5	748	11.5:1	Liquid	Marelli electronic fuel injection	6-speed	Upside down fork 43mm	Single arm rising rate	120/60 X17	180/55 X17	1410	192
748RS	2000	2 Cyl, Desmo, DOHC	88	61.5	748	12:1	Liquid	Marelli electronic fuel injection	6-speed	Upside down fork 43mm	Single arm rising rate	120/60 X17	180/55 X17	1415	172
Monster S4	2001–03	2 Cyl, Desmo, DOHC	94	66	916	11:1	Liquid	Marelli electronic fuel injection	6-speed	Upside down fork 43mm	Single shock rising rate	120/70 X17	180/55 X17	1440	193
ST4S (ABS)	2001–05	2 Cyl, Desmo, DOHC	98	66	996	11.5:1	Liquid	Marelli electronic fuel injection	6-speed	Upside down fork 43mm	Single shock rising rate	120/70 X17	180/55 X17	1430	212 (217)
996R	2001	2 Cyl, Desmo, DOHC	100	63.5	998	11.4:1	Liquid	Marelli electronic fuel injection	6-speed	Upside down fork 43mm	Single arm rising rate	120/70 X17	190/50 X17	1410	185
MHE900	2001–02	2 Cyl, Desmo, SOHC	92	68	904	9.2:1	Air	Marelli electronic fuel injection	6-speed	Upside down fork 43mm	Single arm rising rate	120/65 X17	170/60 X17	1415	183
620IE Monster	2002–	2 Cyl, Desmo, SOHC	80	61.5	618	10.5:1	Air	Marelli electronic fuel injection	5-speed (6-speed)	Upside down fork 43mm	Single shock rising rate	120/60 X17	160/60 X17	1440	177
750IE Monster	2002	2 Cyl, Desmo, SOHC	88	61.5	748	9:1	Air	Marelli electronic fuel injection	5-speed	Upside down fork 43mm	Single shock rising rate	120/60 X17	160/60 X17	1440	179
998/S	2002–04	2 Cyl, Desmo, DOHC	100	63.5	998	11.4:1	Liquid	Marelli electronic fuel injection	6-speed	Upside down fork 43mm	Single arm rising rate	120/70 X17	190/50 X17	1410	198 (187)
998R	2002	2 Cyl, Desmo, DOHC	104	58.8	999	12.3:1	Liquid	Marelli electronic fuel injection	6-speed	Upside down fork 43mm	Single arm rising rate	120/70 X17	190/50 X17	1410	183

Model	Years	Engine	Bore (mm)	Stroke (mm)	Displ (cc)	Comp ratio	Cooling system	Fuel system	Transmission	Front suspension	Rear suspension	Front tyre	Rear tyre	Wheel base	Weight (kg)
800IE Monster	2003–04	2 Cyl, Desmo, SOHC	88	66	803	10.4:1	Air	Marelli electronic fuel injection	5-speed	Upside down fork 43mm	Single shock rising rate	120/60 X17	160/60 X17	1440	179
1000IE/S Monster	2003–05	2 Cyl, Desmo, SOHC	94	71.5	992	10:1	Air	Marelli electronic fuel injection	6-speed	Upside down fork 43mm	Single shock rising rate	120/70 X17	180/55 X17	1440	189
620 Sport	2003	2 Cyl, Desmo, SOHC	80	61.5	618	10.5:1	Air	Marelli electronic fuel injection	5-speed	Upside down fork 43mm	Single shock rising rate	120/70 X17	160/60 X17	1405	181.6
800 Supersport/ Sport	2003–04	2 Cyl, Desmo, SOHC	88	66	803	10.3:1	Air	Marelli electronic fuel injection	5-speed	Upside down fork 43mm	Single shock rising rate	120/70 X17	170/60 X17	1405	183
1000 Supersport	2003–	2 Cyl, Desmo, SOHC	94	71.5	992	10:1	Air	Marelli electronic fuel injection	6-speed	Upside down fork 43mm	Single shock rising rate	120/70 X17	180/55 X17	1395	185.2
749/S	2003–	2 Cyl, Desmo, DOHC	90	58.8	748	11.7:1	Liquid	Marelli electronic fuel injection	6-speed	Upside down fork 43mm	Single shock rising rate	120/70 X17	180/55 X17	1420	199
999/S	2003–	2 Cyl, Desmo, DOHC	100	63.5	998	11.4:1	Liquid	Marelli electronic fuel injection	6-speed	Upside down fork 43mm	Single shock rising rate	120/70 X17	190/50 X17	1420	199
999R	2003–	2 Cyl, Desmo, DOHC	105	58.8	999	12.3:1 (12.4:1)	Liquid	Marelli electronic fuel injection	6-speed	Upside down fork 43mm	Single shock rising rate	120/70 X17	190/50 X17	1420	192 (181)
Monster S4R	2003–	2 Cyl, Desmo, DOHC	96	68.8	996	11.2:1	Liquid	Marelli electronic fuel injection	6-speed	Upside down fork 43mm	Single arm rising rate	120/70 X17	180/55 X17	1440	193
Multistrada	2004–	2 Cyl, Desmo, SOHC	94	71.5	992	10:1	Air	Marelli electronic fuel injection	6-speed	Upside down fork 43mm	Single arm rising rate	120/70 X17	180/55 X17	1462	196
ST3 (ABS)	2004–	2 Cyl, Desmo, SOHC	94	71.5	992	11:1	Liquid	Marelli electronic fuel injection	6-speed	Upside down fork 43mm	Single shock rising rate	120/70 X17	180/55 X17	1430	201 (204)
749R	2004–	2 Cyl, Desmo, DOHC	94	54	749	12.7:1	Liquid	Marelli electronic fuel injection	6-speed	Upside down fork 43mm	Single shock rising rate	120/70 X17	180/55 X17	1420	192
Multistrada 620/Dark	2005–	2 Cyl, Desmo, SOHC	80	61.5	618	10.5:1	Air	Marelli electronic fuel injection	6-speed	Upside down fork 43mm	Single shock rising rate	120/60 X17	160/60 X17	1459	183
Monster SR2	2005–	2 Cyl, Desmo, SOHC	88	66	803	10.5:1	Air	Marelli electronic fuel injection	6-speed	Upside down fork 43mm	Single shock rising rate	120/70 X17	180/55 X17	1440	173
PS1000	2006–	2 Cyl, Desmo, SOHC	94	71.5	992	10:1	Air	Marelli electronic fuel injection	6-speed	Upside down fork 43mm	Single shock swingarm	120/70 X17	180/55 X17	1425	181
Sport 1000	2006–	2 Cyl, Desmo, SOHC	94	71.5	992	10:1	Air	Marelli electronic fuel injection	6-speed	Upside down fork 43mm	Single shock swingarm	120/70 X17	180/55 X17	1425	179
GT1000	2006–	2 Cyl, Desmo, SOHC	94	71.5	992	10:1	Air	Marelli electronic fuel injection	6-speed	Upside down fork 43mm	Twin shock swingarm	120/70 X17	180/55 X17	1425	192
Monster S4RS	2006–	2 Cyl, Desmo, DOHC	100	63.5	998	11.4:1	Liquid	Marelli electronic fuel injection	6-speed	Upside down fork 43mm	Single shock rising rate	120/70 X17	180/55 X17	1440	177
Monster S2R1000	2006–	2 Cyl, Desmo, SOHC	94	71.5	992	10:1	Air	Marelli electronic fuel injection	6-speed	Upside down fork 43mm	Single shock rising rate	120/70 X17	180/55 X17	1440	178
Monster 695	2006–	2 Cyl, Desmo, SOHC	88	57.2	695	10.5:1	Air	Marelli electronic fuel injection	6-speed	Upside down fork 43mm	Single shock rising rate	120/60 X17	160/60 X17	1440	168

INDEX